MARTIAL RACES
OF
UNDIVIDED INDIA

Martial Races of Undivided India

Rs. 630

ISBN: 978-81-7835-775-1

Published in 2009 in India by
Kalpaz Publications
C - 30, Satyawati Nagar,
Delhi - 110052
E-mail: kalpaz@hotmail.com
Phone: 9212729499

Printed at: Singhal Print Media, Delhi

Contents

SECTION: II

Preface

Martial Races Theory is an idea which is absolutely based on the hypothesis that some ethnic races are naturally more martially disposed than others. The term, Martial Race, was in the first place used by the Britishers, who saw that the race of Scottish Highlanders were more ferocious in battle than others races, and they applied this notion to India. They differentiated each of the ethnic group into one of two classes; Martial Race and Non-Martial Race. Martial Races were considered brave and well-built for fighting. Non-Martial Races were those whom the British considered to be unfit for fighting.

This volume examines these Martial Races through their history, culture, people, their sub-divisions, martial traditions, contribution to Armed Forces, gallantry award winners and their famous people. This book covers all important Martial Races such as Ahirs, Awans, Baloch, Dhangar, Gakhars, Garhwalis, Gujjars, Gurkhas, Jat, Kamboj, Kurmis, Marathas, Nagas, Nairs, Pashtuns, Rajputs and Sikhs.

An extensive bibliography guides interested readers to in-depth resources on various topics. This volume is most interactive and highly educative and we hope that it will be very useful and popular among scholars, students and readers who are interested in Martial Races.

We have tried to span the complete imformation pertaining to all Martial Races and to be as accurate as possible, but some mistakes are sure to come in. In preparation of this book, the author has heavely drawn upon from various sources including large number of books, journals and electronic sources. I owe my sincere debt and gratitude to all of them. Suggestions for further improvement of this book are not only welcome but also greatly appreciated.

Introduction

Several efforts have been made, under the British rule and afterwards, to sort the population of India in accordance with a racial classification. After the freedom in 1947, in pursuance of the Government's policy to put off community distinctions founded on race, the 1951 Census of India eliminated racial classifications.

In India, Dravidian, Indo-Aryan, and related words are commonly regarded as linguistic terms, rather than ethnic terms. Some scholars of the colonial era attempted to find a method to assort the various groups of India as per the principal racial theories popular at that time in Europe. This pseudo-scientific racial categorization was used by the British census of India. It was frequently mixed with considerations about the caste system, as well as linguistic groups with "races".

The Martial races theory was a British philosophy established on the hypothesis that some peoples were more martially disposed as opposed to the general populace or other peoples. The British divided the entire range of Indian racial groups into two categories: martial race and a non-martial race". The martial race was looked upon as typically brave and well built for fighting but was also depicted as "unintelligent". The non-martial races were those whom the British assumed to be unfit for battle because of their inactive lifestyle, but were considered as cleverer.

The Indian revolt of 1857 might have played a role in British support of the martial races theory. Throughout this rebellion, some Indian troops, especially in Bengal, rebelled, but the "loyal" Sikhs, Punjabis, Dogras, Gurkas, Garhwalis and Pakhtuns (Pathans) did not join the mutiny and fought on the side of the British Army. Recent scholars have proposed that this theory was used to the limit to increase enlisting from amongst these races, while deterring enlistment of "disloyal" Indians who had sided with the rebel army during the war.

The Indian subcontinent has been home to a innumerable range of racial groups throughout the history, making it one of the most genetically rich areas on the world today. Comparatively insulated from the rest of

Eurasia by the Himilayas, Indian Ocean to the west, east and south, India has managed to shelter some of the oldest races outside of Africa, while also absorbing and assimilating waves of later human populations, ensuing in a greatly enriched genetic, linguistic and cultural heritage.

The aboriginal habitants of India belonged to an ancient population of unsure origins who mainly populated the jungle environments of the subcontinent, much like the modern day Pygmies of Africa and the Negritos of Southeast Asia. We can only presume that the morphological features shared by these last two geographically diverse populations, such as very small-stature, dark skin, woolly hair, scant body hair and occasional steatopygia, must also have characterised the ancient Indian homunculi.

The 2nd wave of migrants to enter India, around 60,000 years ago, followed a coastal route out of eastern Africa, using a bare form of watercarft to cross the small span of water between the Red Sea and the Gulf of Aden. Living on a largely marine diet, a number of these nomadic hunter-gatherers stayed in the Indus and proceeded inland along river systems of the landmass. Others pressed on into Southeast Asia, eventually giving rise to the Australian Aborigines. Genetically the Proto-Australoids are associated with the mtDNA haplogroup M, the earliest lineage outside of Africa. Veddoid peoples were characterised by gracile body types, dark skin and wavy hair, broad, flat noses and fleshy, protruding lips. They had long heads with low foreheads and prominent eye ridges, thick jaws, large teeth and small chins. The Australoids laid the foundation of Indian civilization. They cultivated rice and vegetables and made sugar from sugarcane. Their languages have survived in the Central and Eastern India. At present this race includes a large number of groups of peoples stretching from Iberia to India. The characteristic type appears in late Natufian times in Palestine and may have been differentiated in the southern steppes of Northern Africa and in Asia, and spread westwards and eastwards.

The Out of India Theory imagines Aryans to have originated from Indian and afterwards migrated to different parts of Central Asia and outside. The Aryan migration theory says that Aryans migrated from Central Asia towards Persia and India giving rise to the early Persians and the Indo-Aryans. Aryans pressed through the passes of the Hindu Kush and broke into the rich Indian plain.

Martial Race was a identification formed by officials of British India. The British faced furious resistance in some areas while easily inhibiting some others. This led the British officials to conclude that the peoples of these regions were naturally militant 'races' which possessed characters such as courage, loyalty, self sufficiency, physical strength, resilience, orderliness and fighting tenacity and were hard-working and skilled in military tactics. These 'martial races' tended to be hunting or agricultural cultures from hilly or craggy regions with a history of struggle, whether internally or with external groups, who were considered better capable of surviving hardship than the habitants of the hot, flat plains of the country who were thought to be unwarlike and unsound for military service.

Still others were omitted due to their 'ease of living' or branded as subversive agitators. The philosophy of 'martial races' postulated that the characters that make a useful soldier are hereditary and that most Indians, with the exception of the specified groups, didn't have the required genes that would make them warriors. The British enrolled heavily from the 'martial races' for service in the colonial army. Sensing the differences and fierce commitment to one's tribe or group of the diverse native peoples of the subcontinent, the British found chance to use it to their own great advantage. These already wide divides were a fertile breeding ground to inculcate pride in one's identity based on 'race'. This served the British in two ways. On the one hand it made sure that there was no repeat of the Indian rebellion of 1857 by ensuring there was no unity among the different subjects of the Raj. On the other hand it encouraged a sense of competition among the different 'races'.

The British found eager Indians to aid and assist them in the suppression of the rebellion to begin with. A British general and scholar, Lieutenant General Sir George Fletcher MacMunn wrote "It is only necessary for a feeling to arise that it is impious and disgraceful to serve the British, for the whole of our fabric to tumble like a house of cards without a shot being fired or a sword unsheathed". To this end, it became British policy to recruit only from those tribes whom they classified as members of the 'martial races' and the practice became an integral part of the recruitment manuals for the Army in the British Raj. "The Martial Race theory had an elegant symmetry. Indians who were intelligent and educated were defined as cowards, while those defined as brave were uneducated and backward." The British regarded the 'martial races' as valiant and strong but also intellectually challenged, lacking the initiative or leadership qualities to command large troops. They were also regarded as politically subservient or docile to authority. For these reasons, the 'martial races' theory didn't apply in the case of officer recruitment, which was based on social class and loyalty to the British Raj.

One source calls this a "pseudo-ethnological" construction, which was popularised by Frederick Sleigh Roberts, and created serious deficiencies in troop levels during the World Wars, compelling them to recruit from 'non-martial races'. In fact, Winston Churchill was reportedly concerned that the theory was abandoned during the war and wrote to the Commander-in-Chief, India that he must, "rely as much as possible on the martial races". After Indian Independence, the Indian Army abandoned this theory and recruitment took place without discrimination. Critics of this theory state that the Indian rebellion of 1857 may have played a role in reinforcing the British belief in 'martial races'. During this event some Indian troops (known as 'Sepoys'), particularly in Bengal, mutinied, but the 'loyal' Punjabis, Gurkhas, Kumaunis and Garhwalis didn't join the mutiny and fought on the side of the British Army. From then on, this theory was used to the hilt to accelerate recruitment from among these 'races', whilst discouraging enlistment of 'disloyal' Bengalis and high-caste Hindus who had sided with the rebel army during the war.

It is in this manner, that the Punjab Regiment became the senior most regiment of the Indian Army as it developed from the first Madras Native Infantry battalions. The British often marked the Sikhs 'the greatest of the martial races'. The Sikh Regiment is one of the Indian Army's most highly decorated infantry regiments, with many battle honours being won in its long history. The Marathas were classified as 'non-martial', ignoring the military achievements of the Maratha Empire or the Maratha Regiment's contribution against the Turks during the First World War, when they were recruited by the British Indian Army. The South Indian troops who had demonstrated their valour in the battlefields of central and south India were disbanded after 1857 to make way for more martial races.

In the Poorabiya regiment, the Bihari Rajputs and Bhumihar Brahmins made up the bulk of the soldiers. The Nairs of Kerala were initially included in the list, however after the Nairs of Travancore rebelled against the British under Velu Thampi Dalawa, they were recruited in lower numbers. Though seldom used in today's context, it has been alleged that Pakistan Military believed in the concept of martial races and they thus felt that they should easily defeat India in a war, especially prior to the Second Kashmir War Based on this belief in the martial supremacy, it was popularly hyped that one Pakistani soldier was equal to four to ten Hindus/ Indian soldiers (including a large number of Sikh soldiers and officers), and thus numerical superiority of the foe could be overcome.

SECTION: I

1

Baloch

The Baloch (Baluch, Balouch, Bloach, Balooch, Balush, Balosh, Baloosh, Baloush) are people of Iranian ancestry inhabiting the area of Balochistan in the southeast corner of the Iranian plateau in Southwest Asia, including parts of Iran, Afghanistan, and Pakistan.

The Baloch speak Balochi, which is a northwestern Iranian language. They majorly inhabit mountainous terrains, which have allowed them to maintain a distinct cultural identity and resist domination by neighbouring rulers. The Baloch are predominantly Muslim, with most belonging to the Hanafi school of thought of Sunni Islam, but there are also a significant number belonging to Shia school of thought in Balochistan. Some 60 percent of the total Baloch population live in Pakistan. Approximately 25 percent inhabit the contiguous area of southeastern Iran. Baloch population is estimated at approximately 8,800,000. In Pakistan the Balochi people are divided into two groups, the Sulaimani and the Makrani, separated from each other by a compact block of Brahui clans.

Origin & History

Research scholars have different opinions. Some say they (Baloch) belong to the northern areas of Elburz, now inhabited by Ashkanis, originally Aryans. Some historians maintain that they came from Halab, Allepe, and are Semites. It is also believed that they from the old stock of Sumerians of Mesopotamia, while others regard the Baloch as the remnants of indigenous population of the region. The historians, nevertheless, mostly concern themselves in tracing the Baloch racical ancestry either from amongst the Indo-Europeans or the Semites.

The origin of the word 'Baloch' is still unknown. Some believes that it is derived from brza-vaciya, which came from brza-vak, a Median word standing for a loud cry, in contrast to namravak, quiet, polite way of talking. Some writers maintain that the Baloch owe their name to Babyloian King 'Belus', also the name of their God. It is also believed that the word is a nick-name standing for a `cock's comb`. As the Baloch forces who fought against Astyages (585-550 BC.) wore distinctive helmets adorned with a cock's comb, the name `Baloch' is said to have been derived from the token of cock. Some writers believe that etymologically it is made of two Sankrit words, `Bal` and `Och`. `Bal` means strength or power, and `Och`, high or magnificent.

The word `Baloch' therefore, means very powerful and magnificent. Yet another erroneous version is that Baloch mean `nomad` or `wanderer`. This has been presumed perhaps because of the innocent use of the word for nomadic people, and may be due to the fact that the term may be used by indigenous settlers for the Baloch nomads. The ancient of Baloch (fathers and grand fathers of Baloch) been called "Qaffas" in Syria (Belad al-shaam). It means in Arabic Cage. Some research scholars said that the word Baloch which is in Arabic Balosh came from a mountain which is located in Belaad al-shaam. This mountain is called Balos and Baloch people lived on this mountain that is why they called them Balosh.

The history of the Baloch is, nevertheless, still in dark. Research scholars have different opinions. Some say they belong to the northern areas of Elburz, now inhabited by Ashkanis. Some historians maintain that they came from Halab (an archaeological site in the Al Hasakah governorate of northeastern Syria, near the Turkish border, just opposite Ceylanpýnar), Allepe, and are Semites. It is also believed that they from the old stock of Sumerians of Mesopotamia, while others regard the Baloch as the remnants of indigenous population of the region. The historians, nevertheless, mostly concern themselves in tracing the Baloch racial ancestry either from amongst the Indo-Europeans or the Semites. Neither should one object on these methods for historical research, nor doubt the fact that there had been an admixture of various people with Baloch like the Scythians, Pathians, Ashkanis, Sakas, Kushans, Huns, Turks and many others; nor contest the proposition that Baloch, culturally, were greatly influenced by Tigris-Euphrates civilization at different stages of history.

People & Culture

Groups of people broadly known as the Baloch have inhabited remote, mountainous and desert areas in Pakistan, Afghanistan, and Iran for over 1000 years. The ancestry of the Balochis are still subject to debate amongst scholars and nationalist Balochi movements. The most common myth that is used to attempt to unify the Baloch people claims that they originated from Aleppo (which is now in Syria) shortly before the time of Christ.

Traditionally, the Baloch were nomadic peoples and even today many survive through a combination of subsistence farming and semi-nomadic pastoralism. The Balochis in Pakistan are composed of two major groupings: the Makrani or Western Balochis who speak Balochi and the Brahuis of the central Kalat plateau who speak Brahui (this language is not related to Balochi but contains a heavy Balochi admixture). The vast majority of Balochis adhere to the Hanafi school of the Sunni sect of Islam; nevertheless, religion and religious leaders are not significant aspects of Balochi life. Rather, the major divisions and rivalries amongst the Baloch stem from their hierarchical organization into clans and sub-clans where the highest allegiance and loyalty is owed to the chief or sardar.

The national language of the Baloch is Balochi. In Balochistan, their second-most commonly spoken language is Brahui which belongs to the Dravidian language family, and Farsi.

The Baloch do not only live in Balochistan but also are in Sindh, South Punjab, Southern Afghanistan, Eastern Iran, Gulf States and Mari area of Turkmenistan. There are also Baloch who migrated and still live on the East African coast in cities such as Mombasa and Dar es-Salaam. The Baloch Talpur Leghari reigned Sindh before the British annexation of Sindh to the British Raj. The Baloch in Sindh, South Punjab speak Sindhi and Saraiki.

Baloch society is divided in many sects and Sub-sects, some clans speak Brahui and some speak Balochi, and there are many who speaks both and as well as Sindhi and Siraiki. The Bijaranis and the Bugtis speak Balochi. Mengals speak Brahui and they live in Chagai, Khuzdar, Kharan and in southern parts of Afghanistan, The Langos who live in central Balochistan in the Mangochar region, speak Balochi as their first language and Brahui as their second. The Bizenjos that live in the Khuzdar, Nal and parts of Makkura, along with the Muhammadsanis, speak both languages. The Bangulzais speak Brahui but a sub-sect of the Bangulzai, the Garanis, speak Balochi and are known as Balochi-speaking Bangulzais.

The Mazari in Rajanpur speak Balochi, while the Leghari the largest Baloch community living in Dera Ghazi Khan and Rahim Yar Khan speak Saraiki. In Dera Ghazi Khan, their leader is ex-President of Pakistan Sardar Farooq Ahmed Khan Leghari. The Leghari in Sindh speak Sindhi & Saraiki both. Ahmedan clan is the largest in terms of number both in Sindh and Punjab. In Punjab, the clan is majorly settled in Dera Ghazi Khan division.

A village has also been named as Mana Ahmedani in honour their elder 'Mana Khan' (late). Also exists other Baloch clan Nizamani living in Dera Ghazi Khan (Punjab) and also in Sanghar (Sindh) and other parts of Sindh and the majority of Nizamani Baloch speak seraeki. The Bijarani settled in Sindh speak Balochi. Kolachi Baloch living in the Punjab and Sindh province of Pakistan speak Saraiki, while those living in Sibi district of Balochistan speak Balochi. The Talpur, Mastoi, Jatoi, Gabol, Lashari, Chandio, Bozdar,Samma, Jiskani and other Baloch clans settled in Sindh speaks, Sindhi and Balochi and Siraiki. Qaisrani Baloch living near Taunsa Sharif speak Saraiki, while their clansmen living the Dera Ghazi Khan regions speak Balochi. Rind Baloch settled in Sindh speak Sindhi and Siraiki.

Sects

The following is a list of major Baloch Sects:

- Ahamdanis
- Ameeri
- Askani
- Badezai
- Badini
- Bagayzanii
- Bahawalanzai
- Balochs
- Bangulzai
- Banulzai
- Barazani
- Barija
- Barzoi
- Bhutani
- Bijarani
- Bizenjo
- Bozdar
- Brahmani
- Bugti
- Buledi
- Gyandar
- Hasni
- Hooth
- Indhar
- Ismailzahi
- Jadgal
- Jamaldini
- Jamali
- Jarwar
- Jatoi
- Jatt Baloch
- Jattak
- Jiskani
- Kahodai
- Kalmati
- Kalpar
- Kambarzahi
- Kashani
- Khetran
- Khosa
- Mondrani
- Moosiani
- Narooie
- Naukri
- Nauri
- Nausherwani
- Nothazai
- Nutkani
- Pirkani
- Qaisrani
- Qasimzahi
- Rahija
- Rahimi
- Rahmanzai
- Raisani
- Raisi or Rais
- Ramzahi
- Rigi
- Rind
- Rodeni

- Bulfati
- Buzdar
- Chakerzehi
- Chang
- Chutani
- Damanis
- Dannarzai
- Dareshak
- Dashti
- Dehani
- Dehwar
- Drakhshaan
- Fatahni
- Gamshadzehi
- Gashkori
- Ghanbarzehi
- Ghazini
- Gichki
- Gola
- Gorgage
- Gorshani
- Gurmani
- Kizilbash
- Kolachi
- Kupchanis
- Kurd
- Laghari
- Lamba
- Langhani
- Lanjwani
- Lari
- Lasi
- Lehri
- Loharani
- Malghani
- Mamhdani
- Marri
- Mastoi
- Masuri
- Mazari
- Mengal
- Mirani
- Mobaraki
- Mohammadzahi
- Roonjha
- Sadozai
- Sakhani
- Samma
- Saravani
- Sardaizai
- Sargani Baloch
- Sethwi
- Seyahsawar
- Shah Bakhsh
- Shambhani
- Shambhani
- Sherzai Baloch
- Shirani
- Sundrani
- Taherza
- Tanwri
- Umrani
- Yarahmadzahi
- Zarakzahi
- Zarrani
- Zehi
- Zehri

Demographics

The Baloch people is estimated to be in the range of 10 to 15 million (Population Census Organization, Government of Pakistan, 2006). Nevertheless, the exact number of Baloch and those who are or claim to be of Baloch ancestry is difficult to determine.

It is possible that there are more Baloch than simply those who claim Balochi as their mother tongue. This, nevertheless, raises the question as to who is and is not a Baloch as many surrounding peoples claim to be of Baloch descent, but do not speak Balochi. The Brahui, having resided in proximity to the Baloch, have absorbed substantial linguistic and genetic admixture from the Baloch and in many cases are indistinguishable.

Despite very few cultural differences from the Baloch, the Brahui are still regarded as a separate group on account of language difference. The higher population figure for the Baloch may only be possible if a large number of "Baloch" are included who speak a different languages, such as Saraikis, Sindhi, and Brahui, and who often claim descent from Baloch ancestors. Many Baloch outside of Balochistan are also bilingual or of mixed ancestry because of their proximity to other ethnic groups including the Sindhis, Brahui, Persians,Saraikis and Pashtuns. There are also a large number of Baloch who have been migrating or have been living in adjacent provinces to Balochistan for centuries. In addition, there are many Baloch located in other parts of the world with the bulk living in the GCC countries of the Persian Gulf.

There is a significant population of Baloch in western countries such as Sweden and Australia. It is known that many Baloch settled in Australia in the 1800s and now fourth generation Baloch still live in Australia, majorly in Perth.

The Balochistan area is divided into three parts: Pakistani Balochistan, Iranian Balochistan and the southern parts of Afghanistan Balochistan (Afghanistan). Research also has been done by several authors, that the Baloch ancestry goes back to the Median Empire era, when the Baloch people or Kurd people were sent to protect the borders of the Median empire in areas of Makran and Toran.

Regions with significant populations are:

Area	Population
Pakistan	8 million
Iran	4.1 million
Afghanistan	1.1 million
Oman	407,000
United Arab Emirates	215,000
Turkmenistan	55,000
Kuwait	20,000
Qatar	13,000
Saudi Arabia	12,000
Somalia	8,200

Source: Carina Jahani, *Standardization and Orthography in Balòchi Language*.

Martial Traditions

Martialy, the history of the Baloch has certainly always been interesting. As the last to arrive of the major ethnic groups of Pakistan they were faced with the need to displace the peoples already settled in Balochistan. Some they more or less successfully subjugated or assimilated, like the Meds of Makran and other now subordinate groups. From others they faced a greater challenge, notably from the Brahui clans occupying the hills around Kalat.

The origins of the Brahuis are even more puzzling than those of the Baloch, for their language is not Indo-European at all, but belongs to the same Dravidian family as Tamil and the other languages of south India spoken over a thousand miles away. One theory has it that the Brahuis are the last northern survivors of a Dravidian-speaking population which perhaps created the Indus Valley civilisation, but it seems more likely that they too arrived as the result of a long migration, at some earlier date from peninsular India.

As they moved eastwards, the Baloch were initially successful in overcoming the Brahuis. Under Mir Chakar, who established his capital at Sibi in 1487, a great Baloch kingdom briefly came into existence before being destroyed by civil war between Mir Chakar's Rind clan and the rival Lasharis, whose battles are still celebrated in heroic ballads. Although the Baloch moved forward into Punjab and Sind, the authority of the Mughals stopped them establishing permanent kingdoms there, although the names of Dera Ghazi Khan in Punjab and Dera Ismail Khan in NWFP are still reminders of the Baloch chiefs who conquered these lands in the 16th century. The Baloch who settled in the plains gradually became largely domesticated, forgetting their native language and increasingly assimilated to the local population, with their origins remaining little more than a proud memory.

In Balochistan itself, which came only briefly under the authority of the Mughals, the tables were turned on the Baloch by the Brahuis who succeeded in re-establishing their power in Kalat. Throughout the 18th century, the Khans of Kalat were the dominant local power, with the Baloch settled to the west and to the east of them being forced to acknowledge their suzerainty.

The greatest of the Khans was Mir Nasir Khan (1749-1817), whose military success owed much to the regular organisation of his army, with its separate divisions recruited from the Sarawan and Jhalawan areas which constitute the northern and southern parts of the Brahui homeland.

The Khanate of Kalat became the nearest thing there has ever been to an independent Balochistan. This extended beyond the modern boundaries, since Mir Nasir Khan's authority ran as far as the then insignificant town of Karachi. Although dominated by the Brahuis, they themselves became increasingly "Balochified". Today, for instance, the Brahui language only keeps the first three of its old Dravidian numbers. From "four" upwards Brahuis count in Balochi, in which most are anyway bilingual.

With the British expansion into northwestern subcontinent and their disastrous first Afghan war (1839-41), internal power struggles within Kalat prompted the first British military interference, and the signing of a treaty in 1841. The British annexation of Sind in 1843 from the Talpur Mirs, themselves a dynasty of Baloch descent, and the subsequent annexation of Punjab meant that Kalat and the other regions of Balochistan were now part of the sensitive western borderlands of British India, where the possibility of Russian interference induced a permanent state of imperial neurosis. Although the eastern Baloch were partially pacified by the efforts of Sir Robert Sandeman, it was thought easiest to leave the Khan and his subordinate chiefs in control of most of the rest of Balochistan.

A further treaty was signed in 1876, which forced the Khan to 'lease" the strategic Quetta region to the British but left him in control of the rest of his territories with the aid of a British minister. Granted the rank of a 19-gun salute to mark the size if not the wealth of Kalat, the Khans were for a while content to pursue the eccentric lifestyle characteristic of so many south Asian princes of the time. One Khan became legendary as a passionate collector of shoes, and made sure no pair would ever be stolen by locking up all the left shoes in a dungeon below the Fort at Kalat.

With the last ruler of Kalat, Mir Ahmad Yar Khan (1902-79), the Khanate again briefly entered the political arena. Exploiting the opaque clauses of the 1876 treaty, which left some doubt as to just how independent Kalat was supposed to be, he hesitated to join Pakistan in 1947. The brief independence of Kalat finally ended in 1948 when the Khan signed the necessary merger documents, followed by his formal removal from power and the abolition of the state's boundaries in 1955. The present shape of Balochistan was finally rounded out in 1958 when the Sultan of Oman sold Gwadar, given to one of his ancestors by the Khan of Kalat, back to Pakistan.

The E.I.C. got involved in Balochistan in the context of the First Anglo-Afghan War of 1839-1842. In 1843 the E.I.C. annexed most of Sindh and thus became neighbour of Balochistan. In 1858, the E.I.C.

possessions in India were taken over by the British government; India became a crown colony.

In 1871, an Anglo-Persian agreement partitioned Balochistan into a Persian and a British sphere of interest, divided by the Goldsmid Line. In 1876, the British assumed direct administration of Quetta and environs. In 1893 the Durand Line established the border between Afghanistan and Balochistan.

Within British Balochistan, the lands on the border to Afghanistan and the environs of Quetta were under direct British administration; most of the country was nominally independent - the Khanates of Kalat (1638-1955) and Las Bela (1742-1955) - and placed under indirect rule. In 1940, in a measure directed against the Khan of Kalat, the administration of British India decided to recognize the 'independence' (that is, from the Khan of Kalat) of the State of Kharan (a vassall of Kalat from 1697 to 1940).

For the administration of British India, Balochistan was of purely strategic importance, securing the border to Afghanistan. In Balochistan, pastoral nomadism dominated; there was limited agriculture. The absence of major rivers and the rugged mountainous landscape prevented large-scale irrigation, as in adjacent Sindh and Punjab. The urban centers were small and, from the perspective of the administration of British India, remote, the most prominent being Quetta. The economic policies of the administration of British India had hardly any impact on Balochistan, the social policies (education), by comparison to other regions of British India, limited impact; in Balochistan, Islam and the traditional feudal structures were more influential than the British & missionary-indiced modernization.

The concept of a future Muslim state in India (Pakistan), propagated by the Muslim League since 1930, found a limited echo in Balochistan, for a number of reasons. In Balochistan, the Islamic nature of the state was not an issue as Islam already was the uncontested dominant religion. The vast majority of the Balochis was illiterate and, in regard to politics, accustomed to follow their feudal leaders. The most prominent of these leaders was the Khan of Kalat, who favoured an independent Kalat (Balochistan) over a solution which provided for Balochistan becoming part of Pakistan.

During British control of the Indian subcontinent, the region was largely governed through a combination of direct and indirect rule (four princely states). Upon independence, local Baloch leaders were granted wide autonomy in their traditional spheres of influence. In 1955, the Pakistani government merged its territories in the West to form one single province known as West Pakistan. The merger sparked expectations of major social change amongst the Balochis, who were and remain the weekest of Pakistan's habitants. In 1970, provincial status was restored to Balochistan and West Pakistan's three other major regions. (Balochistan is Pakistan's largest province, encompassing approximately 40% of the total region of the nation).

In Balochistan, growing dissatisfaction over the limited benefits from the central government led to the election of the National Awami Party (NAP) in the 1970 provincial elections. Further, two Baloch nationalists, Mir Ghaus Baksh Bizenjo and Sardar Ataullah Khan Mengal were installed as governor and chief minister of the province, respectively.

Following the secession of East Pakistan, a new constitution was drafted under the leadership of Zulfikar Ali Bhutto. The constitution provided for many guarantees of the rights of ethnic minorities, including their separate legal status and the right to their own language and culture. In reality, the Bhutto government refused to release its strong central control over the provinces.

In 1973, the conflict between the Balochis and the Bhutto government escalated leading to a full-fledged Balochi rebellion that was not contained till 1977. The precipitating incident in February of 1973 was the Pakistani government's seizure of a cache of illegal arms from the residence of the Iraqi military attache in Islamabad. The government alleged that these arms were destined for Baloch separatists. Bhutto then proceeded to dismiss the provincial NAP government on the grounds that it encouraged violence and smuggling and opposed modernization efforts. Key leaders of the NAP and other opposition parties were arrested and in 1975 the NAP was banned. Balochi guerrillas responded by ambushing army convoys and attacking government troops. At its height in 1974, around 55,000 Balochis were engaged in battle with 80,000 to 100,000 government troops. The violent conflict between the two sides continued till the Bhutto government was removed in 1977. Bhutto's successor, General Zia ul-Haq released 6-11,000 Balochi leaders from jails and declared an amnesty for the guerrillas that had fled to Iran or Afghanistan. It is estimated that over the four year rebellion, over 5,000 insurgents and 3,000 government troops were slained. During the imposition of martial law in Pakistan (1977-1985), President Zia's government actively sought to promote economic and social programs in Balochistan. But despite some limited efforts by the Pakistani government, Balochistan still remains the most economically disadvantaged province. Further, Balochis are underrepresented in the bureaucracy, armed forces, and government at both the provincial and national level. Balochistan contains reserves of coal and natural gas that provide for most of Pakistan's needs. The exploitation of these resources by the Pakistani government has often been opposed by Balochis on the grounds that they are not reaping the benefits from the revenue that is generated.

Two other issues dominated the agenda in Balochistan during the 1980s: the rate of migration into the province and the refugee flow into Pakistan as a result of the war in Afghanistan. Of the 4.1% of the Balochi population in Pakistan, only 56% live in Balochistan while the others have settled in Sindh or the Punjab or emigrated to the Gulf States. Balochistan has seen an influx of Sindhi, Pashtu and Punjabi speakers, many of whom have tended to occupy the better jobs in the province, in both the public and private sector. This has heightened fears amongst the Baloch about becoming a minority in the province. The war in Afghanistan further deepened Balochi discontent over the ethnic composition of their province. Approximately 20% of the over three million Afghan refugees fled to Balochistan; most of these were Pashtuns.

Periodically, the Afghan opposition groups used their bases in Balochistan to launch attacks against the Soviet-backed Afghan government, leading to retaliatory action in Balochistan. For the Balochis, the cross-border attacks threatened to draw them further into the Afghanistan quagmire and the large number of refugees exacerbated Baloch fears of being overwhelmed by other ethnic minorities.The last insurgency broke out in the mid-1970s and it took several army divisions and aerial bombardment to overwhelm the defiant members of the Marri clan. Valour, martial prowess and honour are key elements of Baloch custom. Ballads from the 15th century about the great war between two Baloch blocs, respectively governed by Chakar Rind and Gowaram Lashari, are still regarded as the ultimate in chivalric tradition. As recent as the mid-1990s, the warring Mazari and Bugti clans spawned a new generation of ballads extolling their bravery and paying homage to those that had died in the conflict.

In 1973 Islamabad engineered the dismissal of the first elected Balochistan government, then headed by the Marri and Mengal chiefs. The chief of the Bugtis, who nursed a perceived insult from these rival sardars (chiefs), agreed to become Islamabad's newly appointed provincial governor.He then sent a discreet message to his rivals, the Marri and Mengal sardars, that he would reinstate their government provided they made peace by visiting him at his official governor's residence. The ensuing negotiations eventually culminated in a major anti-Islamabad rebellion. It led to the death of hundreds of men at the hands of the army.

Contribution to Defence Services

The achievements of the Baloch Race of today's Pakistan are considerable. Awards and decorations are not always an accurate gauge of their supreme sacrifices. Almost 0.06 per cent of army comprises from Balochistan. They have their own regiment named Baloch Regiment.

Baloch Regiment

Regimental Motto: Who dares Wins

War Cry: "Iman, Taqwa, Jihad fi Sabilillah" (Faith, Piety, to strive in the path of Allah, puting aside all your physical needs)

The Baloch Regiment is an infantry regiment of the modern Pakistan Army. It was established in April 1956 from an existing unit of the same name, merged with the 8th Punjab Regiment and the Bahawalpur Regiment. Newly raised additional units brought the strength of the Regiment to nearly 50 battalions.

Under British rule the British Indian Army included the 124th Duchess of Connaught's Own Balochistan Infantry (raised 1820), the 126th Balochistan Infantry (raised 1825), the 127th Queen Mary's Own Baloch Light Infantry (raised 1844 as the Scinde Balochi Corps), the 129th Duke of Connaught's Own Balochis (raised 1846 as the 2nd Baloch Battalion) and the 130th King George's Own Balochis (raised 1858 as Jacob's Rifles). Following World War I all five units were merged into a single large regiment: the 10th Baloch Regiment, which became part of the Pakistan Army in 1947.The Baloch regiments earned battle honours for service in Afghanistan, East Africa, China, Persia, Aden, Central India, Abyssinia, Hyderabad and Burma. Until 1914 their full dress uniforms included red trousers worn with rifle green or drab tunics and turbans.

This regiment was earlier called the Baloch Regiment, after the Pakistan province of Balochistan. This spelling and pronunciation were, however, inherited from colonial days. The Pakistani pronounciation of the Baloch is Baloch, with the ch as in change. The Baloch regiment is second in seniority after the Punjab Regiment in the Pakistan Army. Its oldest battalion was raised more than two hundred years ago, in 1798 AD at Masulipattam, as the Macleod Ki Paltan (Macleod's force), now the 1st Baloch. After raising, it later became the 89th Punjabis and was followed by 90th, 91st and 93rd Punjab Battalions. Combined these arms were given the title of the Madras Native Infantry.

It was the Madras Army that was responsible to oust the French from the India. The battalions fought valiantly in expeditions that resulted in the unification of the territories which now make up India and modern Burma'.Storming through the jungles of Burma in the same century, uttering their blood-chilling battle cries, the Balochis also led the fight to conquer that country and their name became immortalized as the 'Burma' battalions. In honour of their courage and valor the battalions were presented with an image of the mythical Burmese god, Chinthe, Which they adopted as their cap badge.The Balochis are formidable fighting men. Through two centuries their lustrous deeds in campaigns throughout the sub-continent and in World War I and afterwards are writ large in the history of valor.

One of the battalions raised in the first half of 19th century so distinguished itself on the battlefields of Europe and Palestine; it earned the name of the 'Bombay Toughs'. Another, the 124th, raised in 1905, became the 'War Babies'- for their youth and the courage they displayed in Palestine in 1918.Many awards for courage were won the Balochis in the First World War and subsequently in campaigns across the sub-continent and in the Second World War.These including the first Victoria Cross ever awarded to an Indian soldier, not only a Muslim but also a Balochi: Lance Naik Khudad Dad Khan of the old 4th Baloch, now 11th Baloch. For their fighting distinction and sheer courage in WWI, the British Government in India bestowed a noble onument in the gardens of Frere Hall, Karachi commemorating the officers, JCOs and men of the 10th Baloch Regiment who fell in battle which still stands.

Another unique distinction in the regimental honour is that of the George Cross, Britain's peacetime equivalent of the Victoria Cross, which was awarded to Captain Durrani of the 1st Bahawalpur Regiment, now the 8th Baloch.Altogether in its first 150 year, the regiment gathered one of the most distinguished records for bravery in military history, including fourteen Victoria Crosses, one George Cross, one CMC, 36 DSOs, 158 MCs, Service medals and civil honours and more than 350 mentions in dispatches.

The Baloch Regiment like the Punjab Regiment and the Frontier Force Regiment are three British origin infantry regiments in Pakistan Army. The British ruled this area nearly 200 years and an Army Commander-in-Chief was always number two in rank after the Viceroy/Governor General in the sub-Continent. "Sub-Continent" means present day Pakistan, India, Bangladesh and Burma. The British originally had three different armies to control this region, Bengal Army, Bombay Army and Madras Army. These three armies were united in 1895 as British Indian Army. More than 500 states were also working under British India, most of them, especially big states, had their own state forces.

Present Baloch Regiment have its origin in Bombay Army, Madras Army and in State Forces of Bahawalpur in southern Punjab. Part of the Baloch Regiment's origin is from the old Bombay Army raised in early nineteenth century, the senior battalion originated in the 2nd (Marine) Bn of the 12th Regiment of Bombay Native Infantry raised in 1820. In 1838, as the 24th Regiment of Bombay Native Infantry, they stormed Aden (Yemen), bringing that hotbed of pirates under the British flag. The 26th Bombay Native Infantry was raised in 1825 as the 2nd Extra Bn of Bombay Native Infantry, changing its name a year later. Sir Charles Napier raised two regiments in Karachi - the 1st and 2nd Baloch Regiments - for local service within Sind in 1844 and 1846 respectively.

The 129th in the 3rd (Lahore) Division, was the only battalion of the regiment to serve on the Western Front, the first Indian regiment to attack the Germans, the first also on two other counts - to lose the first British officer and to earn the first Victoria Cross, this by Sepoy Khudadad Khan at Hollebeke. Wounded, he recovered to enjoy the distinction of being the first Indian soldier to receive the King Emperor's most coveted gift. Prior to 1911, Indian soldiers had not been eligible to receive the Cross.

In August 1947, the sub-continent was freed from British rule and dived between Pakistan and India. 10 Baloch, 8 Punjab, and Bahawalpur State Forces were allotted to Pakistan. Dogra companies of 10 Baloch remained in India and transferred to, among other regiments, The Indian Grenadiers. The Regimental center was shifted to Quetta in 1946.

10 Baloch Regimental Center was at Quetta had 50% Punjabi Muslims (PMs), 25% Pathans and 25% Dogras. After the departure of Dogras, new composition was 50% each PMs and Pathans.

On transfer of power, the active battalions were the 1st, 2nd, 3rd, 4th, 5th and 7th. 1 Baloch had 50% PMs, 25% Pathans and 25% Dogras was stationed at Secunderabad, in Aug 1947 moved to Kasur/Lahore. PMs from 5/6 Rajputana Rifles replaced Dogras. 2 Baloch consisted of 3 companies of PMs and one of Dogras was stationed at Razmak. 3 Baloch 50% PMs, 25% Pathans and 25% Dogras was stationed at Quetta. 4 Baloch 50% PMs, 25% Pathans and 25% Dogras was stationed at Nowshera. In 1948 it moved to Kashmir. 5 Baloch 50% PMs, 25% Pathans and 25% Dogras was stationed in Fort Sandeman (Zhob). In March it moved to Quetta and in Dec in Sialkot. 7 Baloch 50% PMs, 25% Pathans and 25% Dogras was stationed at Kanpur when it received orders to move to Fort Sandeman (Zhob). In July, the unit received orders to move Karachi before 7 August and prepare for ceremonies in connection with Independence of Pakistan.

The Battalion had the distinction of providing the first guard of honour to the Quaid-I-Azam as he stepped on the soil of Pakistan. Major Shukat Ali commanded the guard of honour. On 14th August the Subedar Major (the battalion's senior warrant officer) unfurled the first flag at the Governor General's residence. The flag was later presented to 7/10 Baloch by Quaid-I-Azam.

The 8th Punjab Regiment was allocated to Pakistan and the Sikh companies returned to India, principally to replace Punjabi Muslim companies in battalions of The Sikh Regiment and to help in creation of new Sikh battalions.

The regular battalions on transfer of power were the 1st, 2nd, 3rd and 4th.Bahawalpur Regiment was raised among the Bahawlpur state forces. The Bahawalpur Regiment had two active battalions 1 Bahawalpur, 3 Bahawalpur. 4 Bahawalpur was raised from the officers and men from 2 Patiala (raised in 1919) in July 1948.

In 1947, men of Baloch Regiment were assigned the task of escorting the weary refugees fleeing India, earning the regiment-honoured name of Ghazi Balochi. Based at Abbottabad since Dec 1957, the Baloch fought with great courage in the 1947-48 Kashmir Conflict, and in the two wars with India in 1965 and 1971, winning 279 awards for bravery- Including three Hilal-e-Jurats, one of Pakistan's highest awards for valor and 73 Sitara-e-Jurat.

The Regiment's long list of battle honours dates from the battle of Cochin in 1809 to battle of Qaiser-I-Hind in 1971. In 1957, a major re-organization took place in infantry Regiments of Pakistan most of the regiments organized in 1922/23 were re-organized and the regimental centers reduced from 11 to 5.

The Baloch Regiment was re-organized by merging the 10 Baloch, 8 Punjab and Bahawalpur Regiments.The new regimental center was set up at Abbottabad in December 1957.

The badge of the Baloch Regiment depicts crossed swords within a crescent, under a Muslim star, appearing above a title scroll. All ranks wear a rifle green beret with a cherry coloured backing to the badge. Bandsmen wear the traditional green and red full dress of the old Bombay Army Baloch regiments, as described above.

The current Colonel-in-Chief of Baloch Regiment is General Ashfaq Parvez Kayani, who is also the Chief of Army Staff. The Colonel Commandant of the regiment is Lt General Shafaatullah Shah who was installed as the 16th colonel commandant on 26 April 2008. Previous colonel commandants have included Ashfaq Kayani, Lt General Syed Parwez Shahid, and Lt General Jamshaid Gulzar Kiani, who were the 15th, 14th, and 13th colonel commandants respectively.

Performance in W.W. I: 124th Duchess of Connaught's Balochistan Infantry - India, Mesopotamia, Persia. 2/124th (formed in 1916)- Persia, Mesopotamia, Egypt, India. 3/124th (formed in 1917)- India, Persia, Mesopotamia. 126th Balochistan Infantry - India, Egypt, Muscat, Aden, Mosopotamia. 2/126th (formed in 1918) - India. 127th Queen Mary's Own Baloch Light Infantry - India, East Africa, Persia. 2/127th (formed in 1918) - India, Egypt. 129th Duke of Connaught's Own Balochis - India, France, East Africa. 2/129th (formed in 1917) - India, Mesopotamia. 130th King George's Own Balochis (Jacob's Rifles) - India, East Africa. 2/130th (formed in 1918) - India.

The 129th in the 3rd (Lahore) Division, was the only battalion of the regiment to serve on the Western Front, the first Indian regiment to attack the Germans, the first also on two other counts - to lose the first British officer and to earn the first Victoria Cross, this by Sepoy Khudadad Khan at Hollebeke. Wounded, he recovered to enjoy the distinction of being the first Indian soldier to receive the King Emperor's most coveted gift. Prior to 1911, Indian soldiers had not been eligible to receive the Cross.

89th Punjabis - India, Aden, Egypt, Gallipoli, France, Mesopotamia, Greece, Russia. 2/89th Punjabis (raised in 1917) - India, Mesopotamia 90th Punjabis - India, Mesopotamia 2/90th Punjabis (raised in 1918) - India 91st Punjabis - India, Mesopotamia, Egypt 2/91st Punjabis (raised in 1918) - India, Egypt 92nd Punjabis - India, Mesopotamia, Egypt 93rd Burma Infantry - India, Egypt, France, Mesopotamia, Burma Following the return of Indian troops after the war, all the second battalions were disbanded with the exception of the 2/89th Punjabis.

Post W. W. 1: After the First World War, a major re-organization of British Indian Army took place. Most of the wartime units were disbanded and merged with each other. A new Regiment in the name of 10 Baloch was formed in 1922/23 At Rajkot (Rajasthan) with composition of Punjabi Muslims, Pathans, Balochis and Brahuis. Balochi and Brahuis are two great communities of Balochistan province (now in Pakistan). Balochies are also constituted a major part of population of Sindh Province (also in Pakistan). Pathans are great warriors from the NWFP and West Punjab (both are also in Pakistan). The Baloch Regiment is the only one which represents all of Pakistan's provinces.

The badge chosen for the 10th Baloch Regiment in 1923 was a Roman 'Ten' within a crescent moon, a crown above and title scroll below.

The line-up of battalions for the new regiment was as under: 124th Duchess of Connaught's Own Balochistan Infantryredesignated as1st Bn. 126th Balochistan Infantry - redesignated as2nd Bn 127th Queen Mary's Own Baloch Light Infantry - redesignated as 3rd Bn (Queen Mary's Own) 129th Duke of Connaught's Own Balochis - redesignated as 4th Bn (Duke of Connaught's Own) 130th King George's Own Balochis - redesignated as 5th Bn (King George's Own) (Jacobs Rifles) 10th Baloch Regiment. 2/124th Duchess of Connaught's Own Balochistan Infantry - redesignated as 10th Bn

There was no Territorial battalion but the 5/10th was selected for Indianisation. It was not among the initial six infantry battalions nominated in 1923, but it featured in a supplementary list in 1933.

8 Punjab (now part of Baloch regiment) was also formed by the union of the following regiments of Punjabis: The new line-up was as follows:

89th Punjabis redesignated as 1st Bn 8th Punjab Regiment 90th Punjabis redesignated as 2nd Bn 8th Punjab Regiment 91st Punjabis (Light Infantry) redesignated as 3rd Bn 8th Punjab Regiment 92nd (Prince of Wales's Own) Punjabis redesignated as 4th Bn 8th Punjab Regiment (Prince of Wales's Own) 93rd Burma Infantry redesignated as 5th Bn 8th Punjab Regiment (Burma) 2/89th Punjabis redesignated as 10th Bn 8th Punjab Regiment The 92nd had been made 'Prince of Wales's Own' in 1921 for their services during the war.

The badge chosen for the 8th Punjab Regiment on its creation in 1923 was probably one of the most interesting and heraldically appealing. In the light of the former history of the constituent regiments, it was appropriate that the new regiment should adopt the Chinthe, the mythical lion-dragon, the guardian of Buddhist pagodas, above the numerical '8' and the title scroll.

Performance in W. W. II: 1st Battalion - India, Iraq, Iran, Syria, Egypt. 2nd Battalion - India, Malaya. Captured in Singapore in February 1942. Reformed in April 1946 from cadre of 9/10 Baloch. 3rd Battalion - India, Iran, Iraq, Egypt, Sicily, Italy. On return to India, the battalion was nominated for conversion to a parachute role to join 2 Indian Airborne Division. 4th Battalion - India, East Africa, Egypt, Cyprus, Italy. 5th Battalion - India, Burma. 6th Battalion - raised in Karachi on 1 Jan 40. India. Disbanded 1 Feb. 47. 7th Battalion - raised in Benares on 10 Oct 40. India. Burma. 8th Battalion - raised in Karachi on 1 Feb. 41. India, Burma. Disbanded 22 Dec 1946. 9th Battalion - raised in Nasirabad on 1 Feb. 41. India. Disbanded 25 Apr 46 but almost 500 men went to reform the regular 2nd Bn. 14th Battalion - raised in Karachi on 1 Feb. 41. India, Burma, Malaya, Siam. Disbanded 15 Sep 46. 16th Battalion - raised in Karachi on 15 Oct 41. India, Burma, Malaya. Disbanded March 1946. 17th Battalion - raised November 1942 by conversion of 53 Regt IAC, India, Iraq, Palestine, Greece, Libya. 18th Battalion - raised originally as 25 Garrison Bn, it became an active battalion and was redesignated 18/10th. India. Disbanded May 1944. 25th Garrison Battalion - raised in Karachi in July 1941. On conversion to active status, it was redesignated the 18/10th. 26th Garrison Battalion - raised in Karachi in March 1942. India. Disbanded 1946. Machine Gun Battalion - raised in Karachi on 15 Apr 42. Converted to 53 Regt IAC August 1942. Redesignated 17/10th November 1942. In common with many other Indian Infantry regiments, the 10th Baloch Regiment lost its number and, at the end of 1945, became The Baloch Regiment.

The Battalions: Current Baloch regiments are 6th, 7th, 10th, 11th, 12th, 14th, 15th, 16th, 17th, 18th Baloch and 19th Baloch.

Class Composition: Punjabi Mussalmans, Pathans, Balochis and Brahuis.

Battle Honours:

Pre 1947: Aden, Reshire, Bushire, Koosh-ab, Persia. Delhi 1857, Central India, Abyssinia, Kandahar 1880, Cochin, Maheidpore, Ava, Afghanistan 1878-80, Egypt 1882, Tel-el-Kebir, Burma 1885-87, British

East Africa 1896, British East Africa 1897-99, China 1900, Messiness 1914, Armentieres 1914, Ypres 1914-15, Gheluvelt, Festubert 1914, Givenchy 1914, Neuve Chapelle, St. Julian, Loos, France and Flanders 1915, Egypt 1915, Megiddo, Sharon, Palestine 1918, Aden, Kut-al-Amara 1917, Baghdad, Mesopotamia 1916-18, Persia 1915-18, NW Frontier, India 1917, Kilimanjaro, Behobeho, East Africa 1915-18, Afghanistan 1919.Macedonia 1918, Helles, Krithia, Gallipoli 1915, Suez Canal, Egypt 1915, Megiddo, Sharon, Palestine 1918, Tigris 1916, Kut-al-Amara 1917, North Malaya, Jitra, Gurun, Malaya 1941-42, The Trigno, Perano, The Sangro, Villa Grande, Gustav Line, Monte Grande, The Senio, Italy 1943-45, Gallabat, Barentu, Massawa, The Cauldron, Ruweisat Ridge, El Alamein, North Africa 1940-43, Landing in Sicily, Sicily 1943, Castel Frentano, Orsogna, Arezzo, Monte Cedrone, Citta di Castello, Monte Calvo, Gothic Line, Plan di Castello, Croce, Gemmano Ridge, San Marino, San Paulo-Monte Spacata, Monte Cavallo, Cesena, Savio Bridgehead, Casa Bettini, Idice Bridgehead, Italy 1943-45 Donbaik, North Arakan, The Shweli, Myitson, Kama, Burma 1942-45; Athens, Greece 1944-45, North Malaya, Machang, Singapore Island, Malaya 1941-42, Kuzeik, North Arkan, Point 551, Maungdaw, Shwebo, Kyaukmyaung Bridgehead, Mandalay, Capture of Meiktila, Defense of Meiktila, The Irrawaddy, Pegu 1945, Sittang 1945, Burma 1942-45.

Post 1947: Kashmir (1947), Kashmir (1965), East Pakistan (1971)

The Regimental Centre: The regimental centre ia at Abbottabad, Pakistan.

Famous Personalities

The Baloch people is a strong ethnic group spread out over Pakistan, Afganistan and India, and with large populations living in the US, Canada and UK. This is a list of famous jat Peoples:

Armed Forces

Gallantary Award Recipients

Sepoy Khudadad Khan on 31 October 1914 at Hollebeke, Belgium, although himself wounded, continued working his gun after all the other five men of the detachment had been killed. For his heroic deeds, he was awarded Britain's highest medal for valour, the **Victoria Cross**.

Naik Fazal Din on 2 March 1945 near Meiktila, Burma, during an attack, was held up by fire from the enemy bunkers, whereupon he personally attacked the nearest bunker and silenced it, then led his men against the other. For this deed he was awarded **Victoria Cross.**

Caption Mahmood Khan Durrani was awarded the **George Cross** in 1946, for his heroism in withstanding Japanese torture during the Second World War. He was the only prisoner of war taken by the Japanese to both be awarded the George Cross and survive his captivity.

Others

General Muhammad Musa Khan (1908-1991) was the Chief of Army Staff, Pakistan; he succeeded Field Marshal Ayub Khan, who was then President. He was posted to the 6th Royal Battalion,the 13th Frontier Force Rifles as a Platoon Commander in 1936.

General Rahimuddin Khan (born 1926) is the only man to hold all four posts of Corps Commander, Governor of Balochistan, Governor of Sindh, and Chairman of the Joint Chiefs of Staff (having held the first two capacities in simultaneity) in the history of Pakistan.

Politicians

- Zafarullah Khan Jamali: Former Prime Minister of Pakistan (2002-2004)
- Ataullah Mengal: Former Chief Minister of Balochistan (1972-1973)
- Mir Ghaus Bakhsh Bizenjo: Former Governor of Balochistan (1972-1973)
- Farooq Ahmad Khan Leghari: Former President of Pakistan (1993-1997)
- Asif Ali Zardari: Current President of Pakistan (Since Sept. 9, 2008)

Artists

- Abdur Raham Kurd: Poet
- Faiz Mohammad Baloch: Folk Singer
- Alam Lohar: Singer
- Sain Akhtar: Singer
- Tufail Niazi: Singer

2

Garhwalis

The Garhwali are a people of the hilly Garhwal Division of Uttarakhand, India. The Garhwali language belongs to the Pahari (Northern) subgroup of Indo-Aryan. Garhwal is an ancient land that has many layers of history, culture, ethnicity and religion reaching far back into pre-history, and co-existent in present times. Naturally, the lifestyle of its people reflects this rich diversity. The fact that the ancient kingdoms existed in the remote mountain fastnesses allowed an outstanding measure of autonomy to its people. It was also a sanctuary for those seeking to flee the ever turbulent plains of North and Central India. This has meant that the Garhwali has held his liberty very dear and has accepted change only voluntarily.

So the land is the bastion of tradition, soldiery and the home of spiritual learning. It is where some of Hinduism's most holy shrines exist and where Hindus perform the mandatory pilgrimage to Badrinath, which opens the path to Moksh or liberation from the cycle of births and deaths.

Origin & History

The Garhwali people have descended from many Hilly places like Jammu and Kashmir, some parts of Himachal, and many from the Uttaranchal itself. About their ancestry there is not any specific hypothesis or story. No specific account is found anywhere about the real ancestry of the Garhwali people. Garhwal is among the largest districts in the hill state of Uttarakhand, India. Its administrative headquarters is at New Tehri. The district has a population of 604,747 (2001 census). It is surrounded by Rudraprayag District in the east, Dehradun District in the west, Uttarkashi District in the north, and Pauri Garhwal District in the south.

The name Tehri has been derived from 'Trihari', signifying a place that washes away the three types of sins - sins born out of Mansa, Vacha and Karmana or thought, word and deed, respectively. 'Garh' in Hindi means fort. Prior to 888 AD, the area was divided into 52 garhs which were governed by sovereign kings. These garhs were brought under one province by Kanakpal, the prince of Malwa. Kanakpal, on his visit to Badrinath, had met the then mightiest king Bhanu Pratap who later married his only daughter to the prince and handed him his empire. Kanakpal and his descendents steadily conquered all the garhs and governed the whole of Garhwal area for the next 915 years, up to 1803 AD.

People & Culture

Garhwal is a area which comprises of people of various communities. Garhwalis have their ancestral land in this region. It constitutes immigrant Brahmin, Khasi Brahmin, Thakur Rajput, Khai Rajput, Kols, Doms and others. People like Kols or koltas are the original habitants of Garhwal. They are believed to be of pre-Dravidian ancestry. The Kols or Koltas are dark complexioned people and in the bygone ages resided in the forests of Garhwal by hunting and food gathering. Later on, they made small clearings and settled down. They worshipped demons and goblins and later on also Nag and Narsingha.The Rajputs of Garhwal are believed to be of Aryan ancestry. They came as waves of settlers either from the south or from the adjoining tracts of Himachal Pradesh, where they had come from the Hindu Kush through Kashmir. Later Rajput settlers to Garhwal also came from Rajasthan to escape from the invasions of the Muslims/Mughals.

There are other sects like Jaunsaris of Jaunsar-Bawar, Jadhs of Uttarkashi, Marchas of Chamoli (Mana and Niti valleys), Van Gujjars. The Bhotias are businessmen and born mountaineers. The Bhotias of Uttarakhand claim descent from the Rajputs, who came from Kumaon and Garhwal and settled in the higher valleys.The Bhotias are to be found all along the Tibetan border from Nepal in the east to Uttarkashi in the west. Garhwal area consists of people who have different dresses. The languages spoken by the people slightly differ in their accent in the upper and lower hills. Similarly food taken by the people of Garhwal is somewhat different in every area.There are generally division of people who are either living in upper hilly regions, lower areas and middle areas.The People living in the higher or major Himalayan ranges belong to this dietary regime.

Their diet is both meat and vegetable based. The people eat coarse grains like barley, mandua and jhangora. In the recent past, more and more people of this tract have taken to cereals like wheat, rice and pulses.People living in the lower hill, dun valleys and Siwaliks of Garhwal belong to this dietary regime. They are both non-vegetarian and vegetarian. The major cereals eaten by the people of this tract are wheat, rice and pulses, which are cultivated on a large scale.There is distinct style of hill temple architectures. Garhwali people believe in snake worship.They have settled in many interior valleys of Garhwal.

Mountain people, the world over, are a special breed. The people of Garhwal are not very different. The difficult circumstances in which they live has inculcated in them a grand love of life and an abiding reverence for nature and the Almighty. These hardy people have made the endless struggle for survival a joyous expression of their unvanquished souls. There is not a single aspect of their lives that is not steeped in religion, music, dance and art. Indeed, it is this that sustains them through the bleak, snowbound winters and the other extremes of nature that they have to endure.

To try and specifically state what constitutes their culture would be to reflect their lives in the entirety. There are many aspects of their culture that you can find in other parts of this site. Here, we bring to you merely those parts that do not easily find a place elsewhere. The Garhwali lives on the mountains, in the deep valleys, by magnificent rushing rivers, but he is, spiritually, their equal. He is within himself, the mountain, the valley, the forests and the rivers. This is what makes him a good friend and a formidable adversary.

Sects

Present day Garhwal is inhabited by people from many ethnic back grounds. They can be divided into the following groups or sects:

Kols: They are the original habitants of Garhwal believed to be of pre-Dravidian ancestry. The Kols or Koltas are dark complexioned people and in the bygone ages resided in the forests of Garhwal by hunting and food gathering. Later on, they made small clearings and settled down. They worshipped demons and goblins and later on also Nag and Narsingha.

Rajputs: The Rajputs of Garhwal are believed to be of Aryan ancestry. They came as waves of settlers either from the south or from the adjoining tracts of Himachal Pradesh, where they had come from the Hindu Kush through Kashmir. Later Rajput settlers to Garhwal also came from Rajasthan to escape from the invasions of the Muslims/Mughals.

These people fought and subdued the Kols or Koltas or Doms, who were living in Garhwal at that time. Initially, the Rajputs took to settled agriculture as they had brought new skills with them. Later on, they took to other professions. They also joined the armies of various kings of Garhwal in large numbers.

At present, the Rajputs can be found in most professions-agriculture, business and government service. Many Garhwali Rajputs are in the Armed Forces of India, particularly in the Army.

Brahmins: The Brahmins of Garhwal are primarily considered to be the descen- dants of the priests who migrated from the plains or the Brahmins who came to visit the religious places in Garhwal. As a matter of fact, those Brahmins, too, are settled in Garhwal, who came during the migration of the Rajputs or even later.

Both, the Rajputs and Brahmins penetrated into the valleys of Garhwal to escape the rule of the Muslim invaders in the plains of India. There they established villages or colonies, most of which were named after the places from where they had migrated. Some examples are:

a. Ajmer patti and Udaipur patti, and

b. Telangi after Telangana.

In other cases, the people still retained their surnames or named themselves after the place from where they had came. Some examples are:

a. Karnatak and Telang after Mysore (Karnataka), and

b. Rawat and Joshi of Rajasthan and Maharashtra.

Tribal Garhwalis: The tribals of Garhwal live in the upper, e.g. northern tracts. Some are of mongoloid ancestry and have a nomadic or semi-nomadic way of life. Nevertheless, now-a-days, most of these people have taken to a settled life and are engaged in animal husbandry, agriculture, trade and other occupations. Important clans of Garhwal are listed below:

Bhotias: The Bhotias are businessmen and born mountaineers. The Bhotias of Uttarakhand claim descent from the Rajputs, who came from Kumaon and Garhwal and settled in the higher valleys.The Bhotias are to be found all along the Tibetan border from Nepal in the east to Uttarkashi in the west.

Those living close to the Mana pass near Badrinath and those by the Niti pass are known as Tolchas and Marchas, respectively. The people living by the Untadhura pass are Joharis and Saukas. To the south of Johar are the Bhotias or Jethora Bhotias, who are cultivators.

Bhotias are worshippers of the peaks of Nanda Devi, Pancha Chuli etc. and those who are inclined towards Hinduism worship Gabla (the

Weather God), Runiya and Suniya gods, protect their animals from disease, and Sidhuwa and Bidhuwa gods, who help them find lost animals.

Jadhs: The Jadhs are a community inhabiting the cold dry tracts of Uttarkashi District. There are two major villages - Nelang and Jadhang, both situated at an elevation of approximately 3,400 m. The entire community used to migrate from these high altitude villages in the winter, some families staying back at a settlement called Dunda, while the rest of them moved onto the forests around Rishikesh.

This community has close social and economic ties with the people living in the adjoining tracts of Himachal Pradesh and other parts of Uttarkashi. Most Jadhs considered themselves to belong to a superior caste and the task of weaving was left to the Kols, who were considered to be of a lower caste. The Jadhs have typical Mongoloid features and speak a Tibetan dialect. They also speak Garhwali and Pahari.

Jaunsaries: Jaunsar - Bawar forms the northern half of Dehradun District and the people living there are called the Jaunsaries. They are probably of very pure Aryan ancestry. This region had links with the ancient cultural waves, which swept over the northern part of India, particularly during the Vedic, Mahayan, Kushan and Gupta periods of ancient Indian history.

The people follow many of the old customs even today, distinct from their compatriots elsewhere in Garhwal, Kumaon and Himachal Pradesh. Even the art and architecture has its unique features, with profound use of woodwork. The most important festival of the Jaunsaries is the Magh Mela. During festivals, they wear the Thalka or Lohiya, which is a long coat.

Thangel folds like tight-fitting trousers. Digwa or the cap is the traditional Jaunsari head dress made of woolen cloth. Women wear the Ghagra, Kurti and Dhoti and are fond of ornaments. The Jaunsarie still practice polyandry, which are said to be the conse- quence of their having had a close connection with the legendary Pandava brothers of the Mahabharata, who had a common wife, Draupadi.

Van Gujjars: This is a race of nomadic Muslims, who are believed to have come to Garhwal as the dowry of a princess of Sirmaur. This race extends along the Himalaya from Kashmir, Himachal Pradesh to Garhwal. They retain many of the cultural practices of the time before they were converted to Islam. They are purely vegetarian, living basically on milk based products to supplement their consumption of cereals.

They practice transhumance, migrating in the summer to the high mountain meadows, with their herds of buffaloes and cows, and withdrawing to the forests of the low lying tracks in the winters. Much of the milk supply of the hills during the pilgrimage season is provided by them. They are well-known for their command over forest lore. All communities have tremendous knowledge of traditional medicine systems and herbs.

Demographics

As per latest census (2001), the total population of Garhwalis is 6,71,541 with male population of 3,26,380 and female population of 3,45,160. There is an increase of 8.34% in population in comparison of 1991 census.

The proportional distribution of the ethnic groups of Garhwalis is given below:

Group	Population (%)
Khasi Brahmin	13%
Thakur Rajput	15%
Khasi Rajput	23%
Kols or Doms	25%
Immigrant Brahmin	10%
Others	14%

The majority of the population lives in villages as indicated by the rural population of 5,90,359.

The religion wise populations as per latest census is:

Religion	Population (%)
Hindus	97%
Muslims	2.3%
Christians	0.24%
Sikhs	0.17%
Other Religions	0.12%

Martial Traditions

The people of Garhwal have a very memorable history of valour and courage. From very ancient times they have shown their courage and braveness. It is obvious that the life of hills are rather very hard than the plains. And these people are nurtured from their birth to survive in that atmosphere of tough life.

From the Vedic period we can find many stories of their brevity. In British period an Army group was founded for these Garhwali people and they named it Garhwal Rifles. The Garhwal Rifles is a well known infantry rifle regiment of the Indian Army. During the World Wars and the wars fought after Independence, the regiment not only showed exemplary courage but also maintained its unique identity. Majorly comprised of Garhwali soldiers, this regiment fought with grand valour during the Kargil conflict.

Garhwal originally consisted of 52 petty chieftainships, each chief with his own independent fortress (garh). The rulers of Garhwal remained sovereign and repeatedly expelled the attacks of the Mughal rulers of Delhi. During the 19th century, the Gorkhas attacked Garhwal and drove the rulers of Garhwal down to the plains. Thereafter the rulers of Garhwal took the help of the British forces in India and regained their empire. The rulers of Garhwal gave away 60% of their empire for the support the British gave them in driving back the Gurhkas.

Tehri Garhwal or Garhwal Empire, the homeland of Garhwali's was a princely state, governed by Panwar (Shah) dynasty. Later it became a part of the Punjab Hill States Agency of British India, which consisted of present-day Tehri Garhwal District and most of Uttarkashi district. It had a region of approximately 4180 m^2/11,655 km^2 and a population of 268,885 in 1901. The ruler was originally titled Raja and since 1913 Maharaja; the salute state was entitled to 11-guns and had a privy purse of 300000 rupees, acceeding to India on 1 August 1949.

In 1803 AD, the Gorkhas took over Garhwal. Gorkha warriors Subba Amar Singh, Hastidal Chautariya, Bamshah Chautariya and Ranjor Thapa commanded a huge army in the crusade against King Pradyumna Shah and his sons Kuwar Parakrama Shah and Kuwar Pritam Shah. A 12,000 strong army fought with the Gorkhas at Khurhbure where the king was slained. Steadily, Gorkhas captured Dehradun, Saharanpur, Kangada and Shimla and later on extended their empire up to Kangara.

Around1812 AD, Gorkhas captured nearly 200 villages falling under East India Company. British argued with the king of Nepal but to no avail. Finally, the Gorkha War (Anglo-Nepalese War) began in 1814, when an army of 8000 under Major General Marley attacked Kathmandu,

4000 soldiers under Major General Wood started operation from Gorakhpur, and 3500 soldiers attempted to take over Dehradun under Major General Zileswy, where Gorkha army of 300–400 was led by Balbhadra Thapa. Gorkhas fought a fierce battle and crushed the British, which was reinforced by soldiers and cannons. Finally, British army captured Dehradun on 30 Nov 1814.

British Army then moved towards Kumaon. After a fierce battle Gorkha commanders Hastidal and Jayrakha were slained at Vinayathal. The war ended under the Sugauli Treaty, signed on December 2, 1815 and ratified by March 4, 1816, with Gorkha supreme commander Bamshah and thus, British rule started in hills. East India Company then merged Kumaon, Dehradun and east Garhwal in British Empire while west Garhwal was given to Sudarshan Shah which was then known as Tehri Riyasat.

King Sudarshan Shah founded his capital at Tehri city and later on his successors Pratap Shah, Kirti Shah and Narendra Shah founded their capital at Pratap Nagar, Kirti Nagar and Narendra Nagar, respectively. Their dynasty governed over this area from 1815 to 1949. During the Quit India Movement people of this area actively participated for the independence of the nation. Ultimately when the nation was declared independent in 1947, the habitants of Tehri Riyasat started their movement for getting themselves freed from the clutches of Maharaja.

Because of the movement the situation became out of his control and was difficult for him to rule over the area. Consequently the 60th king of Pawar Vansh Manvendra Shah accepted the sovereignty of Indian government. Thus, in 1949, Tehri Riyasat was merged in Uttar Pradesh and was given the status of a new district. Resultantly on 24 February 1960 the state government separated its one tehsil which was given status of a separate district named as Uttarkashi.

In the 1960s Tehri Garhwal went much further east that it currently does. In 1997 much of the eastern portion of Tehri Garhwal was detached and merged with portions of Pauri Garhwal district and Chamoli district to form Rudraprayag district.

"Garhwal" this word consists of word "garh" which means forts. Garhwal was made of many small forts which were governed by chieftains. So the history of garwhal before the dynastic rule of the "Panwar" rulers was not known.It came into light during the rule of Kanak Pal. He came from what is now called the state of Maharastra.

"Panwar" is made of two words, 'pan' and 'mar' which means he who crushes enemies. The origin of the state can be traced back to 2nd century BC when it was governed by the Khasias and was popular as Khashdesh. Several evidences have been excavated recently which point toward the fact that this area was under the domain of Kunidas. It was a race who practiced early form of Shavism.There are also indications of Ashokan edict in the areas of Garhwal area. There was the rule of Chand dynasty between 10th and 18th centuries.With the decline of the Chand dynasty the area became under the Garhwali Kings until the Rohillas took charge of the land in 1744 AD.

Katyuris of Garhwal- there is no evidence of any kind for quite a long time after that, and the next prominent rulers of the valley were the katyuris of Garwhal.The region was overtaken by Gorkhas in 1803.For approximately two decades until 1815 it was under the rule of "Gorkhas".Gorkhas were very cruel people. They use to levy heavy taxes on people. They would often inflict severe punishments on the people.They were evacuated by the British people after they lost the battle in 1815. Garhwal also consists of district of Tehri Garhwal. It was formely a princely state of British India, named after its capital. Pauri garhwal, including today's Chamoli and Rudraprayag (partly) district came to be called British Garhwal till India's independence in 1947. Tehri, at he meeting point of the rivers Bhagirathi and Bhilangna, became the new Capital of Tehri Garhwal.

Contribution to Defence Services

Garhwalis are considered martial race since the days of British colonial rule and form a major part of Indian Army. The military has always heavily recruited Garhwalis and as is consistent with the past, the race continues to produce a considerable number of recruits who occupy many of the senior ranks of the Army.

Prior to 1887, there was no separate Battalion of the Garhwali soldiers. They used to be recruited in the various Gorkha Battalions, Bengal Infantry and Punjab Frontier. Impressed by their honesty, courage and dedication, the British Government decided to form a separate battalion for Garhwali soldiers. The Garhwal Rifles was raised in 1887 to give the Garhwali Hillmen their own Regiment. This was propagated by Field Marshal Sir FS Roberts VC, who realised that many Garhwalis had served in Gorkha regiments, and a large proportion of the early awards to Gorkha Regiments were actually won by Garhwalis.

Garhwal Rifles

Regimental Motto: Yudhaya Krit Nischya (Fight With Determination)

War Cry: Badri Vishal Lal Ki Jai (Victory to the Great Lord Badri Nath)

The Garhwal Rifles is a well known infantry rifle regiment of the Indian Army. During the World Wars and the wars fought after Independence, the regiment not only showed exemplary courage but also maintained its unique identity. Chiefly comprised of Garhwali soldiers, this regiment fought with grand valour during the Kargil conflict. More than 25,000 soldiers of this regiment are at present engaged in the task of safeguarding the motherland.The Rifles are basically infantry soldiers with higher mobility. Riflemen traditionally walk 140 steps a minute vis a vis normal infantry soldiers's 120 steps a minute. They also wear black badges of ranks against that of brass by the rest of the army for better camouflague. The Riflemen take grand pride in being different than rest of the infantrymen.

Soldiers recruited into the Garhwal Rifles are from the Garhwal Hills, among the most beautiful regions of the Himalayas and are known for their hardiness, simplicity and upright manner. Garhwal consists almost entirely of rugged mountain ranges running in all directions, and separated by narrow valleys which in some cases become deep gorges or ravines. The only level portion of the district is a narrow strip of waterless forest between the southern slopes of the hills and the fertile plains of Rohilkhand.

Millions of Uttar Pradesh boys have left their mountain villages of Uttarakhand in search of good fortune or a better life than in the hills. Brave Uttarakhandi soldiers of the bygone era were originally bhagoras (deserters) of their village. Since time immemorial, the running away of village boys from the hills in search of wonderland has been a common practice. In fact it has become a tradition in Uttarakhand, which still continues unabated. The sole source of solace for the hills has been the Indian army. Most appropriately, it is the only institution that has somehow been able to check the migration of village youth. Paharis "Of the mountains" have always played a formidable role in defending the frontiers of India. Twenty-three battalions of Garhwal Rifles and nineteen battalions of the Kumaon Regiment clearly reflect the participation of hill people in the defence forces.

On May 5, 1887 the first Battalion was constituted under the command of Lt. Col. EP Mainwaring at Almora. On November 4, same year, this Battalion reached Kalundanda in Garhwal. In 1890, Kalundanda was renamed as Lansdowne after the then Viceroy of India. In the First World War, the Garhwal Rifles had among the finest fighting records of any regiment in the Indian army. During the first World War, Nk. Darban Singh and Rfn. Gabbar Singh were awarded Victoria Crosses. As a result of their outstanding bravery in France and Flanders, the Garhwal Rifles was the only Indian Infantry Regiment given the title of Royal The Fifth Royal Gorkhas also earned such a title. During the Kotkai war in 1920, Lt. WD Kenny of the Garhwal Regiment won the third Victoria Cross.

The Regiment fell into disfavour with the British because a detachment of Garhwali troops employed at Peshawar refused to open fire on unarmed civilians. In April 1930 at Peshawar, a part of a battalion of The Royal Garhwal Rifles did not open fire against nationalist satyagrahis who were protesting for the unlawful arrest of Khan Abdul Ghaffar Khan. The soldiers of the 2/18 Garhwal Rifles under the leadership of Chandra Singh Garhwali refused to fire upon the non-violent Pathan demonstrators, in spite of the communal instigation by their British officers. A total of 67 soldiers and others were punished, some receiving life imprisonment. A court martial sentenced 17 Garhwali troops to various terms of transportation for life and lesser forms of imprisonment. This incident galvanised the entire freedom movement.

While 721 soldiers of the Rregiment laid down their lives during the first World War, 349 soldiers made the supreme sacrifice during the second World War.

After the formation of India in 1947 and the subsequent merger of the various states in India at the time, the Garhwal Rifles was merged in with the Indian Army. Soldiers from this unit were amongst the first to receive the Victoria Cross - the highest decoration for a soldier in the British Army.

So far the Regiment has won 30 battle honours of which five were awarded in the post-Independence period. The regiment has participated in all the wars fought after Independence. The Regiment has won one Ashok Chakra, four Maha Vir Chakra, 13 Kirti Chakra, and 52 Vir Chakra for exceptional gallantry. In the operation Blue Star, Nk. Bhavani Datt Joshi sacrificed his life while fighting the terrorists in Amritsar and was awarded Ashok Chakra. While Lt. Col. Kaman Singh was awarded Maha Vir Chakra during the Indo-Pak war in 1948. Lt. Col. B.M .Bhattacharya and Rfn. Jaswant Singh (posthumously) were awarded Maha Vir Chakra after the Indo-China war of 1962. Capt. Chandranarayan Singh was posthumously awarded Maha Vir Chakra in the 1965 war.

The Garhwal Rifles played a significant role in the India-China War of 1962. The sacrifice along the frontier of Garhwali lives was enormous, as the Indian Army was ill-prepared for the rapidly advancing Chinese. Badly equipped for high altitude combat, short on supplies, and reconnaissance of the enemy, the Indian troops struggled valiantly onward, despite fighting a losing war to both the invaders and frostbite. Indeed, one battalion of the Garhwal Rifles was captured, and many widows were made of the short, but bloody engagement.

Founded as a single class Regiment, the Garhwal Rifles remained so until 1984. Following a national policy, the 18th Garhwal Joint Battalion was constituted in 1985 along with the merger of companies of Jat, Dogra and Maratha Regiments.

The Garhwal Rifles had the proud privilege of playing a decisive role in dislodging Pakistani forces and recapturing Tiger Hill during the Kargil conflict. The Chief of Army Staff made a special instant award of "Unit Citation" to 18th Battalion, The Garhwal Rifles for their meritorious and gallant performance during the battles of Point 5140 on night 19/20 June and Point 4700 on night 27/28 June 1999, in Dras Sector. The unit performed with distinction during Operation "Vijay" and displayed exemplary valour and grit in the face of the enemy.

The overall performance of 18th Battalion, The Garhwal Rifles along with 13th Battalion, The Jammu and Kashmir Rifles was exceptional and marked with exemplary valour and grit in the face of the enemy. The brave troops of a battalion of The Garhwal Rifles have captured three more positions North of Point 4927, viz, BumpI, II and III on night 08/09 July 1999. 18th Battalion, The Garhwal Rifles also acquitted itself with distinction in the battles of Point 5140 on night 19/20 June and Point 4700 on night 27/28 June 1999. The peak had been held by approximately 30 Pakistan soldiers along with some militants as a composite task force. While the enemy suffered heavy casualties, 11 other ranks from the Garhwal Rifles were also slained. Capt. Sumit Roy was lost in heavy artillery exchange with the enemy.

With so many families in the hills of Garhwal and Kumaon who have sons (and daughters) in the military, the conflict in Kashmir has taken a heavy toll. The Garhwal Rifles, as well as other Himalayan regiments (the Gorkha Rifles, Ladakh Scouts, Naga Regiments, and Jammu and Kashmir Infantry) were all entrusted with operations in Kargil in 1999. They joined their Sikh, Rajasthani, Ahir,Mahar, and Bihari brothers as a multicultural and multi faith force on the frontlines, suffering the brunt of casualties in defense of the state.

The 18th Garhwal Joint Battalion was converted into a pure Garhwali Battalion in December 1999. A special team of the Indian Army successfully removed 800 kg of environmentally hazardous garbage from the Nanda Devi Biosphere Reserve, a famous world heritage site closed for visitors since 1982.

The 40-member team of the Garhwal Rifles Regiment successfully scaled the India's second highest peak. Nanda Devi, and collected the non-biodegradable garbage left behind by previous expeditions in the 2000-sq kin bio-reserve. The team scaled the 7,817-meter peak in September 2001 and collected the garbage through the expedition. The peak, even though isn't among the highest 20 peaks in the world, at one point in time, enjoyed the singular status of being the highest mountain in the British empire - the reason being the Mount Everest lay in Nepal and K2 lay in the princely state of Kashmir.

Class Composition: 100% Hindu Garhwalis

Battle Honours

Pre 1947: La Bassee, Armentiers, Festubert, Neuve Chapelle, Aubers, Egypt, Khan Baghdadi, Sharquat, Mesopotamia, Macedonia, Afghanistan, Gallabat, Barentu, Keren, Massawa, Amba Alagi, North Africa, Malaya, Citta di Castello, Yenaungyaung, Monywa, North Arakan, Ngakyedauk Pass, Ramree, Taungup, Burma, Punjab Frontiers, France, Flanders and Kauntam.

Post 1947: Tithwal, J&K 1947-48, Ladakh 1962, Nuranang, Buttar Dograndi, Gadra Road, Punjab 1965, Rajasthan 1965, Hilli and East Pakistan 1971.

Honours & Awards: 1 Ashok Chakra, 7 Param Vishisht Seva Medals, 4 Maha Vir Chakras, 10 Kirti Chakras, 1 Uttam Yudh Seva Medal, 12 Ati Vishisht Seva Medals, 43 Vir Chakras, 30 Shaurya Chakras, 7 Yudh Seva Medals, 120 Sena Medals and 2 Bars, 24 Vishisht Seva Medals, 92 Mention-in-Despatches, 1 Jeevan Raksha Padak, 305 COAS' Commendation Cards with 3 Bars and 164 GOC-in-C's Commendation Cards.

The Regimental Centre: Lansdowne is the Recruitment Centre of the Garhwal Battalion. On October 1, 1921 the Regimental Centre celebrated its first founder's day. Now October 1 is celebrated as the raising day of the battalion. After Independence, the name of the centre was changed to Garhwal Rifles Regimental Centre. The rigorous drills during the training helps to infuse a sense of discipline in every recruit. Special emphasis is laid on physical fitness, mental hardness and weapon handling. After successful completion of 34-week training, a Garhwali youth is turned into a soldier. The soldier is then trained for two more weeks in counter-insurgency operations.

The Regimental Centre is considered the hub of training for the regiment. Approximately 2500 recruits are trained here as soldiers every year. Earlier, the recruitments were held only at Lansdowne but now the recruitments take place at other places in the area as well. The centre has trained more than 60 thousand soldiers since Independence.

The Battalions

2nd Battalion: The second battalion of the Garhwal Rifles is now over one hundred years old. The battalion was raised by Lt Col JT Evatton on March 1, 1901 at Lansdowne. Soon after raising, the battalion got on to the business of training and achieved the desired field service efficiency. Besides training, troops also had to build their own barracks, known till date as Evatt Lines at Lansdowne, which is a testimony to the solid foundation of the battalion. In September 1906, the battalion relieved 1 Garhwal Rifles at Chitral (Afghanistan). The battalion after a year's duty was relieved in October 1907. During the return journey, the battalion was caught in a severe blizzard and snowstorm while negotiating the Lowari Pass. One other rank, 10 followers and 59 mules died of exposure. The Commander-in-Chief commended the officers and men of the battalion for their conduct and good service which saved numerous lives during this natural calamity. In January 1912, the battalion was specially selected to attend the King George V Coronation Durbar in Delhi. On August 4, 1914, the Great War broke out.

The battalion, which was at Lansdowne at its permanent station in India, was mobilised and it set sail to France through Karachi. The war saw many heroic deeds of the battalion. Late Rifleman Gabar Singh Negi won the coveted Victoria Cross. The battalion won the battle honour Neuve Chappelle and also established itself as a fighting force to reckon with during the battles in Mesopotamia and Turkey. The battalion bagged 1 Victoria Cross, 5 CMGs, 10 DSOs, 10 IDMs, 12 IDSMs and 1 Russian

Cross of St George. The intervening period from 1922 to 1927 saw the battalion in action at Waziristan wherein it was deployed for internal security duty to quell the Mashud Rebellion. Bold action by the battalion found the Mashuds scurrying for cover in a short span of two years. This could be termed as the first exposure of the battalion to fighting insurgency. Having restored peace, the battalion returned to its permanent abode at Lansdowne in 1924 and remained there till 1927. In 1928, the battalion again moved to Waziristan and was stationed at Razmak as part of the Razmak Brigade. During the tenure, the battalion established a temporary garrison at Tauda China and Khyber and undertook counter-insurgency operations. In April 1930, the battalion was deployed in the Peshawar city where two platoons refused to open fire on the unarmed civilians participating in the Civil Disobedience movement.

As an aftermath of the incident, the battalion was disarmed. However, as the Court of Inquiry opined, the battalion was rearmed on May 17, 1931. The battalion was deployed in West Bengal at Bankura and Midnapur from 1932 to 1934 and successfully undertook counter-terrorist operations. The second battalion embarked at Bombay on October 27, 1940 under the command of Lt Col LH Cockram and was ordered to proceed as Garrison Battalion to Kuantan on the East Coast of Pahang in Malaya Peninsula.

The battalion was the only infantry battalion in Kuantan. Its role was to deny the airfield to the enemy and to protect vital points, which involved holding ground to the north of the town with wide dispersion. An observation post was established at the mouth of the Pahang River to give early warning of any enemy movement up the river through which it was possible to reach Jerrantut. By December 1941, the battalion had been milked twice to assist in forming new battalions which resulted in a large number of recruits in the rank and file of the battalion. This inevitably affected the fighting efficiency of rifle companies. Contact with enemy was established on December 29. The overwhelming superiority of the Japanese forced the battalion to withdraw after a series of successful delaying action battles till February 1, 1942 when the battalion reached the Johore Straits.

The causeway for further move to Johore Bheru was destroyed by the Japanese. Since 80 per cent of the troops were non swimmers, it was decided to surrender. At the time of surrender, the strength of the battalion was about 280 all ranks. For conspicuous acts of gallantry, three MC, one MBE and one MM were won by the battalion. On May 11, 1946 the battalion was reconstituted from the remnants of the 4th Battalion at Yol

Camp. Immediately after re-raising, battalion was assigned the task of guarding POW camp at Yol wherein Italian POWs were housed. In August, 1947 the battalion moved to Kolkata and on August 15 the national flag was hoisted at Fort William by Maj (later Brigadier) Hari Singh. Thereafter, the battalion was deployed for internal security duties in the wake of post-Independence communal riots. The battalion was subsequently given the task of escorting the refugees' train to Pakistan and back. In May 1948, the battalion concentrated at Jallandhar and was tasked to construct family accommodation which was completed with usual elan and zeal.

This complex was named as Jawanabad by Brig B M Kaul who expressed his satisfaction at the high standard of discipline and training of the battalion. The battalion also got mentioned in his book, The Untold Story. The battalion was stationed at Fort William from 1957 to 1960 wherein dussehra was celebrated with usual fervour and enthusiasm. Training also received the required impetus and time which enabled all ranks to achieve the desired standards. For the second time after 1954, the battalion was selected to provide a marching contingent for the Republic Day Parade in 1957 which was led by Capt K B Gurung. The battalion moved to Sarol (J&K) on October 1, 1963. It had earlier served in the same sector, so the bhullas were on home turf while manning the picquets on the ceasefire line opposite Pakistani formations.

The battalion headquarters was at Sarol and rifle companies were deployed on picquets. Lt Col Ujagar Singh succeeded Lt Col SS Rana on January 3, 1964. The battalion was part of the battle during operation Hill. On October 6/7, 1965 the battalion was nominated by the GOC for the task of attacking and capturing the area where the Pakistani infiltrators had managed to build up their defences. The attack by the battalion was launched with great courage and determination. However, due to wrong intelligence assessment of enemy strength and disposition with insufficient time to reorient itself and very little fire support, the battalion suffered heavy casualties and the attack was beaten back by a battalion strength of Pakistanis. The battalion took part in second attack on enemy position in conjunction with other battalions.

In this operation, B company laid an ambush and captured one Pakistani officer. Capt C N Singh of the "Superb Second " won the only MVC of the regiment during the 1965 operations. Reacting to specific information about presence of infiltrators, Capt CN Singh attacked them with great ferocity and valour. In a close quarter hand-to-hand fight, he was fatally wounded and later succumbed to his injuries. For his gallant leadership and valour, he was awarded the coveted Maha Vir Chakra.

The battalion won 1 MVC, 2 SMs and 5 COAS Commendation Cards. During Cactus Lily in 1971, the battalion was poised for action but did not participate in the operations. Consequent to the war, battalion moved to Allahabad and was tasked to guard the POW camp. The battalion moved to Chaubatia in 1975 where it carried out its routine training and administrative activities. In one such training activity, the battalion undertook a route march from Chaubatia to Asan field firing ranges to participate in field firing.

Next two years saw the battalion holding extended defences based on DCB at Pallanwala. During the tenure at Kharian from 1978 to 1982, sports teams performed exceedingly well and brought laurels to the battalion. Its Pipes and Drums were adjudged best in the division for two years in succession. The battalion's mine-laying team topped in corps competition and football team won the Garhwal Cup. The unit moved to Arunanchal Pradesh and was commended for constructing permanent defences for a 'Battalion Defended Area' in high altitude. From 1985 to 1988, the battalion was located at Samba. The unit pipers and drummers were highly acclaimed for their performance in the Republic Day Parade in 1986. During this tenure, a number of senior officers visited the battalion and expressed their satisfaction at the overall standard achieved by the battalion.

After a stint of three years on the Line of Control at Budhwal (J&K), the battalion moved to Kolkata and had the good fortune of staying in proper KLP accommodation after 1967. During this tenure, the battalion had the opportunity of providing a guard of honour to the President of India. The unit also had the rare distinction of providing guard to the 'Z' category Army Commander for a period of eleven months which bears testimony to the high professionalism and faith with which the battalion was looked upon. During this period, the battalion was awarded 29 GOC-in-C Commendation Cards. Ayodhya riots in December 1992 saw the unit in action in IS duties which enabled the unit to earn six COAS Commendation Cards. The conduct of IS duties in communally sensitive Kolkata was appreciated by the Government of West Bengal.

The battalion was deployed in J&K from May 1994 to September 1996 for operation Rakshak. The battalion performed exceedingly well and virtually exterminated militants from the battalion's area of responsibility. Due to the efforts of the battalion, 67 militants were killed and 101 apprehended whereas 32 militants surrendered. The arms captured by the battalion included 93 rifles, 4 UMGs, 34 pistols and 3

RPGs. Not only did the battalion achieve distinction in containing militancy in the area of responsibility but it also undertook a number of successful civic action projects to win the hearts of the people. The battalion was handpicked to provide security during Amarnath Yatra of 1994.

The efforts were lauded by one and all as the Yatra passed off without a single attack. The unit was awarded the coveted Chief of Army Staff and General Officer Commanding-in-Chief, Northern Command citations for the excellent work done during operation Rakshak. Gen K V Krishna Rao (Retd), the Governor of J&K visited the battalion. Later, he presented a silver plaque in recognition of the sacrifices of all ranks of the battalion. The battalion won 1 Shaurya Chakra, 9 Sena Medals, 1 Vishisht Seva Medal, 10 COAS Commendation Cards and 9 GOC-in-C's Commendation Cards. Consequent to a gruelling tenure during operation Rakshak, the battalion moved to Meerut for a well-deserved peace tenure. Training and welfare activities were accorded the desired priority.

The unit held the rare distinction of hosting a Chinese delegation which was on a training visit to the formation. The battalion got deployed on western borders in June 1999 for operation Vijay. In October 1999, the battalion moved to the heavenly abode of Joshimath. A sudden move and deployment of the battalion in January 2000 for operation Rakshak truncated the tenure at Joshimath. The battalion not only successfully checked the infiltration but also unearthed a series of caches. The unit was highly appreciated for holding a medical camp at a stones throw distance from the Line of Control.

3rd Battalion: 3rd Battalion was raised in 1916.

4th Battalion: 4th Battalion was raised in 1918.

5th Battalion: Raised during World War II.

6th Battalion: Raised during World War II.

7th Battalion: Raised during World War II.

8th, 9th, 10th, 11th, 12th, 13th, 14th, 15th, 16th and 17th battalion were raised after independence.

18th Battalion: Raised in 1985.

Famous Personalities

Given below is the list of famous Garhwal peoplefrom different sphere of life:

Armed Forces

Gallantary Award Recipients

Lt. Col. Kaman Singh on 16 May 48, during Kasmir Operations, displayed a fine example of inspiring leadership, high sense of duty and great personal courage. He was awarded **Maha Vir Chakra** for his gallant action.

Lt. Col. B. M. Bhattacharya was awarded the **Maha Vir Chakra** for his gallantry in the Indo-China war of 1962.

Rifleman Jaswant Singh Rawat won the **Maha Vir Chakra** Award. during final phase of the Sino-Indian War in November 1962.

Capt. Chandranarayan Singh for his heroism was posthumously decorated with the **Maha Vir Chakra** during the war of 1965.

Nk. Bhavani Datt Joshi in the operation Blue Star in year 1984, sacrificed his life while fighting the terrorists in Amritsar and was awarded **Ashok Chakra**.

Capt. Vivek Mishra got the **Shourya Chakra** in 2003 for his bravery, leadership qualities and dedication to his duty.

Others

General Bipin Chandra Joshi was the head of the Indian Army in 1993.General B C Joshi was awarded the Param Vishisht Seva Medal (PVSM) and the Ati Vishisht Seva Medal (AVSM) for dedicated service to the nation. He passed away on 19th Nov 1994 when he was the head of the Indian Army.

Lt. Gen. K. Mahendra Singh (PVSM) was commanding officer of Garhwal Rifles from 1979 till1987.

Lt. Gen. Paramjit Singh is a graduate of Defence Service Staff College and National Defence College. He has the distinction of commanding 2 Garhwal Rifles and Infantry Brigade in J&K on the Line of Control. He has also been Instructor at the IMA Dehradun.

Lt. Gen. Mohan Chandra Bhandari is Director General NCC since 2006.

Brig. Jagmohan Rawat is former commanding officer of Garhwal Rifles.

Politicians

- Murli Manohar Joshi:Former HRD Minister (1999-2004)

Artists

- Manohar Shyam Joshi: Writer
- Mohan Upreti: Pioneer in Indian theatre music
- Gaura Pant Shivani: Hindi story writer
- Himani Bhatt Shivpuri: Actor
- Varun Badola: Actor
- Vishvamohan Badola: Singer
- Prasoon Joshi: Ad man

3

Gorkhas

Gorkhas claim their descent from the ancient Hindu Rajputs and Brahmins of Northern India, who immigrated in present day Nepal from the west. It is presumed by the scholars and historians that Guru Gorkhanath had a Rajput Prince-disciple, the legendary Bappa Rawal, born Prince Kalbhoj, founding father of the Royal house of Mewar, who later became the first Gorkha and is said to be the forefather of the present day Royal family of Nepal.

Origin & History

It is said in the legendary stories of Nepal that Bappa Rawal was a teenager in hiding, when he met the warrior saint while away on a hunting expedition with friends in the forests of Rajasthan. Bappa Rawal preferred to stay behind, and care for the warrior saint, who was in deep meditation. When Guru Gorkhanath woke up, he was pleased with the devotedness of Bappa Rawal. The Guru gave him the Khukri (Khukuri) knife, the notable curved blade of the present day Gorkhas. The legend goes forward that he told Bappa that he and his people would henceforward be known as Gorkhas, the disciples of the Guru Gorkhanath, and their braveness would become world renowned. He then taught Bappa Rawal, and his Gorkhas to block the advance of the Muslims, who were invading Afghanistan (which at that time was a Hindu/Buddhist nation). Bappa Rawal took his Gorkhas and liberated Afghanistan (in the first place named Gandhara), from which the present day Kandahar gets its name. He and his Gorkhas blocked the initial Muslims infiltration of the eighth century in India.

Many other stories further state that Bappa Rawal (Kalbhoj) went further inhibiting Iran and Iraq before he retired as an ascetic at the feet of Mt. Meru, having captured all encroachers and enemies of his faith. It is a wrong idea that the Gorkhas took their name from the Gorkha area of

Nepal. The area was given its name after the Gorkhas had laid down their command of these domains. In the early sixteenth century some of Bappa Rawal's descendents went further east, and won a small state in present-day Nepal, which they referred as Gorkha in honour of their patron saint. By the year 1769, with help of the leadership of Sri Panch Maharaj Dhiraj Prithvi Narayan Shahdev (1769–1775), the Gorkha dynasty had taken over the region of modern Nepal. They recognised Hinduism as the state religion, although with trenchant influences of Rajput warrior and Gorkhanath.

People & Culture

Gorkhas are drawn from a number of Nepalese ethnic groups including the Gurung (who contribute the greatest percentage of their population of all the groups), Magar, Tamang, Sunwar, Limbu, and Rai. Gorkhas lay claim their Descent from the warlike Rajputs of Chittaur, in Rajasthan, saying they were driven therefrom to the Nepalese hills by the Muslim invasions. The Gorkha military custom can be deciphered back to the sixteenth century when the empire of Gorkha was conquered by the first kings of the Shah Thakuri dynasty. By the end of the eighteenth century the Gorkha Empire, as it was then known, had expanded command over much of what is now Nepal and had started out pushing north into China and Tibet. Expansion south into India was resisted by the British (who were expanding northward), but in 1815 the Nepalese were overcame.

What is Gorkha culture cannot be determined by any specific area any longer. Or on the other hand it will be conceived an imposition process. The Gorkhas in India today are of two kinds. One from the warriorlike races of the lineage of the Gorkha Sena of Nepal-BritishGorkha -Indian Gorkha. The other are from non-martial societies primarily in the east and another kind further North-east. The various backgrounds impress their individual cultures and this should be taken into account by all Gorkha practioners or researchers. While the call of Gorkhaland is for Darjeeling, but what is Gorkha culture, language, customs, eating habits, etc should not be determined from Darjeeling to west or further east. While darjeeling may comprehend Nepali culture as Gorkha culture. In the west, the Gorkha culture is further changed from the archetype Nepali culture.

In the Northwestern Indian Gorkha guilds, the Gorkha grooms do not wear grass garlands and the brides wear a nose-ring (called natha-of different sizes) which is considered essential. Maaltika (on the forehead) is common. The HP Gorkha grooms put on yellow or pink turbans, carry a sword and shield and the khukri. The impact is from the pre-British Gorkha warriors who wore turbans and acquitted shield and swords and the khukri. Their language also had many Persian, urdu, arabic words. Perhaps in impact of interactions with the neighbouring Mughal dynasty. Therefore Amar Singh Thapa was known as Bara Kazi, which intended High Minister. They wore long length chaubanda kurtas. Nowadays, the Gorkha civilization, traditions and language has a lot of diversity.

Sects

Gorkhas can be subdivided into following sects:

- Gurung
- Limbu
- Magar
- Rai
- Sunwar
- Tamang

Demographics

Gorkhas are basically found in Nepal. The Gorkhas' total population is around 8 millions. In India Gorkha people are found chiefly in states of Uttaranchal, Jammu and Kashmir, Himachal Pradesh, Assam, Meghalaya, Nagaland, Manipur, Mizoram, Tripura, Arunachal Pradesh and Sikkim. Around 21 lakhs of Gorkhas are permanently domiciled in India. In the district of Darjeeling and the Province of Assam, they are concentrated to a certain extent. Their number in these two areas is about 14 lakhs and the rest are scattered throughout India.They are also found in foreign countries like Combodia, Indonesia, China, Hong-Kong, Bhutan, Tibbet, UK and USA. Given below is the table of Gorkha population in the world.

Gorkhas in Nepal

Ethnic Group	Population	Percent of Total
Magar	1,622,421	7.14
Tamang	1,282,304	5.64
Rai	635,151	2.79
Gurung	686,000	2.39
Limbu	359,379	1.58
Sonar	145,088	0.64

Gorkhas Overseas

Country	Population
India	2,050,000
Bhutan	40,000
Hong Kong	15,950
Australia	7,000
UK	6,000
Canada	3,780
United States	2,616

Source: Nepal census of 2001 and CIA factbook.

Martial Traditions

More or less 300 years ago, the empire of Nepal was divided into small States and Principalities. The tiny rulers had no unity among themselves. They often disputed with each other for territorial integrity and sovereignty. The Kathmandu valley itself was parted into three kingdoms, Kathmandu, Bhaktapur and Patan. There were at least three herculean realms in the east-Makawanpur, Vijaypur and Chandandi. Likewise, there were twenty-four princedoms in the western-Gandaki area known as Chaubisi Rajya, and twenty-two princedoms in the far western,Karnali area known as Baisi Rajya.

The twenty-four princedoms (Chaubisi Rajya) were as follows:- Gorkha, Lamjung, Tanahun, Kaski, Nuwakot, Dhor, Satahun, Garahun, Rishing, Ghiring, Paiyun, Parbat, Galkot, Palpa, Gulmi, Argha, Khanchi, Musikot, Isma, Dhurkot, Bajhang, Bhirkot, Piuthan, and Butwal. In the same manner, the twenty-two principalities in the far- western Karnali area were as under:- Jumla, Doti, Jajarkot, Bajura, Musikot, Gajur, Biskot, Malneta, Thalahara, Dailekh, Dullu, Duryal, Dang, Sallyana, Chilli, Phalawagh, Jehari, Darnar, Atbis Gotam, Majal, Gurnakot, and Rukum. Various historians have listed many names of these Chaubisi and Baisi Rajya. However, on the basis of the names given by Balchandra Sharma, Kirkpatrick and Hamilton, these names are ordinarily used.

There was a strong demand to consolidate all these states into a Nation. The credit for this integration goes to the Shah Kings of the Gorkha empire. The Gorkha realm, thus, turned into a united Nepal, just as Prussia was ploughed into the German Empire, Sardinia into Italy,

Castela into Spain, and Wessex into Great Britain. Prithvi Narayan Shah sent his force beneath the command of Kazi Biraj Thapa to attack Nuwakot. Biraj Thapa did not attack instantly after reaching Nuwakot, but he commenced to study the stength of the Nuwakot army and the position of the realm. Prithvi Narayan Shah did not like the delay of Biraj Thapa and so he sent another force under the control of Maheswar Panta.

The Gorkha troops in the control of Maheswar Panta attacked Nuwakot immediately but the Gorkha troops were badly overcame. Thus, Nuwakot was winning against the Gorkha invasion for the second time. At that time, the Gorkhali Army was unknown around the geographical position of Nuwakot. During the war, the two Gorkhali commanders held responsible each other. They did not try to fight to get victory. On the other hand, the Nuwakot soldiers were cognisant of the strategic points and they fought at the risk of their lives to save the reign of their empire.

Shah Kings of Gorkhas: As per Bhasa Bansabali, the Shah Kings of Gorkha were went down from a noble family of Chitor (India) who belonged to the Chandrabansi Rajput dynasty. The founding father of this dynasty was Rishi Raj Bhattarak. The 33rd king of this dynasty was Bhupati Ranjee. He had three sons named Udaya Bom, Fatta Singh and Manamath. Fatta Singh had a beautiful daughter named Sadul. The Muslim King Allaudin Khilzi wanted to marry Sadul. But, Fatta Singh rejected to fulfill his wish. So Allaudin Khilizi of Delhi intruded on Chitor and captured it. After the Muslim invasion, Manamath went to Ujjain and resided there.

He had two sons, named Brahmin and Bhupal. But Brahmin and Bhupal did not want to shack up. The youngest brother Bhupal left Ujjain and came to Ridi. He lived there for some time. After some days, Bhupal left Ridi and reached Bhirkot. He started to settle there. He had two sons named Harihar Singh and Ajaya Singh, they were also known as 'Khancha Khan' and 'Mincha Khan'. Khancha Khan had instituted a small princedom of Dhor. Khan founded a small princedom of Nuwakot. Then he started to rule over there.

Kulamardan Shah: Kulamardan was the descendent of Mincha. He governed over Nuwakot, and, in due course of time took over Kaski to his empire. He was a herculean king and gained the titoe of 'Shah' from the emperor of Delhi. Since then, the 'Shah' surname has been used by the kings of Gorkha. He had seven sons. At that time there was no king in Lamjung. The people of Lamjung neared Kulamardan Shah and solicited one of his sons to rule over the empire of Lamjung.

Kulamardan Shah sent his second son, Kalu Shah with them. The people of Lamjung made Kalu Shah, their king, but he died shortly. After the death of Kalu Shah, the people of Lamjung once more asked Kalumandan to give his youngest son. Now Yashovarma Shah was sent to rule over Lamjung. Yashovarma had two sons, Narahari Shah and Drabya Shah. Narahari Shah dominate over Lamjung and Drabya Shah inhibited Gorkha and established an independent kingom.

Drabya Shah: Drabya Shah was a brave, clever and an aspirational man from his childhood. He was not satisfied with himself residing under the shadow of his brother. He wanted to lay down an empire of his own. In those days, there were various small princedoms in the locality of Gorkhs. The Kinghom of Gorkha was governed over by Khadkas. The people of Gorkha, in particular the Brahmins and the Kshatriyas, were not satisfied with the rule of the Khadka kings. Some of the leaders of the people, like Ganesh Pande, Bhagirath Panta, Ganga Rana and Naryan Aryal, were contriving to dethrone the Khadka king and to replace him by a Kshatriya king.

They were the well wishers of Drabya Shah. Narayan Aryal was also an astrologist. They met Drabya Shah and helped him to inhibit Lig Lig which was under the rule of a Ghale King of the Magar clan. There was a particular system electing the ruler. In each year, on the day of Bijaya Dashami, a racing contest was held in Lig Lig. On the race, the winner would be made king. On that day, all the people of Lig Lig were employed in choosing the ruler, Drabya Shah assaulted Lig Lig and seized it. Then Drabya Shah came to Gorkha and steadily, he flourished his power and captured Gorkha. He became the ruler of Gorkha on 27th Sept. 1559 AD. Thus, Drabya Shah established the ruling dynasty of the Gorkha empire. He also inhibited Siranchowk, Azirgarh and Dhading.

The growing power of Drabya Shah excited the jealousy of his brother Narahari Shah, the king of Lamjung. Narahari Shah began to claim the kingdoms assumed by his brother, Drabya Shah. But Drabya Shah did not think about his claim. So, there arose a quarrel between the two brothers. In order to pacify them, their mother determined the limit of the Chepe river dividing the dominions of her two sons.

They did not quarrel so long as their mother was alive. Narahari Shah was decided to kill his brother, however, after the death of their mother, Narahari Shah invited Drabya Shah to execute the 'Shradha' ceremony. He had planned to kill on that occasion. But, Drabya Shah came to know the evil purpose of his brother. He fled away from there and reached Gorkha. After some days, Narahari Shah attacked Gorkha but he was repulsed. Drabya Shah made his empire a mighty one. He announced himself to be a Gorkhali king and earned the popularity of his people. He allowed the people to celebrate their festivals in their own way and did not handicap their local customs and traditions. He enrolled the local people of Gorkha in the military force and nominated them in the higher posts of administration concording to their merit.

Thus, he became a popular and productive ruler of Gorkha. He found short time for administrative reforms. He governed for eleven years and died in 1570 AD. After Drabya Shah, his son Purandar Shah governed for thirty-five years. After Purandar Shah, his son Chhatra Shah governed only for seven months and died. After his demise, his brother Ram Shah moved up to the throne of Gorkha.

Ram Shah: Ram Shah moved up to the throne of Gorkha in 1606 AD. He governed for twenty-six years. He was a good reformist, able administrator and a grand warrior. He annexed all the small principalities surrounding Gorkha. He prolonged his empire as far as Kerung and Rasuwa in the north, Trishuli in the east, Marshyangdi in the west and the Mahabharat range in the south.

The king of Lamjung made an abortive plot to kill Ram Shah while on a hunting expedition. Ram Shah was not only a conqueror but also an able administrator. He preserved friendly relationships with the kings of Palpa, Jumala and Patan. He also sent presents to the Mughal emperor of India. Ram Shah brought radical modifications in the society by bringing in several reforms.

Contribution to Defence Services

The cry of "Ayo Gorkhali" or "The Gorkhas are upon you" is much feared in battle. The Gorkha soldier wields a unique weapon, the Khukri, a curved fighting knife. Despite the fact that, Gorkhas were armed with rifles in the later years, they preferred to use their Khukri. Traditionally, when the Khukri was unsheathed, blood must be drawn. Thus should it be drawn in a non-combative situation, the Khukri must be satiated and blood was drawn from the Gorkha himself with a self-inflicted nick.

Gorkhas in Indian Army: Currently there are 7 Gorkha regiments serving in the Indian Army. Six regiments were transfered from the British Indian Army, one regiment was formed after independence. The following is a list of the Gorkha Regiments currently serving in the Indian Army:

1 Gorkha Rifles

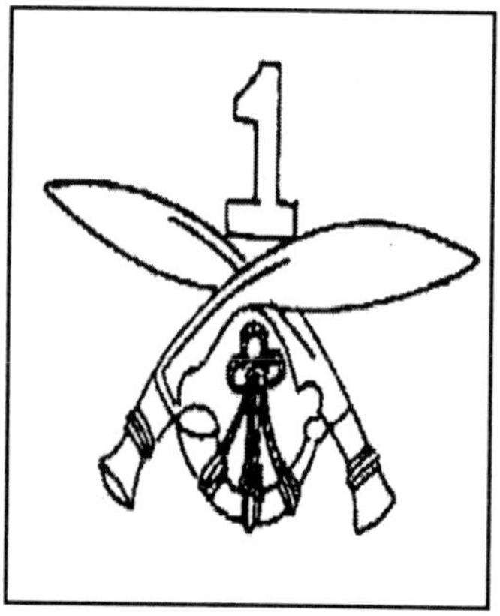

Regimental Motto: Kayar Hunu Bhanda Marnu Ramro (It is better to die than to be a coward).

War Cry: Ayo Gorkhali (The Gorkhas Are Here).

The 1 Gorkha Rifles is a Regiment of the Indian Army and was transferred from the British Indian Army at the time of India's independence in 1947.The Gorkha War was fought between the Gorkha kings of Nepal and the British East India Company as a result of border tensions and ambitious expansionism especially into Kumaon, Garwhal and Kangra hills. The British east India army defeated the Gorkhas army lead by general Amar Singh Thapa but were impressed by its skills and courage during the siege of Malaun fort in Bilaspur. On April 24, 1815 at Subathu, East India Company formed a regiment with the survivors of Thapa's army calling it the First Nusseree (or Nasiri) (friendly or loyal).

The Regiment soon saw its first battle when, in 1826, it took part in the Jat War where it helped in the conquest of Bharatpur, gaining it as a Battle Honour, the first Battle Honour awarded to the Gorkha units. In 1846 the First Anglo-Sikh War began and the Regiment was heavily involved in the conflict. It was awarded two Battle honours for its involvement in the war; at the Battle of Aliwal which saw the Sikh forces, who had invaded British India thus provoking the war, routed by the British forces and at Sobraon which saw the Sikh forces resoundingly defeated.

The Regiment experienced numerous names changes during the 1800s; one name change in 1850 saw it gain a new numerical designation to become the 66th Gorkha Regiment of Bengal Native Infantry after the original 66th had mutinied. The Regiment saw service during the Indian Mutiny which began in 1857. The following year Lieutenant John Adam Tytler won the Regiment's first Victoria Cross (VC) for the Lieutenant's actions against rebels at Choorpoorah.

In 1861 the Regiment gained its present numeral when it became the 1st Gorkha Regiment. In 1875 the Regiment was sent abroad for the first time, when it took part in the effort to quell a rebellion in Malaya during the Perak War. During the conflict Captain George Nicolas Channer was awarded the Victoria Cross for his valiant actions against the Malayans. The Regiment took part in the Second Afghan War in 1878 where they were part of the 2nd Infantry Brigade and won the Theatre Honour "Afghanistan 1878-80".

In 1886 the Regiment became the 1st Gorkha Light Infantry and a 2nd Battalion was raised in February. In 1891 the Regiment was designated a Rifle regiment when it became the 1st Gorkha (Rifle) Regiment and in consequence of this the Regiment's Colours were laid up; Rifle regiments by tradition did not possess Colours. The Regiment took part in operations in Burma and the North-West Frontier campaigns in the 1890s; at Waziristan in 1894 and the Tirah campaign in 1897.

In August 1914 the First World War began; the United Kingdom, France and its Allies against Germany and its Allies.

The 1st Battalion was deployed to France (Western Front) in December that year as-part of the Sirhind Indian Infantry Brigade, 3rd (Lahore) Division. The Battalion quickly began its participation in the Western Front campaign when they took part in the defence of Givenchy in December during the Winter which was no-doubt a culture shock to the Gorkhas.

On 10 March 1915 the Battalion took part in the Battle of Neuve Chapelle which lasted until 13 March. In April the Battalion took part in the Second Battle of Ypres, fighting in the subsidiary Battle of St. Julien which began on 24 April and concluded on 4 May. Later that month the Battalion took part in the Battle of Festubert and in September the Battle of Loos began, the last major engagement on the Western Front that the 1st Battalion took part in.

In 1919 the 1st and 2nd battalions saw service during the Third Afghan War for which they gained the Theatre Honour "Afghanistan 1919".

In 1937 the Regiment's name was altered slightly when it became the 1st King George V's Own Gorkha Rifles (The Malaun Regiment); the only change being the addition of a V.

In September 1939 the Second World War commenced between the UK and its allies against Germany. In December 1941 the Japanese entered the war when it launched a surprise attack on Pearl Harbor and launched a number of swift invasions of British and other countries territories. During the course of the war the Regiment raised a further three battalions, the 3rd in 1940, the 4th in 1941 and the 5th in 1942; the

Regiment saw much service in the war but most notably in Malaya and Burma.

The Regiment, in consequence of the Tripartite Agreement between India, Nepal and the UK, was transferred to the Army of the newly-independent India. The Regiment retained its name until 1950 when it became the 1 Gorkha Rifles (The Malaun Regiment), also adopting the Indian spelling of Gorkha, following India's transition to a republic. The regiment remains in existence and comprises 5 battalions. In 1961 Captain Gurbachan Singh Salaria won the posthumous Param Vir Chakra (PVC), the Indian equivalent of the Victoria Cross, for his actions in the Congo when the 3rd Battalion, of which he was part, was on United Nations service.

Battle Honours: Kalidhar, Darsana.

Honours & Awards: 1 Param Vir Chakra, 7 Maha Vir Chakras, 16 Vir Chakras, 1 Kirti Chakra, 3 Shaurya Chakras, 1 Yudh Seva Medal and 22 Sena Medals.

The Regimental Center: Subathu, Himachal Pradesh, India.

3 Gorkha Rifles

Regimental Motto: Kafar Bhanda Marnu Ramro (Better to die than live like a coward).

War Cry: Ayo Gorkhali (The Gorkhas Are Here).

The 3 Gorkha Rifles was a Gorkha regiment of the British Indian Army formed in 1815. They were present at a number of actions and wars including the Siege of Delhi in 1857 to the Great War and World war II. After partition they were one of the Gorkha regiments transferred to the Indian Army as part of the Tripartite Agreement signed between India, Nepal and Britain at the time of Indian independence. Prior to independence, the regiment was known as the 3rd Queen Alexandra's Own Gorkha Rifles.

In August 1914 World War I began and the regiment's battalions actively participated on the Western Front and in the Middle East.

In 1916, a clerical error gave the regiment a 4th Battalion when 4/3rd, instead of 3/4th, was written on the order for the raising of a battalion for the 4th Gorkha Rifles. The following year a 3rd Battalion for the 3rd

Gorkhas was formed. The regiment, as in WWI, was actively involved in World War II and re-raised the 3rd Battalion in 1940 and the 4th Battalion the following year. India gained its independence in 1947 and the regiment was one of 6 Gorkha regiments (out of 10) to be allocated to the Indian Army as part of the Tripartite Agreement between Britain, India and Nepal. The regiment retained its title until 1950 when India was proclaimed a Republic and the regiment became the 3 Gorkha Rifles. It remains in existence and consists of five battalions.

The Regiment won the Battle Honour 'Pir Kanthi' in the Uri Sector in 1948 and 'Shingo' in the Kargil Sector in 1971. 1/3 GR has the distinction of being the first battalion in the post-independence period to carry out amphibious operations during the 1971 Indo-Pak War. Colonel J.R. Chitnis, CO 1/3 GR, was honoured with the Ashoka Chakra posthumously - India's highest peacetime medal for valour - in Nagaland in 1956.

On December 3, 1997, a statue was unveiled in London in honour of the Gorkhas. A quote from Sir Ralph Turner, a former officer in the 3rd Gorkhas, was inscribed on the memorial: "Bravest of the brave, most generous of the generous, never had country more faithful friends than you."

Battle Honours: Pir Kanthi and Shingo River.

Honours & Awards: 1 Ashok Chakra, 1 Kirti Chakras, 5 Vir Chakras, 5 Shaurya Chakras, 1 Yudh Seva Medal, 19 Sena Medals, 1 Bar to Sena Medal, 4 Param Vishist Seva Medals, 5 Ati Vishist Seva Medals, 9 Vishist Seva Medals, 2 McGregor Medals, 26 Mentioned-in-Despatches, 46 COAS' Commendation Cards and 19 GOC-in-C's Commendation Cards.

Regimental Centre: Varanasi, Uttar Pradesh.

4 Gorkha Rifles

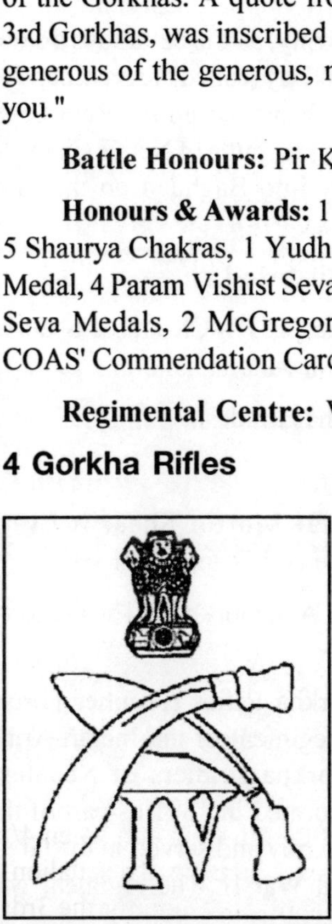

Regimental Motto: Kaphar hunnu bhanda marnu ramro (Better to die than live a coward).

War Cry: Ayo Gorkhali (The Gorkhas Are Here).

The 4 Gorkha Rifles is a regiment of the Indian Army and was transferred from the British Indian Army at the time of India's independence in 1947. The regiment was formerly known as the 4th Prince of Wales's

Own Gorkha Rifles was originally a Gorkha regiment of the British Indian Army.

In 1857, it was decided to augment the existing Gorkha regiments by raising another. Initially, this was known as the Extra Goorkha Regiment, before being numbered as the 19th Regiment of Bengal Native Infantry. In 1861 it was finally ranked as the 4th Goorkha Regiment.

The regiment's first major action was during the Second Afghan War, also seeing service on the North-West Frontier and during the Boxer Rebellion in 1900.

Following India's independence in 1947, the 4th Gorkhas was one of the Gorkha regiments to be allocated to the Indian Army, becoming the 4 Gorkha Rifles in 1950. The third battalion fought a fine action at Bilafond La, at heights of nearly 20,000 feet in 1987. The First battalion was awarded the COAS Unit Citation in 2002, for its outstanding performance in counter terrorism operations in Kupwara dist, Kashmir.

The Regiment is unique in the Indian Army, as the battalions do not celebrate individual Raising Days. Regimental Day (called Neuve Chapelle - Baghdad Day) is celebrated on 11 March by the entire Regiment, commemorating the First Battalion's entry into the Battle of Neuve Chapelle in France and the Second Battalion's entry into Baghdad on that day (different years), during the First World War.

Battle Honours: Punch, Gurais and Bilafond La.

Honours & Awards: 4 Maha Vir Chakras, 16 Vir Chakras, 5 Shaurya Chakras, 1 Yudh Seva Medal and 26 Sena Medals.

Regimental Centre: Sabathu, Himachal Pradesh.

5 Gorkha Rifles

Regimental Motto: Shaurya Evam Nistha (Courage and Determination).

War Cry: Ayo Gorkhali (The Gorkhas Are Here).

The 5 Gorkha Rifles (Frontier Force) is an infantry regiment of the Indian Army comprising Gorkha soldiers of Nepalese origin. It was formed in 1891 as part of the British Indian Army and served in the Great War and World War II. The regiment was one of the Gorkha regiments that was transferred to the Indian Army following independence. The regiment was formerly known as the 5th Royal Gorkha Rifles.

The regiment was raised in 1858 as the 25th Punjab Infantry. The soldiers of the regiment originated from the Kingdom of Nepal and in 1861 it was renamed the 5th Gorkha Regiment. The regiment's first major action was during the Second Afghan War, where they were awarded their first battle honour at Peiwar Kotal and Captain John Cook was awarded the Victoria Cross. In 1891 the regiment was afforded the prestigious title of a Rifle regiment and became 5th Gorkha (Rifle) Regiment which was shortened to 5th Gorkha Rifles in 1901.

The regiment spent most of its time up to the end of the 19th century based in the Punjab as part of the Punjab Frontier Force, more famously known as PFF or Piffers. This was reflected when in 1903, when the regiment was renamed the 5th Gorkha Rifles (Frontier Force).

The 2nd Battalion served in the Far East in the Burma Campaign as part of the 17th Indian Infantry Division and was involved in the retreat of the British Indian Army from Burma, they were one of four battalions chosen to fight as the rearguard at the Sittang River, which formed the border with India. When the bridge over the river was blown up preventing the Japanese forces from entering India, many of the regiment were left on the wrong side. The regiment was involved in the re-entry into Burma in 1943 where three members of the regiment were awarded the Victoria Cross. At the end of the war the 2nd Btn was part of the British Commonwealth Occupation Force of Japan.

The 4th Battalion was raised in 1941 and also served in the Burma Campaign as part of the 7th Indian Infantry Division, fighting in five epic battles at North Arakan, Buthidaung (Battle of the Admin Box), Kohima, Pokkoku (Irrawaddy) and Sittang. The Battalion had the unique distinction of getting Four Battle Honours for the Five Battles Fought. Major I M Brown of the 4th Battalion was one of the few soldiers of the Second World War that was awarded the Military Cross three times.

On Independence, the 5th Royal Gorkha Rifles was one of the six Gorkha regiments that remained part of the new Indian Army, they were renamed the 5th Gorkha Rifles (Frontier Force) in 1950. The Regiment now has a total of six Battalions and has, participated in virtually every major action the Indian Army has undertaken in its four wars with Pakistan, including the first airborne operations undertaken by the army during the 1971 war.

Battle Honours: Zoji La, Kargil, J&K 1947-48, Charwa, Sehjra, Slyhet, J&K 1971 and East Pakistan 1971.

Honours & Awards: 1 Ashok Chakra, 8 Maha Vir Chakras, 5 Kirti Chakras, 23 Vir Chakras, 4 Shaurya Chakras, 1 Yudh Seva Medal, 49 Sena Medals and 27 Mentioned-in-Despatches.

Regimental Centre: Shillong, Meghalaya.

8 Gorkha Rifles

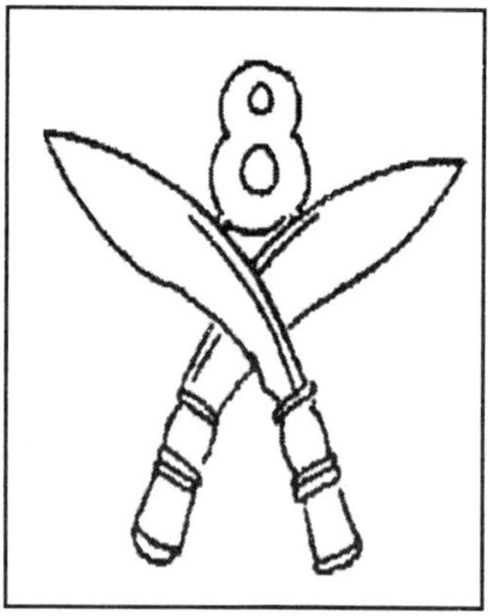

Regimental Motto: Kafar Hunu Bhanda Marnu Niko (Better to die than live like a coward).

War Cry: Ayo Gorkhali (The Gorkhas Are Here).

The 8 Gorkha Rifles is a Gorkha regiment of the Indian Army. It was raised in 1824 and later transferred to the British Indian Army. The regiment served in the Great War and World War II, before being one of the Gorkha regiments transferred to the Indian Army after independence. The regiment is one of the most celebrated regiments of the Indian Army, receiving numerous citations for bravery in the field of battle, and even producing one of the two field marshals, Field Marshal Sam Manekshaw, of the Indian Army.

The Shiny Eight, as the regiment is popularly known in the Gorkha fraternity of the Indian Army, finds its roots of lineage to 16 Sylhet Local Battalion raised in 1824 and since then the identity of the Regiment has undergone a number of transitions to its present designation as the 8 Gorkha Rifles in 1907.

Military assignments commenced as soon after the raising of the Regiment when the first battalion formed the spearhead for operations in Burma War of 1824-25. The services of the Regiment were to be requisitioned again when the British went to War with Bhutan in 1864. Two battalion columns of the Regiment sallied forth, shoulder to shoulder to crush the Bhutanese revolts and the stronghold of Devnageri. The first Victoria Cross (VC) came to the Regiment in October 1879 in its first ever operation mission when its units were summoned to deal with Nagaland Rebels.

This was the first time that a regular army unit was ever employed in the Naga hills. The Younghusband Expedition of 1904 was another jewel in the crown that brought a VC again to the Regiment, awarded to John Duncan Grant, for his actions during the British expedition to Tibet. Braving the high altitude climes of Tibet, the expeditionary force successfully stormed the Tibetan fortress of Gyantse at 19,000 feet.

Soon after partiti€on, 1/8 Gorkha Rifles saw action in the Jammu and Kashmir operations of 1948. In the action against Pakistan in the Kashmir area. Lieutenant Colonel Hari Chand with a handful of men marched on an unconventional route from Kulu to Leh at an altitude of 18,000 feet and destroyed the Pakistan guns, which forced them to withdraw from this sector and saved Leh from falling into Pakistani hands. In this action, Lieutenant-Colonel Hari Chand was awarded Maha Vir Chakra (MVC).

One Param Vir Chakra was awarded to Major Dhan Singh Thapa, of the 1/8 Gorkha Rifles, during the Sino Indian War. To date this is the only recipient of the Param Vir Chakra for the Regiment.

The Regiment was also involved in the 1965 and 1971 Indo-Pakistan conflicts during which members of the regiment were awarded 4 Maha Vir Chakras. The Regiment was also actively involved in the operations in Sri Lanka where again members of the regiment were awarded for gallentry winning one Maha Vir Chakra and four Vir Chakras.In 1979 when the 1/8 became a Mechanised Infantry Regiment a further battalion was raised on July 1, 1979 and named the 7/8 Gorkha Rifles.

The regiment has produced one Army Chief, Field Marshal SHFJ Manekshaw, MC and is incidentally the most celebrated personality of the Regiment. His contribution in the 1971 Indo-Pak War is a legend in the military history of India's Armed Forces.

Battle Honours: Punch, Chushul, Sanjoi and Mirpur.

Honours & Awards: 1 Param Vir Chakra, 4 Ashoka Chakras, 1 Padma Vibhushan, 1 Padma Bhushan, 4 Param Vishist Seva Medals, 7 Maha Vir Chakras, 1 Uttam Yudh Seva Medal, 2 Kirti Chakras, 8 Ati Vishist Seva Medals and 1 Bar, 22 Vir Chakras, 13 Shaurya Chakras, 1 Yudh Seva Medal, 34 Sena Medals and 12 Vishist Seva Medals.

Regimental Centre: Shillong, Meghalaya.

9 Gorkha Rifles

Regimental Motto: Kaphar hunnu bhanda marnu ramro (Better to die than live a coward).

War Cry: Ayo Gorkhali (The Gorkhas Are Here).

The 9 Gorkha Rifles is a Gorkha regiment of the Indian Army. The regiment was one of the Gorkha regiments transferred to the Indian Army after independence as part of the tripartite agreement signed between India, Nepal and Great Britain.

The history of the 9 Gorkha Rifles dates back to 1817, when it was raised at Infantry Levy at Fatehgarh. In 1823, it became a regular unit as part of the Bengal Native Infantry. After the reorganisations post-1857, the designation was changed to 9 Bengal Native Infantry with one of its companies formed by Gorkhas and other hillmen. By then the Regiment had fought at Bhartpur and in the difficult Battle of Sobraon in the First Anglo-Sikh War. In 1901, the Regiment was designated 9 Gorkha Rifles.

9 GR fought in the Great War in Europe and in the inter war years took part in the operations in the North West Frontier. In World War II, it fought in Italy and North Africa.The 3/9 GR and 4/9 GR formed part of the Chindit operations in Burma, and earned a reputation in the long range penetration operations.

Since 1947 the regiment has fought in the 1962 Indo-China War, the 1/9 GR fought under the most demanding conditions on the Namka Chu in (Arunachal Pradesh). The Regiment was also involved in the 1965 and 1971 was with Pakistan.

Battle Honours: Phillora, Kumarkhali and Dera Baba Nanak.

Honours & Awards: 1 Ashok Chakra, 5 Param Vishist Seva Medals, 5 Maha Vir Chakras, 3 Kirti Chakras, 6 Ati Vishist Seva Medals, 17 Vir Chakras, 7 Shaurya Chakras, 13 Sena Medals and 14 Vishist Seva Medals.

Regimental Centre: Varanasi, Uttar Pradesh.

11 Gorkha Rifles

Regimental Motto: Yatraham Vijayastatra (I - The Metaphor for Victory).

War Cry: Jai Mahakali, Ayo Gorkhali (Victory to Mahakali, The Gorkhas Are Here).

The 11th Gorkhas was raised as an ad hoc unit in 1918 with troops and officers being drawn from the various Gorkha Regiments. This regiment saw service in both Palestine and Mesopotamia at the end of World War I, as well as during the Third Afghan War in 1919, before being disbanded in 1922 and the troops being reverted to their original units. There were no separate insignias authorized for this regiment and the personnel wore the badges of distinction of their parent units, though there have been instances where unofficial badges were made and worn by some personnel.

Following India's independence in 1947, the Gorkha regiments of the British Indian Army were divided between the new Indian Army and the British Army. A referendum was held among the soldiers of the four regiments that would transfer to the British as to whether they wished to join the British Army, as the decision to do so was made entirely voluntary. In the event, large numbers of men from the 7th Gorkha Rifles and the 10th Gorkha Rifles, which recruited predominantly from Eastern Nepal, decided not to join their regiments as part of the British Army. So, in order to retain a contingent from this area of Nepal, the Indian Army made the decision to re-raise the 11th Gorkha Rifles.

The 11 Gorkha Rifles was officially re-raised on January 1 1948 with regimental centres at Palampur and Santa Cruz, Mumbai. The regiment was raised with strength from the non-optees of the 7th Gorkha Rifles and the 10th Gorkha Rifles. As the regiment was raised by the Indian Army after independence, it was decided not to retain the honours and traditions of the first 11th Royal Gorkha Rifles of the British Indian Army.

Today, the regiment has a total of six regular and one Territorial Army battalions. The regiment took part in all major military operations India has undertaken since independence including the 1947 India Pakistan War, 1948 Operation Polo, 1965 India Pakistan War, 1971 India Pakistan

War, and in the 1999 Kargil Conflict. The regiment has won a single Param Vir Chakra, which was won by Lt Manoj Kumar Pandey of the 1st Battalion during the 1999 Kargil Conflict.

Battle Honours: Shingo River, Bogra and Batalik.

Honours & Awards: 1 Param Vir Chakra, 3 Ashok Chakras, 1 Padma Bushan, 6 Param Vishist Seva Medals, 2 Maha Vir Chakras, 8 Ati Vishist Seva Medals, 11 Vir Chakra, 4 Shaurya Chakras, 30 Sena Medals, 14 Vishist Seva Medals and 18 Mentioned-in-Despatches.

Regimental Centre: Lucknow, Uttar Pradesh.

Gorkhas in British Army: The Gorkhas, men from Nepal have been an integral part of the British Army since the early 18th Century, forming The Brigade of Gorkhas. They have served with distinction in various theaters of war, firstly against the Afghans in the North West Frontier, then the First World War in Gallipoli, Palestine and France and in Burma, Malaya, North Africa, Italy and France in the 2nd War. The Gorkhas unlike regular British troops in battle, charge at the enemy at close quarters, with drawn kukris (Gorkha swords) instead of fixed bayonets and with their customary shrill piercing cry "Aayaaoo Gorkhali" translated as "The Gorkhas are coming" in Hindi and Gorkhali, a cry so piercing and terrifying that hearing the cry alone can cause the enemy to flee in terror. Today's Gorkhas play an important role in British Army commitments, serving in the Gulf, the Falklands, and Afghanistan.

Gorkhas in Singapore Army: The Gorkha Contingent (GC) of the Singapore Police Force was organized on 9 April 1949 from selected ex-British Army Gorkhas. It was raised to replace a Sikh unit which had lived prior to the Japanese business throughout the Second World War and is an inherent part of the Police Force.

The GC is a well trained, committed and disciplined body whose primary role is as a specialist guard force. In times of crisis it can be deployed as a reaction force. Throughout the turbulent years before and after independence, the GC acquitted itself well a number of times throughout outbreaks of civil disorder. The Gorkhas exhibited the courage, self restraint and professionalism for which they are renowned and gained the respect of the society at large. Recently the GC can be seen patrolling the streets and have substituted local policemen to guard key facilities. Before the 9/11 attacks, they were rarely seen in public. The latest deployment of the GC was to render additional security for the Singapore Airshow, Asia's largest airshow and the hunt for the got away terrorist, Mas Selamat.

Brunei Gorkha Reserve Unit: The Gorkha Reserve Unit is a special guard force in the Sultanate of Brunei. The 2,000 strong Gorkha units are made up of British Army veterans. The unit functioned primarily as a praetorian guard that protected the sultan, the Royal Family and oil installations.

Hong Kong: A large number of ex-Gorkhas and their families live in Hong Kong, where they are especially well represented in the private security profession (G4S Gorkha Services, Pacific Crown Security Service, and Sunkoshi Gorkha Security) and among labourers. Ex-Gorkhas left barracks and moved into nearby urban area. There are significant Nepalese communities in Yuen Long and Kwun Chung.

Malaysian Armed Forces: Since the Federation of Malaya became independent from the United Kingdom in August 1957, many Gorkhas become soldiers in the Malayan armed forces, particularly in the Royal Ranger Regiment. Others became security guards, chiefly in Kuala Lumpur.

United States Navy: The United States Navy employs Gorkha Guards as sentries at its base in NSA Bahrain. The Gorkhas work alongside Navy members in day to day operations. Gorkhas are also sometimes employed to render security for ships in foreign ports.

Famous Personalities

Some famous Gorkha personalities are given below fromvarious fields.

Armed Forces

Gallantary Award Recipients

Rifleman Kulbir Thapa of 3rd Gorkha Rifles was awarded **Victoria Cross** for his courage in France on 25/26th September 1915.

Subedar Lal Bahadur Thapa of 2nd Gorkha Rifles was awarded **Victoria Cross** for his courage in Tunisia on 5/6 April 1943.

Rifleman Karna Bahadur Rana of 3rd Gorkha Rifles was awarded **Victoria Cross** for his courage in Palestine on 10th April 1943.

Lance Naik Bhanbhagta Gurung of 5th Gorkha Rifles was awarded **Victoria Cross** for his courage in Burma on 27th May 1943.

Havildar Gaje Ghale of 5th Gorkha Rifles was awarded **Victoria Cross** for his courage in Burma on 27th May 1943.

Rifleman Ganju Lama of 7th Gorkha Rifles was awarded **Victoria Cross** for his courage in Burma on 12th June 1944.

Rifleman Tul Bahadur Pun of 6th Gorkha Rifles was awarded **Victoria Cross** for his courage in Burma on 23rd June 1944.

Subadar Netra Bahadur Thapa of 5th Gorkha Rifles was awarded **Victoria Cross** for his courage in Burma on 25/26 June 1944.

Rifleman Agam Singh Rai of 5th Gorkha Rifles was awarded **Victoria Cross** for his courage in Burma on 26th June 1944.

Rifleman Sher Bahadur Thapa of 9th Gorkha Rifles was awarded **Victoria Cross** for his courage in Italy on 18/19 September 1944.

Rifleman Thaman Gurung of 5th Gorkha Rifles was awarded **Victoria Cross** for his courage in Italy on 10th November 1944.

Havildar Lachhiman Gurung of 8th Gorkha Rifles was awarded **Victoria Cross** for his courage in Burma on 12/13 May 1945.

Lance Corporal Ram Bahadur Limbu of 10th Gorkha Rifles was awarded **Victoria Cross** for his courage in Borneo on 21st November 1965.

Major Dhan Singh Thapa (1928– 2005) was an Indian Army major in 1st Battalion, 8th Gorkha Rifles Regiment. He was awarded the **Param Vir Chakra**, India's highest military decoration For his gallant act on 20 October 1962 against the Chinese forces.

Others

- Major General M. S. Karki
- Major General Basant Singh
- Major General N. S. Rana
- Major General R. S. Pradhan
- Major General Shakti Gurung

Politicians

- **Bimal Gurung:** The chief of the Gorkha Janamukti Morcha.
- **Damber Singh Gurung:** Only Gorkha in the nation's Constituent Assembly, which was setup to draft the Constitution of Independent India.
- **Subash Ghising:** He was the chairman of the Darjeeling Gorkha Hill Council in West Bengal, India. He spearheaded the Gorkhaland movement in the 1980s and till the late 80's the movement had gained tremendous momemtum.

Artists

- Prashant Tamang: Indian Idol Winner

4

Jats

The Jat people are an ethnic group native chiefly to the Punjab area of India and Pakistan. The Jat people have a cultural history that can be traced back to ancient times and have traditionally been an agricultural community. The Jat people are a strong ethnic group of people mainly found in thePunjab region of India and Pakistan. Other regions include Balochistan, NWFP, Rajasthan, Haryana, Uttar Pradesh, Madhya Pradesh, Gujarat, Maharashtra.

The Jat people are considered to be the merged descendants of Indo-Aryans, Indo-Scythian people of the region, merging to form the Jat people. The Jat people follow different faiths and are engaged in different professions. They have a discrete and distinct cultural history that can be historically traced back to ancient times.

The Jat people of India and Pakistan are not related to the Jats of Afghanistan, who are a distinct ethnic group.

Origin & History

Some 19th century writers have identified the Jats with the ancient Getae. Sir Alexander Cunningham, former Director-General of the Archeological Survey of India, connected the name of the Scythian Xanthii. He considered the Jats to be the Xanthi, who he also considered very likely to be called the Zaths (Jats) by early Arab writers.

The Hindu mythological account in Deva Samhita traces the ancestry of Jats to Shiva's locks. The earliest attestation of the Jats is in a Pali inscription dated to AD 541 (as Jit). There are two major hypotheses, but nothing certain is known about the ancestry of the Jats: The ancestry of the Jats is discussed in terms of native Indo-Aryan ancestry on one hand, and intrusive Indo-Scythian admixture on the other.

Authors postulating Indo-Scythian ancestry were Alexander Cunningham, B. S. Dhillon, Sir Mountstuart Elphinstone Grant Duff, Arthur Edward Barstow, James Todd and Bhim Singh Dahiya. Authors emphasizing "indigenous" Indo-Aryan lineage include E. B. Havell, KR Qanungo, Sir Herbert Risley, C.V.Vaidya, and Thakur Deshraj.

Jats find a mention in Mahabharata and other ancient Indian literature. Mahendra Singh Arya believe that the shloka Jat Jhat Sanghate in renowned Sanskrit scholar Panini's Astadhyayi refers to the Jat people as a federation. G. C. Dwivedi says that the Persian Majmal-ut-Tawarikh mentions Jats and Meds as the descendents of Ham (son of Noah), living in Sind on the banks of the river Bahar. S.M. Yunus Jaffery believes that the Jat people have been mentioned in Shahnama, a well-known Persian epic.

People & Culture

Today, besides agriculture (which is there main occupation), Jat people are engaged in trade and commerce. Though they continue to be a rural populace, their presence in cities and district headquarters can be noted because of migration, which undoubtedly explains their distance from agriculture and animal husbandry.

Jat people are considered a Forward class in the vast majority of states in India, with a few exceptions in a small number of regions were they are Other Backward Class (OBC). In Rajasthan, the Jat people are classified as OBC, except in Bharatpur and Dhaulpur districts. In Rajasthan the Jat people are a wealthy and rich section of society but in 1999, they were granted OBC status. Some specific clans of Jats are classified as OBC in some states. Examples are Muslim Jats in Gujarat and Mirdha Jat people (except Muslim Jats) in Madhya Pradesh. Land reforms, particularly the abolition of Jagirdari and Zamindari systems, Panchayati Raj and Green revolution, to which Jat people have been major contributors, have immensely contributed to the economic betterment of the Jat people.

Adult franchise has created enormous social and political awakening amongst Jat people. Consolidation of economic gains and participation in the electoral process are two visible outcomes of the post-independence situation. Through this participation they have been able to significantly influence the politics of north India. Economic differentiation, migration and mobility could be clearly noticed among Jats.

The culture of Jats is full of diversity and approaches most closely to that ascribed to the traditional Aryan colonists of India. The Jat lifestyle was designed to foster a martial spirit. Whenever they lost their kingdoms,

Jat people retired to the nation-side and became landed barons and the landlords with their swords girded round their waists. They would draw the sword out of the scabbard at the command of their panchayat to fight with the invaders. Jat people have a history of being brave and ready fighters. They are fiercely sovereign in character and value their self respect more than anything, which is why they offered heavy opposition against any foreign force that treated them unjustly. They are known for their pride, bravery and readyness to sacrifice their lives in battle for their people and kinsmen. In the government of their villages, they appear much more democratic. they have less reverence for hereditary right and a preference for elected headmen.

In Gujarat, Rajasthan and part of Haryana Jat people are mostly vegetarians. Some practise the Arya Samaj sect of Hinduism. Their staple food is wheat or bajra (pearl millet), vegetables and plenty of milk and ghee. In Punjab, the Jats usually eat meat, especially goat meat. Punjabi Jat people are also fond of saag (made from mustard leaves) with cornflour roti. Nevertheless, food habits within individual families can be completely different, so no universal "Jat diet" can be identified. Mathura's Jat people are pure vegetarian. Their food includes dal, milk, ghee, matha, and bajra ki roti. Some Jats consider non-vegetarian food undesirable, but many Jats, particularly the ones who belonged to the martial/warrior ancestry and defied Brahmin orthodoxy, customarily ate meat. For example, meat is part of regular diet for Jat non-practicing Sikhs and segments of Warrior clan Hindu Jats (now scattered in parts of Haryana and Uttar Pradesh) who formed part of the erstwhile Jat royalty/aristocracy/nobility. No doubt meat consumption was essential for sustained warfare and only the purely agrarian Jats of peaceful farming habits who did not have much to do by way of taking to martial ways and adversities of wars, could remain purely vegetarian.

To an extent, the incidence of Jat meat consumption is higher in regions where Jats have historically had higher social status, particularly during the medieval/aristocratic periods. For example, meat consumption is particularly high in the Punjab area (including modern day Haryana), where the king was a Jat, and is almost non-existent in Rajasthan (except in Bharatpur and Dholpur, where there was likewise a Jat king).

The Jats have always organized themselves into hundreds of patrilineage clans, Panchayat system or Khap. A clan was based on one small gotra or a number of related gotras under one elected leader whose word was law.

The big Jat clans now are so big that individual in them are only related to each other by individual that lived typically hundreds years ago. Mutual quarrels of any intensity could be settled by orders of Jat elders. In times of danger, the whole clan rallied under the banner of the leader. The Jat Khap or Panchayat "system is territorial and highly democratic. District and a number of Khaps form a 'Sarva Khap' embracing a full province or state. Negotiations with anyone were done - at 'Sarva Khap' level.

In addition to the conventional Sarva Khap Panchayat, there are regional Jat Mahasabhas affiliated to the All India Jat Mahasabha to organize and safeguard the interests of the community, which held its meeting at regional and national levels to take stock of their activities and devise practical ways and means for the amelioration of the community.

All Jats, irrespective of their official or financial positions in life, have equal social status. The only criterion of superiority is age. The Jat people are ethnically and culturally required to marry within their community. With the advancement of modern civilization, as people are becoming less dependent upon and more tolerant towards each other, the joint family system is going out of vogue. It is still prevalent in the less advanced regions.

Jat people are followers of many faiths. Today they follow Hinduism, Islam, and Sikhism. Jats of Pakistan are chiefly Muslim by faith and nearly six million Jats of India were mostly divided into two large groups of about equal strength: one Sikh, concentrated in Punjab, the other Hindu.

The Jat Muslims are organized in hundreds of groups tracing their descent through paternal lines; they were mostly labourers. Those of India and of the Punjabi regions of Pakistan are more often landlord farmers. Numerically, Jats form the largest percentage of the Sikh community. Some scholars attribute Sikh military tradition largely to its Jat heritage.

Jat people usually speak Hindi and its dialects (Rajasthani, Haryanvi, Malvi), Punjabi and its dialects, Urdu, Dogri, Sindhi or Gujarati. Sikh and Muslim Jats from the Punjab mostly speak Punjabi and its various dialects (such as Maajhi, Malwi, Doabi, Saraiki, Pothohari, and Jhangochi).

Sects

The Jat people sect names are unique. List of Jat Clans have been compiled by many Jat historians like Ompal Singh Tugania, Bhaleram Beniwal Dr Mahendra Singh Arya and others, Thakur Deshraj, Dilip Singh

Ahlawat, Ram Swarup Joon etc. Thakur Deshraj, Ram Swarup Joon and Dilip Singh Ahlawat have mentioned history of some of Jat gotras.

The following is a list of major clans of the Jat people:

- Agre
- Ahlawat
- Ajmeria
- Ansari
- Arneja
- Atwal
- Bachak
- Bagga
- Bagri
- Bains
- Bajwa
- Balhara
- Bhati
- Brar
- Budania
- Budhwar
- Chahal
- Chaudhry
- Chauhan
- Chauhan
- Cheema
- Chhina
- Dabas
- Dahiya
- Dalal
- Deol
- Deshwal
- Dhadwal
- Dhaliwal
- Dhariwal
- Dosanjh
- Gahlot
- Gaina
- Gill
- Grewal
- Hooda
- Jaglan
- Jaswal
- Johal
- Joon
- Kak
- Kakkar
- Kharvel
- Kothari
- Lamba
- Maan
- Malik
- Nehra
- Pandher
- Panwar
- Parihar
- Pawar
- Rajawat
- Rana
- Randhawa
- Rathi
- Rathore
- Rawat
- Sahi
- Sandhu
- Sangwan
- Sehrawat
- Sidhu
- Sindhu
- Solanki
- Tanwar
- Tevatia
- Tiwana
- Uppal
- Vaire
- Virdi
- Virk
- Wainse
- Waraich
- Waseer

Demographics

Professor Kalika Ranjan Qanungo mentioned in his famous book "History of Jats", that the religion wise percentage of Jats in year 1925 was as follows:

Religion	Population %
Hinduism	47%
Sikhism	20%
Islam	33%

The last census which enumerated caste was conducted in 1931. According to which, the jat population was:

Name of Area	Population (1931)
Punjab region*	6,068,302
Rajasthan	1,043,153
Uttar Pradesh	810,114
Jammu & Kashmir	148,993
Balochistan	93,726
North-West Frontier Province	76,327
Bombay Presidency	54,362
Delhi	53,271
Central Provinces and Berar	28,135
Ajmer-Marwar	29,992

*The Punjab Region included present day Punjab (Pakistan), Punjab (India), Haryana and Himachal Pradesh. Bombay Presidency comprised the present-day state of Gujarat, the western two-thirds of Maharashtra state, and northwestern Karnataka state of India; It also included Pakistan's Sindh province.The Central Provinces and Berar comprised much of present-day Madhya Pradesh, Chhattisgarh and Maharashtra states.The province consisted of the present day districts of Ajmer and Marwar.

As per Professor B. S. Dhillon in his book "History and Study of the Jats", the Jat population for 1988 has been estimated at 30 million. As per earlier censuses, the Jati or Jat people accounted for approximately 25% of the entire Sindhi-Punjabi speaking region. A regional breakdown (approximation) of the total Jat population is given in the following table.

Name of Area	Population (1988)
Punjab (India)	13,353,530
Punjab (Pakistan)	9,356,225
Rajasthan (India)	3,75,6008
Uttar Pradesh (India)	2,845,244
Jammu & Kashmir (India)	581,477
Balochistan (Pakistan)	369,365
North-West Frontier Province (Pakistan)	302,700
Maharashtra Area (India)	216,139
Delhi (India)	187,072
Madhya Pradesh Area (India)	98,473

Martial Traditions

In the seventeenth century a (Hindu) empire was founded in the region of Bharatpur and Dholpur (Rajasthan) in northern India; it was the outcome of many centuries of rebellion against the Mughal Empire, and it lasted until 1826, when it was beaten by the forces of the British East India Company. Farther north, in the Punjab, in the early years of the eighteenth century, Jat (chiefly Sikh) organized peasant uprisings against the predominantly Muslim landed gentry; subsequently, with the invasion of the region—first by the Persian King Nadir Shah and then by the Afghan Ahmad Shah Abdali—they controlled a major part of the region through close-knit bands of armed marauders operating under the leadership of the landowning chiefs of well-defined territories. Due to their martial traditions, the Jat, together with certain other communities, were classified by British administrators of imperial India as a "martial race," and this term had certain long-lasting effects. One was their large-scale recruitment into the British-Indian army, and to this day a very large number of Jat are soldiers in the Indian army.

When Muhammad bin Qasim invaded Sind, the Kaikan area in Sind was in sovereign possession of Jats. The first Arab invasions in the area were repelled by the Jats. Jats of the Panwar clan governed Umerkot in Sind prior to Mughal ruler Humayun. Susthan area in Sindh was governed by Chandra Ram, a Jat of Hala clan. Chandra Ram lost his empire (known as Halakhandi) to the Muslim invaders sent by Muhammad bin Qasim.

There is no information of any important Jat state in a period of two centuries following Kushan rule. Nevertheless, in the starting of fifth century, there is evidence of the Jat ruler Maharaja Shalinder ruling from "Shalpur" (the present-day Sialkot); his territory extended from Punjab to Malwa and Rajasthan. This is indicated by the Pali inscription obtained by James Todd from village Kanswa in Kota state in year 1820 AD.

There were several small Jat states in what is now Rajasthan. The Bikaner area (then known as Jangladesh) in the desert area of Western India was dominated by the Jats. At what period the Jat people established themselves in the Indian desert is not known. By the fourth century they had spread up to Punjab in India. The small Jat population in the area were Jat clans governed by their own chiefs and largely governed by their own customary law.

There were several Jat rulers of small regions in North India. These included the Garhwals of Garhmukteshwar, Kaliramnas (who governed near Mathura), Khirwars of Brij and Narsinghpur, Nauhwars (who governed the region surrounding the Noh lake region near Mathura), Koils of Kampilgarh (the region that is now Aligarh), Halas, Kuntals, Pachars, Thenuas, Toouts, and Thakureles. The Jats also dominated the Malwa area, under rulers like Harshavardhana, Shiladitya, Singhavarma, Vishnuvardhan, and Yasodharman.

In 1699, the Jats of the Gokula area around Mathura rebelled against the mighty Mughal rulers. The rebellion resulted from political provocation aggravated by the economic discontent, and further aggravated by the religious persecution and discrimination.

In the disorder following Aurangzeb's death in 1707, the Jat opposition resumed, organized under the leadership of Churaman (1695–1721). Churaman's nephew, Badan Singh (1722–1756), founded an empire centered at Deeg, from which he extended his rule over Agra and Mathura. Badan Singh's eldest son and successor, Maharaja Suraj Mal (1707–1763), extended his empire to include Agra, Mathura, Dholpur, Mainpuri, Hathras, Aligarh, Etawah, Meerut, Rohtak (including Bhiwani), Farrukhnagar, Mewat, Rewari and Gurgaon. He has been described as among the greatest Jat rulers. Suraj Mal moved the capital from Deeg to Bharatpur in 1733. Rustam, a Jat king of the Sogariya clan, had previously laid the foundation of the modern town of Bharatpur. During the British Raj, the princely state of Bharatpur covered a region of 5,123 sq.km, and its rulers enjoyed a salute of 17 guns. The state acceded to the dominion of India in 1947.

As per Cunningham and William Cook, the town of Gohad was established in 1505 by the Jats of Bamraulia village, who had been forced to leave Bamraulia by a satrap of Firuz Shah Tughluq. Gohad developed into an important Jat state, and was later captured by the Marathas. The Jats of Gohad signed a treaty with the British and helped them capture Gwalior and Gohad from the Marathas. The British kept Gwalior and handed control of Gohad to Jats in 1804. Gohad was handed over to the Marathas under a revised treaty dated 22 November 1805 between the Marathas and the British. As a compensation for Gohad, the Jat ruler Rana Kirat Singh was given Dhaulpur, Badi and Rajakheda; Kirat Singh moved to Dhaulpur in December 1805.

Ballabhgarh was another important princely state founded by the Jats of the Tewatia clan, who had come from Janauli village. Balram Singh, the brother-in-law of Maharaja Suraj Mal was the first mighty ruler of Ballabhgarh. Raja Nahar Singh (1823–1858) was another notable king of this princely state.

Patiala and Nabha were two important Jat states in Punjab, governed by the Jats of Siddhu clan. The Jind state in present-day Haryana was established by the descendents of Phul Jat of Siddhu ancestry.

Maharaja Ranjit Singh (1780–1839) of the Sandhawalia Jat clan of Punjab became the Sikh emperor of the sovereign nation of Punjab and the Sikh Empire. He united the Sikh factions into one state, and conquered vast tracts of territory on all sides of his empire. From the capture of Lahore in 1799, he rapidly annexed the rest of the Punjab. To secure his empire, he invaded Afghanistan, and defeated the Pathan militias and clans. Ranjit Singh took the title of "Maharaja" on April 12, 1801 (to coincide with Baisakhi day). Lahore served as his capital from 1799. In 1802 he took the town of Amritsar. In the year 1802, Ranjit Singh successfully invaded Kashmir.

Other Jat states of the eighteenth and nineteenth centuries included Kuchesar (governed by the Dalal Jat clan of Mandoti, Haryana), and the Mursan state (the present-day Hathras district in Uttar Pradesh) governed by the Thenua Jats.

The Jats also briefly governed at Gwalior and Agra. The Jat rulers Maharaja Bhim Singh Rana (1707-1756) and Maharaja Chhatar Singh Rana (1757-1782) occupied the Gwalior fort twice, Maharaja Bhim Singh Rana from 1740 to 1756, and Maharaja Chhatra Singh Rana from 1780 to 1783. Maharaja Suraj Mal captured Agra Fort on 12 June 1761 and it remained in the possession of Bharatpur rulers until 1774. After Maharaja

Suraj Mal, Maharaja Jawahar Singh, Maharaja Ratan Singh and Maharaja Kehri Singh (minor) under resident ship of Maharaja Nawal Singh governed over Agra Fort.

Contribution to Defence Services

Jat people formed part of almost all successful armies of Indian feudal states. They offered a vigorous resistance to the Arab invaders. The Jat people are one of the longest serving and most decorated of the Indian Army. They have won many battle honours.

In India the Jats maintained the high reputation they had created for themselves on the battle-fields of France and Flanders, Libya, Malaya and Burma to name a few. In Jammu and Kashmir 1947-48, the China War 1962, the conflicts with Pakistan in 1965 and 1971, and in Sri Lanka and Siachen, they have added to the laurels of the Army.

Jat Regiment

Regimental Motto: Sangathan Va Veerta (Unity And Valour)

War Cry: Jat Balwan, Jai Bhagwan (Brave Jat, Victory to God)

The Jat Regiment is an infantry regiment of the Indian Army, it is one of the longest serving and most decorated regiments of the Indian Army. The regiment has won 19 battle honours between 1839 to 1947 and post independence 5 battle honours, eight Maha Vir Chakra, eight Kirti Chakra, 32 Shaurya Chakras, 39 Vir Chakras and 170 Sena Medals.

Over its life of more than 200 years, the regiment has participated in various actions and operations both in the pre and post-independence India and abroad, including the First and the Second World Wars. Numerous sections of the Jat regiment fought in the First World War including the 14th Murray's Jat Lancers.

The Regiment claims its origins from the Calcutta Native Militia raised in 1795, which later became an infantry battalion of the Bengal Army. The 14th Murray's Jat Lancers were formed in 1857. After 1860, there was a substantial increase in the recruitment of Jats in the British Indian Army, however the Class Regiment, The Jats, was initially created as infantry units in 1897 from old battalions of the Bengal Army. In January 1922, at the time of the grouping of the Class Regiments of the Indian Army, the IX Jat Regiment was formed by bringing under a single regiment, four active and one training battalion.

The Jat people are the merged descendents of Indo-Scythian Central Asian and Indo-Aryan communities. In Mughal times, they preserved their independence and power in Delhi.

Jat society is a republican form of society, epitomized by the Sarv Khap, a body, a council, based at Shoron, district Muzaffarnagar, U.P, India, that united the Jats from the Punjab to Central India and organized the resistance to the feudal forces and the invaders.

They formed principalities like Bharatpur, Dholpur, Gohad (Bhind), Patiala, Nabha, Jind, Kuchesar (UP) and Bahadurgarh.

Conservative by nature, the Jats rarely marry people from other ethnic groups. Great pride is placed in their ancestry. In fact, all the Jats in a particular village consider themselves to be the descendants of the man whom they believe founded it.

The British in their quest for power and domination in India came into conflict with the Jat people and recorded that they caused them the maximum trouble along with the Jat Sikhs. So impressed were they by the soldierly qualities of the Jats that they soon started recruiting them in ever-increasing numbers into all branches of the Bengal Army. The 1st Battalion was raised as the 22nd Bengal Native Infantry in 1803.

The 2nd and 3rd Battalions were raised in 1817 and 1823 respectively. All three battalions had distinguished records of service including the winning of many honours during WW1. The 1st Battalion in particular served with great distinction in France and Iraq (then Mesopotamia) and was conferred the signal honour of being declared 'Royal' in addition to being made Light Infantry.

1947 saw the Regiment undergoing a great deal of change at last becoming a one-class Regiment of Jats, as it should have been from the beginning. The Punjabi Musalmans and Hindustani Mussalmans/Ranghars left for Pakistan being replaced by the Jats from the 15th Punjab Regiment, a Pakistan Regiment. Though 50% of the Regiment left for Pakistan and there were insufficient numbers of Jats to replace them someone in Army HQ had the foresight to give the Jats their due and make the Jat Regiment at last a true image of the proud yeoman it represented.

In free India the Jats maintained the high reputation they had created for themselves on the battle-fields of France and Flanders, Libya, Malaya and Burma to name a few. In Jammu and Kashmir 1947-48, the China War 1962, the conflicts with Pakistan in 1965 and 1971, and in Sri Lanka and Siachen, they have added to the laurels of the Regiment and the Army. But the actions of 3 Jat under Lt. Col. Desmond Hayde initially on 1st September and then again on Sept 21-22 of crossing the Ichhogil Canal and capturing Dograi right up to Batapore-Attocke Awan and knocking on the very doors of Lahore speaks for itself about the battalion's leadership and the bravery of the troops.

Recently in the 1999 Kargil conflict five of the Regiment's battalions took part and once again displayed the soldierly qualities that have made the Jats so well known amongst the community of fighting men. The performance of the Regiment's battalions during the UN missions in Korea and Congo has been in keeping with its high standards. Again, it performed very well in the counter-insurgency operations that have kept the Indian Army busy ever since independence. Nowadays, it fights the foreign mercenaries in Kashmir with its traditional martial spirit.

Class Composition: The Jat Regiment's class composition is 100% Jats from Haryana, Rajasthan, Delhi, and Uttar Pradesh and other parts of India except for 3 Battalions whose ethnic make-up is as follows:

12th Battalion: All India All Class.

15th Battalion: The Battalion recruit Ahirs, Jats, Gujjars and Rajputs, the classes with a common heritage. This was done as an experimental measure to test whether the mixing of these inter-linked classes could lead to fulfillment of the dream of a section of the politico-bureaucratic hierarchy; a mixed Army.

20th Battalion: Raised by General Vaidya the then Army Chief with a mixed class composition of Jats, Dogras, Garhwalis, and Marathas.

Battle Honours

Pre-1947

- Nagpur, Afghanistan (1839)
- Ghuznee, Ali Masjid, Candahar (1842)
- Cabool (1842)
- Maharajpore, Sobraon, Mooltan, Punjab, China (1858-59)
- Kandahar (1880)
- Burma (1885-87),
- Afghanistan (1879-80)
- China (1900)
- La Basee (1914)
- Festubert (1914-15)
- Shaiba, Ctesiphon, Khan Baghdadi, Kut al Amara (1915)
- Neuve Chappelle, France and Flanders (1914-15)

- Defence of Kut al Amara, Tigris (1916)
- Mesopotamia (1914-18)
- North West Frontier (India) (1914-15) (1917)
- Afghanistan (1919)
- Razabil, Kampar, Burma (1942-45)
- Jitra, Malaya (1941-42) Ninshigum, North Africa (1940-43)

Post-1947

- Rajauri (1947)
- Zoji La (1947)
- Dograi (1965)
- Phillora (1965)

Honours & Awards: 8 Maha Vir Chakras, 5 Kirti Chakras, 1 Uttam Yudh Seva Medal, 34 Vir Chakras and 12 Shaurya Chakras.

Unit Citations: Citations are given instead of Battle/Theatre Honours when a unit is decorated for Counter Insurgency Operations.

- 4th Battalion Nagaland (1995)
- 7th Battalion J&K (1997)
- 34th Battalion Rashtriya Rifles J&K (1997)
- 17th Battalion Operation Vijay (1999)

The Regimental Center: The Regimental Centre was originally raised in July 1795 at Calcutta. Ever since the raising of the Regiment in 1922 the Regimental Centre has been located at Bareilly in Uttar Pradesh.

The Battalions

1st Royal Jat Battalion: 1st Royal Jat Battalion was originally raised in 1803 at Fatehgarh. It was affiliated to the Mechanized Infantry Regiment in 1980 and became its 2nd Battalion. Its class composition now is All India All Class.

2nd Battalion: 2nd Battalion (Mooltan) was raised at Bombay, October 1817. With the transfer of 1st Jats to the Mechanized Infantry Regiment in 1980, this is now the senior battalion. The battalion was part of the 2nd Brigade of the Bengal Force during the first Afghan War in 1838. During this war, the battalion retrieved sandalwood gates from the tomb of Sultan Mahmud Ghazni and brought them back to India. Mahmud of Ghazni looted these from the Somnath Temple in 1024 AD. The gates are currently at Agra Fort under the aegis of Archaeological Survey of

India. The battalion was crested with the title 'Light Infantry' on October 4, 1842 for having marched 1100 miles in 33 days and for its distinguished service during the Afghan war. On its return, the battalion saw action in Gwalior Campaign.

The battalion again rose to the occasion during the second Afghan War on November 21, 1878. It entered the Khyber Pass to counter Ali Masjid defences. The troops of the battalion achieved victory the very next day.

To suppress the Boxer uprising in China, the 1st Battalion arrived in Hong Kong on September 1, 1900, where it was posted to the 3rd Brigade of the Chinese Expeditionary Force. It was deployed in the province of Shantung. On July 3, 1901, it embarked for India after successfully suppressing the revolt.

During the second world war, the battalion was deployed at Mandalay Fort in Rangoon. As part of 16 Infantry Brigade (17 Infantry Division) it fought the Japanese when their offensive was launched in December 1941. The battalion repulsed and held the Japanese at various positions, from Rangoon upto Imphal. During this war, the battalion was actively involved in operations in Malaya and Burma against the Japanese.

For the third time in the second world war, the battalion embarked from Calcutta and reached Rangoon on July 10, 1945. It joined 114 Independent Infantry Brigade (7 Infantry Division) to operate against the retreating Japanese. The battalion was later employed to guard the Japanese prisoners of war till the surrender of Japan in January 1946.

During the 1962 war, the battalion proved its mettle once again. While fighting against Pakistan in 1965 war, the Royal Jats fought the ensuing battles with great gusto and tremendous perseverance in which they repulsed two Pakistani counter attacks on the Ichhogil Canal and destroyed seven Sherman tanks.

From October 1967 to February 1969, the battalion was deployed in Mizoram Hills to suppress insurgency. It was the first regular battalion to be inducted in south of Lungle and had many encounters with the Mizo rebels. Braving adverse vagaries of terrain and weather, the Jats emerged as victors again and captured and killed a number of hostiles apart from recovering of large number of weapons. Sub Man Singh was awarded Shaurya Chakra for his gallant action during the counter-insurgency operations in the Mizo Hills.

In 1971, during its stay at Jhansi, the unit was converted into a Mechanised Infantry battalion and was fully equipped with Topaz armoured personnel carriers. In October 1971, during Indo-Pak war, the battalion went to Najabat Kokri (in Punjab) where it remained in a defensive position till the end of operations, as part of 1 Armoured Division. From 1972 to 1981, the battalion was garrisoned at Babina from where it moved to Patiala. At Patiala, the battalion was re-designated as 2nd Battalion, the Mechanised Infantry Regiment [1 Jat (LI)]. In 1984, the Jat Regimental Centre built a monument at Fatehgarh to mark the birth of the 1st Royal Battalion.

In 1984, during Operation Blue Star, the battalion was placed under the operational control of 4 Infantry Division. Subsequently, it was grouped with 57 Mechanised Brigade and moved to Hissar in September 1986. It was presented with new colours on February 24, 1988 by the then President Dr R Venkataraman. In 1989, the first lot of BMP-2 infantry combat vehicles were given to the battalion and the battalion commenced its conversion training.

3rd Battalion: 3rd Battalion (Dograi) Was raised on 13 July 1847 at Dinapur.

4th Battalion: 4th Battalion (Asifwala) was raised on July 1795 at Calcutta. Amalgamated with the 10th Training Battalion on 1 February 1922. Reraised 15 July 1940 at Jhelum. Lost after it surrendered at Singapore on 14 February 1942. Reraised 15 January 1962 at Bareilly. Served in Sri Lanka 4 Oct 1988 to June 1990.

5th Battalion: 5th Battalion (Ladakh) was raised on 1 February 1941 at Banaras. This battalion arrived in Ladakh in April of 1962 and was assigned to 114 Infantry Brigade (Leh). Its assignment, as part of India's "forward policy", was to protect the Central Sector, from the Galwan River to the Lunkung defile, which lay on the north end of Pangong Tso. One forward position, named Galwan post, was commanded by Major S.S. Hasabnis and about 60 men. The post had initially been set up by 1/8 Gorkha Rifles and had been surrounded by the Chinese from before the Jats took over. Movement to and from the post was mainly by helicopter. On October 20, 1962, the Chinese attacked this post with approximately 600 men. According to Major-General Jagjit Singh (Retired), then Brigade Major of 114 Brigade and author of the book The Saga of Ladakh, in the following battle 30 troops were killed, including two JCOs and Captain Paul, the medical officer at the post, and 18 were wounded, including Major Hasabnis. General Jagjit Singh notes that the post - in common with almost all others established as part of the forward policy - was located in a tactically unsound manner, and while this was clearly understood by Major Hasabnis and his men, there was nothing anyone could do about it as orders came from the highest level. After the first phase of Chinese attacks, the brigade HQ was ordered from Leh to Chushul as part of the reorganization of Indian forces in Ladakh. The battalion now found itself split between the two extremes of the 80-km long Central Sector. One company was deployed at the Taska La on the southern end, protecting the right flank of the brigade against a possible Chinese advance against Chushul from that direction. The rest of the battalion, supported by a troop from 32 Heavy Mortar Battery and a machine-gun detachment of the Mahar Regiment was deployed at the Lunkung defile. In the event, no further fighting was in store for 5 Jats. Their service in the area, and the defense of Post Galwan earned this battalion the right to append "Ladakh" to their name.

6th Battalion: 6th Battalion was raised on 1 February 1941 at Bareilly. Served in Siachen 1993-94.

7th Battalion: 7th Battalion was raised on 15 November 1962 at Bareilly.

8th Battalion: 8th Battalion (Poonchh) was raised on 14 December 1959 at Bareilly.

9th Battalion: 9th Battalion (Chhamb) was raised on 1 June 1962 at Bareilly.

11th Battalion: 11th Battalion was on raised on 1 April 1964 at Bareilly. Originally raised as 31 Jat as an 'I' Battalion on a special T/O for CI Ops in the North-East using specially selected personnel from the Jat Regiment, Sikh Regiment, Punjab Regiment, Dogra Regiment and Grenadiers. Converted to a standard infantry Battalion in 1972. Now has an All India All Class Composition. Served in Siachen 1988-89.

12th Battalion: 12th Battalion was raised on 7 June 1970 at Bareilly. Served in Sri Lanka 12th June 1988 to January 1990, and in Siachen 1998-99.

14th Battalion: 14th Battalion was raised on 1 October 1963 at Bareilly. Served in Sri Lanka 14 December 1987 to December 1989.

15th Battalion: 15th Battalion was raised on 15 May 1976 at Bareilly. Known as the AJGAR battalion.

16th Battalion: 16th Battalion was raised on 1 October 1964 at Bareilly. Served in Siachen 1990-91.

17th Battalion: 17th Battalion was raised on 1 June 1966 at Jabalpur.

18th Battalion: 18th Battalion was raised on 1 October 1966 at Secunderabad.

19th Battalion:19th Battalion was raised on 1 August 1980 at Bareilly.

20th Battalion: 20th Battalion (The Jat Regiment's 'Vaidya' Battalion) was raised on 27 February 1985 with a mixed class company composition of Jats, Dogras, Garhwalis and Marathas. However, on 9 August 1998 orders were received for the re-organization of the Battalion as a 100% Jat unit. The following were the departures/arrivals: Departures: 1.Dogras to 19 Dogra 2.Garhwalis to 18 Garhwal Rifles. (This company, who proudly style themselves as the Garhwali Jats, took a stellar part in Operation Vijay, capturing Point 4700 and winning a number of gallantry awards.) 3.Marathas to the Maratha Light Infantry Regimental Center. The fourth rifle company was raised from personnel sent from the Centre and other battalions. The re-organization of the 20th Battalion as a pure Jat unit was complete was completed on 31 December 1999. Served in Siachen 1989-90.

21st Battalion: 21st Battalion was raised on 1 November 1987 at Bareilly. Served in Siachen 1991-92.

114 Battalion: 114 Battalion (Territorial Army) was raised on 1 October 1960 at Dehra Doon.

Famous Personalities

The Jat people is a 31 million strong ethnic group spread out over of north west India and Pakistan and with large populations living in the EU, US, Canada, Australia and UK. This is a list of famous jat Peoples:

Armed Forces

Gallantary Award Recipients

Subedar Richhapal Ram Lamba (1899- 1941) was twice the winner of prestigious **Victoria Cross** award, the highest and most prestigious award for gallantry in the face of the enemy that can be awarded to British and Commonwealth forces.

Major Hoshiar Singh was awarded the **Param Vir Chakra** for his gallantry on India's western front in December 1965, against Pakistani soldiers.

Flying Officer Nirmaljeet Singh Sekhon, on the 14th December 1971, engaged six Pakistani Sabre jets above Srinagar airfield. He hit one directly and set another ablaze. Out numbered, he was shot down and killed, but his struggle was not in vain. India honoured this young and valiant martyr with its highest honour for gallantry- **Param Vir Chakra**.

Lt. Col. Dharam Singh, on the night of November 7/8, 1948, led his battalion extremely well over a difficult country and against a determined enemy. His conduct in carrying out the attack was an inspiration to all his men, which eventually led to the capture of the feature at dawn. For his gallantry he received the **Maha Vir Chakra**.

Maj. Malkait Singh Brar was awarded **Maha Vir Chakra** for exceptional gallantry in Feb 1948 during the Jammu and Kashmir operations for defending his position from enemy forces.

Maj. M. S. Chaudhary was able to inflict more than 100 casualties on 9th October, 1962, on the enemy and was later killed. For his bravery he was awarded the **Maha Vir Chakra** on 20th October, 1962.

Maj. Gen. Swarup Singh, during 1965 Indo-Pakistan War, planned and executed operations to hunt the infiltrators, capture their bases and block routes of infiltration. He succeeded in his mission by showing exemplary leadership, determination and courage in the best traditions of the Indian Army. He was awarded the **Maha Vir Chakra** on 5th August, 1965.

Brigadier K. K. Singh, commanded his Armoured Brigade in action in the Sialkot Sector in 1965.The force under Brigadier Singh destroyed over 75 enemy tanks. He was awarded the **Maha Vir Chakra**.

Subedar Ajit Singh gallantry during 1965 Indo-Pak war, inspired his comrades and they routed the enemy. He was posthumously honoured with the **Maha Vir Chakra**.

Lt. Col. Kulwant Singh Pannu, during the war of 1971, was awarded the **Maha Vir Chakra** for his exceptional leadership in capturing of Mirpur bridge.

Lt. Col. Narinder Singh Sandhu, during the 1971 war, was decorated with the **Maha Vir Chakra** for his skillful leadership.

Captain Devinder Singh Ahlawat, in the 1971 India-Pakistan war, sacrificed his life for his country at the young age of 24 and was awarded the **Maha Vir Chakra** (MVC) posthumously.

Subedar Randhir Singh won the **Vir Chakra** award in Kargil War of 1999 in the battle of Tiger Hill, but at the cost of his life. He was killed in this action.

Hawaldar Shish Ram Gill, on 9 July 1999, during Kargil conflict drove away the Pakistani intruders beyond the Line of Control and killed five intruders. Meanwhile he was attacked and killed. He was awarded the **Vir Chakra**.

Lt. Arvind Kumar Burdak got **Shaurya Chakra** on 2 November 2002 for his acts of bravery in killing three terrorists in J & K on 1 July 2001 at an altitude of 13200 feet in a headon encounter.

Sepoy Virendra Kumar won **Sena Medal** in Kargil War in 1999. He was from Unit-17 Jat Regiment. He was killed in the action.

Others

Air Chief Marshal Arjan Singh, was Chief of Air Staff of the Indian Air Force from 1964 to 1969. He was honoured with the rank of Marshal of the Indian Air Force (equivalent to the Army's Field Marshal), on the Republic Day of 2002.

Lt. Gen. Joginder Singh Dhillon (1914-2003) was a decorated celebrated Indian and Sikh military war hero. He was commissioned into Bengal Engineer Group in 1936, was the first Army Officer to be awarded 'Padma Bhushan' on 24 November 1965. Gen Dhillon, was the General Officer Commanding a forward Corps.

Lt. Gen. O.S. Lohchab (retd) was Director-General of Military Intelligence, at Army Headquarters, Delhi. He actively participated in the wars in 1965 and 1971 and also played a major role in the Kargil operations in 1999. He was awarded the 'Param Vishisht Seva Medal', 'The Ati Vishisht Seva Medal' and The Vishisht Seva Medal' during 40 years of his distinguished service in the Army.

Brigadier N.L. Poonia, is a Sena Medal awardee of 1965 Indo-Pak war. He commanded 19 Grenadiers, and an operational brigade in the desert. During his service, he was actively associated in the process of staff selection and promotion of recruits, gentleman cadets, officers, JCOs, other ranks, NCC cadets/officers and civilians.

Lt. Gen. Sarabjit Singh Dhillon, is the Indian General Commander of Kashmir (GoC) since 2005, and is Master General of the Ordnance of the Indian Army. He is one of the most respected Generals currently serving in the Indian Army.

Brigadier Ran Singh was commander of 3 Jat and Jat Center Barriely.

Brigadier J.P. Nehra of the Indian Army is the Acting Force Commander of United Nations Interim Force in Lebanon(UNFIL).

Lt. Col. Chanan Singh Dhillon (retd) (born 1920), is a famous Punjabi Indian Sikh World War II hero and veteran. He fought in world war two in the British Indian army. He was later taken prisoner (PoW) by the Germans in 1943. He stayed in PoW camps in Italy, France and Germany. In Germany he remained confided to POW Camp XII in Limburg near Frankfurt. In addition, the International Red Cross, Geneva who was responsible for the welfare of POWs, appointed him Chief Man of confidence. He escaped many times.

Capt. Bhagwan Singh Chahar (1916 – 1995) was a unique diplomat, a radical student leader, army officer, Indian Administrative Service officer, High Commissioner of India to Fiji and a devoted social worker.

Sepoy Ganpat Singh Dhaka was the hero of Kargil war who belonged to the village Sihot Chhoti in Sikar district in Rajasthan. He died on 27 July 1999 during Kargil war. He was in Unit-16 Grenediers.

Sepoy Moola Ram Bidiyasar is a hero of Kargil war. He was in Unit-04 Jat Regiment of Indian Army. He died on 15 May 1999, in Kargil war fighting with bravery in war with Pakistan Army.

Politicians

- Amarinder Singh Sidhu: Former Chief Minister of Punjab (2002–2007)
- Chaudhary Bansi Lal:Former Chief Minister of Haryana (1927–2006)
- Chaudhary Charan Singh: Former prime Minister of India (1902-1987)
- Harkishan Singh Surjeet: Former General Secretary of the Communist Party of India (1916– 2008)
- Parkash Singh Badal: Current Chief Minister of Punjab (born 1927)
- Pratap Singh Kairon: First Chief Minister of the Punjab (1901–1965)
- Surjit Singh Barnala: Current Governor of Tamil Nadu, India ((born 1925)
- Bhupinder Singh Hooda: Current Chief Minister of Haryana
- Om Prakash Chautala: Leader of Indian National Lok Dal. He has been Chief Minister of Haryana of the state, for record five times.

- Chaudhary Ajit Singh: A prominent Jat leader from Western Uttar Pradesh, India. He is the son of former prime minister of India and Jat leader Choudhary Charan Singh.
- Mahendra Singh Tikait: A popular leader of farmers from Uttar Pradesh in India.
- Sahib Singh Verma: He was an Indian politician of the Bharatiya Janata Party. He served as Chief Minister of Delhi (1996-1998) and as member of parliament (1999-2004).
- Sajjan Kumar: Indian politician belonging to the Indian National Congress party. He currently is a member of 14th Lok Sabha representing Outer Delhi constituency.

Artists

- Bano Qudsia: Writer, intellectual, playwright
- Dharmendra: Actor
- Gurdas Mann: Music
- Harbhajan Mann: Actor
- Harbhajan Mann: Music

5

Marathas

The Marathas form an Indo Aryan group of Hindu warriors hailing mostly from the present-day state of Maharashtra, who created the expansive Maratha Empire, covering a major part of India, in the late 17th and 18th centuries. They were also considered as Kshatriyan warriors.

The "Maranthas" were known by that name since their native tongue was almost invariably Marathi, nevertheless, not all those whose native tongue is Marathi are Marathas. Historically "Maratha" was a common term used for people of Maharashtra area that speak Marathi. In present time, the term "Maratha" refers only to those Marathi-speaking people who also belong to certain specific Hindu sects:. Thus, the terms "Marathi people" and "Maratha people" are not interchangeable and should not be confused for each other.

Origin & History

The Marathas originated as a social class of Marathi speakers (Indo-Aryans). They belong to the Kshatriya (Warrior) class. The etymology of the words "Maratha" and "Marathi" is uncertain. It may be a derivative of the Prakrit word Marhatta found in Jain Maharashtri literature, itself from Sanskrit Maharashtra "great realm" (from maha "great" and rashtra "nation, dominion, district"). One theory holds that a reference to a clan known as Rashtika in some of Ashoka's inscriptions alludes to a people of the Deccan who were progenitors of the Marathi-speaking people; that the later "Maharachmri Prakrit" is linked with these people

Other theories link the words Maratha and Rashtri with Ratta, supposedly a corruption of Rashtrakuta, the name of a dynasty that held sway over the Deccan from the 8th to 10th centuries. All theories nevertheless affirm, as do linguists, that the modern Marathi language has developed from the Prakrit known as Maharashtri.

Although some Paleolithic remains have been discovered, Maharashtra enters recorded history in the second century BC, with the construction of its first Buddhist caves. These lay, and still lie, in peaceful places of grand natural beauty, but could never have been created without the wealth generated by the nearby caravan trade routes between north and south India.

The name Maharashtra first appeared in a 7th century inscription and in a Chinese traveller's account. Its name may have originated from rathi, meaning "chariot driver" and referring to builders and drivers of chariots who formed a maharathis, a "fighting force." This area seems to have attained prominence as early as 90 AD., when king Vedishri made Junnar the capital of his empire, thirty miles north of Pune. For the 900 years ending in the early fourteenth century, with the overthrow of the Devgiri Yadavs by the northern Muslim powers, no historical information in this area is available. In 1526, first Mughal king, Babar, established his prominanace in Delhi and soon the Mughal power spread out to the southern India. The Mughals were to dominate India until the early eighteenth century.

The areas's first Hindu rulers, based in Badami, appeared during the sixth century, but the eighth-century Rashtrakutas achieved a greater authority. Buddhism was almost entirely supplanted all over the entire nation by the twelfth century, in what has been characterized as a peaceful popular revolution attributable largely to the popular poet-saints. Maharashtra was one of the major channels that helped the emotional and emotional bhakti school of Hinduism spread out from southern to northern India, Jnanesvara (1271-1296) whose commentary on the Bhagwad Gita, the Jnanesvari, was significantly written in the day-to-day spoken language, Marathi, as opposed to classical Sanskrit. The most renowned of his contemporary poet-saints was the tailor Namdev (1270-1350), whose passionate devotional hymns caught the popular imagination. The tradition they founded continued to flourish, even when forced underground by Islam, reaching its zenith in the plain faith of the anguished Tukaram (1598-1650), whose wife and son died in a famine, and Ramdas, the "Servant of Rama" (1608-1681). Ramdas, both ascetic and political activist, provided the philosophical underpinning behind the campaigns of Maharashtra's greatest warrior, Shivaji.

People & Culture

The Marathi people or Maharashtrians are an Indo-Aryan ethnic group, that inhabit the Maharashtra area and state of western India. Their language

Marathi is part of the southern group of Indo-Aryan languages. Although their history goes back more than a millennium, the community came to prominence when Maratha warriors under Shivaji Maharaj founded the Maratha Empire in 1674.

The Marathi people are also known as Maharashtrians. The whole community was called Maratha or Marathe (plural of Maratha) between the 17th and 19th centuries. Nevertheless, at the starting of 20th century, because of the efforts of Shahu Maharaj of Kolhapur, the peasant Marathi class called Kunbi started using the word Maratha to describe themselves. So that in current usage, the term Maratha applies chiefly to the group mentioned before rather than the wider Marathi community. In the Marathi language, they refer to themselves as marathi manoos. They are called Marathi people due to the language they speak, Marathi.

As Maharashtra is a vast state, the people of this colourful state wears different types of dresses, take different cuisines, has different forms of dances and music as per the physical features of their locality. Generally, men wear dhoti and pheta in olden days, while women wear choli and saree. But with the change of time, young Maharashtrians too are fast attracting to the latest fashions imported from the western countries.

Maharashtrian cuisines are a bit strong in pepper and spice, but it is the speciality of the dishes of this state that world knows about. And everybody knows about the unbeatable taste of the Mumbai chaats.

The dance forms like Povada, Lavani and Koli with mesmerizing music and rhythmic movements entertain the Maharashtrians. Dhangri Gaja, Dindi, Kala and Tamasha are the folk dances that attach to the heart of the people of this state.

The cuisine of Maharashtra is largely influenced by the landscape, the people and the crops grown in various areas. It is not only memorable for its subtle variety and strong flavours, but also due to the legendary hospitality of Maharashtrians.

The exotic Konkani food of the West coast of Maharashtra, be it the mild, naturally fragrant vegetable mixture served with local papads, or a spicy-hot fish and meat curry with a coconut milk base, is a gourmet's dream come true.

Vidarbha's cuisine is spicier and more exotic than that of the coastal and southern areas. The ingredients commonly used are besan, or chickpea flour, and ground peanuts.

The food of Peshwas and Brahmin communities of Pune is delicate, sparsely designed and entirely vegetarian. 'Puneri misal', 'thalipeeth', 'puri bhaji' and 'dalimbi usal' are not only tasty and nutritious, but inexpensive to make.

Kolhapur is renowned for its spicy meat curries. Popularly called 'Matnacha rassa', red-hot meat dish is served with robust chappatis, a white gravy to dilute its pungency or a chilli gravy for the bravehearts.

Aurangabad's food is much like Moghlai or Hyderabadi food, with its fragrant pulaos and biryanis. Meat cooked in fresh spices and herbs is a speciality, as are the delectable sweets.

The Nagpur food is generally spicy, with a good amount of ghee, and peanuts, dried copra and dal are often the basis of the flavours. Presented with its rich culture and traditions, Maharashtra has different types of dance forms. Povada is the dance form that showcases the lifetime achievements of the Maratha ruler Shivaji Maharaj. Lavani and Koli dance forms entertain the Maharashtrians with its mesmerizing music and rhythmic movements. Dhangri Gaja dance pays respect to their God by the Dhangars of Sholapur. Dindi and Kala are the religious folk dances, which expresses of religious ecstasy of Lord Krishna. Tamasha is the folk dance that is so popular all over the state.

Every festive occasion is accompanied by song, music and dance in Maharashtra. Talking about the music of Maharashtra won't complete without the mention of Natya Sangeet, numerous folk songs and its grand saint poets. Although music in Maharashtra like Marathi literature has an ancient tradition, the popularity of classical music in Maharashtra began through Gwalior. Miraj city of Sangli district is known as the 'city of music'. The world renowned Indian musical instrument the Sitar is made in this city.

Folk songs are an inseparable part of the daily lives of the rural Maharashtra. Folk forms like lavani, nautanki and tamasha music are very renowned. Nevertheless, a lot of these art forms are dying out as performers are finding it difficult to sustain.

Among the saint poets, Jnandev, Namdev, Tukaram, Jani and Soyara are imorptant to mention. They believed in the fusion of Bhakti (devotion) with Jnana (knowledge). They taught to worship and merge into oneness with the God.

Sects

There are many different sects & communities of Marathi people, with their own traditions. All Communities respect the Warkari movement which started in around 13th century.The feudal Marathas caste make up more than 35% of the Marathi Hindu demographics. The 96 kulin Marathas claim to be the descendents of the Maratha kings and knights (sardar). The farming Maratha-Kunbi community accounts for the largest agricultural and political group in the Maharashtra area. The Maratha-Kunbi community is now the dominant political group in Maharashtra area. They also dominate Police and Military jobs in Maharastra.

The Marathi Brahmins, although they make up only 4% of the Marathi population, have made a significant contribution to the culture of Maharashtra. They are divided into six groups - Saraswat, Deshastha, Chitpavan, Devrukhe,Karhade and Daivadnya.The Marathi Brahmins have long been linked with the freedom struggle,arts, literature, sports and social reform.

The Dalits make up approximately 11.0% of Maharashtra population and fourth of the total Marathi population. Major Marathi dalit sects are Mahar, Chambhar and Mang. They are concentrated in Vidarbha. There are several other artisan communities like Shimpi (tailor caste), Sutar (carpenter caste), Sonar, Teli (oil presser), Gurav and Nabhik (Barber).

Chandraseniya Kayastha Prabhu (CKP for short) is a highly educated Kshatriya-Kayastha community. Members of this community traditionally competed with brahmins for clerical and administrative positions under Maratha & British rule. Baji Prabhu Deshpande and Bal Thackeray are the noted historic and contemporary members of this community respectively.

Pathare prabhu is another enterprising and highly educated Marathi Hindu community chiefly based around Mumbai. The Indian government does not collect data on the "upper castes". Other groups include Marathi Muslims. Marathi muslims from the Konkan area have retained many of their preconversion practices including the Marathi language. Other muslims in Maharashtra tend to identify with the islamic culture of North India and mostly speak an Urdu dialect called Dakhni. The Indian government does not collect data on the "upper castes". Nevertheless, their present numbers may be calculated from the census carried out by the British Raj government a century or more ago.

Demographics

The population of Marathas as per the Population Census 2001 was 9.69 crore, which contributes to 9.4 per cent of the total population (102.86 crore) of India. Most of the population is concentrated in Mumbai, Thane and Pune district which have more than 5 million of population. They are followed by districts Nagpur, Sholapur, Kolhapur, Nasik and

Ahmedanagar, which have a population between 3 to 5 million. The population density has been increasing consistently, with the greatest density of population in districts of Mumbai, Thane, Pune, Nagpur, Nasik and Ahmedanagar. The consistent rate of increase in population also indicates uniformity in the trend of population increase.

The population is quite evenly divided as urban and rural population, with 42% of the population in urban region, which is quite high to the All India level of just 28% of the population living in urban areas. The number of males and females are also uniformly distributed within these areas.Over the years, the rural urban divide in the population has only been decreasing, with the urban population continuously at a greater increase in the last few years, than the rural population which indicates the increasing industrial and business activities in the state over the years.

Martial Traditions

The early history of the Marathas is a tale of the rise and fall in the importance of the dynasties ruling the various areas. Over time the center of political influence shifted south from the Godavari Basin to the Krishna Valley. From the 1300s on, the Maratha rajas held territories under Muslim kings and paid tribute to them. Feuds amongst the local Muslim Kingdoms and later their confrontation with the Mogul dynasty, which was eager to extend its power to the Deccan, allowed Maratha chieftains to become independent. One such successful revolt was that of Shivaji, a Maratha prince who fought against his Muslim Bijapur overlords in the name of establishing a Hindu empire. The local Muslim rulers, weakened by their fights with the Moguls, succumbed to the guerrilla attacks of Shivaji's light infantry and cavalry.

In the sixteenth century, regional Muslim powers like Nizamshahi, Adilshahi, and Qutubshahi established their prominence in the Deccan area. They basically served the Mughal empire but were autonomous to an extent. One of them, Nizamshahi was located in Ahmednagar, a city 95 miles east of Pune. Maloji Bhosle, Grandfather of Shivaji served for the Nizam as a Sardar. In 1595, Bahadur Nizam II honoured him as 'Raja' for his courage in a battle with Mughals and gave him the estates of Pune and the fort of Chakan, near Pune. This is generally considered as the starting point of the Maratha history.

Shivaji Bhosle, founding father of the Maratha empire, was born in 1627, in the fort of Shivneri, 40 miles north of Pune. In 1629, Shivaji's father Shahaji, who had succeeded his father Maloji, in Pune and Chakan, disengaged himself from the service of the Nizamshahi. Consequently, in

1635 the Nizam's army attacked Pune. Shahaji surrendered and his estates were returned to him. Soon, Shahaji put Dadaji Kondadev in charge of Pune,and as a caretaker for the Shivaji while he joined the Adilshahi in Vijapur, aprox. 400 miles south of Pune, which was soon to emerge as the most important power in the area as the other local powers slowly diminished.

In Pune, Dadoji built a palace 'Lal Mahal', for Shivaji and his mother Jijabai. At the age of sixteen (1643 AD), Shivaji took great delight in stirring up his friends' hopes and nursed the thought of becoming independent. He took the oath to make the land free at the fort Torna at the age of sixteen. This was the start of his lifelong struggle against Mughals and other Muslim powers. By 1647, Shivaji had captured two forts and had the complete charge of Pune. In 1657, he committed his first act of hostility against the Adilshahi by plundering a large booty in Ahmednagar. Thus, began a sequence of attacks on the Adilshahi.He slowly started capturing forts in the area, Purandar, Rajgad, Torna being most notable of his first achievements.

Disturbed by his continuing success, Adilshahi sent a renowned Sardar, 'Afzalkhan' to destroy Shivaji. Afzalkhan knew that Shivaji's army, which was much smaller than his huge force would be unable to fight him on open land. He tried all the tricks in the book to make him fight on plains, but Shivaji was no less clever. He convinced Khan that he was very much afraid of him and requested him for a meeting at a place near Vai (100 miles south of Pune) which was densely wooded, mountainous area, and ideal for his army to fight. Khan still had plans to kill him in the meeting and Shivaji knew it well. Ultimately it was Khan who was slained and his unsuspecting army was completly washed out by Shivaji. After this, Shivaji went on a winning spree and spread out his reach until Panhala near Kolhapur.

Meanwhile, Aurangzeb got concerned by Shivaji's rise to power. It was now clear that local Muslim Powers were unable to stop him. So he sent a huge Army, led by Mirzaraje Jaisingh to defeat Shivaji (1666). Jaising's army was much stronger than Shivaji and soon he lost most of his important forts. Realising that he was fighting a losing battle, he signed a treaty with Mirza and agreed to serve Aurangzeb, his young son, Sambhaji being made a sardar. He went to Delhi with Mirza to meet Aurangzeb. Aurangzeb gave a humiliating treatment to Shivaji and soon put him under house imprisonment under some excuse. It looked certain that Shivaji will be slained sooner or later by Aurangzeb. But this was not to happen, fortunately, for Maratha empire. Shivaji made a clever plot to escape and escaped with Sambhaji to south.

After this turning point, Shivaji never looked back and slowly regained his lost glory. By 1673, he had control over most of western Maharashtra and had made Raigad his capital. He was cerémeniously enthroned as a sovereign king in 1673. By 1680, the year of Shivaji's death, nearly whole of the Deccan belonged to his empire. He had developed an efficient administration and a mighty army. He also encouraged a spirit of independence amongst the Marathas that enabled them to withstand for 150 years all attempts to conquer them. Shivaji's achievements among monumental difficulties were really spectacular and that is why he holds the highest place in Maratha history.

Shivaji was succeeded by his son Sambhaji. He showed the same vigor as his father, but was taken prisoner and executed by the Mughal ruler Aurangzeb, in 1689. Rajaram, Sambhaji's younger brother then took the throne, since Sambhaji's son, Shahu was still a minor. The death of Rajaram in 1700 seemed to end the power of the Marathas, but Tarabai, the elder widow of Rajaram, put her young son Shahu on the throne, at the tender age of ten, and continued the struggle against Aurangzeb who had come to south with the sole purpose of destroying Maratha empire. Between 1700 and 1703, Aurangzeb captured the fort of Sinhagad, near Pune. During the siege, his son prince Muhuil-Mulk died; so Aurangzeb changed Pune's name to Muhiabad, in the prince's honour. Shahu continued to fight against the Mughals and captured Rajgad, the former capital of the Maratha territory. The fight against the Mughals ended with the death of Aurangzeb in 1707 which was another turning point in Maratha history. After Aurangzeb, Mughal power never regained its status as major power in India and Balance of power shifted towards Marathas, which was soon to be controlled by Peshwas.

In 1712, Shahu died of smallpox and his minister or peshwa, Balaji Vishwanath took over the throne. Negotiations between the Mughal court of Delhi and Balaji Vishwanath enabled him to send a large Maratha delegation to Delhi to assist the Mughals. The year 1718 marked the starting of the Maratha influence in Delhi, to which they remained closely acquainted, until 1803. Balaji Vishwanath's health had suffered considerably, and he died in 1721.

Bajirao, his elder son was awarded the title of peshwa after the death of his father. It was Bajirao's dream to extend the Maratha empire to North India. By this time, Pune had regained its status as capital of

Maratha Empire from Rajgad. Rajgad was made capital by Shivaji beacuse it was a safe place, high in the moutainous, wooded region. As Pune was in plains, it always had a threat. By 1720's, Maratha power was spreading in large regions and the threat of local battles fought over forts did not exist much. Pune remained the capital until the end of Maratha empire in 1818.

In 1734, Bajirao captured the Malwa territory in the north, and in 1739, his brother Chimnaji drove out the Portuguese from almost all their possessions in the northern Western Ghats. Bajirao diedi in 1740 and left three sons behind him. It was Bajirao who built the 'Shanivarwada', the residence and ruling place for the Peshwas.

Nanasaheb succeeded Bajirao as Peshwa in 1740. He had two brothers, Raghunathrao, who later betrayed the Marathas and joined hands with the British, and Janardan, who died in his early youth.

Nanasaheb was ambitious and a multifaceted person. In 1741, when his uncle Chimnaji died, he returned from the northern districts and spent nearly a year improving the civil administration of Pune. The period between 1741 and 1745 was of comparative calm in the Deccan. Nanasaheb encouraged agriculture, protected the villagers and brought about a marked improvement in the state of the territory.

The scene changed in 1751, when the Mughals, supported by the French, advanced towards Pune, totally destroying every village in their way. The Marathas fought with grand determination, and nothing but the French artillery saved them from total defeat. In 1754, Raghunathrao, Nanasaheb's brother started on an expedition to conquer Gujarat, the state north of Bombay. In 1756, Nanasaheb marched south to attack Karnatak. In the meantime, news spread that the war had broken out between the English and the French, in Europe.

In 1756, the fall of the formidable navy formed by Shivaji gave British their chance to regain importance in the area. The navy was headed by Kanhoji Angre and its destruction was a cruical blow to Maratha sea power. It was a sad outcome of neglect of navy by Marathas which turned out to be a horrible mistake. Marathas never regained control of the sea after that.

In 1761, the Marathas were defeated at the third Battle of Panipat against Ahmadshah Abdali, a grand warrior from Afganistan. Marathas were fighting to save Delhi Sultanat and consequently their power in the north. NajibUddowla was the person responsible for calling Abdali. 14th

January, 1761 was the D-Day. This was a cruical blow to the rising Maratha power from which they never recovered. They lost more than 100,000 men and dozens of important Sardars in the battle. Nanasaheb Peshwe (Balaji Bajirao) lost his brother, Sadashivrao (After whom the Sadashiv Peth in Pune is named), and also his first son, Vishwasrao, in this battle. This news shattered Balaji Bajirao, who died shortly later on, in the temple on Parvati hill in Pune. The Maratha power was at the zenith of its glory during Balaji Bajirao's (also called Nana Saheb Peshwa) reign. It never fully recovered from the crushing defeat at Panipat.

Madhavrao, his second son then took over, but had to constantly face administrative disputes with his uncle, Raghunathrao. Despite of this, he achieved many remarkable victories and restored the shattred Maratha empire to a large extent. His outstanding achievements included defeat of Nizam (Hyderabad), Hyder (Karnataka) and Bhosle of Nagpur. He also had to fight wars with Raghunathrao whose greed for power never waned. Ultimately, Madhavrao took Raghunathrao prisoner in 1768; the same year when the Nizam attacked Pune.He was eventually defeated. Madhavrao, also called 'Thorale'or Greatest Madhavrao, is entitled to special praise for supporting the poor and for his sense of justice. Ramshastri Prabhune, the chief justice, has become a legend for his work. The people who rose to power in his rule were Mahadji Shinde, Nana Phadnis and Haribhau Phadke who became the key figures in the power structure after his death. He took ill in 1771 and died in 1772 at an early age of 27, causing yet another blow to recovering Maratha power.

Narayanrao, Balaji Bajirao's third son succeeded the throne at Shaniwarwada as the next Peshwa. He neither had the courage to take any bold decisions nor administrative skills and soon became very unpopular amongst the people. In 1773, Raghunathrao, who had been imprisoned by Madhavrao, in a room in the palace in Pune, escaped with the help of the Gardi people. Narayanrao was murdered at the Shaniwar wada, owing to a conspiracy by Anandibai, Raghunathrao's wife.

Raghunathrao was proclaimed the next peshwa, although he was not heir to the title. Narayanrao's widow gave birth to a son, Sawai Madhavrao, who was legally the next peshwa. Raghunathrao tried to maintain his empire by signing treaties with the English, and relied on them for manpower in exchange for money and territory. Nevertheless his plans did not succeed. Raghoba was displaced from power by a clever plot by the 12 Maratha sardar's " Barambhainche karasthaan" (Plot by 12 people) including Nana, Holkar, Phadke Shinde. Sawai Madhavrao was then declared the next Peshwa. As he was only one year old at that time, Nana Phadnis became the major administrator with Phadke, Shinde, Holkar taking care of Military duties. These people handled the Peshwai well and with great unity until the premature death of Sawai Madhaorao in 1795. They defeated the rising British Power in 1784, near Pune and halted their advancements, temporarily. Sawai Madhaorao's death was the last blow to the Maratha empire and all the unity amongst its leaders vanished after his death causing a downfall of Peshwai in a short time.

Raghunathrao died in 1782, leaving behind him, two sons; Bajirao, who in 1817 confronted the British at the Battle of Kirkee, in Pune; and the younger, Chimnaji Appa. Bajirao became the next Peshwa after Madhaorao's death. Nana was still the administrator and the Peshwai remained in stable condition until his death owing to his superb administrative skills. Nana died in 1800 and Pune fell into the hands of the Sindia's (Shinde); the former chiefs of Nana's army. They remained in power for a short while and in 1802, Bajirao reestablished himself in Pune, by signing the treaty of Bassein with the British. This essentially ended Peshwai, establishing British supremacy in the area. The capturing of the Ahmednagar fort in 1803, proved British supremacy in the Deccan. In 1804, General Wellesly proclaimed the Deccan in a state of chaos, established military rule and the Peshwas remained rulers for name's sake.

Towards the end of 1805 Sir James Mackintosh, the Chief Justice of Bombay (1804-1811), came from Bombay to visit Colonel Close, the Resident at Pune. The Residency on the 'Sangam' (confluence of the Mula and Mutha rivers) Mackintosh describes as a set of bungalows, fitted conveniently and luxuriously. Pune city had its principal streets paved with stone, and was reckoned one of the best built native cities in India. The Peshwa's residence, that is the Shaniwar wada, added to Pune's glory. Between 1805 and 1811, under Colonel Close and for a short while under Mr. Russel, affairs went smoothly in Pune.

In 1811, Mr. Russel was succeeded by Lord Mountstuart Elphinstone. Bajirao was very disloyal to the British, and in November of 1817, he declared war against them. This battle was fought at Kirkee, that is the Cantonment region, in the east of Pune. The Peshwa fled and the power of the nation passed from the Peshwas to the British by 1819. The rest of the nineteenth century witnessed a few minor uprisings in and around Pune, but the British established their supremacy. As the Maratha's were the key power in India at this time, their fall clearly marked the begining of British Rule in India.

The first step towards establishing a municipal government in the city of Pune, was taken in 1856, when the Pune Municipality came into existence under the Act of 1850. The fact that Pune is not recognized as a major tourist center, is probably because it cannot boast of outstanding artistic specimens of architecture, like those of Delhi or Agra. Yet, it is rich in its associations with the past.

In the early 20th century, the whole of India was in revolt against the British; yearning for freedom. Mahatma Gandhi launched his movement of nonviolence, and people participated by the thousands in the 'Chale Jao' ('go away') struggle. Paradoxically, Pune witnessed violence when the Chaphekar brothers slained a British police officer by the name of Mr. Rand. On one hand, as the violence overrode the city, improvements were made in the education of women and the abolition of child labor. Independence was attained in 1947, but that was not the end of violence.

The British fought the three Maratha wars, supporting one faction against the other, and in each case the British gained territory and power over individual chiefs. At the end of the Third Maratha War in 1818 the British routed the Peshwas so completely that they abolished their position and directly incorporated vast regions of Maratha territory into the British Empire as a part of Bombay Presidency. In 1960 by an act of Parliament the modern state of Bombay was divided into the linguistic states of Maharashtra, with Bombay as its capital, and Gujarat. The legacy of the Maratha State lingers on in the memory of the people, who revere Shivaji as a modern hero. A more negative aspect of Maratha consciousness has led to intolerance of other communities who have settled in Bombay, the premier commercial, industrial, and cultural center of India. Political parties like the Shiv Sena, a labor union-based organization, have sought to politicize Maratha consciousness by demanding the ouster of "foreigners" like Tamils and Malayalis from Bombay.

Contribution to Defence Services

The Marathas were a potent force in 16th, 17th, and 18th century India. Their military qualities were brilliantly optimised in their historic campaigns against the Mughals and the British, under the leadership of King Shivaji and succeeding Maratha rulers.Maratha armies, comprising both infantry and light cavalry, with the Maratha naval power had dominated the military scene in India for three centuries.

The true fighting qualities of the Marathas were discovered during the First World War (1914-1918) when, in the long drawn out Mesopotamia campaign, three Marhatta battalions the 103rd, 114th and

117th covered themselves with glory. In the ferocious battles that took place, the battalions at times lost 50 percent of their strength in casualties but never lost an inch of ground nor left their objectives uncaptured.

Maratha Light Infantry

Regimental Motto: Duty, Honour, Courage.

War Cry: Bol Shri Chhatrapati Shivaji Maharaj Ki Jai (Say Victory To King Shivaji).

The Maratha Light Infantry (MLI, also called Ganpats) is a light infantry regiment of the Indian Army. It was formed as the 103rd Maharattas in 1768, making it the most senior light infantry regiment of the Army. The regiment recruits from the Indian state of Maharashtra. Their regimental center is in Belgaum, Karnataka. The battle cry of Maratha Light Infantry is, Bol Shri Chattrapati Shivaji Maharaj ki Jai! ("Cry Victory to King Shivaji!"), in tribute to the Maratha conqueror Shivaji Bhosle.

One of the most famous regiments of the Indian Army, the history of MLI spans over 235 years.The Second World War saw the Marathas in the forefront in almost every theatre of operations from the jungles of South East Asia, to the deserts of North Africa, and the mountains and rivers of Italy. The war also saw the expansion of the regiment when thirteen new war service battalions were raised. Most of these were later demobilised after the war, whilst two were converted into artillery regiments.

During the war the courage and determination of the Maratha soldier reached its pinnacle when Naik Yeshwant Ghadge and Sepoy Namdeo Jadhav were decorated with the Victoria Cross in the Italian campaign. The 130 other decorations awarded to the MLI was a tribute to the fighting qualities of its men. Apart from being the first light Infantry of the Indian Army,Kali Panchwin was the first Indian Battalion to participate in World War II,first to have lost its Commanding Officer in action,Col Chitty-battle of jebel Hamrin,1917,First Maratha Battalion to participate in UN Mission.Later,It earned the Indian Army's first Ashoka Chakra in the North-East.

The Indian independence saw the Regiment reverting back to the original five battalions, with the 3rd Maratha Light Infantry converting to the airborne role and becoming 2nd Bn, the Parachute Regiment in April 1952. With the integration of the erstwhile princely states, the 19th, 20th, 22nd battalions were amalgamated, from the state forces of Kolhapur, Baroda, and Hyderabad, with the Regiment. The expansion of the Indian Army to meet the omnipresent threat to its borders has seen the Regiment grow to its present total of 18 battalions and two TA battalions whilst the period also saw the conversion of 21st Bn into 21 Para (Special Forces) and the 115 Infantry battalion (TA) being grouped under the Mahar Regiment.

Since Independence, battalions of the MLI have taken part in every armed conflict – Jammu and Kashmir (J&K) operations in 1947-1948, entry into Junagarh, Liberation of Hyderabad, Goa, Daman and Diu, the Chinese aggression in 1961, conflicts with Pakistan in 1965 and 1971 against the Chinese on the Sikkim watershed in 1956, the operations in Sri Lanka, the on going operations in the Siachen glacier and in counter insurgency operations.

The conduct and performance of its troops in Korea, Laos and the Gaza strip as part of UN Peace keeping missions have drawn worldwide acclaim. The Regiment has conducted itself creditably whenever called upon for peacetime duties and combating insurgency and terrorism and reposed the confidence and faith.

The Ashoka Chakra awarded to Captain Eric Tucker (2 Maratha LI) and Colonel N. J. Nair (16 Maratha LI),Col Venugopal (9 Maratha LI), the five Maha Vir Chakras and the numerous other war and peace time gallantry awards bear testimony to the frontline leadership and courage of the Regiment's Offrs, JCOs and men. Over the past two and a quarter centuries the Regiment has won a number of honours and awards.

Various Battalions of the Maratha Light Infantry are 1 Battalion (Jangi Paltan), 2 Battalion (Kali Panchwin), 4 Battalion, 5 Battalion, 6 Battalion, 7 Battalion, 8 Battalion, 9 Battalion, 11 Battalion, 12 Battalion, 14 Battalion, 15 Battalion, 16 Battalion, 17 Battalion, 18 Battalion, 19 Battalion, 22 Battalion, 26 Battalion, 101 Infantry Battalion, 109 Infantry Battalion, 17 RR Maratha LI, 27 RR Maratha LI, 41 RR Maratha LI and 56 RR Maratha LI

Two special forces battalions of the Parachute Regiment (2 PARA (SF) & 21 PARA (SF), one mechanized battalion (10 Bn, Mechanised Infantry Regt), two Arty regiments (34 Medium Regiment & 36 Medium

Regiment) one guided missile destroyer (INS Mumbai) and a fighter squadron (20 Sqn Air force) are also affiliated to the regiment.

Battle Honours

Pre-1947: Mysore, Seedaseer, Seringapatanam, Beni-bu-Ali, Kahum, Mooltan, Goojrat, Punjab, Central India, China, Abyssinia, Afghanistan, Burma, British East Africa, Basra, Shaiba, Ctesphon, Kut-el-Amra, North West Forntier, Baghdad, Meggido, Sharon, Nablus, Palestine, Sharqat, Messopotamia, Persia, Tobruk, Shangro, Tengnoupal, Sangshak, Gothic Line, Ruywa and Senio.

Post-1947: Naushehra, Jhangar, Burki, Hussainiwala, Jamalpur, Burj and Suadih

Honours & Awards: Honours & Awards: 5 Maha Vir Chakras, 3 Ashok Chakras, 5 Uttam Yudh Seva Medal.

Regimental Headquarters: Belgaum, Karnataka.

Famous Personalities

The Marathi people are an Indo-Aryan ethnic group that inhabit the Maharashtra region and state of western India. Some famous marathi people are given below.

Armed Forces

Gallantary Award Recipients

Naik Yeshwant Ghadge on 10 July 1944 in the Upper Tiber Valley, Italy performed gallantly and died fighting bravely. For his brave action he was awarded the **Victoria Cross** posthumously.

Sepoy Namdeo Jadhav on 10 July 1944 in the Upper Tiber Valley, Italy performed gallantly. For his brave action he was awarded the **Victoria Cross**.

Major Rama Raghoba Rane, during his 21 years' service with the Army, he earned five Mentioned-in-Despatches. He served with distinction during the 1947-48 Jammu and Kashmir operations. He was awarded the **Param Vir Chakra** for his courage and gallaranty during the war against Pakistan.

Naik Vishwanath Bhosale withstood Chinese intrusion at Natu La in 1963. Nk Vishwanath Bhosale was the first gallantry award (**Veer Chakra**) winner of the battalion.

Others

General Arun Shridhar Vaidya (1922-1986) was the 13th Chief of Army Staff (CoAS) of the Indian Army. General Vaidya retired and took residence in Pune, India. On August 10, 1986 he was shot to death by Sikh militants while driving his car home from the market.

Air Marshal Bhushan Ghokale is former Vice-chief of Indian Air Force.The Air Marshal was commissioned into the IAF's fighter stream in 1968 and has flown every combat aircraft in the IAF's fleet. A veteran of the 1971 Indo-Pak conflict he has been actively involved in the planning and conducts of the IAF's operations during the Kargil conflict.

Admiral Vishnu Bhagwat is a former Chief of the Naval Staff of India. Vishnu Bhagwat was commissioned into the Indian Navy on 1 January 1960. In his years of service he had a vast and varied experience. He was actively associated with the 1961 Goa Liberation Operations. During the 1971 Indo–Pak war his ship was in the escort groups for missile boats responsible for humbling the adversary. A Specialist in Communication and Electronic Warfare, he was Flag Lt. to Chief of the Naval Staff in 1968–70 and Naval Assistant to Chief of the Naval Staff in 1986-87.

Col. Prakash Khandekar: Retired Army Officer and mentor to over 500 officers in the Indian Army

Capt. Vinayak Gore: First officer to be martyred in Operation Rakshak, 1995

Politicians

- Babasaheb Ambedkar: Architect of Indian Constitution
- Balasaheb Thackeray: Founder of Shiv Sena
- Lokmanya Tilak: National leader of pre-Gandhi era
- Madhav Sadashiv Golwalkar: RSS leader
- Pratibha Patil: President of India
- Sharad Pawar: Founder of NCP
- Shivraj Patil: Current Home Minister of India
- Vilasrao Deshmukh: Current CM, Maharashtra

Artists

- Arun Kolatkar: Great poet of 20th century marathi poetry
- Asha Bhosle: Legendary Singer

- Ashok Patki: Popular Marathi music composer
- Lata mangeshkar: Popular singer
- Suresh Wadkar: Popular trained classical singer
- V.S. Khandekar: Jnanapeeth awardee
- Vishram Bedekar: Novelist

6

Nagas

The Naga people are found in Nagaland, parts of Manipur, Assam, Arunachal Pradesh in North-East India, and parts of Myanmar (Burma) such as Sagaing Division. Of mixed Yunnanese and Burmese ancestry, they speak dialects belonging to the Tibeto-Burman family.

The Nagas are a mountain people, of one million individuals, who live at the meeting-point between China, Myanmar (former Burma) and north-eastern India, a remote and inaccessible area of dense forest, broken up by steep valleys and watched over by the imposing Saramati (almost 4,000 metres high). The ancestry of the name Naga is still disputed. Some philologists say it derives from a Sanskrit word meaning "mountain men", others from "naked people", and the latest research points to the word nok, or "people", of some Tibetan languages. However, the term was not used by the Nagas themselves till a few years ago. They were given this name by the people of the plains and later by the British colonists.

Some of the oldest accounts referring to the Naga cultures appear in literature written in Sanskrit, which as per the anthropologist Verrier Elwin described the Nagas as "mountain men who live mainly from hunting, on fruit and roots, dress in skins, have a warlike appearance and carry formidable weapons. They were good-looking people and emphasis is always placed on their golden colour, unlike the dark skins of other peoples of the plains". Elwin also describes the Nagas as "excellent people...strong and self-sufficient with the free and independent appearance of mountain people everywhere...with an innate instinct for colour and design, friendly and cheerful, with a good sense of humour, talented, with splendid dances and a love of singing".

Origin & History

It is not clear how the name "Naga" was derived. There have been several attempts made by the anthropologists and historians to trace out the origin of this word. Yet as Verrier Elwin points out, "the derivation of the word is still obscure." Even three decades after Elwin made this observation the problem remains unsolved. An attempt has been made to present the explanations made by different scholars and find out the correct position. The issue is complex because of the continuing process of identity assertion, formation and expansion movement of the Naga themselves.

In the Ramayana and Mahabharata, there are references to the Kiratas who have been identified with the Indo-Mongoloid people of North East India. (The Puranas and the Epics refer to many Naga dynasties (Naga Vansa). In the Mahabharata, Arjun, the great Pandava here is to said to have married Ulupee, a Naga Princess. Indian scholars have attempted to identify the Nagas of the ancient Sanskrit literature with the Nagas of North East. This is evidently not correct. The Nagas of the Sanskrit literatures may be identified with the Nagas, who in their climax of glory came to rule in Northern India, after the fall of the great Kushanas before the rise of the imperial Guptas in Northern India, the descendents of whom may be the present Naga Sadhus of central India. Thus it is hard to accept the theory of "Naga" originating from Sanskrit "Nag" meaning serpent. There is no snake worship cult amongst the Nagas, though the Python is revered sometimes and its killing is done ceremonially and elaborately. Some have connected the "Naga" with Sanskrit "Nag" meaning mountain as the people live mostly in the hills, thus implying "hill men."

In the middle ages, the records of the Ahom kings of Assam, specially "Ahom Baranji" refer to the Naga, who fought against them. The first reference to "Naga in the Ahom records dates back to the 9th century AD. when the Ahom-Tais or Shans were living in Upper Burma and had not crossed over to the Brahmaputra vallley: This reference to "Naga" in G.C.Barua (Ed.) Ahom Buranji has been doubted, as the Shan and Burman name for the Nagas was Khyen or Khen.

The early 19th century opinions is well expressed by William Robinson (1814) when he observes, The origin of the word Naga is unknown; but it has been supposed to have been derived from the Sanskrit word (Nanga) and applied in derision to the people, from the paucity of their clothings but there seems little foundation for the etymological derivation, as the term has never been, known to be applied by the Bengalees to either the Khasias or the Garos with whom they were better acquainted.

Despite the "Nanga" theory of the Nagas which became popular with the Naga's fight against British their renowned head hunting practice a new theory of the origin of the "Naga" was propounded by a British explorer and tea cultivator, S.E. Peal that it came the word "Nok" meaning man in some of the Tibet Burman languages like that of the Ao, Nocte, Garos, etc. The clans, it is true, call themselves mostly man or people indicative of the absence of any class or distinction in social order E.A. Gait, the great historian of Assam in 1906, wrote on the subject. "The collective designation by which they are known to the Assamses seems to be derived, as suggested by Holcombe and peal, from "Nok" which means folk in some of the dialects when strange parties meet, they are said to ask each other term Noke or Noke meaning "what folk are you?" and Nok range, "the people of the sky." In this connection it is worth nothing that the khonds call themselves "Kui Luika" and the Orans 'Ku Nok'. The lengthening of the first vowel sound in the Bengali and English rendering of the word is probably because of the old idea that is connected with snake worship."

Chief authority of the Naga clans, J.H.Hutton, originally thought that it was a corruption of the Assamese Noga (Pronounced Naga) probably meaning a mountaineer from the Sanskrit naga, a mountain or inaccessible place. Later the reluctantly recanted this opinion in view of the fact that Ptolemy in the 2nd century and shihabuddin in the 17th century speak of the Nagas as Nanga or Naked.

People & Culture

The Nagas belong to the Indo-Mongoloid family. The fourteen major Naga clans are the Angami, Ao, Chakhesang, Chang, Khemungan, Konyak, Lotha, Phom, Pochury, Rengma, Sangtam, Sema, Yimchunger and Zeliang. The Chakhesangs were earlier known as Eastern Angamis and are a combination of the Chakri, Khezha and Sangtam sub-clans. Now the Chakhesang clan is spilt further; Pochury's who were earlier a part of it now claim a distinct entity. Each clan has their own languages and cultural features. Literacy is 61.30 %. The population has shown a steady upward trend.

The Naga's have different stories about their ancestry. The Angamis, Semas, Rengams and the Lotha's subscribe to the Kheza-Kenoma legend. It is said that the village had a large stone slab having magical properties. Paddy spread on it to be dried doubled in quantity by evening. The three sons of the couple who owned the stone used it by rotation. One day there was a quarrel between the sons as to whose turn it was. The couple, fearing bloodshed, set fire to the stone which as a result cracked. It is believed that the spirit in the stone went to heaven and the stone lost its miraculous properties. The three sons thereafter left Kheza-Kenoma, went in different directions and became the forefathers of the Angami, Sema and the Lotha clans. As per another legend, to which the western Angamis subscribe, the first man evolved from a lake called Themiakelku zie near Khonoma. The Rengmas believe that till recently they and Lothas formed one clan. The Aos and the Phoms trace their ancestry to the Lungterok (six stones) on the Chongliemdi hill. Some people believe that these Indo-Mongoloids are 'kiratas' frequently mentioned in the old Sanskrit literature of whom 'Nagas' were a sub-clan.

The hill communities in the regions now known as Nagaland had no generic term applicable to the whole race. The word 'Naga' was given to these hill people by the plains people. This proved to be an outstanding unifying force to the clans now classified as Naga. Nagas are of sub-medium height, the facial index is very low, the nasal index corresponds to a medium nose, the hair is generally straight, and the skin is brownish yellow. The eyes significantly do not show Mongolian form.

It could broadly be said that they are straight forward people, honest, hardworking, sturdy and with a high standard of integrity. They are lacking in humility and are inclined to equate a kind and sympathetic approach with weakness. The Nagas have a very strong sense of self respect and would not submit to anyone riding roughshod over their sentiments. The Angamis are politically the most conscious group. The Zeliang and Pochury clans in Kohima district are comparatively plain and unsophisticated. The Tuensang clans are un-spoilt children of nature. A striking characteristic of the Naga clans is their hospitality and cheerfulness. To be greeted with a smiling face while traveling on the roads is a common experience. A visitor to Naga village is heartily received and entertained with a surfeit of rice-beer, which is generally served by the lady of the house or her young daughter with warmth which is unforgettable.

The clans of Nagaland are, Sumi, Lothas, Angami, Ao, Kuki, Chakhesang, Chang, Khiamniungan, Konyak, Phom, Pochury, Rongmei, Rengma,Sangtam, Yimchungru, Zeliang, of which the Angamis, Aos, Lothas and Sumis are the largest Naga clans. Clan traditions and loyalties play an important part in the life of Nagas. Weaving is a traditional art handed down through generations in Nagaland. Each of the major clans has its own unique designs and colours, producing shawls, shoulder bags, decorative spears, table mats, wood carvings and bamboo works. The dances of the Nagas give an insight into the inborn reticence of the people. War dances and dances belonging to distinctive clans are a major art form in Nagaland. Some of these are Moatsu, Sekrenyi, Tuluni, Tokhu Emong and Gan-Ngai.

They live in a mountainous area on the border between northeast India and western Burma. Once feared as fierce warriors and headhunters on the margins of the British colonial empire, they were at the same time admired for the beauty of the material culture they produced. After India became independent in 1947, the Naga territory, comprising approximately thirty ethnic groups, was declared a no-go region because of protracted political unrest. It was only after 2001 that foreign visitors were allowed back into Nagaland, which had gained statehood within the Indian Union in 1963. This setting forms the background to two exhibitions that are being shown in the Museum der Kulturen Basel and the Volkerkundemuseum der Universität Zurich. The two events provide an ideal opportunity to rediscover the cultural heritage of the Naga people.

The status-conscious Naga people and their culture, renowned for their grand feasts of merit and headhunting as well as the extraordinary aesthetic appeal of their clothing, ornaments and artefacts quickly attracted the attention of colonial officers, travellers and anthropologists alike. The fascination for this unique culture and people soon resulted in numerous detailed ethnographic monographs and collections, which today rank as important testimonies of traditional Naga culture.

Nagas speak 60 different dialects belonging to the Sino-Tibetan family of languages. Nagamese, a variant language form of Assamese and local dialects is the most widely spoken market language. Every clan has their own mother tongue language but communicate with each other in Nagamese. As such Nagamese is not a mother tongue of any of the clans and nor is it a written language. English, the official state language is widely spoken in official circles and is the medium for education in Nagaland.

Christianity is the predominant religion of Nagaland. The census of 2001 recorded the state's Christian population at 1,790,349 (90.02% of the state's population), making it one of the three Christian-majority states in India, and the only state where Christians form 90% of the population. The state has a very high church attendance rate in both urban and rural regions. The largest of Asia's churches dominate the skylines of Kohima, Dimapur and Mokokchung. Amongst Christians, Baptists are the predominant group constituting more than 75% of the state's population.

Nagaland is known as "The most populated Baptist state in the world". The state's population is 1.988 million, out of which 90.02% are Christians. 75% of the state's population profess the Baptist faith.

Catholics, Revivalists, and Pentecostals are the other Christian denomination numbers. Catholics are found in significant numbers in parts of Wokha district as also in the urban regions of Kohima and Dimapur. Hinduism and Islam are minority religions in state, at 7.7% and 1.8% of the population respectively. A small minority, less than 0.3%, still practise the traditional religions and are chiefly concentrated in Peren and the Eastern districts.

Sects

Their major sects are:

- Ancho
- Angami
- Angkhul
- Angtam
- Ao
- Chakesang
- Chang
- Engma
- Katcha
- Khiamnungan
- Konyak
- Liangmei
- Lotha
- Mao
- Maram
- Nocte
- Ongmei
- Phom
- Pochuri
- Poumai
- Sumi
- Tangsa
- Tutsa
- Yimchunger
- Zeliangrong
- Zemei

Demographics

The population of Naga is 1.99 million according to 2001 census . Nagaland state has the density of 120 persons per sq. km, As against decadal growth rate of 21.54% at the national level, the population of the State has highest grown in NE states by 64.53% over the period 1991-2001. The sex ratio of Nagaland at 900 females to 1000 males is lower than the national average of 933. Female literacy of the State rose to 61.92% from 54.75% in 1991.

Christianity is the predominant religion of Nagaland. The census of 2001 recorded the state's Christian population at 1,790,349 (90.02% of the state's population), making it (with Meghalaya and Mizoram) one of the three Christian-majority states in India, and the only state where Christians form 90% of the population.

Martial Traditions

The military tradition of the Nagas nevertheless is very rich. There are a good many Nagas hereditary names denoting military occupations. This includes Hevage (House of the soldier) in such forms as Golu Hevage, Lama Hevage, Mamu Hevage and Punchi Hevage. Many seem to have distinguished themselves in war and commanded high offices as seen in names such as Ranavirage (House of the war hero) and Henanayakage (House of the Commander-in-chief). They also had clans of bards (Bettage), lance-bearers (Lansage), flag-bearers (Kodikarage), gunners (Kodituvakkuge) and archers (Dunu Vidi Hevage). Then we have family names with Vedage (House of the physician), Guruge (House of the teacher) and Hettige (House of the merchant).

The First World War did not have much impact on the the Naga's, though Naga warriors were recruited for the Labors corps in France, the response of which was remarkable. The Second World War, nevertheless, had a more devastating and far reaching effect. The Japanese penetrated up to Kohima under the Naga Hills District and the Naga's faced the sufferings, dangers and disaster of the modern battle. The Naga's gave invaluable support to the allied forces. Despite floggings, torture, execution and the burning of their villages, they refused to aid the Japanese in any way or to betray the allied troops, instead they guided the allied columns, collected information's, ambushed the Japanese patrols, carried out supplies and helped the wounded in the battlefields.

As far back in 1918 an organization was formed by a group of Naga's who returned from France, Its members were Christian's educated Government officials and headmen from various Naga villages called the Naga Club. This was the first attempt at consolidating a Naga identity and solidarity. Their activities which included a cooperative store and holding discussions were informally supported by local British administrators. During this period the Indian Independence movement had begun to gain momentum and the British Government was negotiating the future of the nation. The Naga's club felt that in order to preserve the Naga's identity they should be allowed to decide their future for themselves.

They feared that Naga culture would be engulfed by that of the plains people which they had come to see as the antithesis of their own. As, Second World War ended, the Naga Club and the councils that had been formed along its lines had merged and evolved into an organization called the NNC (Naga National Council) which dedicated to reforming Nagaland from the scratch of the war and advocated Independence for Nagaland. It held that the Naga's being fundamentally different from the mass of the Indian people and had lived independently before the British conquest of their territory. Therefore, their inclusion into the Indian Union would be an artificial and forced one. A delegation led by Mr. Z.A.Phizo met with Jawaharlal Nehru to reiterate this stand. The Indian Government maintained that the Naga Hills were an integral part of the British India, and the Naga Hills District was handed over to India with the rest of the British India.

It is unthinkable for them to dress now as they did a generation ago. There are only a few older people who regularly wear the traditional ornaments, beads, feathers, shells, brass, tiger's teeth, boar's tusk, cane and ivory put together with a truly artistic sense of form and colour. Otherwise, those who still own ornaments only wear them as dresses. Complete traditional outfits are chiefly worn while taking part in the official celebrations or welcoming comities putting up a performance for VIPS.

When change has brought about so many social ills and so much disillusionment, Naga's are starting to look to the past and the traditions that Naga's grew up on.

They were expected to model themselves after an alien culture; first that of the Christian Europe, then of mainstream India, rather then develop along their own lines. The results have had negative repercussions on every Naga. When a Naga Christian dies, he is given a Christian burial but usually an object that he particularly cherished is put into the coffin just as a deceased's prized possessions were displayed on his funeral platform. Before burial, family members address words of farewell to the deceased with an emphasis on the statement that he should not grieve as he goes to the other world nor should he return to search for those he has left behind (Naga's believe that the dead returns to take with them members of their family). This wake is held in the traditional ways. Naga Christians do not see these traditions that belong to a pre-Christian era as in any way clashing with Christian way of living.

There are also to be found family names of a religious character such as Kovilage (House of the temple), those denoting pastoral pursuits such as Enderage (House of the herdsman) and those concerned with a literary tradition such as Liyanage (House of the scribe). Indeed, the Nagas have distinguished themselves as the literati of the Sinhalese because of their excellent command of the Sinhala language. Amongst the prominent Nagas literary personalities may be included Munidasa Kumaratunga, founding father of the Hela Havula school and Editor of Subasa, Devaraja Dampasangina, the author of the Dalada Sirita, Malavara Kavsekara, the composer of the Rabel Asna and the renowned poetess Dona Isabel Cornelia Senaratna Perumal alias Gajaman Nona. How is it then that the Portuguese designated the Nagas as Chandas and labelled them as 'toddy tappers', a designation that has stuck to this day.

Contribution to Defence Services

The Nagas traditionally are a organized people with a strong warrior tradition, The British first came into contact with the Nagas when they took over Assam and the Brahmaputra Valley in the 1820s and moved into the hill areas in order to stop Naga raids, especially from the Angami clan. During 1960, the delegation of the Naga Peoples Convention put forward a proposal for a separate regiment to fulfill their desire of playing a greater role in the Defence Forces of India. In 1970, the First Battalion of the Naga Regiment was raised in Ranikhet. It is the youngest Regiment of the Indian Army.

Naga Regiment

Regimental Motto: Prakramo Vijayate (Valour Triumphs)

War Cry: Jai Durga Naga.

The Naga Regiment was the first infantry regiment to be raised in the post-Independence India. In 1957, when the Naga hills area was simmering with insurgency, a convention of the Naga people took place and it came out with a charter of demands including statehood for Nagaland and a separate entity for the Naga people in the Indian defence forces. Nagaland attained its statehood in 1963 and the Naga Regiment was formed seven years later. Nevertheless, a remarkable fact about its raising was that several ex-militants were given a fair chance to prove their newfound nationalism and made to join the Indian Armed Forces, many of them were directly appointed junior commissioned officers.

But even before their training could be completed and the recruits were administered oath, trouble began brewing on our eastern border. Bypassing the training schedule, the Naga Regiment was ordered to move into the concentration areas. And thus the youngest regiment of the Indian Army was pushed into the war with scanty preparedness. Still it held the Tri-colour aloft, it should be attributed jointly to the natural instincts of the Naga warriors and to the inherent valour of Kumaunis, Garhwalis and Gorkhas, the other hill communities to be drawn into the Naga Regiment.

The remarkable achievement of the Naga Regiment laid the way for raising of the second Naga battalion. Subsequently, the second Naga battalion was inducted into Keran sector of Kupwara district, where it was responsible for ensuring the sanctity of approximately 24 kilometres of Line of Control (LoC) and also to counter anti-national elements and their operations. It was in this sector the second Naga battalion participated in one of the landmark operations - Operation Romeo. The goal of this operation was to dominate the LoC, which was wrongly occupied by the enemy. The entire operation was carried out with clockwork precision and without any casualties to our troops. This was the first proactive operation in the divisional sector and has been a trend-setter.

Over the years, the Naga Regiment has carved out a niche for itself against insurgency operations. The Chief of Army Staff made a special instant award of "Unit Citation" to 2nd Battalion, The Naga Regiment for their meritorious and gallant performance during the battles of Twin Bump on night 07/08 July and raid on enemy mortar position North West of Point 4875 on 08 July 1999, in Dras Sector.

During Operation "Vijay", the unit performed with distinction and displayed indomitable resolve and valour in the face of the enemy. The renowned warriors of the |Naga Regiment, fighting against heavy odds in the Tiger Hill complex, captured North Bump killing 15 Pakistan Army soldiers including one officer, Captain Imtiaz of 69 Field Regiment. The Naga's lost Captain Prem Raj, an artillery Forward Observation Officer and 10 soldiers of their battalion.

With so many families in the hills of Garhwal and Kumaon who have sons in the military, the conflict in Kashmir has taken a heavy toll. The Garhwal Rifles, as well as other Himalayan regiments (the Gorkha Rifles, Ladakh Scouts, Naga Regiments, and Jammu and Kashmir Infantry) were all entrusted with operations in Kargil in 1999. They joined their Sikh, Rajasthani, Mahar, and Bihari brothers as a multicultural and multifaith force on the frontlines, suffering the brunt of casualities in defense of the state.

Although the Naga youths earned accolades in the Kargil War, desertions were also frequent. The Army conducted a special recruitment drive for all category of posts to recruit 325 Naga youths across the State. GOC, Nagaland, Major General R. N. Kapur said at least 3,000 Naga youths would be recruited in the Army, Assam Rifles and India Reserve Battalion this year and hoped the youth would avail the opportunity to join the armed forces.

The 2nd battalion of Naga Regiment, affectionately known as Head Hunters, celebrated its 19th raising day in February 2003. The event was attended by war widows, ex-servicemen, families of martyrs and a large number of serving officers and other ranks of the paltan. A band display was organised for the families by the regimental brass band and unit's pipe band. A variety entertainment programme added colour to the celebrations.

Naga Regiment is known for its valour and has more than once proved its mettle in various operations. It has to its credit two unit citations and one GOC-in-C Northern Command's appreciation. Besides, the unit has the honour of having 46 individual awards that include one Maha Vir Chakra and two Vir Chakra.

Raised on February 11, 1985 at Haldwani by Lt. Col. (later Brigadier) P. S. Sajwan, the braves of 2 Naga won unit citation by the COAS and Appreciation of GOC-in-C, Northern Command for the excellent job done in Keran sector in Kashmir valley within a few years of its raising in the year 1997.

It was the role played by the unit during operation Vijay in Mashkoh valley that made it to win the title Head Hunters. The braves of 2 Naga captured Twin Bumps as part of the Point 4875 complex. The battalion raided enemy mortar position resulting in a large number of casualties to enemy troops and captured huge quantities of arms, ammunition, equipment and documents. The unit was once again honoured with unit citation by the COAS. It was within a span of three years and both times in face of enemy that 2 Naga got its both unit citations.

The second battalion of the Naga Regiment (Head Hunters) stepped out of teens on 11 February 2004 when it celebrated 20th raising day. The two-day celebrations included an informal get-together of officers and JCOs, badakhana with troops and a special sainik sammelan. All serving and retired Naga and Kumaoni officers also took part in the celebrations. Brig PS Sajwan (Retd) who raised 2nd Naga on February 11, 1985 at Haldwani was also present on the occasion. He gave away trophies and CO's Banner to the champion company.

The badakhana was attended by war widows, ex-servicemen and families of martyrs amongst others. An exquisite entertainment programme was organised which included Naga, Kumaoni, Garhwali and Gorkha dances and songs. Kumaon Regiment's Military Band and Unit Pipe Band's performance added colour to the celebrations.

The second battalion of the Naga Regiment, within a short period has proved its mettle on various occasions. It has to its credit two unit citations awarded by Chief of Army Staff. The enemy got the taste of fury of the Nagas when the unit, during operation Vijay, captured Twin Bumps (part of Pt 4875 complex) and also raided enemy mortar position in broad daylight, causing large number of casualties to enemy troops. The battalion has also to its credit one Maha Vir Chakra and two Vir Chakra.

Presently Naga regiment has a strength of 3 battalions which are 1st Battalion, 2 Battalion and 3 Battalion.

Honours & Awards: 1 Maha Vir Chakras, 2 Vir Chakra, 1 YSM, 1VSM and nine Sena Medals.

The Regimental Center: Ranikhet, Uttar Pradesh.

Famous Personalities

Armed Forces

Gallantry Awards Recepients

Lt. Keishing Clifford Nongrum was awarded **Maha Vir Chakra** for leading from the front as always,he charged a bunker alone, destroyed it, fought hand-to-hand with enemy soldiers and attacked another bunker before he was finally killed on the night of 30 June/01 July 1999 during Kargil operations.

Sepoy Imliakum showed exemplary courage and determination killing two enemy soldiers during Operation Vijay in 1999. His determination, grit, cool confidence and raw courage in the face of enemy. He was awarded **Maha Vir Chakra.**

Capt. Jintu Gogoi, during Kargil operations, with his men of 17 Garhwal had charged into battle shouting 'Badri Vishal', their battle cry during Kargil operations. Of the four companies that went into battle one officer and eleven jawans did not return. **Vir Chakra** was awarded to him on 15th August 1999.

Captain Nayanjyoti Buragohain was awarded **Shaurya Chakra** for his gallantry in Kargil War in 1999.

Captain Bimlesh Kumar was awarded **Sena Medal** for his gallantry in Kargil War in 1999.

Naik Govind Singh was awarded **Sena Medal** for his gallantry in Kargil War in 1999.

Sepoy Matbar Singh Kandari was awarded **Sena Medal** for his gallantry in Kargil War in 1999.

Politicians

- H. K. Zhimomi: H. Khekiho Zhimomi is a popular leader from Nagaland, India. In 2003 he was elected to the Legislative Assembly of Nagaland. Currently, he serves as a member of the Rajya Sabha.
- Lalhuma: Cheif Secretory of Nagaland
- Neiphiu Rio: Chief Minister of the state of Nagaland. He is currently serving his second term in office having been sworn in on March 12, 2008. His first term was between March 6, 2003 and January 3 2008.
- S.C.Jamir: Sanayangba Chubatoshi Jamir is an Indian politician, currently serving as Governor of Maharashtra. He previously served as Chief Minister of Nagaland and as Governor of Goa.

Artists

- Ajungla Imchen: Painter
- Akup Buchem: Painter
- Arenla Subong: Musician
- Iris Yingzen: Painter
- Moa Subong: Musician

7

Pathans

Pathans also called Pashtuns, ethnic Afghans, or synonymously Afghans, are an Eastern Iranian ethno-linguistic group with populations primarily in eastern and southern Afghanistan and in the North-West Frontier Province, Federally Administered Tribal Areas and Balochistan provinces of western Pakistan. The Pashtuns are typically characterized by their usage of the Pashto language and practice of Pashtunwali, which is a traditional code of conduct and honour.

Pashtun society consists of many clans and subclans which were rarely politically united, till the rise of the Durrani Empire in 1747. Pashtuns played a vital role during the Great Game as they were caught between the imperialist designs of the British and Russian empires. For over 250 years, they reigned as the dominant ethnic group in Afghanistan. They gained worldwide attention after the Soviet invasion of Afghanistan in 1979 and with the rise and fall of the Taliban, since they were the major ethnic contingent in the movement. Pashtuns are also an important community in Pakistan, where they are prominently represented in the military and are the second-largest ethnic group.

The Pashtuns are the world's largest (patriarchal) segmentary lineage ethnic group. There are an estimated 60 major Pashtun clans and more than 400 sub-clans.

Origin & History

The history of the Pashtuns is ancient, and much of it is not fully researched. Since the 2nd millennium BC, areas now inhabited by Pashtuns have seen invasions and migrations, including by Aryan clans (Iranian peoples, Indo-Aryans), Medes, Persians, Mauryas, Scythians, Kushans, Hephthalites, Greeks, Arabs, Turks, and Mongols. There are many conflicting theories about the ancestry of the Pashtun people, some modern and others archaic, both amongst historians and the Pashtuns themselves.

A variety of ancient groups with eponyms similar to either Pashtun or Pukhtun have been hypothesized as possible ancestors of modern Pashtuns. The Greek historian Herodotus mentioned a people called Pactyans, living on the eastern frontier of the Persian Satrapy Arachosia as early as the 1st millennium BC, but their connection to Pashtuns remains unclear. Similarly, the Rig-Veda mentions a community called the Pakthas (in the area of Pakhat) inhabiting eastern Afghanistan and some academics have proposed a connection with modern Pashtuns, but this too remains speculative.

In modern history, Pashtuns were also called Afghans till the advent of modern Afghanistan and the division of Pashtuns by a border called Durand Line drawn by the British in the late 19th century. Al-Biruni refers to Afghans as various clans living along the frontier mountains between India and Persia, a possible reference to the Sulaiman Mountains, and further notes that they were neither Muslim or Hindu, indicative of an indigenous Pre-Islamic religion. Thus, it is believed that the Pashtuns emerged from the region around Kandahar and the Sulaiman Mountains, and expanded from there. In this geographic location they would have often been in close contact with the ancient Persians and Indians, and were Zoroastrians, Shamanists, and later Buddhists before the arrival in the 7th century of Muslim Arabs who brought Islam.

The ancestry of the Pashtuns are eastern Iranian. The Pashto language is classified under the Eastern Iranian sub-branch of the Iranian branch of the Indo-European family of languages. Thus, Pashtuns are classified as an Iranian people, possibly as partial descendents of the Scythians, an ancient Iranian group.

Early precursors to the Pashtuns were Old Iranian clans that spread all over the eastern Iranian plateau. Pashtuns who speak a southern dialect of Pashto refer to themselves as Pashtuns, while those who speak a northern dialect as Pukhtuns. These Pashtuns compose the core of ethnic Pashtuns who are found in western Pakistan and southern-eastern Afghanistan. Like other Iranian peoples, many Pashtuns have mixed with various invaders, neighboring groups, and migrants. In terms of phenotype, Pashtuns are predominantly a Mediterranean people, so light hair, eye colours and pale skin are not uncommon, especially amongst remote mountain clans.

Some anthropologists lend credence to the mythical oral traditions of the Pashtun people themselves. For instance, as per the Encyclopaedia of Islam, the theory of Pashtun descent from Israelites is traced to Maghzan-e-Afghani who compiled a history for Khan-e-Jehan Lodhi in the reign of Mughal Emperor Jehangir in the 17th century.

Other Pashtun clans claim descent from Arabs, including some even claiming to be descendents of the Muslim Prophet Muhammad (popularly referred to as Sayyids). Some groups from Peshawar and Kandahar (such as the Afridis, Khattaks and Sadozais) also claim to be descended from Alexander the Great's Greeks.

Pashtun tradition holds that they are descended from a common ancestor named Afghana who resided in what is now Afghanistan in ancient times. As per some traditional beliefs, Afghana was a grandson of Saul, the first king of ancient Israel.

People & Culture

Pushtan culture adheres to a rigid, unwritten "code of ethics" - the Pushtunwali (the way of the Pushtan). Behavior expected without question includes hospitality and protection for guests, provision of refuge to a fugitive and acceptance of a sincere offer of peace, bravery, steadfastness, persistence, defense of property and family honour and protection of female relations - values for which death is not too high a price to pay.

Hard lives, nevertheless, find joy and relaxation in music that includes folk songs or dancing accompanied by stringed instruments and tambourines. Poetry and storytelling have long been favourite pastimes, as are segregated gatherings just to visit or to have pleasant conversation with friends.

Clothing is plain. Men wear long-sleeved cotton shirts over loose pants with sleeveless vests, and turbans wound in a particular way with the end hanging to the shoulder. In some regions weapons complete this dress. Women must observe Purdah (meaning curtain) which requires wearing a full-length garment known as the burka that features a mesh opening over the eyes for navigation.

Women raise the children and prepare meals. The dietary staple is a flat bread called nan. The rare dish containing meat could include curry or garlic, perhaps accompanied by lentils, spinach, or onions, with cheese to complete the meal. Tea is the favoured beverage - one always offered to guests. Living a limited life, women neither inherit property, appear publicly without a male escort nor expect advanced education. Her identity is linked to a male member of her family, that is, as the wife of (her husband) or the mother of (her eldest son). With increased exposure to the world beyond, nevertheless, and a new democratic-style government some Pushtan customs may eventually change.

Pashtun culture was formed over the course of many centuries. Pre-Islamic traditions, probably dating back to as far as Alexander's conquest in 330 BC, survived in the form of traditional dances, while literary styles and music largely reflect strong influence from the Persian tradition and regional musical instruments fused with localized variants and interpretation. Pashtun culture is a unique blend of native customs and strong influences from Central, South and West Asia.

The Pashtuns speak Pashto, an Indo-European language. It belongs to the Iranian sub-group of the Indo-Iranian branch. It can be further delineated within Eastern Iranian and Southeastern Iranian. Pashto is written in the Perso-Arabic script and is divided into two major dialects, the northern "Pukhtu" and the southern "Pashto".

Pashto has ancient origins and bears similarities to extinct languages such as Avestan and Bactrian. Its closest modern relations include Pamir languages, such as Shughni and Wakhi, and Ossetic. Pashto has an ancient legacy of borrowing vocabulary from neighboring languages including Persian and Vedic Sanskrit. Invaders have left vestiges as well as Pashto has borrowed words from Ancient Greek, Arabic and Turkic, sometimes because of invasions. Modern borrowings come primarily from English.

Most Pashtuns follow Sunni Islam, almost completely the Hanafi school. A minority of Twelver Shi'a Pashtuns exist in Afghanistan and Pakistan.

Studies conducted amongst the Ghilzai reveal strong links between clan affiliation and membership in the larger ummah (Islamic community). Most Pashtuns believe that they are descendents of Qais Abdur Rashid who is purported to have been an early convert to Islam and thus bequeathed the faith to the Pashtun population. A legacy of Sufi activity remains common in Pashtun areas, as evident in song and dance. Many Pashtuns are prominent Ulema, Islamic scholars, such as Dr. Muhammad Muhsin Khan who translated the Noble Quran and Sahih Al-Bukhari and many other books to English. Lastly, non-Muslim Pashtuns are virtually non-existent as there is limited data regarding irreligious groups and minorities. The term "Pakhto" or "Pashto" from which the Pashtuns derive their name is not merely the name of their language, but is synonymous with a pre-Islamic honour code/religion formally known as Pashtunwali (or Pakhtunwali). Pashtunwali is believed to have originated millennia ago during pagan times and has, in many ways, fused with Islamic tradition.

Pashtunwali governs and regulates nearly all aspects of Pashtun life ranging from clan affairs to individual "honour" (nang) and behavior.

Numerous intricate tenets of Pashtunwali influence Pashtun social behavior. One of the better known tenets is Melmastia, hospitality and asylum to all guests seeking help. Perceived injustice calls for Badla, swift revenge. A popular Pashtun saying, "Revenge is a dish best served cold", was borrowed by the British and popularized in the West. Men are expected to protect Zan, Zar, Zameen, which translates to women, treasure, and land. Some aspects promote peaceful co-existence, such as Nanawati, the humble admission of guilt for a wrong committed, which should result in automatic forgiveness from the wronged party. These and other basic precepts of Pashtunwali continue to be followed by many Pashtuns, especially in rural regions.

Sects

A prominent institution of the Pashtun people is the intricate system of clans. The worldwide trend of urbanization has begun to alter Pashtun society as cities such as Peshawar and Quetta have grown rapidly because of the influx of rural Pashtuns and Afghan refugees. Despit this trend of urbanization, many people still identify themselves with various clans.

The clan system has several levels of organization: the clan, tabar, is divided into kinship groups called khels, in turn divided into smaller groups (pllarina or plarganey), each consisting of several extended families called kahols. "A large clan often has dozens of sub-clans whose members may see themselves as belonging to each, some, or all of the sub-clans in different social situations (co-operative, competitive, confrontational) and identify with each accordingly." Pashtun people are divided into four 'greater' groups: Sarbans, Batians, Ghurghusht and Karlans.

Another prominent Pashtun institution is the Jirga or 'Senate' of elected elder men. Most decisions in life are made by members of the Jirga, which is the major institution of authority that the largely egalitarian Pashtuns willingly acknowledge as a viable governing body.

The major Pathan clans are as follows:

- Afridi
- Bangash
- Khattak
- Lodhi
- Masud
- Marwat
- Niazi
- Orakzai
- Wazir
- Yousafzai

Demographics

The vast majority of Pashtuns are found in an area stretching from southeastern Afghanistan to northwestern Pakistan. Additional Pashtun communities are found in the Northern Areas of Pakistan and in Khorasan Province of eastern Iran. There is also a sizeable community in India. A large migrant-worker community resides in the countries of the Arabian Peninsula and in smaller communities in Europe and North America. Important metropolitan centers of Pashtun culture include Peshawar and Kandahar. Quetta and Kabul are ethnically mixed cities with large Pashtun populations. With 3.5 million ethnic Pashtuns, Karachi hosts one of the largest Pashtun populations in the world.

Afghanistan: Pashtuns, are one of the largest ethnic groups in Afghanistan, comprising between 39%to 40% of Afghanistan's population or 13 million people (Dupree, L.: Afghanistan: ethnocgraphy). The term Pashtun is historically synonymous with Afghan, a term currently used to describe a person from the nation of Afghanistan. Kandahar is the second major city in Afghanistan and a stronghold of the Pashtun culture.

Pakistan: Pashtuns are the second largest ethnic group after the Punjabis in Pakistan, comprising over 15% of Pakistan's population or 28 million persons (Population Census Organization, Government of Pakistan (2006). About 3 million are refugees from Afghanistan who migrated there during the Soviet war in Afghanistan. The Pashtuns have considerable influence in the politics, army, government, business and trade of Pakistan. Peshawar and Quetta are Pakistani cities with significant numbers of Pashtuns while Karachi is the world's largest city by number of Pashtuns.

The following lists the population of Pashtun in the provinces of Pakistan (Population Census Organization, Government of Pakistan (2006):

Area	Population
North-West Frontier	14,586,000
Balochistan	2,293,000
Punjab	1,929,000
Sindh	1,052,000
Azad Kashmir	157,000
Islamabad	15,000

In ethnic terms, substantial ethnic communities reside in Attock district and Mianwali. Other communities include large numbers of Muhammadzais in Kasur, and other larger communities have settled around Multan which was formerly part of the Durrani Empire.

India: The larger number of Pashtuns in India are Urdu-speaking. Despite the loss of most of the Raj-era Pashtun population, India still has a large community of Urdu-speaking Muslims who trace their ancestry to Pashtun-invaders and settlers. They are often referred by the Hindi-Urdu pronunciation of the word Pashtun, "Pathan".

Shabbir Hasan Khan Josh, an Urdu-speaking poet of Pakhtun ancestry from Malihabad (UP, India), wrote that the Pathans of India took pride in their ethnicity and considered bravery and aggressiveness a part of it. Major Indian Pathan clans resided in the following regions. While, many persons belonging to these races moved to the Afghan-Pakistan border, others chose to stay and thus, descendents of these clans still reside in the parts of India listed below:

1. Rohillas chiefly live in Uttar Pradesh.
2. Bangashes living in Farrukhabad
3. Yousafzai other than Rohillas living in Tonk, Baroda, and Bhopal
4. Mianas in Southern India
5. Lodhis and Suris of North India

Many Pashtuns worked in the Indian independence movement. While many supported the Muslim League's demand for Pakistan, several Pashtuns opposed it in favour of a united and secular India. These included Khan Abdul Ghaffar Khan, his son Khan Wali Khan, Indian diplomat Mohammed Yunus, Pakistani opposition leader Mufti Mahmud and Balochistan-based Pashtun leader Abdul Samad Achakzai.

Today around 11,904,000 Urdu-speaking people who claim Pathan descent reside in post-partition India. The following table lists the population of Pathans in different states of India ("Pashtun, Northern of India". Joshua Project).

Area	Population
Uttar Pradesh	4,670,000
Maharashtra	1,047,000
West Bengal	988,000
Rajasthan	925,000

Madhya Pradesh	816,000
Karnataka	599,000
Tamil Nadu	467,000
Bihar	306,000
Andhra Pradesh	261,000
Gujarat	231,000

Middle East: A significant population of Pasthuns serving as migrant workers is found in the Middle East particularly in United Arab Emirates, Saudi Arabia, Qatar, Kuwait, Oman and other Arab countries. Majority of them are involved in the import-export business, while others are owners of construction companies.

Martial Traditions

Between the 13th and 16th centuries, several Pashtun clans migrated from Afghanistan to Pakistan, where they founded kingdoms. In Pakistan the death of a king frequently led to fighting between the supporters of different potential heirs.

The Pashtun chieftain Ahmad Shah, who extended his rule from Kandahar, unified the Pashtuns under one government for the first time in 1747. Although Pashtuns dominated the monarchy of Afghanistan from its beginnings till its abolition in 1973, foreign intervention and political intrigue weakened the empire of Ahmad Shah's successors.

In the 19th century, Afghanistan became a buffer state between the British Empire, seeking to protect its colonial possessions in Pakistan and India to the southeast, and the expanding Russian Empire to the north. In 1893 the British secured the agreement of the Afghan shah (king) to delineate a new border between Afghanistan and present-day Pakistan (then part of British-controlled India). The new border divided Pashtun territory between Afghan and British regions of control.

After Pakistan became an independent nation in 1947, the legitimacy of the border was called into question periodically by the Afghan government and by Pashtun clans whose territories straddled the border. The issue caused tensions between Afghanistan and Pakistan, which insisted on the permanence of the boundary.

During the British Raj the Pashtuns were called "Pathans" by the British. The word Afghan also originally meant Pashtun, this use of the word remaining in many parts of Afghanistan. Due to this etymology, the Pashtuns are sometimes referred to as "true Afghans". By that logic,

Farsiwan, Uzbek, Hazaras, and Tajik Afghans are not "true Afghans" (though they may be "true" nationals of Afghanistan).

The British identified the Pathans as one of the martial races of the Indian Subcontinent. All through Pathan history the warrior has been the most revered member of society. The term 'Pakhto' or 'Pashto' from which they derive their name is not merely the name of their language, but the name of a complicated honour code.

Although the Pathan people are extremely protective of their womenfolk from prying 'foreign' eyes, in the home women are undeniably in-charge and society is very matriarchal in nature. All Pathan men are extremely close to their mothers and indeed they are encouraged to espouse the virtues of a chivalrous warrior by their mothers.

Pathan heritage is transmitted from generation to generation in the form of a number of verbal stories or anecdotes that every child becomes acquainted with through his/her parents. For instance mothers often tell their children that a Pathan boy was once asked to get his mother a glass of water while she lay in bed. On his return his mother had fallen asleep so the boy stayed awake all night waiting for her to wake up so that he could give her the glass of water. He did not want to disturb her by waking her up.

Mothers are generally very hard on their male children when it comes to being well-mannered. After a certain age boys are not allowed to be in the presence of their own mothers without their shirts on. Boys are told the story of how a man once accidentaly passed wind in front of his wife. He was so dishonoured by this that he decided to run away from home in shame. Many years later when he mustered up some courage to try and return, he approached his doorstep only to hear his wife scolding his son and telling him his father was a dishonourable man. So the poor man decided to turn around and leave again.

The Pathans are predominantly a tribal peoples, nevertheless, increasing numbers now dwell in cities and urban settlements. Many still identify themselves with various clans. Clan names are increasingly being adapted as western style last names or family names.

Contribution to Defence Services

Pashtun influence within the Pakistani army is considerable. The Pakistani army stands today as the most organized, powerful and influential institution in the country. It has a cohesive and task-oriented profile with a strong esprit de corps. The composition and ethnic make-up of the Pakistani army have a long history. Before the independence of India and

Pakistan in 1947, imperial British rulers defined the recruitment policies and orientation of the British Indian forces for a little under a century.

They were convinced that certain classes of Indians described as martial races were more suitable for army service and would make better soldiers. In the area that is today Pakistan, the British-preferred recruitment hubs were the Punjab, which includes the districts of Rawalpindi, Jhelum and Attock and the North-West Frontier Province (NWFP), which includes the districts of Kohat, Mardan and Peshawar. After partition, Pakistan continued this unwritten policy at least until the late 1970s. From then onwards, it officially discarded this concept and tried to expand its recruitment base. The results today, however, are not any different from earlier times.

Pakistani army is considered a reserve of Pashtuns. A fact is that out of the 11 chiefs of the army, four have been Pashtuns (Generals Ayub Khan, Yahya Khan, Gul Hasan Khan and Waheed Kakar), leading the institution for a total of 18 years. Two of them imposed martial law and remained presidents of Pakistan. Ayub Khan, the first Pakistani commander-in-chief of the army, remained at the helm of affairs for eight years as army chief (1951-58) and an additional 11 years as head of the country (1958-69) (Dawn, October 13). Ayub Khan also promoted himself to field marshal in 1965 and is credited with developing the army into one of the most resourceful and powerful institutions in the country.

Pashtuns are known for their marksmanship, courage and loyalty. Although there are no all-Pashtun regiments, and only one corps of the nine total is headquartered in NWFP, many important training centers for soldiers (Peshawar, Nowshera, Mardan) and the only military training academy for officers (Kakul) are located in the NWFP. Hence, Pashtuns are very well placed within the Pakistani army's infrastructure.

The Frontier Force Regiment

Regimental Motto: Labaik (Here I Come)

The Frontier Force Regiment (popularly known as the "Piffers" or the "FF") is one of six Infantry regiments in the Pakistan Army. At present, the regiment consists of 52 battalions and has its regimental depot at Abbottabad. For that reason Abbottabad is also known as Home of Piffers. Currently the regiment includes both mechanised and motorised infantry battalions. Other than these there are also some Armoured and Artillery battalions which were raised from the strength of Frontier Force or one of its predecessor regiments.

W. W I: Guides Infantry - India, Mesopotamia, Egypt, Palestine (one company to France in 1914, attached to 57th Wilde's Rifles), 2nd Guides - (raised in 1917) - India, Egypt, Palestine, Syria, 3rd Guides - (raised in 1917) India, 51st Sikhs - India, Aden, Egypt, Mesopotamia, 52nd Sikhs - India, Mesopotamia, 54th Sikhs - India, Egypt, Turkey 2/54th - (raised in 1917) India.

The formation of the 12th Frontier Force Regiment in 1922 did not present too much of a problem in re-numbering its battalions. The change was facilitated by the Guides Infantry who,volunteered to become the 5th Battalion. The Territorial battalion, raised on 11 Mar 22 as the 1st (territorial) Bn 51st (The Prince of Wales' Own) in Nowshera, became the 11/12th but wore its own badge, crossed Khyber knives, points down, a crown above and title scroll below. It recruited only Pathans and, on mobilisation on 4 Sept. 39, was the only all-Pathan battalion in the army.

In 1933, the 4/12th was one of the battalions nominated for Indianisation. Most regiments saw service on the North West Frontier in the between-wars years but few had the experience of the Guides Infantry.

In an action in September 1935, the under-strength battalion, barely 370 all ranks, faced an overwhelmingly superior force of Mohmands, an action in which all the British and most of the Indian officers were killed or wounded. Captain Godfrey Meynell MC, the adjutant, went forward to encourage his men and was over-run with them. His action inflicted heavy losses on the clansmen and gained him a posthumous Victoria Cross. Also in 1935, in the Silver Jubilee honours, the 3/12th was made a royal battalion.

W. W II: 1st Battalion - India, Iraq, Syria, Italy. In late 1946, the battalion was nominated for parachute training to join 2nd Indian Airborne Division. 2nd Battalion - India, Malaya, Captured on Singapore Island by the Japanese in February 1942, Reconstituted 30 Apr 46 on a cadre of 9/12th. 3rd Battalion - India, Italian East Africa, Egypt, Iraq, Cyprus, Sicily, Italy, Greece. 4th Battalion - India, Burma. 5th Battalion (Guides) - India, Iraq, Iran. 6th Battalion - raised 8 Aug 40 at Sabathu. India. Disbanded 5 Jul 44. 7th Battalion - raised 7 Aug 40 at Shillong. India. Became a unit of 39 Training Division. Disbanded February 1946. 8th Battalion - raised 1 April 41 at Bareilly. India, Burma. The battalion was not disbanded after the war but continued as a regular unit. 9th Battalion - raised 1 April 41 at

Jhansi, India, Ceylon, Burma, Indo-China, reconstituted as 2/12th on 30 April 46. 11th Battalion - the pre-war Territorial battalion was mobilised on 4 Sep 39, converted to active battalion of 15 Sept 41 and redesignated 14th (Suba Sarhad) Bn. 14th Battalion - formed 15 Sep 41 on conversion of 11th Battalion to active status. India, Burma, Iran, Greece. Disbanded September 1946. 1st Afridi Battalion - raised 1 Apr 42 at Sialkot. India, Iran, Iraq, Syria. Disbanded January 1946 but re-raised as Khyber Rifles. Machine-Gun Battalion - raised 15 Jan 42 at Sialkot, India, Burma, Dutch East Indies. Disbanded December 1946. 25th Garrison Battalion - raised 1 Apr 41 at Sialkot, India. Disbanded 20 May 46. 26th Garrison Battalion - raised 1 Mar 42 at Sialkot, India, Iraq. Disbanded February 1946.

FF is Pakistan's third oldest regiment after the Punjab and Baloch. The regiment's history dates back to 1957, when it was raised through the amalgamation of three Pakistan Army regiments, all with their origins in two regiments which had been transferred to Pakistan from the British Indian Army at the time of the partition of India in 1947. These two regiments were the Frontier Force Regiment and the Frontier Force Rifles. The third component, the Pathan Regiment, had been raised after partition from elements of the former two. The merger took place when a major reorganisation of regiments was carried out in the Pakistan Army.

The FF battalions took active part not only in battles on Pakistan's borders but also served extensively overseas, in Saudi Arabia, and as part of United Nations peacekeeping operations in Somalia. In Somalia, some of the Piffer battalions also participated in the world renowned operations of Battle of Mogadishu (1993). This battle history earned Piffers two Nishan-e-Haider, the highest gallantry award in Pakistan, and many other awards too.

The battalions are divided under independent formations and are commanded by their formation commander. The training and record keeping is done by the regimental depot, which is usually commanded by an officer of the rank Brigadier. The regiment's highest ranking officer is given the honourary title of "Colonel Commandant" and Colonel-in-Chief, if the highest ranking officer is the Chief of Army Staff.

The Pathan Regiment was raised after partition from the 4th battalion of the Frontier Force Regiment and the 4th and 15th battalions of the Frontier Force Rifles. Initially the regimental depot was at Dera Ismail Khan but it relocated to Kohat in 1949 and was later merged into the Frontier Force Regiment with its regimental depot at Abbottabad.

At present the Frontier Force Regiment musters 52 infantry battalions, some of which are mechanised or motorised with the remainder known colloquially as "foot infantry". Each battalion is subdivided into four companies, normally named Alpha, Bravo, Charlie, and Delta. The regiment also includes armoured and artillery units, established from among its strength. All Piffer battalions serve alongside other Pakistan Army units in mixed formations; operational control resides with the appropriate brigade, whereas administrative control remains with the Frontier Force regimental depot. The regiment recruits mostly from the Pashtun clans of the North-West Frontier Province, and is often called a Pashtun Regiment, although officers and other ranks from all over Pakistan have served and continue to serve in the regiment. Prior to 2000 the Piffers had been standardised to include equal numbers of Pashtuns and Punjabis in its non-officer ranks, but in 2000 this composition was amended to include 10% Sindhis and 5% Balochis, reducing the quota of Punjabis to 35%. This measure was intended to diminish segregation within the Army.

Battle Honours: Pegu, Mooltan, Goojerat, Punjaub, Delhi 1857, Ali Masjid, Kabul 1879, Ahmed Khel, Kandahar 1880, Afghanistan 1878-80, Chitral, Malakand, Punjab Frontier, Tirah, Pekin 1900, Somaliland 1901-04. Suez Canal, Egypt 1915, Megiddo, Sharon, Nablus, Palestine 1918, Aden, Tigris 1916, Kut-al-Amara 1917, Baghdad, Sharqat, Mesopotamia 1915-18, NW Frontier, India 1914, 1915, 1916-17, Afghanistan 1919.

Gallabat, Tehamiyam Wells, Agordat, Barentu, Keren, Amba Alagi, Abyssinia 1940-41, Gazala, Bir Hacheim, El Adem, North Africa 1940-43, Landing in Sicily, Sicily 1943, Landing at Reggio, The Sangro, Mozzagrogna, Romagnoli. The Moro, Impossible Bridge, Cassino II, Pignataro, Advance to Florence. Campriano, Gothic Line, Coriano, The Senio, Santerno Crossing, Italy 1943-45, Athens, Greece 1944-45, North Malaya, Kota Bharu, Central Malaya, Kuantan, Machang, Singapore Island, Malaya 1941-42, Moulmein, Sittang 1942, 1945, Pegu 1942, 1945, Taukkyan, Shwegyin, North Arakan, Buthidaung, Maungdaw, Ngakyedauk Pass, Imphal, Tamu Road, Shenam Pass, Bishenpur, Kyaukmyaung Bridgehead, Arakan Beaches, Ramree, Taungup, Mandalay, Myinmu, Fort Dufferin, Kyaukse 1945, Meiktila, Nyaungu Bridgehead, Capture of Meiktila, Defence of Meiktila, The Irrawaddy, Rangoon Road, Pyawbwe, Toungoo, Burma 1942-45.

Honours & Awards: 2 Nishan-e-Haider, 2 Hilal-e-Jurat, 6 Victoria Cross, 4 Military Cross.

The Regimental Centre: Sialkot, Pakistan

Famous Personalities

The Pathan's are a warrior race originally hailing from the North West Frontier Province of the present day Pakistan. Many of them migrated to the Central and the Southern parts of India during the long period of Muslim rule, and made it their home. 'Khan' is a common surname of the Pathan's, though its not necessarily a rule. Many of them have distinguished themselves in the fields of science, art, music and sports.

Armed Forces

Gallantary Award Recipients

Jemadar Mir Dast, on 26 April 1915 at Wieltje, Belgium, led his platoon with great bravery during the attack, and afterwards collected various parties of the regiment (when no British officers were left) and kept them under his command until the retirement was ordered. He was awarded **Victoria Cross** for this act.

Ali Haidar was recipient of the **Victoria Cross,** the highest and most prestigious award for gallantry feet on 9 April 1945 near Fusignano, Italy, in the face of the enemy.

Major Muhammad Akram, during War of 1971, he was posthumously awarded **Nishan-e-Haider**.

Major Shabbir Sharif, on December 3, 1971, was posthumously awarded **Nishan-e-Haider**.

Others

Gen. Muhammad Iqbal Khan is a former four star general of the Pakistan Army who stayed as Chairman Joint Chiefs of Staff Committee from 1980 to 1984. During his career, Iqbal was Deputy Chief of Army Staff (DCOAS), Commander IV Corps, Lahore and Chief of General Staff (CGS) at the Army General Headquarters.

Lt . Gen. Munir Hafeez is the former chairman of the National Accountability Bureau (NAB) of the Government of Pakistan, the body charged with fighting corruption. Before his appointment in 2002 he served in the Pakistani Army for 38 years.

Lt. Gen. Mohammed Attiqur Rahman (1918- 1996) was a distinguished general officer in the Pakistan Army, a noted military historian, as well as a senior government official. He was the martial law administrator of West Pakistan in the General Yahya Khan's military regime.

Maj. Gen. Mian Hayaud Din (1910 - 1965) was a soldier in the early years of Pakistan's existence. He studied at the Royal Military

Academy Sandhurst. He served with distinction on the North West Frontier in the early 1930s. His gallantry/service decorations, plus four Mentions in Despatches, made him the most highly decorated officer of the Pakistan Army, and the only Officer ever to have been decorated by the Governments of Britain; France; Pakistan and the USA. He ended active service in the Pakistan Army upon completing 30 years of service, in the rank of Major General, and retired in December 1960.

Maj. Gen. Mian Ghulam Jilani (1914 - 2004) was a World War II Japanese POW camp survivor at Singapore, who subsequently rose to help negotiate Pakistan's membership in the Baghdad Pact and the Southeast Asia Treaty Organization. An ethnic Pashtun, he retired from the Pakistan Army in 1962.

Politicians

Khan Abdul Ghaffar Khan (1890-1988) was a political and spiritual leader known for his non-violent opposition to British Rule in India. A lifelong pacifist,and a follower of Mahatma Gandhi, he was also known as Badshah Khan (King Khan), and Sarhaddi Gandhi (Frontier Gandhi).

Akram Khan Durrani was the 23rd Chief Minister of Pakistan's North-West Frontier Province (NWFP) on September 29, 2002. He is a prominent member of the Jamiat-Ulema-Islam (F) of Maulana Fazlar-Rehman as well as a prominent member of the religo-political alliance the Muttahaida-Majlis-e-Amal.

Maulana Mufti Mahmud (1919-1980), was an ethnic Marwat Pashtoon He was an Islamic scholar and political activist. Maulana Fazal-ur-Rehman is his son and was the leader of opposition in Pakistan. He fought in the Indian Independence Movement during the 1940s. He was a close ally of the Indian National Congress at the time and opposed the demand for Pakistan.

Artists

- Abdullah Duran: Famous folk singer
- Azmat: Famous Pakistani musician
- Kandi Kuchi: Famous folk singer

8

Rajputs

Rajput constitute one of the major Hindu Kshatriya groups from India. They claim descent from ancient royal warrior dynasties of Kshatriyas. They are identified with the word "Rajanya" found in ancient Indian literature and trace their roots to Rajputana. In ancient times the son of a king was referred as to Rajput- Raja-putra. The Rajputs are comprised of many different clans.

From ancient times they were known for their valor and chivalry in battle. They are considered to be formidable warriors even to this day. It is common to find many of them serving in the Indian Armed Forces. In current days Rajasthan, Madhya Pradesh, Punjab, Haryana, Gujarat, Uttar Pradesh, Bihar, Uttrakhand and Himachal Pradesh are home to most of the Rajputs. Lord Rama of the Hindu Pantheon was a Kshatriya of the Raghuvanshi or Suryavanshi clan which is said to continue to this day in the royal descent of the Udaipur and Jaipur royals.

The Rajputs governed more than four hundred of the estimated six hundred princely states at the time of India's independence. From those princely states, 121 were Salute states in which Rajputs governed 81 of them at the time of India's independence. The Rajputs were classified as a martial race by the British colonial government and recruited for the military establishment during the subcontinent's colonial period.

Origin & History

The theories about the origin of Rajputs can be classified into certain categories. The most ancient theory is that they are the progeny of sun, moon and fire. The reference to solar and lunar dynasties is not traceable in the earliest Indian literature i.e. the Vedas (1500 to 1000 BC.) and the Jatakas (3rd century BC.) but can be traced back to Mahahharata (5th century BC. to 2nd century BC.) and the Puranas (9th century AD.). the theory BC. to 2nd century AD.), Mahahharat, Bhagvatapurana (9th century AD.), the Tamil Poem Purnanuru (6th century AD.), the Sanskrit composition Navasahasanka of Padmagupta (11th century AD.) and Rajasthani composition Prithviraja-raso of Chandravardayi (12th century AD.). This shows that these theories are a concoction of 2nd century BC. to claim superiority over the foreigners like Greeks, Parthians and Scythians or may be that theory of divine origin is a gift from the Achaemenians who claimed the right to rule by the grace of Ahur-Mazda or from Alexander the great who was hailed as son of Amon by the priest of the shrine of the. God Amon Ra (a sun god) in the Sahara desert.

The second theory is that the Rajputs belonged to a foreign stock. This theory was propounded by James Tod who was the greatest admirer of their virtues but could not believe that this heroic race of Rajputs could belong to India. He was followed by A.M.T. Jackson, J. Campbell, Baden Powell, Wiliam Crooke, D.R. Bhandarkar, P.C. Bagchi and following him, R.S. Sharma. Two Europeans have remained very discreet. J. Kennedy thought that Chauhans, Solankis and Gahlots had Indo-Scythic or Gujar origin, the Rajputs of Punjab were of Brahmana stock whereas Rajputs of Uttar Pradesh originated from Brahmanas, Bihars (aborigines) and Ahirs (foreign clan of Abhiras) but thinks that majority of them were Aryanised Sudras. Vicent Smith Agreed with Crooke that fire-pit origin mentioned by Chandravardayi was a cover for purifying the foreigners as Rajputs but about the clans beyond Rajputana and Gujarat he is of the opinion that they sprang from aboriginal people like Gonds, Bhars, Kols etc.

Rajput is a corrupt from of the Vedic word rajaputra which has been used as a synonym of rajanya in Rigveda, Yajurvedic Kathaka Samhita, and Aitareya Brahmana of the Rigveda. In Purusha – sukta of Rigveda Rajanya is used for the generic class of warriors. It has been used in the same sense in Atharvaveda but Manu has used the word rajan in place of rajanya. The term rajan means endowed with kingdom whereas Rajanya means belongings to rajan. The word Kshatriya meant scion of one endowed with kingdom. But difference was made in Kshatriyas and rajanyas in Kaushitaki Upanishad (8th BC.). It is said there that Soma (king) is eating the Kshatiyas and Vaishyas respectively with his two mouths, Brahmana and rajanya was used for the nobles and their scions whereas Kshatriya was in vogue for the warrior class in general. In the light of this Upanishadic reference the meaning of the three terms used separately at a time in Satapatha Brahamana becomes meaningful. There Rajputra, Rajnaya and Kshatraputra, these three terms are mentioned separately. The rajaputras (sons of the kings) were entitled to only quivers, and Kshatriyas were holding simply clubs. Thus as early as 1000 BC. a difference was made between rajaputras, nganyas and Kshatriyas.

In Mahabharata (2nd century BC.) the word rajaputra has been used for the nobles and warriors (Kshatriyas) at different places.This word has been continuously in use; Kautilya (4th century BC.) in his Arthashastra has used it for sons of the king. Asvaghosha in Saundaranada. St Century AD.) Has used it in the sense of nobles and so has done Kalidasa in his Malavikangnimitra (in 4th century AD.) – Banabhatta (7th century AD.) has used it for nobles in Harshacharita and for the scions of the nobles in Kadambari. It is in this sense that the word rajaputra or its corrupt form Rajput became current in early medieval period, i.e. 650 to 1200 AD.

There is one more title rauta, which is still later corrupt form of rajaputra. This was a title of the landlords and nobles but all of them were not rajaputras or Rajputs. In Chandella inscriptions we have Brahmanas and Kayasthas adored with this title. In Rajasthan of modern times we have Rivals among Khandelwal Vaishyas and also a community known as Ravats whose profession is to make plate of leaves (pattal) for dining purpose. It is only the Rajputs or scions of nobles who later became a caste and not all the landowners who got a title Rawat by grace.

As all the landowners were not Rajputs, in the same way all the Kshatriyas were not Rajputs. All the rulers in ancient India were not Kshatriyas nor all the Kshatriyas were actually ruling. Visvarupa, the commentator of Yajnavalkya says it clearly that the title of dominion (rajya) does not belong to every Kshatriya. All the rulers were called rajans and their relatives were called mjaputras. Thus in actual application rajaputra and Kshatriyas did not always coincide. The ruling classes intermarried with rulers of foreign origin also. In ancient times Chandragupta Maurya had married the daughter of Seleucos Nikator. Saka Rudradaman married his daughter to a Satavahana prince and himself had won the hands of number of princesses in Svayamvaras. In the post-classical period Harichandra Pratihar of Mandor, who was a Brahmana, married a Kshatriya Bhadra whose sons passed as Rajputs. All this does not substantiate the theory of foreign origin.

The theory of the foreign origin of the Rajputs can be substantiated only on one basis i.e. that the Aryans in the hoary past came to India from Central Asia and as most of the Rajputs contain Aryan blood they are foreigners. The mixture of the aborigines cannot be denied on the basis of anthropology but no dynasty can be historically proved to have had developed from an aboriginal people into a Rajputs clan. The question arises: what was the historical milieu of all the Rajput clans? The source material for the same is not available. However, the present author has traced the origin of 15 clans about whom some source material is available. Though geographical basis of clan is common to all, in some cases even social milieu could be traced. He has traced the Paramaras, Chalukyas, Pratiharas and Chahamanas to Agney-Brahmanas; Guhilas and Chandellas are also traced to Brahmanical origin; Mauryas and Kalachur are traced to ancient Kshatriyas whereas the ancient social milieu of the Gaudas, Dahimas, Bhatis, Chavaras, Gahadvasa, Rathors and Kachhawa is said to be untraceable before their passing as Rajputs though their original home which is the cause of their name has been traced.

We can thus conclude that Rajaputras were a class upto the classical period, and from Harsha's time up to the time of Prithviraja Chauhan, besides two Kshatriyas clans of Mauryas and Kalachuris, many non-Kshatriya groups – six groups of Brahmanas, one foreign group of Hunas and five non-descript people whose ancient social milieu is not known with certainty entered in to Rajput group and later became clans of this caste. This survey would lad one to the conclusion that Rajputs were a class up to the Rajput period in 1200 AD. and became a caste only after the Turks entered the political field and refused to be Aryanised. For the first time a stumbling block came in the way of the Rajputization of the rules and the practice fell into abeyance and even the local Hindu rulers after that had to be content with power but could not be included among the Rajputs as the Chaturvarnya system received a great set back at the hands of the unbelieving Turks who had brought new society and religion with them.

People & Culture

Rajput constitute one of the major Hindu Kshatriya groups from India. They claim descent from ancient royal warrior dynasties of Kshatriyas. They are identified with the word "Rajanya" found in ancient Indian literature and trace their roots to Rajputana. In ancient times the son of a king was referred as to Rajput- Raja-putra. The Rajputs are comprised of many different clans.

The Sanskrit word Rajputra is found in the Vedas, the Ramayana, and the Mahabharata. It has been used by Panini. The word Kshatriya was initially used for the community of warriors and rulers. After the passage of much time there were many Kshatriyas. Some of them left their traditional occupation. Some were still rulers and warriors. As a custom these kings married only with the daughters of kings. They were abundant in India. It is very clear from the Puranas, Ramayana, Mahabharata, Prithviraj Raso, Akbarnama, and present genealogy that they intermarried with the royal families only. The rule of primogeniture allowed only the eldest male offspring of a king to succeed him. The rest were known as Rajputras. The word Rajput is claimed to be a corruption of Rajputra. Steadily it became a jati within the Kshatriya or warrior caste, nevertheless the Rajputs are often considered the elite of the Kshatriyas - at least by their own members.

The traditional occupations of the Rajputs is military service and at times agriculture. Nevertheless, because of their natural ability in warfare and their discipline, this would give them opportunities to rise through the ranks and eventually become rulers or at least hold high positions in office.

The concept of the Raja-putra, or "son of a king," is mentioned in Vedic literature. Rajput, a shortened version of Raja-putra, is a name that has come to be linked with specific clans that would gain political importance in a given area. Due to the fluid social structure in early medieval India, a clan could gain or lose its status based on its political importance, its occupation, and its survival or extinction. Many clans over the course of time became extinct due to war, or relocated to another location and changed their names. Traditionally, 36 "royal races," or raj-kul, were known as Rajputs.

The Rajput ethos is martial, in spirit, and fiercely proud and independent, and emphasizes lineage and tradition. Rajput patriotism is legendary, an ideal they embodied with a sometimes fanatical zeal, often choosing death before dishonour. Rajput warriors were often known to fight till the last man.

By the late 19th century, there was a shift from on questions regarding the political relations among the Rajputs to a concern with kinship. As per Harlan, many Rajputs of Rajasthan are nostalgic about their past and keenly conscious of their genealogy, emphasizing a Rajput ethos that is martial in spirit, with a fierce pride in lineage and tradition.

The tradition of common ancestry permits a Rajput yeoman to consider himself as well born as any mighty landholder of his clan, and superior to any high official of the professional classes. No race in India can boast of finer feats of arms or brighter deeds of chivalry, and they form one of the major recruiting fields for the Indian army of the day. They consider any occupation other than that of arms or government derogatory to their dignity, and consequently during the long period of peace which has followed the establishment of the British rule in India, they have been content to stay idle at home instead of taking up any of the other professions in which they might have come to the front.

The Rajput lifestyle was designed to foster a martial spirit. Todd describes at length the bond between the Rajputs and their swords. The double-edged scimitar known as the khanda was a popular weapon amongst the Rajputs of that era. On special occasions, a primary chief would break up a meeting of his vassal chiefs with khanda nariyal, the distribution of daggers and coconuts. The Karga Shapna ritual, performed during the annual Navaratri festival, was another affirmation of the Rajput's reverence for his sword.

The festival of Rakhi is typically held in August. The rakhis, or bracelets, are tied to a brother's wrist by his sisters. The belief among Rajputs was that the bracelets would avert evil in battle and designated those who would make a proper return from battle. This festival was and is still celebrated all over India. All recorded instances of Jauhar and "Saka" have featured Rajput defenders of a fort, resisting the invasion of a Muslim force.

Jauhar was originally the voluntary death on a funeral pyre of the queens and royal womenfolk of defeated Rajput castles in order to avoid capture and consequent molestation. The term is extended to describe the occasional practice of mass suicide carried out in medieval times by Rajput women, or by entire Rajput communities, when the fall of a besieged city was certain.

Sects

The rajputs are divided into 36 clans, each clan belonging to one of three basic lineages (vanshas):

1. The Suryavanshi lineage, claiming descent from Surya, the Hindu Sun-god or in English it is known as Solar Dynasty;
2. The Chandravanshi lineage, claiming descent from Chandra, the Hindu Moon-god or in English it is known as Lunar Dynasty;
3. The Agnivanshi lineage, claiming descent from Agni, the Hindu god of fire. Four Rajput clans are considered to be Agnivanshi.They are Chauhans,Paramara,Solanki and Pratiharas.

Each of these Vamshas or lineages is divided into several clans (kula), all of whom claim direct patrilineage for a remote but common male ancestor who supposedly belonged to that Vamsha. Some of these thirty-six major clans are further subdivided into shakhas or "branches", again based on the same principle of patrilineage.

Each shakha or basic sub-clan has its individual genealogical creed, describing the essential peculiarities, religious tenets and original domicile of the clan. This creed is a touchstone of traditional affinities and also provides all information governing the laws of intermarriage.

The list of Rajput clans is given below:

- Agnivanshi
- Ahra
- Baghel
- Banaphar
- Banirot
- Bargujar
- Bhadoria
- Bhalwal
- Bhareh
- Bidawat
- Bika
- Bishen
- Bundela
- Champawat
- Chandel
- Chandravanshi
- Chandrawat
- Chauhan
- Chavda
- Chundawat
- Dahia
- Datia
- Gaur
- Gehlot
- Hariovansh
- Jadeja
- Jadon
- Jadon Bhati
- Jagmanpur
- Jaitawat
- Jamwal
- Janjua
- Janjua
- Jarral
- Jaryal
- Jasrotia
- Jhala
- Jodha
- Johiya
- Kachwaha
- Kalyanot
- Kandhalot
- Karnot
- Katoch
- Khadad
- Khangarot
- Khokra
- Khurmi
- Kumpawat
- Lakhnesar
- Lawtamia
- Madadh
- Mahthan
- Medatiya
- Minhass
- Naruka
- Nathawat
- Paramara
- Pratihara
- Pundir
- Rahaver
- Rajawat
- Ranawat
- Rathore
- Rawat
- Rawatot
- Ruru
- Sambyal
- Sengar
- Shaktawat
- Shekhawat
- Sheobramhpota
- Sisodia
- Solanki
- Somvanshi
- Srinet
- Surwar
- Suryavanshi
- Taparia
- Tomar

Demographics

Majorcountries having Rajput populations are:

Area	Population
India	40,559,000
Pakistan	15,293,000
Nepal	76,000
Bangladesh	30,000

Source: *Josua Project, 2008*

In India, the population of Rajputs is approximately 40,559,000. Major states having Rajput population are:

Area	Population
Uttar Pradesh	9,830,000
Madhya Pradesh	5,224,000
Rajasthan	4,223,000
Bihar	4,044,000
Uttaranachal	2,894,000
Gujarat	2,362,000
Haryana	1,510,000
Himachal Pradesh	1,272,000
Maharashtra	979,000
Delhi	968,000

Source: Josua Project, 2008

In Pakistan, the population of Rajputs is approximately 15,293,000. Major states having Rajput population are:

Area	Population
Punjab	8,969,000
Sindh	4,720,000
Azad Kashmir	643,000
Islamabad	223,000
North-West Frontier	174,000
Balochistan	37,000

Source: Josua Project, 2008

Martial Traditions

The fertile and prosperous plains of northern India had always been the destination of choice for streams of invaders coming from the north-west. The last of these waves of invasions were of people who had previously converted to Islam. Because of geographic reasons, Rajput-governed states suffered the brunt of aggression from various Mongol-Turkic-Afghan warlords who repeatedly invaded the subcontinent.

The Rajputs for centuries were India's line of defense against invaders. They proved their chivalry by fighting with honour and the mercy that they showed to the vanquished. When fighting against the hordes of Arabs, Mughals, Afghans, and Turks, many preferred to die rather than to forsake their ancestors' faith (Hindu dharma) for Islam. While the nations of the Middle East fell in a matter of a few years to the rapid advance of Islam's new followers, the Rajput men and women refused to let them capture India for over 500 years. The heroism and sacrifice displayed by this community is undisputed and unmatched in the records of Indian history.

Within 15 years of the death of the Muhammad, the caliph Usman sent a sea expedition to raid Thana and Broach on the Bombay coast. Other unsuccessful raiding expeditions to Sindh occurred in 662 and 664 AD. Indeed, within a hundred years after Muhammad's death, Muslim armies had overrun much of Asia as far as the Hindu Kush; nevertheless, it was not till 1000 AD that they could establish any foothold in India.

The Rai Dynasty, who governed Sindh in the 6th and 7th centuries and were displaced by an Arab army led by Bin Qasim, is sometimes held to have been Rajputs. As per some sources, Bin Qasim, an Arab who invaded Sindh in the 8th century, also attacked Chittorgarh, and was beaten by Bappa Rawal.

The Pratiharas rebuffed Arab invasion in the ninth century. Significant Muslim invasions were then not attempted till the eleventh century, largely because of the formidable reputation of the Rajput clans.

Certain other invasions by marauding "Yavvanas" are also recorded in this era. By this time, the appellation "Yavvana" (literally: "Ionian/ Greek") was used in connection to any clan that emerged from the west and north-west of present-day Pakistan. These invasions may therefore have been a continuation of the usual invasions into India by warlike but less civilized clans from the north-west, and not a reference to the Greeks or Indo-Greeks. Lalitaditya of Kashmir defeated one such Yavvana invasion in the 8th century and the Pratiharas rebuffed another in the 9th century.

The first Rajput kingdoms are attested to in the 7th century and it was during the 9th, 10th, & 11th centuries that the Rajputs rose to prominence in the Indian history. The four Agnivanshi clans, namely the Pratiharas (Pariharas), Solankis (Chaulukyas), Paramaras (Parmars), and Chauhans (Chahamanas), rose to prominence first.

- Pratiharas founded the first Rajput empire in Marwar in southwestern Rajasthan. Later they established themselves at Ujjain and governed Malwa, and later on at Kanauj in the Ganges-Yamuna Doab, from which they governed much of northern India, from Kathiawar in the west to Magadha in the east, in the ninth century.
- Chauhans established themselves at Ajmer in central Rajasthan
- Solankis in Gujarat
- Paramaras in Malwa.

But there were other Rajputs also who rose to prominence. Clans claiming descent from the Solar and Lunar races, who were originally vassals of the other clans, established their independent states later.

- The Guhilas (Guhilote or Gehlot, later called the Sisodias) founded the state of Mewar (later Udaipur), under Bappa Rawal, who governed at Chittorgarh (Sanskrit name Chitrakuta), which was given in dowry to Bappa in 734 for his bravery. Chittor, was then governed by the Mori clan of Rajputs. Maan Mori was their last king at Chittor. It is believed the word Mori is a corruption of Maurya, the renowned dynasty.
- The Kachwaha (Kacchapghata) founded their rule in Narwar in 8th century. One of their descendent Dulah Rai established his rule in Dhundhar in 11th century, with their capital at Amber, and later Jaipur.
- The Chandela clan governed Bundelkhand after the tenth century, occupying the fortress-city of Kalinjar and building the renowned temple-city of Khajuraho.
- The Tomaras established a state in Haryana, establishing the city of Dhiliki (later Delhi) in 736.

The Kachwahas, Chandelas, and Tomaras were originally vassals of the Pratihara empire before over throwing their rule in the 10th century to establish more power independent kingdoms.

The organization of Rajput clan finally crystallized in this period. Intermarriage amongst the Rajput clans interlinked the various areas of India and Pakistan, facilitating the flow of trade and scholarship. Archaeological evidence and contemporary texts suggest that Indian society achieved significant prosperity during this era.

The literature composed in this period, both in Sanskrit and in the Apabhramshas, constitutes a substantial segment of classical Indian literature. The early 11th century saw the reign of the polymath King Bhoja, Paramara ruler of Malwa. He was not only a patron of literature and the arts but was himself a distinguished writer. His Samarangana-sutradhara deals with architecture and his Raja-Martanda is a renowned commentary on the Yoga-sutras. Many major monuments of northern and central India, including those at Khajuraho, date from this period.

Pratiharas: The Imperial Pratiharas established their rule over Malwa and governed from Bhinmal and afterward Ujjaini in the 8th & 9th century. One branch of the clan founded a state in (Rever) Tarangagadh in the 11th century. Marwar in 6th and 7th century, where they held sway till they were supplanted by the Rathores in the 14th century. Around 816 AD, the Pratiharas of Ujjaini conquered Kannauj, from this city they governed much of northern India for a century. They went into decline after Rashtrakuta invasions in the early 10th century.

Rathore: The Rathore or Rathor or Rathod is a Rajput clan of India. Rathors in India are a Rajput clan from the Marwar area of western Rajasthan, inhabiting Idar state of Gujarat and also the Chhapra and Muzaffarpur districts of Bihar in very small numbers. In India, their native languages are Hindi and its dialects (such as Rajasthani, Marwari and other languages of Rajasthan, Gujarati and Kutchi in Gujarat, as well as Punjabi in the Punjab a dialect of Punjabi called Rathi spoken in Ratia and Tohana in present day Haryana. Rathore are the people from the west Rajasthan. Rathore's have many gotras, most of these gotras are from the name of the great warriors of the past and gotras are being used by their family members. Rathore's were said to be the worshipers of sun. To understand the huge clan of Rathore's we will have understand their regions they occupy. Rathore's of Jodhpur were supreme in present districts such as - Jodhpur, Pali, Ajmer, Nagaur, Barmer, Sirohi. Rathore, s of Bikaner were occupant of the region that included districts Bikaner, Churu, Ganganagar, Hanumangarh.

Dynasties belonging to this clan governed a number of kingdoms and princely states in Rajasthan and neighbouring states before India's independence in 1947. The largest and oldest amongst these was Jodhpur, in Marwar and Bikaner. Also the Idar State in Gujrat. The Maharaja of Jodhpur, is regarded as the head of the extended Rathore clan of Hindu Rajputs. Even in the modern times the clout of this clan in the democratic world is such that a large number of MLAs and MPs have been elected from amongst them. Prominent Sub-clans are Banirot, Bika, Kandhalot, Rawatot, Bidawat, Kumpawat, Champawat, Medatiya, Jodha, Jaitawat, Khokra, Karnot.

Sisodias: The Sisodias claim their descent from Lord Rama, the hero of the renowned Hindu epic Ramayana. It is also said that the group descended from the Sun God and is thus known as the Suryavanshi or Children of Sun. The prince of Mewar is treated as the legitimate heir to the throne of Rama.

They trace their descent from Bappa Rawal, purported scion of the Guhilot or Guhila or Gehlot or Gahlot clan, who established himself as ruler of Mewar in 734 AD, ruling from the fortress of Chittor (or Chittorgarh).

The Mewar flag is disinguished for its "crimson" flag. During both times of war and peace, this standard could always be seen flying high. It depicts the image of a dagger and a flaming sun. Robert Taylor of the Bengal Civil Service records in his book, "The Princely Armory", "...for eight centuries a golden sun in a crimson field has floated over the head of the Rana at feast and fray, and is conspicuous in the ornament of his palace...On the top of the mast is the face of the Sun, embossed in gold. On the triangular Nishan (flag), the human face is embroidered in gold depicting the Sun. It has a gold tassle at the end. A Katar (a type of dagger) with silver threads on the Nishan completes this plain design. The Sun signifies that the Nishan is of the "Surya Vansi" (Sun Dynasty) Maharanas of Mewar.

Prominent Sub-clans include Gehlot, Sisodia, Gahlot, Chundawat, Chandrawat, shaktawat, Dungarpur, Banswara, Mahthan, Ranawat.

Bargujar: The Bargujars (Birgoojur) were the vassals of the Gujjar pratihars. They are one of the most revered and most fierce clan of the rajputs ever known. They constituted the major force in "Haraval" Tukdi the first line of offence in a battle. The bargujars chose to die rather to submit to the supremacy of the Muslim kings. Many bargujars were put to death for not giving their daughters to Muslim rulers. Some bargujars changed their clan name to sikarwar to escape mass genocide carried out against them.

Lava (one of the Sons of King Rama) was their ancestor and so they are also known as Raghav. Raghav was the great great grandfather of Rama. Bargujars take this name as children of Raghav dynasty.

Bargujar is a suryavanshi clan. Prominent sub-clans include Lawtamia, Madadh, Khadad, Taparia.

Pundir: The Pundir are a Suryavanshi branch of Rajputs, one of the thirty six royal rajput clans. The Pundir Rajputs still hold riyasat in Nagaur and Saharanpur where their Kuldevi's are situated. Their Shakha is Koolwal and their Kuldevis are Shakumbhri Devi and Dhadimati Mata with a few of the Gotras shared by them being Bhardwaj, Parashara and Pulastya. Most of the Pundirs are today based chiefly around the North Indian states of Uttar Pradesh, Himachal Pradesh, Uttarakhand, Punjab and Haryana. Elliot writes that Uttar Pradesh (Hardwar area), where they are most prominent today, has over 1,440 villages claimed by Pundir Rajputs with high concentrations in the districts of Dehradun, Saharanpur, Muzaffarnagar, Aligarh and Etawah. As per the British census of 1891 the population of the Pundir Rajputs was recorded at approximately 29,000.

Solankis: Solankis were descended from the Chalukyas of Karnataka who governed much of peninsular India between the 6th and 12th centuries. In the 10th century, a local branch of the clan established control over Gujarat and governed a state centered around the city of Patan. They went into decline in the 13th century and were displaced by the Vaghela.

Paramar: Paramaras originated from the Rashtrakutas and rose to power in the 10th century. They governed Malwa and the region at the border between present-day Gujarat and Rajasthan. Bhoja, the celebrated king of Malwa, belonged to this dynasty. In the 12th century, the Paramaras declined in power because of conflict and succumbed to attack from the Delhi sultanate in 1305. They have families migrated to south-wards in Gujrath, Maharashtra, holding many important positions as regional war-lords and Chiefs of private armies. The origin reference about Naik-Nimbalkar of Phaltan state and Dalvi.

Kachwaha: The Kachwaha (also spelled as Kachavaha,Kacchavahas, Kachhawa, Kuchhwaha & Kushwah including Kacchapghata, Kakutstha, and Kurma) are a Suryavanshi Rajput clan who governed a number of kingdoms and princely states in India such as Alwar, Maihar, Talcher, while the largest and oldest state was Amber (city) later known as Jaipur. The Pachrang flag of the former Jaipur state. Prior to the adoption of the Pachrang (five coloured) flag by Raja Man Singh I of Amber, the original flag of the Kachwahas was known as the 'Jharshahi' (tree-marked) flagJaipur (Jainagara), an extension of the old empire of Amber, was established by Maharaja Sawai Jai Singh II in 1727.The Maharaja of Jaipur is regarded as the head of the extended Kachwaha clan. Overall, sub-clans of the Kachwaha number around 71. Prominent sub-clans of the Kachhawa clan include: Rajawat, Shekhawat, Sheobramhpota, Naruka, Nathawat, Khangarot and Kumbhani. The Kachhawas belong to the Suryavanshi lineage, which claims descent from the Surya and Sun Dynasty of the ancient Kshatriyas. Specifically, they claim descent from Kusha1 younger of the twin sons of Rama, hero of the Ramayana, to whom patrilineal descent from Surya is in turn ascribed. Indeed, the name Kachawaha is held by many to be a patronymic derived from the name "Kusha". Prominent Sub-clans are Shekhawat, Naruka, Rajawat, Nathawat, Kalyanot, Jamwal, Minhas, Manhas, Baghel, Jasrotia, Nindar.

Chandelas: In the early 10th century, the Chandelas governed the fortress-city of Kalinjar. A dynastic struggle (912-914 AD) amongst the Pratiharas provided them with the opportunity to extend their domain. They captured the strategic fortress of Gwalior (950) under the leadership of Dhanga (ruled 950-1008). Dhanga's grandson Vidyadhara (ruled 1017-29) expanded the Chandela empire to its greatest size, from the Chambal river in the northwest to the Narmada River in the south, thus covering a large portion of the present-day state of Madhya Pradesh.

Tomar: Tomar/Tuar Rajputs are the descendents of the Pandava Prince Arjun, through his great grandson Emperor Janamejaya, son of Emperor Parikshit.

Tomars did not lose control of Delhi in battle, but the then Tomar Rajput ruler Anangpal Tomar II appointed his grandson (daughter's son, and son of King of Ajmer), Prithviraj Chauhan, as the heir apparent. Some historians believe that Prithvaraj was merely a caretaker king as long as his grandfather was alive. Prithviraj was never crowned the Delhi, therefore adding weight to the opinion that the Chauhan ruler took over the thrown from his maternal grandfather.

As per records kept by Jagas of Tomar Rajputs, King Anangpal made Prithviraj only as caretaker when he went on a religious pilgrimage, as his own sons were very small at that time. When King Anangpal returned back, Prithviraj refused to hand over the empire.

Following their loss of control at Delhi, a branch of the Tomar clan established itself in the region of modern Gwalior in northern Madhya Pradesh. Man Singh Tomar built the fortress citadel which still stands there.

The Mughal emperor Akbar captured Gwalior in 1559. Some Tomar Rajputs converted to Islam during the Muslim-Mughal rule; Tomar Muslim Rajputs are found in western Rajasthan, Pakistan and Sind.

Tomars moved from Delhi to Haryana (Bhiwani, Mahendergarh and Karnal Districts), Madya Pradesh (Gwalior, and Morena and Bhind Districts), Punjab, and Rajasthan (Patan State and surrounding regions). They are spread from Punjab, to Western Uttar Pradesh (Meerut, Badaun, Bareilly, Baraut, Muzaffarnagar Ghaziabad, Aligarh, Bulandshahr), Eastern U.P, significant parts of Himachal Pradesh, to western Rajastan to Northern Madhya Pradesh and even some in Pakistan.

The great Vikramaditya of the year 56BC is claimed to be an ancestor of the Tuar Rajputs. In the Hindu tradition in India and Nepal, the widely used ancient calendar is Vikrama Samvat or Vikrama's era. This is said to have been started by the legendary king following his victory over the Sakas in 56 BC. Tuar Sub clans include; Pathania Rajputs, Janghara Rajputs and Janjua Rajputs.

Pathania: Pathania is the name of a branch of the Tomara Rajputs. It is one of the ruling Rajput Clans of India. Their Empire was at Nurpur, established in the 11th Century, situated in the Kangra district of Himachal Pradesh. Rana Jethpal (11th Century AD.), the younger brother of Anang Pal II of Delhi, came to Jallandhar Doab also called Bist Doab to carve out a territory for himself. After crossing the Beas river he captured a fort called Bhet, and for this reason it is said, he acquired the name Rana Bhet. After that he became master of the Fort and the city of Paithan, now known as Pathankot, and from then onwards, he came to be known as a Pathania Rajput instead of a Tanwar Rajput. Pathania Rajputs are Dogra Rajputs, descended from Lord Arjuna, the hero of Mahabharata. They mostly live in and around Himachal Pradesh, in North India. The Pathania clan governed the Empire of Nurpur, until 1849 AD.,They were renowned for their opposition against foreign rule, which they proved by giving battle to invaders until 1849 AD., after which the Empire was annexed by the British, the Raja being a minor. This clan has to its credit three Maha Vir Chakra winners in the Indian Army. This clan has also won many other gallantry awards while serving in the British army of India.

Janghara Rajputs: Known as a large and turbulent branch of the Tomar clan, the Janghara Rajputs were readily recruited by the British Indian Army. The turbulent nature of the clan is further enhanced by the origin of the name Janghara being derived from the words, Jang (war) and Ahara (hunger) meaning "the men who hunger for war".

After the fall of Delhi to the Chauhans, the Janghara sept parted from the major Tomar branch in disgust. They entered Rohilkhund under the leadership of the prince Dhapu Dham who's warlike nature was proverbial. A couplet sung by women of the clan states "Below is Earth, above is Ram. Between the two, fights Dhapu Dham"

Chauhan: Chauhans originated as feudatories of the Pratiharas and rose to power in the wake of the decline of that power. Their state was initially centered around Sambhar in present-day Rajasthan. In the 11th century, they established the city of Ajmer which became their capital. In the 12th century, their the then King Prithviraj Chauhan acquired Delhi from his maternal grand father, the then Tomar King Anangpal II Tomar. Their most renowned ruler was Prithviraj Chauhan, who won the First Battle of Tarain against an invading Muslim army but lost the Second Battle of Tarain the following year. This loss heralded a prolonged period of Muslim rule over northern India. After the death of Manik Rae Chauhan (Ruler of Sambhar), his son Chandrapal Dev came and settle at a place called Bhadaura near present place Bah in U.P.,his sons were called Bhadauria and until date this clan is now seen as a sub class of Chauhans. the last chauhan king was in mainpuri district (U.P), who fought in first war of independence in 1857, known as "judev"

Minhas: Minhas or Manhas or Minhas-Dogra is a Rajput clan from the Jammu area of the Indian subcontinent. It is an off-shoot of Jamwal-Dogra Rajputs, the founders of the city and state of Jammu and its rulers from ancient times to 1948 C.E. In antiquity of rule, which is generally considered a benchmark of royalty, they are second to none, but the great Katoch Rajputs of Trigarta and Kangra. Paying tribute to the antiquity of their royal lineage, Sir Lepel Griffin says, "These royal dynasties may have been already ancient when Moses was leading the Israelites out of Egypt, and the Greeks were steering their swift ships to Troy." Minhas Rajputs are Suryavanshis and claim descent from Rama a legendary king of Ayodhya. In Rajputana, their closest cousins are the Kachwaha Rajputs of Jaipur.

They trace their ancestry to the Ikshvaku dynasty of Northern India (The same clan in which Lord Rama was born. He, therefore is the 'kuldevta' (family deity) of the Hindu Minhas Rajputs). Specifically, they claim descent from Kusha younger of the twin sons of Rama, hero of the Ramayana, to whom patrilineal descent from Surya is in turn ascribed.

Prithiviraj III, ruler of Delhi, defeated Muhammad of Ghor at the First Battle of Tarain (1191 AD). Muhammad returned the following year and defeated Prithviraj at the Second Battle of Tarain (1192 AD). In this battle, as in many others of this era, rampant internecine conflict amongst Rajput kingdoms facilitated the victory of the invaders.

Rajputs reestablished their independence, and the Rajput states were established as far east as Bengal and north into the Punjab. Prithviraj Chauhan proved to be the last Rajput ruler of Delhi. The Chauhans reestablished themselves at Ranthambore, led by Govinda, grandson of Prithviraj III. Jalore was governed by another branch of Chauhans, the Songaras. Another branch of the Chauhans, the Hadas, founded an empire in Hadoti in the mid-13th century.

The Maharaja Ranavghansinh ruled Taranga, in the 11th century. The Tomaras established themselves at Gwalior, and the ruler Man Singh built the fortress which still stands there. Mewar emerged as the leading Rajput state, and Rana Kumbha expanded his empire at the expense of the sultanates of Malwa and Gujarat.

The Delhi sultanate was extinguished when Babur defeated Ibrahim Lodi at the First Battle of Panipat in 1526. Rana Sanga, ruler of Mewar, rallied an army to challenge Babur. He was betrayed by one of his Rajput generals and was beaten by Babur at the Battle of Khanua on March 16, 1527; The Rajput rulers agreed to pay tribute to Babur, but most retained control of their states, and struggles between Babur's successor Humayun and the Suri Dynasty for control of the Sultanate preoccupied the Muslims for several decades. It was not till the reign of Akbar that the structure of relations between the Mughal imperium and the Rajput states took definitive shape.

During the Second Jauhar Rana Sanga died soon after the battle of Khanua. Shortly later on, Mewar came under the regency of his widow, Rani Karmavati. The empire was menaced by Bahadur Shah, ruler of Gujarat. As per one legend, Karmavati importuned the assistance of Humayun, son of her late husband's foe. The help arrived, but too late; Chittor was reduced by Bahadur Shah. This is the occasion for the second of the three Jauhars performed at Chittor. Karmavati led the ladies of the citadel into death by fire, while the menfolk sallied out to meet the besieging Muslim army in a hopeless fight to the death.

Contribution to Defence Services

The Rajputs have for long been known as the Prince of Warriors or the blue blooded warriors of the Indian subcontinent. They have carried a long tradition of chivalry, love of battle, fearlessness for the upkeep of their honour and that of their womenfolk.

Rajput Regiment

Regimental Motto: Sarvatra Vijay (Victory Everywhere)

War Cry: Bol Bajrang Bali Ki Jai (Say Victory to Lord Hanuman)

The Rajput regiment is a regiment in the Indian Army that is composed primarily of the Rajput clans from India. The British designated the Rajputs as a martial race and subsequently employed large numbers of these warriors in the British Indian Army.

The association of the Rajputs with the army started in 1778, when the 3rd Battalion was raised as the 31st Regiment Bengal Native Infantry. Two other battalions the 1st and 2nd were raised in 1798. The 3rd Battalion fought against Hyder Ali and captured Cuddalore. It was after this battle that the crossed daggers (also known as katars) as a badge was granted in recognition of gallantry, this since has been adopted as the badge by the Rajput Regiment. The 1st Battalion fought at the battle of Delhi (1803), which broke the power of the Marathas at the Imperial court. This battalion was in action again at the siege of Bharatpur (1805), of the 400 men who went into the assault at least 50 percent became casualties.

The 1st and 4th Battalions participated in the British campaign against the Gorkhas. All the Rajput Battalions (1st, 2nd, 3rd, 4th and the 5th) fought against the Sikhs in the Sikh Wars. The 5th Battalion captured three Sikh standards at the battle of Gujarat. The 1857 mutiny was mostly confined to the Bengal infantry regiments, during which the 2nd, 3rd and 4th Rajputs were temporarily disarmed. The 1st Battalion was at Saugor and stood firm while guarding the treasury and the arsenal. For its role it was awarded the title of Light Infantry.

The Regiment of Lucknow, which later became the 16th Battalion, then the 10th Battalion contributed to the successful defence of the Lucknow Residency. It won two Victoria Crosses and every Sepoy in the regiment was also awarded a medal. The 1st Battalion in 1876 achieved a rare honour by becoming the Queen's Own as well as the Royal regiment.

World Wars: Most of the Rajput battalions saw action during World War 1. The 1st Battalion fought at the Battle of Dujailah in Mesopatamia, where it was nearly annihilated. The 3rd Battalion fought the Battles of

Qurna and Kut-al-Amara against the Turks. In one of the battles the Turks had invaded both the flanks of the 3rd Rajput, during which Jemadar Sital Baksh was severely wounded. Sepoy Jhandu Singh rushed to his rescue, the Jemadar ordered him to leave him behind but the sepoy lifted him on his back and started moving through the marshlands. Soon both the rescuer and the rescued became targets of the Turks and were riddled with bullets. Sepoy Jhandu Singh was awarded a posthumous IOM and Medaille Militaire. A large number of other awards and battle honours were won by the Rajputs and at the end of WW1, a total of 37 battle honours were on the colours of the Rajputs, which exceeded that of any other regiment of the Indian Army.

In 1922 the infantry regiments were reorganised and all the battalion were renumbered as follows: 2nd Rajput became 1st Battalion, 4th Rajput became 2nd Battalion, 7th Rajput became 3rd Battalion, 8th Rajput became 4th Battalion, 1th Rajput became 5th Battalion and 6th Rajput (Regiment of Lucknow) became the 10th Battalion. Also the one class character of most of the infantry regiments were changed and the Rajputs introduced a company each of Punjabi Musalmans and Hindustani Musalmans in each of their battalions.

A number of Rajput regiments participated in World War II. The 1st Battalion was in the Arakan and then took over the defence of Andaman & Nicobar Islands. The 2nd Battalion was also in the Arakan area and a number of actions were fought by it. The capture of Point 551, also called Rajput Hill was the most important. The Japanese holding this feature had turned back repeated attacks by other battalions but the Rajputs carried the day winning an IOM, five MC's and two MM's for this action. The 3rd Battalion was at Suez and Egypt and fought at the Battle of El Alamein. The 4th was also in the Western Desert at Siddi Barrani and El Alamein and on its return to India was posted at the Kohima front. The 5th Battalion was at Hongkong. The action against the invading Japanese was short and swift with heavy casualties to the regiment. The regiment along with the British garrison was forced to surrender and the men became POWs and had to undergo great hardships. 130 men of the 5th Rajput were either beaten or starved to death or just died because lack of medical care. The Japanese wanted Captain M.A. Ansari of 5th Rajput to turn on his fellow men, but he refused. For five months he was subjected to brutal beatings and treatment, as a result of which he could not walk. He was then sent to live with the other ranks instead of the officers. Captain Ansari remained true to the regiment and organised a system for helping escapees. He was again put in jail and tortured but refused to be broken. In the end the Japanese executed him. Captain M.A. Ansari was awarded the George Cross for his heroism.

1947-48 J & K Operations: At the time of partition in 1947 Punjabi Musalmans who formed up to 50% of the strength in most battalions were transferred to the Pakistan Army. The gaps created by their departure were filled in by Gujars, who came over from the Punjab Regiments which were allotted to Pakistan.

Four Rajput Regiments (1st, 2nd, 3rd and 4th) participated in the 1947-48 operations in J&K. The 3 Rajput was the first to be inducted. Its original task was for protection of Ramban and Jammu, but it quickly came under 50 Para Brigade for its relief of Jhangar and Kotli. The advance from Jhangar to Kotli took five days, as the column had to clear 47 road blocks. After the relief of Kotli the column returned to Naushera. 1 Rajput was inducted next and it also formed a part of 50 Para Brigade at Naushera. It had its share of fighting in clearing the raiders from some hill features around Naushera. The raiders meanwhile kept heavy pressure on the Naushera Jhangar road and both 1 and 3 Rajputs fought a number of engagements to keep the road open. In December 1947, 4 Rajput were inducted and deployed in the Chammb- Akhnoor area. 2 Rajput came in next and were employed for L of C duties around Jammu.

Aggressive patrolling was done by 1 and 3 Rajputs around Naushera and Kot. On 06 February 1948 a strong patrol was send out in the area east of Naushera. The patrol was surrounded by an enemy force of approximately 1000 men. Soon a fierce fight started which continued for seven hours. During this time Subedar Gopal Singh's platoon came under heavy pressure. Gopal Singh wounded thrice kept reorganizing his men time and again. At one time Gopal Singh got separated from his platoon and had only three men at his side, one of them was Sepoy Sikdar Singh. When things got tough Subedar Gopal Singh lead a bayonet charge during which he was seriously wounded. Sikdar Singh picked him up and carried him back to the main patrol area. Havildar Mahadeo Singh was another hero. He kept on supplying ammunition to the bren gunners of the platoon, couple of times he walked through heavy enemy fire to get the ammunition through. In one of his attempts he was wounded and fell down, when he scrambled to his feet he was riddled with bullets. In this action the 3 Rajput won 3 VrCs - one each to Subedar Gopal Singh and Sepoy Sikdar Singh and a posthumous one to Havildar Mahadeo Singh.

After the fall of Jhangar, Naushera became the enemy's next objective. Brigadier Mohammad Usman, 50 Para Brigade commander closely watched the situation and drew up defensive plans in which the Rajputs were holding tactical grounds around Naushera. C Company, 1 Rajput was holding the vital Taindhar position, which was vital for the defence of Naushera. Brig. Usman had directed C company to hold this position at any cost in case of an attack. On the early morning hours of 6 February, 1948 the enemy attacked the Taindhar position. The enemy was about 1500 strong and consisted mostly of Pathans with some Pakistani servicemen. The enemy attacked in waves of lines of 200-300 men. Six such attacks were launched and there was heavy hand to hand fighting in some posts. Havildar Daya Ram who was then manning the 3-inch mortar detachment realised that the enemy had gotten very close to the defensive positions. He took the secondary charge out of the mortar bombs, elevated the mortars to their maximum limit and fired the bombs. These bombs landed within 30-50 yards of the Rajput defensive positions and caused havoc among the enemy. Some of the enemy switched and attacked Daya Ram's section, but the position held, Daya Ram was wounded and his bren gunner killed. He picked up the bren gun and started firing at the enemy, for his courage and actions Daya Ram was awarded the Maha Vir Chakra.

The left flank of C Company gave an easy approach to the enemy. This sector was defended by Naik Jadunath Singh and his section. The enemy after failing in the frontal attacks switched the main effort on this sector. Jadunath Singh effectively directed the fire of his bren gun, rifles and grenades. The enemy, however still continued to advance, Jadunath rushed out of his defensive position throwing hand grenades and firing his sten gun, this took the enemy by surprise and he withdrew to regroup. The enemy regrouped and charged again, Jadunath Singh again stood firm and charged out. He was wounded this time but the attack failed again. By this time his section had suffered heavy casualties. The enemy attacked again and Jadunath Singh charged out the third time firing his sten gun and hurling grenades. He was hit by two bullets, one in the head and another in the chest and at last fell making the supreme sacrifice. The enemy had lost heart after this and withdrew, leaving behind a large number of dead and wounded. Naik Jadunath Singh for his gallantry was awarded the Param Vir Chakra.

The 1950s: In 1950 there was another change among the infantry regiments. On raising of the Brigade of Guards, the 1st Rajput was transferred to them and became 4th Battalion Brigade of Guards. Also at this time Bengalis and Muslims started coming into the regiment. When the princely states were amalgamated with the Indian Union, the Bikaner

Sadul Light Infantry and the Jodhpur Sardar Infantry joined the Rajput Regiment and became 19th and 20th Rajput respectively. The Bikaner Sadul Light Infantry traces its origin back to 1464. They fought under the legendary Rana Sanga at the Battle of Kanwa (1527) against Babur. During World War 1, this unit was organized as Camel Corps, called Ganga Risala. It won many gallantry awards including 1 DSO, 1 IOM, 11 IDSMs, 9 MMs and 16 Mentioned-in-Despatches. Jodhpur Sardar Infantry was raised in 1922. During World War 2 it was in Eritrea and then it was part of the American 5th Army when it landed at Salerno in Sept. 1943. Afterwards as part of the 10th Indian Division it operated along the Adriatic coast. During these operations it won 1 DSO, 1 MC, 3 MMs and 17 Mentioned-in-Despatches. 17 Rajputs was in Nagaland during the insurgency operations of 1955 and 1956. It carried forward the high traditions and won seven Kirti Chakras and two Shaurya Chakras.

1962 Indo-China War: Two Rajput battalions witnessed some heavy fighting in NEFA in 1962. The 2nd Rajput under the command of Lt. Col. M.S. Rikh were at Walong in early 1962 and were moved to the banks of the Namka Chu river by October 10th as a part of 7 Infantry Brigade. The brigade was stretched on a twelve mile front along the Namka Chu, with the marching time from one end to the other being five days. The site chosen for their defences was forced upon them by the corps commander, who was working directly with the political authorities instead of the military chain of command. The battalion took up hastily erected defensive positions along the Namka Chu. The battalion was deployed in a trackless wilderness, where no mules could go and no civilian population lived which could help logistically. Lack of winter clothing added to the hardships of the men on these snowy heights. By the time the fighting commenced, the Chinese had occupied all the dominating heights in the area. A massive assault came on the Rajput front and in the fierce fighting that ensured, the battalion repulsed a number of determined attacks. The positions were soon enveloped from both sides and the battalion was cut off. In spite of heavy old against them the Rajputs did not give in and fought until the end.

The story of gallantry beyond the call of duty was re-enacted in many platoons and companies. At the temporary bridge, Naik Roshan Singh's section clung doggedly to its position till every man was killed. Subedar Dasrath Singh's platoon was reduced to seven men and had exhausted its ammunition in repulsing three Chinese attacks. When the fourth Chinese attack came the Rajputs fixed bayonets and charged. In the ensuing hand to hand fighting four men were killed and the three survivors all seriously wounded were captured. Jemadar Bose's platoon was left with only 10 men after halting three Chinese attacks. He too fixed bayonets and charged. He along with most of his platoon were killed. For those interested in more details there is an excellent article in the 'Battles' section of Bharat Rakshak on this battle.

Not a single man from B, C or D Companies was awarded any gallantry medal as there was no one left to write the citations because there was no officer or JCO who was not killed or seriously wounded and taken POW. When the CO, Lt. Col. M.S. Rikh was released from the POW camp, he wrote up the citations but GoI and MoD made lame excuses and did not pay any attention to them. There is a memorial erected to those who fought at Namka Chu, which is a ricktey tin shed with names still missing from it and names of persons who were not there have been put up. Major B.K. Pant's company of 112 men had 82 killed and wounded. What more does a country want from its brave sons and not honour them properly? 2 Rajput, out of 513 all ranks in battle, 282 were killed, 81 were wounded and captured. 90 others were taken prisoners when they tried to break out. Only 60 other ranks, mostly from the administrative elements got back.

4 Rajput under Lt. Col. B. Avasthi was in the Sela-Bomdila area and it too had to face heavy odds. There was conflicting views among the senior commanders. The brigade commander wanted to hold Sela, but the divisional commander wanted to fall back. The divisional commander and the corps commander both agreed to withdraw. This led to total chaos during the retreat as the Chinese had bypassed many positions and ambushed parties of the soldiers withdrawing in a number of places. The battalion broke up into a number of parties, one led by Lt. Col. Avasti was ambushed and he was killed along with 300 men.

1965 Indo-Pak War: After the Rann of Kutch affair, Pakistan switched its attempts towards Kargil and in May 1965 it attacked one of the Indian posts there. 4 Rajput as a part of 121 Infantry Brigade were ordered to capture Point 13620 and Black Rock (15000) also known as Kargil heights to remove any threat to the Srinagar-Leh highway. Both posts consisted of three parts and each of these features was held by a platoon plus of the enemy in addition to a section of 3" mortars and MMGs on Point 13620. On 17 May 1965, B Company under Major Baljit Singh Randhawa, infiltrated deep behind the enemy held posts and attacked them. A grim battles was the fought and the Rajputs were sucessful in evicting the enemy. The Rajputs were awarded a MVC to Maj. B.S. Randhawa (posthumous) and 3 VrCs, one each to Captain Ranbir Singh,

Sepoy Budh Singh and a posthumous one to Havildar Girghari Lal. Black Rocks was captured by A Company in the second phase of the attack. As an act of goodwill by GOI these posts were handed back to the Pakistanis some weeks later. These were again recaptured by another battalion in August 1965.

In August, 4 Rajput were moved to the Hajipir area and Bisali feature was captured by them on the night of 4/5 September. This assault was carried out in face of heavy MMG, mortar and artillery fire. The Pakistanis launched five counterattacks and all these were beaten back. By this time the Rajputs had nearly exhausted all of their ammunition and with no hope of reinforcements, they had to withdraw to other defensive positions.

6 Rajput were in and around Srinagar dealing with the Pakistani infiltrators. A number of raids and ambushes were systematically carried out by them. After the infiltrator menace had died down, 6 Rajput moved to Ahknur area and came under 191 Infantry Brigade, which in turn was directly under HQ 15 corps. The battalion was supplied with RCL guns but without sights. When asking for the sights they were told to "see through the barrels and engage the Pakistani armour."' The battalion held on to a number of forward posts in the area in face of repeated counterattacks and heavy shelling. Some time after the cease fire a Brigadier came around to see the 6 Rajput defences. He asked Naik Nanak Singh, who was in charge of an LMG position as to where his range card was, and how could he fire properly without knowing the primary and secondary arcs. The Naik replied that he would fire from where ever the enemy came. This annoyed the Brigadier and he said that the Naik was not a good NCO. Nanak Singh faced the Brigadier and said, "Sahib, jab golian chal rahi theen to dikhai nahin diye. Ab range card poochh rahe ho." (Sir, when the bullets were flying you were not to be seen and now you are asking for the range card!). That ended the matter.

14 and 20 Rajput were at the Phillora-Chawinda front and after the capture of Charwa on the border, 20 Rajput led the advance for the next 10 days. 17 Rajput were in the southern Lahore sector in the Bedian area.

In 1967, 18 Rajput were carrying out a project of erecting wire fences on the North Shoulder of Nathula. On September 11th, they broadcast taped messages in Chinese to inform the Chinese troops of the intention. When the wire laying party was in the open and laying the fences, the Chinese opened up with machine guns. Major Harbhajan Singh the company commander ordered his men to charge the Chinese. He single handedly rushed forward and bayoneted three Chinese soldiers and then silenced one of the machine guns by throwing a hand grenade. In doing so he made the supreme sacrifice. The Rajputs inspired by their company commander's courage, led by Naib Subedar Raghav Prasad Pandey charged the other machine gun and silenced it. There was firing between the Rajputs and Chinese for the next five days. 61 casualties (22 killed and the rest wounded) were the suffered by the Rajputs. Major Harbhajan Singh was awarded a MVC (posthumous) and Naib Subedar Pandey a VrC (posthumous) for their gallant actions.

1971 Indo-Pak War: Rajput battalions played an active part in liberation of Bangladesh. Starting in West Bengal, near Calcutta and going about in a clockwise direction around Bangladesh the battalions were deployed as follows.

22 Rajput captured Akandabaria and cleared the way to capture Darsana. The Rajputs then led the brigade attack on Kushtia. The Pakistanis had built up the area around Kushtia and they let the Rajputs and the supporting tanks come forward into the area. They then opened up with heavy fire, the leading company of the Rajputs suffered heavy casualties.

16 Rajput participated in the battle of Hilli and then led the brigade advance to Ghoraghat and on to Rangpur. 21 Rajput spearheaded the move to Saidpur and fought in the battle of Khansama during which there was fierce hand to hand fighting. 4 Rajput were in the area Kurigram-Kaligunj-Jaipurhat. 6 Rajput fought in the Sylhet area and led the advance towards Fenchunganj and Kola Bils. Heavy fighting took place at Kola Bils and the battalion suffered 100 casualties, but it obtained the surrender of 22nd Baloch Regiment. The battalion was awarded 1 VrC (posthumous) and 2 SMs for the action at Kola Bils.

18 Rajput were on the Akhaura-Ashuganj axis. Akhaura proved a tough nut to crack, fighting for it took nearly three days. After this the Rajputs rushed forward and captured the Titas bridge intact. They then attacked Ashuganj, which was cleared after a tough fight and moved on to Narsingdi and entered Dacca on the 16th December. 20 Rajput operated in the Belonia bulge and captured Chaudagram and later moved to Chittagong.

On the western front, 20 Rajput (Jodhpur Sardar) were in their elements in the sands of Rajasthan. Covering a distance of 70 km in the first five days of the war the Rajputs reached Chachro. 15 Rajput was in the Fazilka area. It was involved in heavy fighting for the capture of Beriwala bridge and Ghazi post. It suffered heavy casualties during the attacks. Lance Naik Drigpal Singh received a posthumous MVC for his gallant actions. 14 Rajput saw action in the Khalra sector and 5 and 9 Rajputs were in the Chammb area. 9 Rajput operated in the Ratnu Chak area and carried out a number of raids, they also captured a couple of enemy posts.

Since the 1980s a number of Rajput battalions have been involved involved in CI operations in the North East, Punjab and Jammu and Kashmir. 4, 5 and 25 Rajputs formed a part of IPKF in Sri Lanka. In 1980, 18 Rajput transferred to the newly raised Mechanised Infantry Regiment as its 13th battalion. More recently, 27 Rajput were involved in the fighting in the Kargil sector in 1999.

The affiliation between Navy ships and Army regiments was instituted in 1990 when the guided missile destroyer, "INS Rajput", was affiliated to the Rajput Regiment. Battalions of Rajput regiment are 2 Battalion, 3 Battalion, 4 Battalion, 5 Battalion, 6 Battalion, 7 Battalion, 8 Battalion, 9 Battalion, 14 Battalion, 15 Battalion, 16 Battalion, 17 Battalion, 19 Battalion, 21 Battalion, 22 Battalion, 23 Battalion, 24 Battalion, 25 Battalion, 26 Battalion and 27 Battalion.

Battle Honours: Naushera, Zoji La, Khinsar, Madhumati River, Belonia, Khansama and Akhaura.

Honours & Awards: 1 Param Vir Chakra, 1 Ashok Chakra, 5 Param Vishisht Seva Medals, 7 Maha Vir Chakras, 12 Kirti Chakras, 5 Ati Vishisht Seva Medals, 58 Vir Chakras, 20 Shaurya Chakras 4 Yudh Seva Medals, 67 Sena Medals, 19 Vishisht Seva Medals, 1 Bar to Vishisht Seva Medal, 1 Padma Shri.

The Regimental Center: The Rajput Regimental center is in Fatehgarh, Uttar Pradesh. The regiment now a days recruits Rajputs, Gujars, Bengalis, Brahmins, Muslims, Jats, Ahirs, Mazhabi & Ramdasia Sikhs and Dogras. A war memorial was erected at Fetehgarh in 1932. It is in a form of a chattri, with its dome resting on six pillars, each representing a battalion at that time and bearing its crest. The regimental motto is Sarvatra Vijaya, which means Victory Everywhere and the war cry is Bajrang Bali Ki Jai.

Famous Personalities

Armed Forces

Gallantary Award Recipients

Naik Jadu Nath Singh Rathore during the Jammu & Kashmir ops in the winter of 1947, displayed great valour & superb leadership and used his small force in such a manner that the enemy retreated in utter confusion. He was honoured with the highest war-time gallantry medal, **Param Vir Chakra**, posthumously.

Company Havaldar Piru Singh Shekhawat, during the Jammu & Kashmir operations in summer of 1948, was honoured with the highest war-time gallantry medal, **Param Vir Chakra** for his gallantry.

Captain Gurbachan Singh Salaria, on 5 December 1961, showed exemplary leadership, courage, unflinching devotion to duty and disregard for his personal safety and was awarded **Param Vir Chakra**, the highest wartime gallantry medal, posthumously.

Major Shaitan Singh was awarded **Param Vir Chakra**, the highest wartime gallantry medal, posthumously, for his leadership and devotion to duty during the 1962 Indo-China conflict.

Rifleman Sanjay Kumar, for his sustained display of the most conspicuous personal bravery and gallantry of the highest order in the face of the enemy on 04 July 1999, was awarded the **Param Vir Chakra,** India's highest medal for gallantry

Brigadier Rajendra Singh was awarded **Maha Vir Chakra**, posthumously for his outstanding leadership, courage and sense of duty during J &K operations in 1948.

Brigadier Yadunath Singh was awarded the **Maha Vir Chakra** for conspicuous bravery allantry and devotion to duty during J & K operations in 1948.

Major Khushhal Chand was awarded the **Maha Vir Chakra** for his exceptional courage, gallantry and devotion to duty during J & K operations in 1948.

Lieutenant Kishan Singh Rathore was awarded the **Maha Vir Chakra** for conspicuous bravery allantry and devotion to duty during J & K operations in 1948.

Naik Nar Singh was awarded the **Maha Vir Chakra** for outstanding gallantry and devotion to duty, posthumously during J &K operations in 1948.

Sepoy Dewan Singh was awarded the **Maha Vir Chakra** posthumously for his exceptional courage, gallantry and devotion to duty during J &K operations in 1948.

Rifleman Dhonkal Singh was awarded the **Maha Vir Chakra** posthumously for his exceptional courage, gallantry and devotion to duty during J &K operations in 1948.

Lieutenant Colonel Raghubir Singh Rajawat was awarded **Maha Vir Chakra** for his actions during war of 1965.

Major Anup Singh Guhilote was awarded **Maha Vir Chakra**, posthumously for displaying exemplary leadership during the battle of 1971.

Captain Pratap Singh was part of the Indian forces that defended Bana outpost against Pakistani forces in the summer of 1988. He was posthumously honoured with the **Maha Vir Chakra** for his devotion to duty and courage.

Major Rajesh Singh Adhikari was honoured with the **Maha Vir Chakra**, posthumously for conspicuous gallantry and supreme sacrifice during Kargil war of 1999.

Others

General Rajendrasinhji Jadeja (1899-1964) was the second Chief of Army Staff of the Indian army, and the second Indian, after Field Marshal K. M. Cariappa, to head the Indian Army.

Admiral V. S. Shekhawat was Chief of Indian Navy from 1993 till 1996. He was 14th Chief of Naval Staff.

Admiral Madhvendra Singh was chief of Indian Navy from 2001 till 2004. He was the 17th Chief of Naval Staff.

Politicians

- Vishwanath Pratap Singh: Former Prime Minister of India from 2 December 1989 to 10 November 1990.
- Bhairon Singh Shekhawat: Former Vice President of India from 2002 till 200.
- Arjun Singh: (born November 5, 1930) is an Indian politician from the Indian National Congress party. He is the Union Minister of Human Resource Development in the Cabinet of Prime Minister Manmohan Singh, and was earlier in the same post in the 1991 Narasimha Rao government where he was elected from the Satna constituency.
- Maharani Gayatri Devi: Rajmata of Jaipur
- Digvijay Singh: Congress Leader Former Chief Minister of Madhya Pradesh
- Satyendra Narayan Sinha: Congress Leader & Former Chief Minister of Bihar
- Harish Rawat: PCC Chief, Uttarakhand

Artists

- Chandrachur Singh: Actor.
- Diwakar Pundir: Model.
- Lalita Pawar: Actress
- Sonal Chauhan: Miss India
- Sunidhi Chauhan: Renowned Singer.
- Kangna Ranaut: Actress
- Raghavendra Singh Rathore: Renowned Fasion Designer

9

Sikhs

Sikhism, established on the teachings of Nanak and nine successive gurus in fifteenth century Northern India, is the fifth-largest organised religion in the world. This system of religious philosophy and expression has been traditionally known as the Gurmat (literally the counsel of the gurus) or the Sikh Dharma. Sikhism originated from the word Sikh, which in turn comes from the Sanskrit root Sisya meaning "disciple" or "learner", or Sikca meaning "instruction."

The principal belief of Sikhism is faith in Vahigurû—represented using the revered symbol of çk oankar, the Universal God. Sikhism advocates the pursuit of salvation through disciplined, personal meditation on the name and message of God. A key distinctive feature of Sikhism is a non-anthropomorphic concept of God, to the extent that one can interpret God as the Universe itself. The followers of Sikhism are ordained to follow the teachings of the ten Sikh gurus, or enlightened leaders, as well as the holy scripture entitled the Gurû Granth Sahib, which includes selected works of many devotees from diverse socio-economic and religious backgrounds. The text was decreed by Gobind Singh, the tenth guru, as the final guru of the Khalsa Panth. Sikhism's traditions and teachings are distinctively linked with the history, society and culture of the Punjab. Adherents of Sikhism are known as Sikhs (students or disciples) and number over 23 million across the world. Most Sikhs live in the state of Punjab in India and, prior to the country's partition, millions of Sikhs resided in what is now known as the Punjab province of Pakistan.

Origin & History

In the 15th century Sikhism rose in Punjab and now it is of utmost importance all over India. Sikhism is Hinduistic in the sense that it accepts the four-fold principles of Karma-Samsara-Jnana-Mukti. It also adopts a general Hindu opinion of life, poetry and music.

Sikhism was born at a time when India was in a state of political upheaval, social instability and religious ritualism, externalism without much inner illumination and spiritual experience in depth. Sikhism at the hands of the first Guru, named, Nanak was not primarily a political movement. From the social viewpoint it was founded on the rejection of caste and it promoted egalitarianism. Naturally it did not support untouchability.

Sikhism of Guru Nanak was essentially a religious reformist movement in the direction of Saint poets of India. Guru Granth Sahib the revered book of the Sikhs contains four poems of Trilochan, 62 of Namadeva and 240 Sakhis and 227 padas of Kabir. Most of the characteristic teachings of Sikhism like monotheism, crusade against idolatry and caste, externalism (bhaiachara), ritualism could be easily traced to these saint poets, specially Kabir. Kabir appears to be a contemporary of Guru Nanak.

Again, in the starting, terms like Sikh, Saint, Sadhu, Bhakta and Sevak were used in the same sense. Nevertheless, now, the term 'Guru' is to be used for the first ten Gurus and for Adi Granth Sahib. All poets whose lines have been included in Adi Granth Sahib are called 'Saint. But 'Guru' is not to be called 'Saint'. Nevertheless, one can note that Guru Nanak: was greatly influenced by Saint Kabir.

Sikh is really derived from the word 'Sisya'. Therefore, Sikhism is the religion often Gurus and their followers Sisyas. A Sikh is one who is willing to lay down his life for the sake of his Guru.

Guru Nanak was the real founding father of Sikhism. He was born in a village called Talwandi, which is some fifty miles south of Lahore in the year 1469. It is now in Pakistan and has been named "Nankana Sahib". Sikhism preached by Guru Nanak was largely a religious and spiritual movement, but even Guru Nanak advised his followers to resist evil even to the point of sacrifice and martyrdom`. Later on Guru Hargobind Singh girded on two swords `miri" (to defend and pursue political end) and `piri` (for safe guarding spiritual pursuit). But it was the last Guru Gobind Singh who infused martial spirit into his Sikh followers called `Khalsa` and -who were to be called `Singh` (lion). The new order of Khalsa had to fight in defence of their faith, home and hearth and their honour.

1. Guru Nanak (1469-1539).
2. Guru Angad (1504-1552).
3. Guru Amar Das (1479-1574).

4. Guru Ram Das (1534-1581).
5. Guru Arjan Dev (1563-1606).
6. Guru Hargobind (1595-1644).
7. Guru Hari Rai (1630-1661).
8. Guru Hari Krishan (1656-1664).
9. Guru Teg Bahadur (1621-1674).
10. Guru Gobind Singh (1666-1708).

The founding father of Sikhism was Shri Guru Nanak Dev, (1469-1538) who was born in the Punjab region of what is now Pakistan. At Sultanpur, he received a vision to preach the way to enlightenment and God. He is responsible for the saying "There is no Hindu, there is no Muslim" which has since become one of the pillars of Sikhism. He taught a strict monotheism, the brotherhood of humanity. He rejected idol worship, and the Hindu concept of caste. Guru Nanak and Panth (his followers) later built the first Sikh temple at Katarpur.

A succession of nine Gurus (regarded as reincarnations of Guru Nanak) led the movement during the period from Guru Nanak's death till 1708. At that time, the functions of the Guru passed to the Panth and to the holy text, considered the 11th Guru.

Mughal emperors governed a large region of Asia from the 16th century till the end of the 18th century. They attempted to convert the Sikhs to Islam, but were unsuccessful. It has been said of one of the Sikh Gurus (considered by many Sikhs to have been the last guru) that "Had there been no Guru Gobind Singh, the entire country would have gotten circumcised" i.e. been converted to Islam.

In 1801, the Sikh state of Punjab was established in Northern India by Maharaja Ranjit Singh. An invasion by Great Britain triggered the Sikh Wars (1845-1849). The British successfully gained control over all of India. After independence in 1947, occupied India was partitioned on religious grounds into a mostly Muslim Pakistan and mostly Hindu India. A mass migration of Sikhs and Hindus from Pakistan to India and a reverse migration of Muslims resulted, with immense loss of life. Some Sikhs have been seeking an independent homeland since the late 1940's.

People & Culture

Sikhs are also divided along caste lines, although these divisions exist contrary to the teachings of Sikh Gurus. In addition to social divisions, there are a number of Sikh sectarian groups, such as Namdharis, Ravidasis,

Nirankaris and Radhasoamis. These groups differ from orthodox Sikhism, and have their own religious and social organisations. Nihangs tend to have little difference in practice but are considered Sikhs proper by mainstream Sikhism. There is also a sect known as Udasi, established by Sri Chand who were initially part of Sikhism but later developed into a monastic order.

Nanak taught that rituals, religious ceremonies or empty worship is of little use and Sikhs are discouraged from fasting or going on pilgrimages. Nevertheless, during the period of the later gurus, and because of increased institutionalisation of the religion, some ceremonies and rites did arise. Sikhism is not a proselytizing religion and most Sikhs do not make active attempts to gain converts. Nevertheless, converts to Sikhism are welcomed, although there is no formal conversion ceremony.

Upon a child's birth, the Guru Granth Sahib is opened at a random point and the child is named using the first letter on the top left-hand corner of the left page. All boys are given the middle name or surname Singh, and all girls are given the middle name or surname Kaur. Sikhs are joined in wedlock through the anand karaj ceremony. Sikhs are required to marry when they are of a sufficient age (child marriage is taboo), and without regard for the future spouse's caste or descent. The marriage ceremony is performed in the company of the Guru Granth Sahib; around which the couple circles four times. After the ceremony is complete, the husband and wife are considered "a single soul in two bodies."

As per Sikh religious rites, neither husband nor wife are permitted to divorce. A Sikh couple that wishes to divorce may be able to do so in a civil court – but this is not condoned. Upon death, the body of a Sikh is usually cremated. If this is not possible, any means of disposing the body may be employed. The kirtan sohila and ardas prayers are performed during the funeral ceremony (known as antim sanskar).

Sects

The Sikh religion is not an entirely monolithic faith - there are several sects which are not recognized by the majority of Sikhs as orthodox in their teachings and beliefs. One is known as the Udasis, a group of holy men which was established by an elder son of Guru Nanak, Baba Sri Chand. They are celibate and, either nude or while wearing a yellow robe, carry around a begging bowl to receive food or donations (begging is forbidden amongst orthodox Sikhs). They are very similar to Hindu ascetics in their mannerisms and habits and they have been active as missionaries of the Sikh faith.

Another group is known as the Sahajdharis, which means "slow adopters." This actually encompasses several smaller sects, all of which tend to be shaven like Hindus and contrary to Sikh tradition. They have largely rejected the more militant teachings which were promoted by Gobind Singh, the tenth and final human Guru.

The final group is known as the Keshadharis ("hair-wearers") and it, too, encompasses a number of smaller sects. The Nihangs are the most militant of all Sikhs - they regularly carry a variety of weapons and are more willing to take action to defend their religion. They regard themselves as continuing in the tradition of Guru Gobind Singh's Khalsa army and live a semi-nomadic lifestyle. The Nirmalas, on the other hand, are much less militant than average and members tend to lead contemplative lives while secluded in monasteries.

Another group categorized with the Keshadharis are the Nirankaris, established by Baba Dayal (d. 1853). They concentrate on the formless, eternal nature of God and accept the existence of a continuing line of living gurus. The final group is known as the Namdari or Kukas. This is a reform group which developed in the 19th century and they follow a living Guru who is descended from he original gurus.

Demographics

The existance of Sikh communities all over the world is a fascinating story of an immigrant community which originated in the Punjab, India, more than five hundred years ago. Over the centuries, they have acquired a reputation for being sturdy, industrious and adventrous; they are a people who have earned the reputation for being extremely brave and loyal soldiers. They have also become known for being a militant people.

The Sikh homeland is the Punjab, in India, where today Sikhs make up approximately 61% (Census 2001) of the population. This is the only place where Sikhs are in the majority. Sikhs have emigrated to countries all over the world - especially to English-speaking and East Asian nations. In doing so they have retained, to an unusually high degree, their distinctive cultural and religious identity.

Sikhs are not ubiquitious worldwide in the way that adherents of larger world religions are, and they remain primarily an ethnic religion. But they can be found in many international cities and have become an especially strong religious presence in the United Kingdom and Canada.

Large National Sikh Communities

Nation	Population
India	21,500,000
United Kingdom	500,000
Canada	225,000
USA	100,000
Malaysia	50,000
Singapore	20,000

Source: Indian census 2001, UN census data, Sikh Directory U.K.

Places With the Highest Percentage of Sikhs in the Population

Place	Percent	Number
Punjab, India	61	11,000,000
Haryana, India	5.81	956,836
Uttar Pradesh, India	0.49	675,775
Rajasthan, India	1.48	649,174
United Kingdom	1.00	500,000
British Columbia, Canada	2.30	100,000
Himachal Pradesh, India	1.01	400,000

Source: Indian census 2001.

Martial Traditions

Sikhs are the most energetic, sturdy and martial race by nature & compassionate in their acts. A race created by 10th Master i.e., Guru Gobind Singh, in the lineage of Guru Nanak the First who gave not only shape to form and look distinct from Hindus & Muslims though yet within philosophical and cultural dimensions of the duo, proclaimed the eternal Guru in the shape of Shabad i.e. Shri Guru Granth Sahib- reverently & in all divinity, in cosmogenical pursuit called Shabad- Guru.

Although the early Mughal emperors had peaceful relations with the Sikh Gurus, the Sikhs started facing religious persecution during the reign of Jahangir. Guru Arjan Dev, the fifth Guru, was arrested and executed by Jahangir in 1606.

In 1675, Guru Tegh Bahadur, the ninth Guru of the Sikhs was executed by the Mughal emperor Aurangzeb. In 1699, his son and the tenth Guru, Gobind Singh decided to establish a military order to stage opposition against the Mughals. He sent hukmanamas (letters of authority) to his followers all over the area, requesting them to congregate at Anandpur on 13 April 1699, the day of Baisakhi (the annual harvest festival).

Guru Gobind Singh addressed the congregation from the entryway of a tent pitched on a hill (now called Kesgarh Sahib). He drew his sword and asked for a volunteer who was willing to sacrifice his head. No one answered his first call, nor the second call, but on the third invitation, a person called Daya Ram (later known as Bhai Daya Singh) came forward and offered his head to the Guru. Guru Gobind Singh took the volunteer inside the tent, and emerged shortly, with blood dripping from his sword. He then demanded another head. One more volunteer came forward, and entered the tent with him. Guru again emerged with blood on his sword. This happened three more times. Then the five volunteers came out of the tent unharmed. These five, who were willing to sacrifice their lives for their Guru, were called Panj Piare ("the five beloved ones"). These five volunteers were the first Khalsa Sikhs: Daya Ram (Bhai Daya Singh), Dharam Das (Bhai Dharam Singh), Himmat Rai (Bhai Himmat Singh), Mohkam Chand (Bhai Mohkam Singh), and Sahib Chand (Bhai Sahib Singh).

Guru Gobind Singh Ji beheaded the five disciples, and then brought them back to life using divine powers. Guru Gobind Singh then took an iron bowl, and poured some water in it. Sahib Devan (later Mata Sahib Kaur) added some sugar crystals to the water in the bowl, and Guru stirred this mixture with a double-edged sword whilst reciting the panj banis.

These actions allude to the nature expected of the inductees to the Khalsa: that they must have the will and the strength to fight oppression (symbolized by the sword), but must always remember that their actions are born from protection and not hatred (symbolized by the sweetness of the sugar).

Each of the panj pyares were given five palmfuls of the amrit to drink, and had amrit sprinkled in their eyes five times. Each time, they repeated the phrase, "Waheguru ji ka Khalsa, Waheguru ji ki Fateh" ("The Khalsa belongs to God, the victory belongs to God"). Then they received five sprinkles in their hair and sipped from the bowl of amrit.

Guru Gobind Singh gave them all the surname "Singh" (meaning "lion") over their original surnames (which indicated the caste that they originally belonged to) to symbolize the caste-less nature of the order, and indeed of the religion itself. Similarly, every subsequent male who takes the ceremony are also given the surname "Singh", and every female is given the name "Kaur" (meaning "princess," but originally it meant "prince" this was given by Guru Nanak Dev Ji so as to remove distinction between sexes, and bring about equality); the collective body of whom is called the Khalsa.

The Panj Piare were thus the first baptised Sikhs, and became the first members of the Khalsa brotherhood, who symbolically regard Guru Gobind Singh as their "father", and Mata Sahib Kaur as their "mother". Khalsa claims Anandpur, where they were created by Guru Gobind Singh, as their home, and celebrate Vaisakhi as their birthday.

With the creation of Khalsa, Guru Gobind Singh had abolished all existing social divisions as per teaching of Guru Nanak. In their new order the lowest of the low would stand with the highest, all would become one and drink from one vessel. All previous beliefs relating to family, occupation, customs and ceremonies were declared useless by the Guru and salvation could be achieved only by the ways of the Khalsa. This caused uncomfort to those who considered themselves to be superior races and they protested. Many departed from the ceremeony, but the Guru declared that the low sects should be raised and would dwell next to himself.

One of the duties of a Khalsa was to practice arms and be ready to defend the weak. This was deemed necessary because of the rising religious persecution from zealous Islamic Mughal rulers. In this context the Khalsa rose as a group as saint-warriors to withstand the Mughals.

After the death of Guru Gobind Singh, his disciple Banda Singh Bahadur led the Khalsa warriors in an uprising against the Mughals. Banda Singh Bahadur first founded a Sikh empire when he defeated the Mughals at Sirhind. He and his comrades were eventually defeated and executed, but he became an icon amongst the Khalsa Sikhs. By the late 1730s, the Khalsa regrouped as a military force under Nawab Kapur Singh, who gathered local chieftains and created Dal Khalsa, a coalition army. The Dal Khalsa fought with the Mughals and the Afghans, eventually resulting in the establishment of a Sikh empire in the Punjab area.

After the fall of the Mughal empire and the later establishment of a Sikh state in Punjab, the Khalsa became an instrument of the Punjab Maharajas: the Khalsa was a democratic body, and could oppose the Maharaja. By the death of Ranjit Singh in 1839 the regular army of Punjab was assessed by Sir Lepel Griffin at 29000 men, with 192 artillery guns. The irregular levies were estimated at a similar number.

The Khalsa order attracted the vast Jat peasantry of middle and eastern Punjab, and over the years, the Khalsa Sikhs became the orthodox majority in the Sikh community. The rise of Khalsa dominance in the Sikh community is sometimes linked with rise of Jat influence in the Sikh community, and the decline of the Khatri influence (all ten Sikh Gurus were Khatris). Nevertheless, W. H. McLeod states that while the Khalsa may incorporate mighty Jat influences, it would be a "naive interpretation" to regard the Khalsa as an "institutionalized conquest of the (Sikh) Panth by its Jat constituency". Under the Khalsa dominance, the Sikh religion came to be identified with the Khalsa and the Jats, although not all of the Khalsa Sikhs are Jats, and not all Sikhs subscribed to the Khalsa code of conduct.

Today, the Khalsa brotherhood is respected by the entire Sikh community; nevertheless, not all Sikhs are Amritdharis. The issue of Khalsa code of conduct has led to several controversies. In the early 1950s, a serious split took place in the Canadian Sikh community, when the Khalsa Diwan Society in Vancouver elected a clean-shaven Sikh to serve on its management committee. Although most of the early Sikh immigrants to Canada were non-Khalsa, and a majority of the members of the society were clean-shaven non-Khalsa Sikhs, a faction objected to the election of a non-Khalsa to the management committee. The factions in Vancouver and Victorial broke away from the Khalsa Diwan Society, and established their own gurdwara society called Akali Singh.

Contribution to Defence Services

Sikhs by nature are self-respecting, courageous, hardworking and enterprising. Look into their short span of history and you will find their pitcher is full of sacrifices and hard work which has contributed so much towards the nation building. If not for them, the course of Indian History would have been very different. That's what makes them the spirit born people and gives the ability to simply ignore the digs targeted at them. Volumes could be written on the contributions made by the Sikhs, who constitute less than 2% of Indian population.

Sikhs were the only Indian community to be internationally acclaimed as early as 1897, for their heroism and valour. Where in the history of warfare can you find the instance of heroism as demonstrated by 22 Sikh soldiers manning the signal post of Saragahi in North-West province with no ammunition back up. All the 22 of them fought till the last bullet had been fired against an Afghan army of 7000 warriors. The 22 soldiers then charged with their kirpans to be eventually cut down to pieces. The easier way out would have been to surrender but the spirit of Sikhs has always made them do what Gobind Singh, the 10th Guru had said, "Grant me this boon, O Lord, at last when the end of life is near, I may die fighting in the battlefield for the sake of righteousness".

The first battle for freedom from British was won by Sikhs, when after loss of many lives in 1929 they were able to take over the charge of their shrines from British.Contribution of Sikhs towards the Indian Defence Services is the highest with respect to their 2% population size. This community has also won the maximum number of gallantary awards since independence - 5 Param Vir Chakras (PVCs), 40 Maha Vir Chakras (MVCs), 209 Vir Chakras (VrCs).

Sikh Regiment

Regimental Motto: Nischey Kar Apni Jeet Karon (I Fight For Sure To Win)

War Cry: Bole So Nihal, Sat Sri Akal (He who cries God is Truth, is ever Happy)

The Sikh Regiment is one of the oldest and highest decorated Regiments of the Indian Army. The Regimental Centre is located at Ramgarh, South Bihar. With 73 Battle Honours, the largest collection of Victoria Crosses-Param Vir Chakras and equivalent, the Saga of Saragarhi, the young soldiers of the Sikh Regiment are proud to wear the regimental colours of India's highest decorated regiment. Since it's raising more than 150 years ago, the regiment has been in the vanguard of various actions and operations both in the pre and post-independence era in India and abroad.

Maharaja Ranjit Singh brought the well built and courageous people of the then Punjab to "Khalsa Panth" and formed "Khalsa Army". Following numerous heroic and valiant battles by the Khalsa Army, XIV Ferozepur (1 Sikh, now 4 Mechanised Infantry), and XV Ludhiana (2 Sikh) were raised from the soliders of the vanquished force on August 1, 1846. The history of the Sikh Regiment has been replete with examples of gallant soldiering and supreme sacrifice. "It is the highest decorated Regiment of the Indian Army as reported in the Defence Review Annual 1995-96" says Brig R Sharma, the Commandant of the Sikh Regimental Centre.

In September 1897, 4 Sikh was deployed in Khanki valley on Samana ridge in North-West Frontier Province (NWFP) in Pakistan. During those days, 4 Sikh was known as XXXVI Sikh of the British Indian Army. The battalion, deployed in two groups, occupied Fort Lockhart with picquets at Dar, Sartope, Sangar, Carg and Saragarhi. Amongst all the piquets, Saragarhi was the most important one due to its position on the highest point between Fort Lockhart and Gulistan. Twentyone soldiers, under the command of Hav Ishar Singh, held the Saragarhi piquet.

To separate Fort Gulistan and Lockhart, 10000 Orakzai and Afridi Lashkars attacked Saragarhi on September 12, 1897 at daybreak. The attack was initially rebutted with the enemy sustaining a loss of over 60 killed. Lt. Col. J. Haughton, the then Commanding Officer, took all efforts to hold Saragarhi. However, the battalion was forced to retreat initially as the enemy repeatedly attacked Saragarhi. Without losing heart, the Sikhs did not move back from the fort. One Sepoy took control of the guardroom and shot down not less than 20 enemies, before clansmen set the guardroom on fire and burnt him to death. By about 3 pm, men and ammunition ran short and the assailants destroyed the battalion post by putting it on fire. Thus, the brave Sikhs killed 450 clansmen before making the supreme sacrifice.

On receiving the news, British Parliament interrupted the proceedings and gave standing ovation to the Saragarhi Braves. Each hero was awarded an Indian Order of Merit (IOM), the highest award given to an Indian soldier in British Indian Army for valour and sacrifice. Altogether, 21 IOMs were awarded in one day, a record of the sort. The battle of Saragarhi gave the concept of "last man, last round". Now, September 12 is celebrated as "Saragarhi Day" by all the battalions of the elite Sikh Regiment. UNESCO recognises this battle as one among eight battles of the world known for collective bravery.

The fourth battalion of the Sikh Regiment celebrated the 107th anniversary of the battle of Saragarhi in 2004 at its location somewhere in Central Sector. On this occasion, the battle of saragarhi was enacted by the battalion as a highlight of the two-day celebrations. Presiding over the sainik sammelan, Col. S. C. Panwar, Commanding Officer of the battalion underlined the incidents associated with the battle. Earlier, martyrs of the battalion were paid homage at a wreath-laying ceremony held at the battalion war memorial. Gurudwara service, a variety entertainment programme, adventurous sports and a social evening added colour to the celebrations.

In all, the Regiment has to its credit 1652 gallantry awards and honours including 10 Victoria Cross, two Param Vir Chakra, 14 Maha Vir Chakra and 68 Vir Chakra. In addition it has also earned 73 battle honours and 38 theatre honours besides four COAS Unit Citation (including the one bestowed upon 8 Sikh during the 1999 Kargil episode) and two "Bravest of the Brave" citations. The Museum of the Regimental Centre displays a record of the Sikh Regiment in four halls viz., the Religious/ motivational Hall, the Hall of Heritage, the Regimental Glory Hall and the Peripheral Gallery. The two winners of Param Vir Chakra are L/Nk Karam Singh in 1948 during Kashmir operations and Sub Joginder Singh during the Chinese Aggression of 1962.

The Chief of Army Staff made a special instant award of "Unit Citation" to 8th Battalion, The Sikh Regiment for their meritorious and gallant performance during the isolation of Tiger Hill, which facilitated the capture of Tiger Hill top and battles of Helmet and India Gate, features to the West of Tiger Hill top, on night 07/08 July 1999, in Dras Sector. During Operation "Vijay", the unit displayed sterling performance marked with exceptional valour and grit in the face of the enemy.Battalions of Sikh Regiment are 2 Battalion, 3 Battalion, 4 Battalion, 5 Battalion, 6 Battalion, 7 Battalion, 8 Battalion, 10 Battalion, 11 Battalion, 13 Battalion, 14 Battalion, 16 Battalion, 17 Battalion, 18 Battalion, 19 Battalion, 20 Battalion, 21 Battalion, and 22 Battalion.

Battle Honours: Srinagar, Tithwal, Raja Picquet, Burki, OP Hill, Parbat Ali, Punch and Siramani.

Honours & Awards: 2 Param Vir Chakras, 2 Ashok Chakras, 14 Maha Vir Chakras, 14 Kirti Chakras, 64 Vir Chakras, 15 Shaurya Chakras, 75 Sena Medals and 25 Vishisht Seva Medals.

The Regimental Centre: Ramgarh Cantonment, Bihar.

Famous Personalities

Sikhs are leader in various fields of life and has contributed to every aspect of society. Some famous Sikhs and their contribution is listed below.

Armed Forces

Gallantary Award Recipients

Sepoy Ishar Singh, a Sepoy in the 28th Punjab Regiment, Indian Army during the Waziristan Campaign, India, on 10 April 1921, near Haidari Kach (Waziristan) undertook the valient actions which led to the award of the **Victoria Cross**.

Major Parkash Singh was awarded **Victoria Cross**, the highest and most prestigious award for gallantry in the face of the enemy that can be awarded to British and Commonwealth forces for his bravery on 6 January 1943 in Burma against Japanese forces.

Naik Nand Singh was awarded **Victoria Cross**, the highest and most prestigious award for gallantry in the face of the enemy that can be awarded to British and Commonwealth forces for his bravery on 11/12 March 1944 in Burma. On 12th December 1947 he led his platoon of D Coy in a desperate but successful attack to extricate his battalion from an ambush in the hills of Uri in Kashmir. He was mortally injured by a close-quarters machine-gun burst, and posthumously awarded the Maha Vir Chakra, the second-highest Indian decoration for battlefield gallantry.

Naik Gian Singh was awarded **Victoria Cross,** the highest and most prestigious award for gallantry in the face of the enemy that can be awarded to British and Commonwealth forces for his bravery on 2 March 1945 against Japanese.

Lieutenant Karamjeet Singh Judge was awarded **Victoria Cross,** the highest and most prestigious award for gallantry in the face of the enemy that can be awarded to British and Commonwealth forces for his bravery on 18 March, 1945 near Meiktila, Burma against Japanese forces.

Lance Naik Karam Singh is an Indian military war hero who was awarded the **Param Vir Chakra** India's highest wartime military award in 1948.

Captain Gurbachan Singh Salaria, was awarded the **Param Vir Chakra** posthumously for his extraordinary leadership and devotion to duty on 5 December 1961, saving the UN Headquarters in Elisabethville.

Subedar Joginder Singh was awarded the highest wartime gallantry medal, the **Param Vir Chakra**, posthumouslyfor his brave actions on 23 October 1962 against the Chinese forces.

Flying Officer Nirmal Jit Singh Sekhon was an officer of the Indian Air Force and the posthumous recipient of the only **Param Vir Chakra** awarded to an Indian Air Force Personnel. Fg. Off Sekhon's award was in recognition of his lone and fatal defence of Srinagar Air Base during an air raid during the 1971 Indo-Pak War.

Naib Subedar Bana Singh was awarded the **Param Vir Chakra**, the highest wartime gallantry medal in India for his bravery in Kargil War of 1999.

Others

Marshal Arjan Singh (1919-) is the only officer of the Indian Air Force to be promoted to five star rank, equal to a Field Marshal, to which he was promoted in 2002. With the death of Field Marshal Sam Manekshaw in June 2008, he is presently the only living Indian military officer with a five-star rank.

General Joginder Jaswant Singh (1945-) was the first Sikh chief of army staff of India. He served as chief of army staff from January 31, 2005, to September 30, 2007.

Lt. General Jagjit Singh Arora (1916-2005) supervised the surrender of more than 90,000 Pakistani soldiers in East Pakistan (now Bangladesh) during the 1971 India-Pakistan war.

Politicians

Master Tara Singh Malhotra (1885-1967) was a prominent Sikh political and religious leader in the first half of the 20th century. He was instrumental in organizing the Shiromani Gurdwara Prabhandak Committee, in organizing Sikhs politically, and guided the Sikhs during the Partition of India, and later led their demand for a Sikh-majority state in Punjab, India.

Darbara Singh (1927- 1998) was a former Chief Minister of Punjab and former Governor of Rajasthan.

Giani Zail Singh (1916–1994) was an Indian politician and member of the Congress Party. He served as the seventh President of India between 1982 and 1987.

Manmohan Singh (born 1932) is the 17th and current Prime Minister of India. He was the Governor of the Reserve Bank of India from 1982 to 1985 and held the post of the Finance Minister of India from 1991 to 1996. He took oath as the Prime Minister of India on May 22, 2004, becoming the first person of Sikh faith to hold the post.

Pratap Singh Kairon (1901–1965) was the Chief Minister of the Punjab province (then comprising Punjab, Haryana and Himachal Pradesh), and is widely acknowledged to be the architect of post-Independence Punjab Province(or Punjab, Haryana and Himachal as of today).

Buta Singh (born 1934) is a former Union Home Minister under Rajiv Gandhi's Government & more recently governor of Bihar state, India. He took office on November 5, 2004. He was the home minister of India during the early 1990s.

Artists

- Harbhajan Maan: Singer
- Hans Raj Hans: Singer
- Manmohan Singh: Music Director
- Rabbi Shergill: Singer
- Khuswant Singh: Writer
- Major Rajasthani: Singer
- Amrita Pritam: Writer

SECTION: II

10

Ahirs

The Ahir (an altered form of the word, Abhira standing for "fearless") orYadav is a martial race of India. Yadav (Sanskrit) meaning a descendent of Yadu; also a grand race of Hindustan in which Krishna was born. The founding father of this community, Yadu, was the son of Yayati and Devayani, and reigned over the area west of the Jamuna River, next-door to the Kurus.

He was the half-brother of Puru, who became the founding father of the Paurava line of the Chandravansa (lunar dynasty), to which also belonged the Kurus and Pandus. The grandest of the Yadavs in Hindu story was Krishna (therefore he is called Yadav, "son of Yadu"). He founded the Yadavs in Gujarat, his principal city being Dwarka, to which he brought all the habitants of the town of Mathura after he had killed his evil Uncle Kansa who had took over the throne.

A short time after after his death (3102 BC), a disaster took place at Dwarka in which the town and all its habitants were engrossed by the ocean. Only a few members of the clan who were absent from the town were saved. The present Rajas of Vijaya-nagara assert that they are living descendents of the Yadavs.

The Ahir are among the most ancient martial communities of India. They are found in Uttar Pradesh, Haryana, Bihar, Rajasthan, Madhya Pradesh, Gujarat, Maharashtra and Nepal. The Ahirs also share most gotras with the Gujjars and Jats (Abhars) and have the similar bodily look as them. This led to the hypothesis of them being of the similar ancestry.

Origin & History

The Ahirs today claim ancestry from Krishna. Their beginning, nevertheless, is disputable. Some historiographers hold that they were a mighty tcommunity of nomad cowherds from eastern or central Asia who came to India by the way of Punjab area in large droves around the same time as the Sakas and the Yuechis in the first or second century BC and steadily spread over large parts of Northern, Eastern and Central India.

Other opinions are that they came from Syria or Asia Minor around the starting of the Christian era; resided in India long before the Aryan assault; were descendents of the Yadavs of the Lunar family of Pururavas Aila; and that their original home was the area between the Sutlej and the Yamuna from where they migrated beyond Mathura in the East and beyond Gujarat and Maharashtra in the South. The name of the State of Haryana may have been derived from its ancient habitants: Abhlrayana. The name 'Abhira' may havebeen derived from a-bhira standing for fearless.

As per custom, the Abhiras had the merit of establishing the first recorded empire on the banks of the revered river Saraswati. On the other side of the river was the empire of the Suras. The Sarswati steadily went belowground, and the Suras were held responsible for the calamity and accused with sins with which the river was burdened. Both the Suras and Abhiras had to migrate away from their empire and were estranged from the rest of society.

At the starting of the Christian era, the invading Scythians and Kushans forced most of them out of their land to lower Rajasthan in the Arbuda (Aravali area). In Marubhumi (Marwar), Saurashtra and Maharashtra they attended to the local rulers and founded their own rule. Ishwarsena, an outstanding Ahir general, became master of Western Deccan in place of the renowned Satava-hanas. He took the title of Rajan and an era was named after him. His descendents proceeded to rule for nine generations. For centuries the Ahirs were overshadowed as a political power in Haryana till the time of the Pratihara dynasty. In time they became sovereign rulers of Southwest Haryana. In 1150, Vighararaja IV, a Chauhan from Rajasthan forced them to become his vassals. In 1181 they were beaten by Prithviraj Chauhan but only after they had put up a hard opposition. As per some of the records Ahirs also governed the Nepal for some 491 years.

People & Culture

Ahirs lived as the shepherds in Gokul Mathura thousand years ago. Later on, they spread out all over the north and north-west sides of India. There are four major sects of Ahirs in Kutch: Prantharia, Mochhaya, Baureecha and Sorathia. Approximately three lakhs Ahirs of the eighteen million populations of Ahirs in India live in Kutch.

Prantharia Ahirs resided in eastern Kutch and they established a village named 'Vrajvani'. Mochhaya and Baureecha Ahirs resided in Chorad region (Satalpur). Prantharia Ahirs live in Chobari, Ranavav, Amaraper, Ratenper, Khengarper, Lodai, Dhrang, Dhori, Sumerasar, Vang, Dador, Kuneria, Nokhania, Lakhaper and Sataper. Machhaya Ahirs live in Padhar, Vagura, Tapper, Padana and Bhuvad. Sorathia Ahirs live in Anjar, Nagor and Syinai. Baureecha Ahirs live in Anjar, Meghper, Bourichi, Mithirohar, Bharapar Veera, Modsar, Khokhara, Kaniyabe, Jomkha, Kera and Baladia.

Ahirs are mainly farmers who once sold milk and ghee but they have changed their business to transfer due to irregularity of rain in Kutch. Young Ahir women wear most complex dresses. They generally wear skirts of red, green, blue, orange or brown tied and coloured cotton which are bonded and adorned with charming embroidery work. Middle young women wear 'odhanis' of red and black lined with exaggerated border and the old women wear plain black cotton tube skirts.

Ahirs worship Baba Ramdev Pir. The parents of the boys give gives to the parents of the girls when the engagement is concluded. Then, the bride's family and companions give a lot of presents during the marriage. Machhaya Ahirs and Baureecha Ahirs give sets of clothes adorned with mirror work embroidery. The bride's relations also give at least one silver jewellery, one or two gold necklaces, ear-rings, nose pins, anklets and bracelets.

The Ahirs maintain their connections with the nation lying between the Sutlej and the Yamuna. In many districts like Badaun, Etah, Mainpuri, Hissar, Rohtak and Gurgaon, the Ahirs are still in a majority. Ahirs also form a majority in various districts of Eastern Uttar Pradesh and Bihar, including Azamgarh and Madhepura. Most of the Haryanvi ahirs live in the area around Rewari and Narnaul. This place is therefore known as Ahirwal or 'the abode of Ahirs.' In medieval times the Ahirs gave up their arms and took to agriculture. In early British settlement reports they are spoken of highly as farmers. They stand on an equal footing with the Jats, Gujjars and Rajputs in the caste hierarchy, but though they eat with them, they do not intermarry. In appearance, they proclaim their Aryan descent. They are tall and wiry, have dark eyes, long noses, black hair and their complexion varies from wheatish to dark brown. Though mostly agriculturists, they also make good soldiers. Ahirs have been serving the Indian military right from the British period and won the highest of gallantry awards the Victoria Cross and the Parma Veer Chakra. In the annals of Indian military history there is sufficient proof of Ahir bravery that is immortalized in the ballads of Alah and Udal of Bundelkhand.

The Ahir are a caste of cowherds, milkers, and cattle breeders widely dispersed across the Gangetic Plain, especially in the more easternly part (Bihar, Bengal, and eastern Madhya Pradesh). The Ahir must number well over a million today: they numbered 750,000 in the Central Provinces and Berar in 1911, ranking as the sixth-largest caste in terms of numbers. In many sects there is a separate division of Ahirs, such as the Ahir Sunars, Sutars, Lohars, Shimpis, Salic, Guraos, and Kolis. The name "Ahir" is derived from "Abhira," a clan mentioned several times in inscriptions and the Hindu revered books. "Goala," standing for a cowherd or "a protector of cows," is the Bengali name for the caste, and the term "Gaoli" is now used in Madhya Pradesh State to signify a dairy worker.

Some dialects named after the Abhira or Ahirs are still spoken. One, known as Ahirwati, is spoken in the Rohtals and Gurgaon districts, the Punjab, and near Delhi. The Malwi dialect of Rajasthani is also known as Ahiri; there is a dialect of Gujarati called Khandeshi, also known as Ahirani. These linguistic survivals are an indication that the Ahirs were early settlers in the Delhi nation of the Punjab, and in Malwa and Khandesh.

The Ahir were seemingly among the immigrant races from central Asia who came to India during the early Christian era. The Ahir have been for centuries a purely occupational caste, majorly recruited from the indigenous communities. As cattle must graze in the forest during hot weather, there is a close relationship between Ahirs and many of the forest clans. Many Ahir in Mandla, for instance, are barely considered Hindus, because they live in Gond villages.

Only approximately 30 percent of the Ahirs are still occupied in breeding cattle and dealing in milk and butter. Approximately 4 percent are domestic servants, and nearly all the remainder were cultivators and laborers in 1931. Formerly the Ahirs had the exclusive right to milk cows, so that on all occasions an Ahir had to be hired for this purpose even by the lowest caste.

The caste has exogamous sections, which are of the usual low-caste type, with titular or totemistic names. The marriage of persons belonging to the same section and of first cousins is prohibited. A man may marry his wife's younger sister while his wife is living. The practice of exchanging girls between families is permissible.

The Ahir have a special relation to the Hindu religion, owing to their connection with the revered cow, which is itself revered as a goddess. Amongst the special deities of the Ahirs is Kharsk Deo, who is always located at the place of assembly of the cattle. Mater Deo is the god of the pen. A favourite saint is Haridas Baba. The major festival is the Diwali, falling around the starting of November. All people observe this feast by illuminating their houses with many small saucer-lamps and with fireworks.

Sects

Major Sects of Ahirs are:

- Abhirs
- Banaphar
- Bhati
- Gaddi
- Gaurs
- Gawlis
- Ghosals
- Golla
- Gope
- Gowdas
- Jadeja
- Jadon
- Jambavas
- Kalchuri
- Pradhans
- Puhanian
- Raos
- Rauts
- Rawals
- Saini
- Souryasaini
- Surabhirs
- Surasena
- Taljunghi
- Yadavas
- Yadavulu

Demographics

Ahirs, Yadavs or Yadavs are to be met with all over the India especially in Haryana. They include the Abhiras or Ahirs of northern India, Raos of Haryana, Gwallas of Uttar Pradesh, Mandals of Bihar, Pradhans of Orissa, Yadavs of Rajasthan, Ghoshals of Bengal, Gopas and Reddis of Andhra Pradesh and Wadeyars of Karnataka. The Yadav contribution to the composite culture of India is immense: the nomadic art forms, the Abhira language (Apabhramsa), the Raslila and certain ragas life Ahir-Bhairav, Abhirika, Gopixa, Kannadaguala and perhaps most of all, the Krishna cult.Beside India, Ahirs are also found in Nepal, Pakistan and Bangladesh.

Major countries having Ahir populations are:

Area	Population
India	54,711,0000
Nepal	1,132,0000
Bangladesh	214,0000
Pakistan	7,500

Source: Joshua Project 2008.

In India, the population of Ahirs is approximately 54,711,000. Major states having Ahir population are:

Area	Population
Uttar Pradesh	12,445,000
Bihar	12,383,000
Andhra Pradesh	7,440,000
West Bengal	4,539,000
Orissa	3,387,000
Tamil Nadu	2,884,000
Madhya Pradesh	2,312,000
Jharkhand	2,294,000
Chhattisgarh	2,080,000
Maharashtra	1,254,000

Source: Joshua Project 2008.

Martial Traditions

The ahirs (Yadavs) faced many foreign assaults, right from 326 BC when Alexander, the Great came to conquer the fertile Indus valley and beyond; and the Persians and the Afghans in the 10th & 11th centuries. Therefore, it is in the field of battle, that, the Ahirs first claimed fame. The poignant 'last man last round' stand of the ahir rifle company of 13 Kumaon Regiment in the Sino Indian of October/November 1962, in the epic battle of Rezangla, is stuff that legends are made of.

The Ahirs have been a clan to themselves. Right from the times of the Shakyas, the Kushans and the Synthians (6000 BC) they have been warriors par excellence, and only then agriculturists and farmers. They are the only community that; perhaps with the sorry exception of the Bhuttos of Sindh; who defied the devout and very severe Muslim Mughal Emperor Aurangzeb's might and parried repeated attempts at conversion to Islam.

In the 1st AD, invading Scythians and Kushans forced Ahirs out of their land to lower Rajasthan in the Aravali Region. In Marwar, Saurashtra and Maharashtra they served the local rulers and established their own Kingdoms. Ishwar Sena, a great Ahir General, became master of the Western Deccan and became King whose descendants continued to rule the region for nine generations. For centuries the Ahirs were eclipsed as a political power in Haryana until the time of the Pratihera dynasty. In time they became independent rulers of south-western Haryana.

The Ahir hold over Haryana must have remained intact for centuries after the battle of the Mahabharat. At the starting of the Christian era the invading Scythians and Kushans forced most of them out of their land to lower Rajasthan in the Arbuda (Aravali area). In Marubhumi (Marwar), Saurashtra and Maharashtra they served the local rulers and founded their own Raj. Ishwar Sena, a grand Ahir general, became master of western Deccan in place of the renowned Satavahanas. He took the title of Rajan and an era was named after him. His descendents continued to rule for nine generations. For centuries the Ahirs were eclipsed as a political power in Haryana till the time of the Pratihera dynasty. In time they became sovereign rulers of south-western Haryana.

Rao Tula Ram was one of the most important Ahir leaders of the 1857 War of Independence. He was born on 9 Dec1825 in the well known Rao family in village Rampura in Rewari. He was educated according to the then prevalent customs and knew Persian, Urdu, Hindi and a smattering of English. In November 1839, Rao Tula Ram ascended the throne on the death of his father. Along with Meerut, the people of Rewari under the dynamic leadership of Rao Tula Ram and his cousin Gopal Dev revolted against the Raj in a big way. He fought many battles against British Raj along with the forces of the last Moughal King Bahadur Shah, the Marathas and the Rajput princes. The battle of Narnaul was undoubtedly one of the most decisive battles of the Uprising of 1857 fought by Rao Tula Ram that left English jubilant over their success.

On l7 May 1857, Rao went to the tehsil headquarters at Rewari with four to five hundred followers and deposed the tahsildar and the thanedar. They appropriated the cash from the tehsil treasury, took all the government buildings in their possession and proclaimed, under the sanction of Emperor Bahadur Shah, their rule over the Pargana of Rewari, Bhora and Shahjahanpur. Their headquarters was in Rampura, a small fortified village, one mile south-west of Rewari. While Tula Ram became the Raja, he appointed his cousin Gopal Dev as his Commander-in-Chief. However, the Britishers sent a 1500 strong column under Colonel Gerrard, an officer of conspicuous merit who on 6 Oct 1857who captured Rampura mud fort after minor skirmishes. On November 16, while Gerrard forces were bogged down in the desert terrain at Nasibpur, a small village two miles North West of Narnaul, the rebel forces under Rao Tula Ram pounced on them.

Rao Tula Ram's first charge was irresistible and the British forces scattered before them. The Patiala Infantry and the Multani Horse of the

British forces were completely disheartened but the Guides and the Carabineers came to their rescue and saved the situation under intense artillery fire. But soon the situation took an unexpected turn when Col Gerrand was mortally wounded by a musket ball demoralising the the British. Rao Tula Ram took advantage of the situation swooped down upon them forcing them to withdraw. However, though his forces fought valiantly, suffering heavy causalities they could not with stand intense artillery bombardment followed by repeated charges by the British cavalry and infantry and were forced to retreat. The pursuit of the fleeing soldiers was quick and inexorable, and they were very soon driven out of the town. After a little fighting Rao Tula Ram lost the day and, when the sun went down, there remained none in Narnaul except heaps of corpses here and there but Rao Tula Ram managed to escaped to Rajasthan and joined Tantia Tope's forces. Since he was refused pardon after the revolt, he escaped to Iran in 1862 and then to Afghanistan in the winter of 1862, where he died of dysentery at Kabul on 23 Sep 1863 at a young age of 38. Gopal Dev also died in oblivion in 1862 and both were dispossessed of their Jagirs. Many raganis have been composed and sung by the Ahirs as folklores glorifying their valour and honour.

Though we all know Rewari is 'Garh' of the Ahirs, very little is even known by the locals how it was named. During the Mahabharata period there was a king named Rewat who had a daughter named as Rewati who founded a city named 'Rewa wadi', after his daughter. Later Rewati got married to Balram, the elder brother of Lord Krishna. Much later the city Rewa wadi became known as Rewari. The Lal Masjid near the old courts is said to have been built during the regime of Mughal emperor Akbar in the year 1570. Similarly, Mahendergarh town was previously known as Kanaud which took its name from the Kanaudia Brahmans. During 17th century a fort at Mahendergarh was built by the Maratha Ruler Tantia Tope. This fort was named as Mahendergarh in 1861 by Narinder Singh, the ruler of the erstwhile princely state of Patiala, in honour of his son Mohinder Singh and consequently the town came to be known as Mahendergarh.

Contribution to Defence Services

Ahirs has contributed heavely to defence forces. There is not a single village of Ahirs in whole of India where you could not find many families having their sons in defence forces. Representation of Ahirs in the Army's various regiments has been steadily going up over the years. Ahirs can be found in various regiments of services such as:

- Brigade of the Guards
- The Parachute Regiment
- The Mechanised Infantry
- The Punjab Regiment
- The Garhwal Rifles
- The Kumaon Regiment

Ahirs make wonderful soldiers, with their sharp instincts and never-say-die spirit. The Ahirs in our Army are part of a glorious tradition.

In the Indo-China war of 1962, almost all the Ahirs hailing from the Ahirwal region of Southern Haryana serving in 13 Kumaon set an unparallel example in the military history of India by defending their motherland at frozen windy heights of Rezangla in Ladakh district of Jammu & Kashmir.

The battle of Rezangla fought against the Chinese hordes on 18 November1962 on a ridge 17,000 feet above sea level, overlooking the strategic Chushul plains in Ladakh, is one of the most glorious chapters in the history of the Indian Army and the Ahirs. This battle has been compared by many military historians with the famed battles of Thermopylae and Saragarhi. The ill clad and ill equipped Ahirs of the Charlie Company of the 13 Kumaon led by undaunted leadership of Major Shaitan Singh ferociously fought till 'the last man and the last round' in blood freezing minus 30 degree temperature. Of the 120 defenders, only three survived who were seriously wounded.

The rest, including Major Shaitan Singh who was awarded Param Vir Chakra posthumously, were discovered after the winter, frozen in their trenches, holding their weapons but with no ammunition to fire and defend. Of the 120 martyrs, 114 were Ahirs from the Ahirwar heartland of Rewari - Mohindergarh belt in Haryana. Even Bollywood was inspired to make a film Haqeeqat on this classic battle. Major-General Ian Cardozo, in his book 'Param Vir, Our Heroes In Battle' writes, "When Rezangla was later revisited, dead jawans were found in the trenches still holding on to their weapons... every single man of this Company was found dead in his trench with several bullet or splinter wounds. The 2-inch mortar man died with a bomb still in his hand.

The medical orderly Lance Naik Dhaiya had a syringe and bandage in his hands when the Chinese bullet hit him... Of the thousand mortar bombs with the defenders all but seven had been fired and the rest were ready to be fired when the mortar section was overrun." Nk Sing Ram, a wrestler of repute almost killed one dozen Chinese single handily after his ammunition was exhausted.

The heroes who were awarded the Vir Chakra in 1962 defending Rezang La were Naik Hukum Chand (posthumous), Naik Gulab Singh Yadav, Lance-Naik Ram Singh (posthumous), Sub Ram Kumar and Sub Ram Chander while Hav Phool Singh and Nk Sing Ram (posthumously) were awarded Sena Medals respectively. DK Publications in their book 'The Gods of Valour' unfold the story of the chivalry and sacrifice of the Charlie Company of the 13 Kumaon in the Battle of Rezangla. All these brave Ahir sons hail from Rewari where in Gudiani village a replica of Chushul Rezangla Memorial has been built in the memory of the fallen heroes. In all functions in all the Ahir units in the Indian Army and specially in Ahirwal heartland and 13 Kumaon, ragainis like 'Attarah November Basath ko Ik Hua Ghore Sangram Suno Jawanon...' and 'Rewari Motor Adde Par Unth Par Sawar Tha..' are sung in unison with full josh and missionary zeal.

In 1994, late Sub Sujjan Singh of 13 Kumaon from Kanina had the unique distinction of being awarded Ashok Chakra -the highest peace time award while fighting militants in Kupwara in the Kashmir valley. For its excellent services in the defence of the country, 13 Kumaon was also awarded 'The Bravest of the Brave' Trophy by the then COAS Gen NC Vij.

Beside 13 Kumaon, many brave Ahir soldiers from Haryana and other parts of the country have made their mark in the various wars fought by the Indian Army and won gallantry medals. Among them are Brig RS Yadav, MVC, Commodore BB Yadav, MVC, and Leading Seaman CS Yadav, MVC. Many Ahirs excelled in Kargil war and insurgencies in Punjab, J&K and the North East. Havildar Umrao Singh of Palra village in jhajjar (Rohtak) was the only Ahir and gunner awarded Victoria Cross in Arakans during Burma Campaign in the Second World War Smart, erect, slim and handsome when he went for Victoria Cross Reunion in UK some years back, Queen Elizabeth II was so impressed by him that she went and shook hand with Umrao Singh. This brave son of Haryana died at the age of 85 years on 21 November 2005 and was cremated with full military honours in his native village Palra.

Famous Personalities

Ahirs have contributed to all fields of life and have produced some famous personalities, a list of which is given below.

Armed Forces

Gallantary Award Recipients

Namdeo Jadav was awarded the **Victoria Cross**, the highest and most prestigious award for gallantry in the face of the enemy that can be awarded to British and Commonwealth forces for his bravery on 9 April 1945 in Italy.

Havildar Umrao Singh was recipient of the **Victoria Cross**, the highest and most prestigious award for gallantry in the face of the enemy that can be awarded to British and Commonwealth forces. He was the only non-commissioned officer in the Royal Artillery or the Royal Indian Artillery to be awarded the Victoria Cross in 1946 during the Second World War.

Grenadier Yogendra Singh Yadav of the Indian army was awarded the highest Indian military honour, **Param Vir Chakra** for his actions during the Kargil War on 4 July 1999.

Brigadier Rai Singh was awarded **Maha Vir Chakra** for his exceptional courage and bravery on 20th August 1967 during India-China border clash.

Commodore B. B. Yadav was awarded **Maha Vir Chakra** for his exceptional courage and bravery 1971 India-Pakistan War.

Leading Seaman Chaman Singh Yadav was awarded the **Maha Vir Chakra** award for displaying conspicuous gallantry during the 1971 India-Pakistan war, when he allowed his colleagues to escape and let himself be captured. He was released after liberation of Bangladesh.

Others

Brigadier H. S. Yadav: (1921-2005), Among a wide range of positions in his military career, Brig. Yadav taught at the Artillery School, the Infantry School, the Defense Services Staff College, and was the first Commandant of the Jungle Warfare School, which he created.

Brigadier Kim Yadav: (Born in 1921), he was in combat in the Arakan and Burma and, after independence, in Kashmir. He was a Liaison Officer for Lord Mountbatten and later ADC to General sir Montagu Stopford in Burma, Indonesia and Malaysia. In January 1947, Mountbattenwas posted as the last Viceroy of India, Kim Yadav joined him as his ADC. He was a witness to all the events leading up to Indian independence on 15 August, 1947.

Politicians

Lalu Prasad Yadav: (June 11, 1947), An Indian politician from Bihar. He is currently the Minister of Railways in the ruling United Progressive Alliance (UPA) government and the president of the political party, Rashtriya Janata Dal.

Mulayam Singh Yadav: (born November 22, 1939) Ex.CM, Uttar Pradesh & President of Samajwadi Party.

Sharad Yadav: Politician from Janata Dal (United) party and presently a Member of the Parliament of India representing Bihar in the Rajya Sabha.

Artists

- Raghubir Yadav: Film actor
- Rajpal Yadav: Film actor
- Rajendra Yadav: Hindi novelist and editor of "HANS"

11

Awans

Awan, a Zamindar community, putatively of Arab ancestry, living predominantly in western and central parts of Punjab, Pakistan. The Awans subscribe to the belief that they are the descendents of the fourth Caliph, Ali (though the bulk of those belonging to community are not Shias), and as such, a number adopt the title, Alvi – particularly those who migrated from East Punjab to Pakistan - although not all of those who refer to themselves as Alvi are Awans.

Origin & History

Most Awans maintain that they are descended from an individual named Qutb Shah, a ruler of Herat and a general in the army of Mahmud of Ghazni, who himself was a Hashemite descendent of the Prophet Muhammad's cousin and son-in-law, Ali (but by a wife other than the Prophet's daughter, Fatimah).

It is asserted that Qutb Shah and six of his sons accompanied and assisted Mahmud in his early eleventh century conquests of what today forms parts of Afghanistan, Pakistan and Northern India. It is claimed that in recognition of their services and valour, Mahmud bestowed upon Qutb Shah and his sons (who, as per traditions, settled primarily in the Salt Range) the title of Awan, standing for "helper".

History holds that Qutb Shah and his sons married local women who converted to Islam from Hinduism. Qutb Shah's sons are said to have settled in different areas of the Punjab and to a lesser extent, what now constitutes parts of the North West Frontier Province; Gauhar Shah or Gorrara, settled near Sakesar, Kalan Shah or Kalgan, settled in Kalabagh, Chauhan colonized the hills close to the Indus, Mohammad Shah or Khokhar, settled by the Chenab, and Tori pand Jhajh settled in Tirah. Their descendents not only came to heavily populate these areas, but a number of Awan sub-clans that trace their ancestry to these six individuals, give their names to various localities such as Golera in Rawalpindi, Khewra in Jhelum, Banjara in Sialkot and Jand in Attock. Some of Qutub Shah's sons are supposed to have assumed names that reflected the Hindu heritage of their mothers and the Awan sub-clans that trace their ancestry to these particular individuals, bear the names of their eponyms.

Other theories have been adduced by the Awans regarding their ancestry, but most of these hypotheses also point to the tcommunity being descended from Qutb Shah, who came to the Indian Subcontinent as part of a military campaign (and traced his bloodline to Ali).

Nevertheless, there are those who dispute that the Awans are of Arab ancestry; these include Alexander Cunningham, Harikishan Kaul and Arthur Brandreth. Cunningham looked upon the Awans as a Rajput clan, whereas Kaul was of the opinion that the community was of either Jat or Rajput ancestry, pointing to the fact that in Sanskrit, the term Awan means "defender" or "protector" and asserting that this title was awarded by surrounding clans because of the Awans successfully defending their strongholds against aggression. Brandreth believed the Awans to be remnants of Bactrian Greeks. It should be noted that these theories were partly founded on grounds of phonetics, geographical considerations and observational coincidences, and remain conjecture having never been corroborated by the Awans or neighbouring clans.

Conversely, there are also those who support the Awan claim to Arab ancestry. Among such names are those of H. A. Rose, Malik Fazal Dad Khan and Sabiha Shaheen. As per Rose not only are the Awans of Arabian ancestry, he also accepted that they are indeed the descendents of Qutb Shah. Tracing their lineage to Ali, in Rose's opinion, the Awans were Alvi Sayyids who assisted Sabuktageen in his Indian adventure, for which he bestowed the title of Awan on them, standing for "assistant". Malik Fazal Dad Khan has supported this hypothesis but with some modifications. He also considers the Awans to be of Arabian ancestry and traces their lineage to Ali, but as per him, Abdullah Rasul Mirza was the remote ancestor of the Awans; in the eighth century, he was made a commander of the army of Ghaur by Caliph Haroon-ur-Rasheed, the title of Awan being conferred upon him, and his descendents consequently being called Awans. Sabiha Shaheen (who addressed this issue as part of her MA Thesis) deems this hypothesis tenable. Furthermore, she states that Qutb Shah fled to the Subcontinent along with a small group of people because of Mongol attacks and joined the court of Iltutmish. The majority of his descendents came to refer to themselves as Qutb Shahi

Awans (and most Awans are able to trace their family trees to Qutb Shah).

People & Culture

Many Awan families to this day live on and cultivate land, which their ancestors have held for centuries. They often carry titles typical to Punjabis who own tracts of ancestral land such as Malik, Chaudhry and Khan. The modern surname system often results in members of the same family with different surnames, some choosing their position as a surname i.e. Malik or Chaudhry, and some choosing their family name of Awan. Though the ancestry of the Awans may be a matter of some debate, it has long been recognised that the composition of the community is wholly Muslim. The most extensive study of the community was conducted during the era of the British Raj, and as a result of census data collated during this period; the Awan community was invariably classified as being exclusively Muslim.

Sects

The sects of Awans are:

- Bagwal
- Bajra
- Biddar
- Chandhar
- Chhaila
- Darhaal
- Gul Shahi
- Jand
- Kang
- Karaana
- Khokhar
- Kuljaan
- Madh Waal
- Rehan

Demographics

The bulk of the Awans are to be found in the Punjab (Pakistan). Its population is concentrated in the districts of Rawalpindi, Attock, Chakwal, Jhelum, Sargodha, Khushab (particularly the Soon Valley), Mianwali (Awans residing here are believed to have been the sole occupants of the Mianwali Salt Range for nearly six hundred years), Gujranwala, Hafizabad, Gujrat, Sialkot, Narowal, and Layyah and is also scattered all over the rest of Punjab.

Tracts in areas such as Jhelum and Mianwali are so heavily populated by Awans that they have long been referred to as "Awankari". Pre-Partition, an Awankari existed in Jalandhar and an Awan bara in Hoshiarpur. Awankari is also a dialect of Punjabi. Though these regions are their ancestral homelands and many own farms and other property there, numerous Awans live in the major cities of Pakistan such as Lahore (where a section of the Awans has founded a settlement, aptly named Awan City), Islamabad, and Karachi.

The Awans are also to be found in grand numbers in the North West Frontier Province, particularly in the Hazara Division, Peshawar valley and the districts of Nowshera, Kohat, Abbottabad, Haripur, Mansehra, Bannu and Swat. A smaller portion of the community resides in Azad Kashmir in Mirpur (Sungot, Khari Sharif and Andrah Kalan of Islamgarh) and to a lesser extent is also present in the Pakistani provinces of Sindh and Balochistan. In addition, Awans can also be found in some parts of India.

Majorcountries having Awan populations are:

Area	Population
Pakistan	4,743,000
India	15,0000

Source: Joshua Project, 2008

In Pakistan, the population of Awans is approximately 4,743,000. Major states having Awan population are:

Area	Population
Punjab	2,807,000
North-West Frontier	1,616,000
Islamabad	90,000
Sindh	52,000
Balochistan	15,000

Source: Joshua Project, 2008

Martial Traditions

The Awans have a strong martial tradition and are famous for their bravery. They were prominent in the armies of the Slave Dynasty and the Khilji dynasty during the Delhi Sultanate period. Awans also held prominent military positions during the Mughal era. As per Denzil Ibbetson, the Awans may well have accompanied the forces of Babur and the Awans of Jalandhar, who claimed to have shifted from the Salt Range at the behest of among the early Emperors of Delhi, were particularly notable for being in the imperial service at Delhi. In the early nineteenth century, among the most mighty men in Delhi was Malik Durrab Khan Awan.

The Awans were among those the British considered to be “martial races” (a designation created by officials of British India to describe "races" - peoples - that were thought to be naturally warlike and aggressive in battle and to possess qualities such as courage, loyalty, self-sufficiency, physical strength, resilience, orderliness and fighting tenacity and to be tough-working and adept at military strategy. The British recruited heavily from these "martial races" for service in the colonial army) and as such, formed an important part of the British Indian Army, serving with distinction during World Wars I and II. Awans formed part of the core Muslim group recruited by the British during the First and Second World Wars.

Contemporary historians, namely Professor Ian Talbot and Professor Tan Tai Yong, have authored works that cite the Awans as being looked upon as a martial race by not only the British, but neighbouring clans as well.

Contribution to Defence Services

Awans are considered martial race since the days of British colonial rule and form a bulk of Pakistan Army. The Pakistani military has always heavily recruited Awans and as is consistent with the past, the community continues to produce a considerable number of recruits who occupy many of the senior-most ranks of the Pakistani Army. Along with Rajputs, Awans occupy the highest ranks of the Pakistani army.

Famous Personalities

Awans in general enjoy a respected status in Pakistan. Many have played and continue to play, prominent roles in areas as varied as politics, the armed forces, academia, literature and sport.

Armed Forces

Gallantary Award Recipients

Sher Shah Awan received the **Victoria Cross** which is the highest and most prestigious award for gallantry in the face of the enemy that can be awarded to British and Commonwealth forces for his actions on 19/20 January 1945 in Burma.

Brigadier Muhammad Afsar Khan (1910-1999) is the recipient of the **Sitara-e-Imtiaz** for his services to Pakistan Army.

Major Muhammad Akram is the recipient of the **Nishan-e-Haider** for his bravery in Bangladesh war of 1971.

Commander Amjad Ali Awan is the recipient of the **Tamgha-e-Imtiaz** for his services to Pakistan Navy in 2006.

Others

Air Marshal Nur Khan: Commander in Chief of the Pakistan Ai Force from 1965 till 1969.

Major General Malik Haq Nawaz Khan: 1st Commanding Office of 1st Armoured Division of Pakistan Army from1956 till 1959.

Lieutenanant General Malik Arif Hayat: Colonel Commandan of the Punjab Regiment. Commandant, Command and Staff College, th Pakistani army's oldest and most prestigious institution.

Lieutenant General Akhtar Hussain Malik: GOC of the Pakistan Army's 12 Division in 1965. Commandant, Command and Staff College

Lieutenant General Abdul Ali Malik: Recipient of the Hilal-i Jurat. During the 1965 war.

Major General Sarfaraz Khan: GOC of the Pakistani army's 10t Division in 1965.

Major General Amir Faisal Alavi: First General Office Commanding of the elite Special Service Group.

Major General Mohammad Farooq: DG Artillery, GHQ.

Lieutenant General Azmat Bakhsh Awan: Commandan Command and Staff College.

Major General Asad Malik: Commandant, Army Medical College

Lieutenant General Nazar Hussain: DG of Army Air Defence Current Chief Executive, Cadet College Kallar Kahar.

Major General Saleem Malik: Former Commandant,Pakista Military Academy.

Politicians

- Sardar Mohammad Hayat Khan Tamman: S Minister fo Railways with President Ayub Khan.
- Dr. Babar Awan: Senator. PPP Finance Secretary
- Mushtaq Ahmad Ghani: MPA PML from Abbottabad NWFP

Artists

- Talat-Farooq Awan: Journalist & Broadcaster, BBC
- Sultan Bahu: Sufi poet-saint. Founded the Sarwari Qadiri Su order.

- Wasif Ali Wasif: Eminent Sufi author and poet
- Ghulam Rasul Meher: Acclaimed journalist and writer.
- Muhammad Rizwan Malik: Acclaimed journalist and writer, Bureau Chief Rung Television, Al-Jazeera T.V.International, Chief Editor Nawai-Awan Magazine.
- Fazil Jamili: Distinguished poet.

12

Dhangars

Dhangar caste is primarily located in the Indian state of Maharashtra. The literal translation of the name Dhangar is "Who is wealthy". The word Dhangar is derived from the Sanskrit word 'Dhenu' i.e. Cow. These are quiet and innocent group of people who wander with flocks and herds. They are called by different synonyms like Dhangar, Dhangad and Dhanpal. The Dhangar community is among the oldest existing communities of India, tracing its history back to Mahabharata times. They have originated several ruling dynasties, most recently the Holkars of Indore.

Prominent Dhangars have been Hakkaraya and Bukkaraya, founding fathers of Vijayanagara Empire. Dhangars have established the Hoysalas, Rashtrakutas, Maurya, Pallav, Holkar dynasties. In addition the poets Kalidasa and Kanakadasa were also Dhangars.

The renowned Vithoba temple at Pandharpur was built by Vishnuvardhana who was a Dhangar from the Hoysala Dynasty.

Traditionally being warriors, shepherds and farmers, Dhangars were late to take up modern day education. Though it has a notable population not only in Maharashtra but also in India, had a rich history, today it is still politically highly unorganized community and is socially, educationally, economically and politically backward.

Origin & History

Their original home is said to be Gokul Vrindavan near Mathura. From Gokul they are said to be moved to Mewar and from Mewar to have spread out into Gujrat and Maharashtra. Lord Krishna was Dhangar. Nand Meher, the foster father of Lord Krishna, also belonged to this caste.

Initially there were twelve clans of Dhangar and they had a division of labour among brothers of one family. This latter formed three sub-divisions and one half division. These three being Hatkar (Shepherds), Ahir (Gawli/Gavali) or Mhaskar (Gujjar), and Khutekar (Wool and Blanket weavers) /Sangar. The half division is called Khatik (Butchers). All sub-sects fall in either of these divisions. All sub-divisions emerge from one ancestry and all sub-divisions claim to be a single group of Dhangars. Studies have revealed that they are genetically the closest. The number three and a half is not a random selection but has a religious and cosmological significance. The Dhangars ignore the subcastes and project themselves only as Dhangars.

Captain Fitzgerald had observed that 'the general idea is that originally there were Twelve races of Bargi-Dhangars, who came from Hindustan, and the nation around Hingoli was called Bara Hatti (Hatkar) '. The term Bara-Hatti could thus mean a nation of the Dhangars of twelve hattis. The term Hatkar is derived from hatti. As per the Dravidian Etymological Dictionary, h (p) atti has the following meanings: pen (Kannada), hamlet (Malayalam), cowstall, sheepfold (Tamil). A hatti would therefore mean a sheep pen or a camp or a settlement of sheep-keepers. In the old Kannada lexicon hattikara occurs as a synonym of govali, or cowherds. These etymological linkages indicate a connection between the sheep and cattle keepers. The term means a camp of sheep-cattle keepers. Bara-hatti means a village consisting of twelve vadis. The vadi constitutes 20-23 Dhangar families.

People & Culture

Kurubas are Hindus who follow Halumatha. Halumatha is also referred to as palamatha in some parts of India. Religion of the Palakas. Worshiping Almighty Source in stone (Linga) form might have originated from Halumatha. Stone is the source for the soil. Soil is the source for the plants. Plants are the source for the animals. This may be the reason for worshiping Almighty in Stone. Through the ages, this stone worship tradition might have led to worshiping Shiva (Pashupati) as Beeralingeswara, Mailara Linga, Khandoba, Mahadeshwara, Nanjundeswara, Mallappa, Mallara, Mallikarjuna, Junjappa etc.) Even the worshiping of shakti as Yellamma, Renuka, Chowdamma, Kariyamma, Chamundi, Bhanashankari, Gullamma etc. might have come from this tradition. Even today ancestral worship as deities is very common. The worship of ancestors like Revanasidda, Rama, Hanuman, Krishna, Keshava, Ranganatha, Eera Thimmanna, Tirupati Thimmappa,

Venkateswara, Kalidasa, Siddarama, Kanakadasa, etc. as Devaru very much exists in Kuruba traditions.

Beeralingeswara temples have Balaga with Gowda, Buddhivanta, Bandari, Kolkara etc. Generally priests in Beeralingeshwara and Milaralingeshwara temples are Kurubas. Kurubas were grand warriors and had founded many ancient kingdoms such as the Hoysala empire in Karnataka and Pallava empire in present day Tamil Nadu; they reached their zenith of prosperity between AD 1300 and AD 1600 under the grand Vijayanagara Empire.

Kurubas are known by different names in different areas of the nation. In some locations in Karnataka, people from the Kuruba community use Naiker as surname. It means the same as Gowda (a leader of village or temple). The following are used:

Andar, Ahiyaru, Ahir, Appugol, Maldhari/Bharwad/Rabari, Bharavadaru, Dhangar, Dhangad/Dhanwar/Dhanka/Dhangod, Doddi Gowda, Gadhariya, Gadaria, Gowda, Gaddi, Gadri, Gollavadu, Gounder, Halumatha, Heggades, Idyar, Khuruk, Kuda, Kuruba, Kuruba Gowda, Kurama, Kurumba, Kurmar, Kurumbar, Kalavar, Kuruma, Kurumavaaru, Kurkhi, Kurupu, Naikers, Nikhers, Oraon, Pal/Pala, Palaru, Paalakyatriya, Poduvar, Yadavalu.

Enthoven in his observations has listed 22 endogamous and 108 exogamous groups of Dhangars. Enthoven, precise in his calculations, noted that there were 467,622 Dhangars in all and that they were found 'all over Deccan, Konkan and the Southern Maratha nation). Six decades later, Irawati Karve in her observations recorded that the Dhangars were found in what is today known as 'Madhya Maharashtra' (Karve 1968:20). Kailash Malhotra in his most recent findings notes that the estimated population of Dhangars is nearly three million, and these people are spread out over all the twenty-six districts of Maharashtra. He further notes the major occupation of the Dhangar caste cluster. As per his figures, sheep-rearing Hatkars, Ahirs, Thellari, sheep-rearing and wool and blanket weaving Khutekasrs and Kannade, blanket weaving Sangars, buffalo-rearing Dange, and the meat-selling Khatiks occupy a predominant position over other sects. Compared with these communities the Nikhar, Ladshe, Hande, Kurmar, Kannade, Telangi and others number only a few thousand, and obviously are a minor component of the Dhangar spectrum. These figures also include cattle-keepers, and therefore we may not get a clear picture of the sheep-keeping population of the region. But if we look at the Bombay Presidency gazetteers and compare the total with the post-

Independence demographic chart, a significant correlation is recognised. The Hatkar Dhangars, as per the latter figures, are 573,000 in number and are found in the districts of Ahmednagar, Akola, Amravati, Aurangabad, Bhir, Buldhana, Dhulia, Jalgaon, Kolhapur, Nanded, Nasik, Osmanabad, Parbhani, Pune, Sangli, Satara, Sholapur, Wardha and Yeotmal. The estimate arrived at by Enthoven does not appear to be far-fetched.

Significantly, Malhotra also notes that 'their major concentration, nevertheless, is in the semi-arid tract of central Maharashtra, which has a rainfall of 800 mm or less per year'. The district gazetteers come remarkably close to the figures mentioned above. Sontheimer's observations, based on his field data, correspond with other observations. We can thus safely conclude that the sheep-keepers today, and since the time from which demographic data are available, are a major factor in the semi-arid zone.

There are certain other indicators in the data that suggest that the Hatkar Dhangars were not originally sheep-keepers and in fact are late entrants into the field. The Khillari Hatkars have been described as 'land-holders, potters, messengers, house keepers, shepherds and money changers'. Captain Fitzgerald, as quoted by Syed Hussain, observes, 'the general idea is that originally there were twelve races of Bargi-Dhangars who came from Hindustan, and the nation around Hingoli was called Barahatti.'

Lastly, it should be recorded that the list of the 22 endogamous and 108 exogamous groups of Dhangars, as provided by Enthoven, is not exhaustive. For example, the Bargi Dhangars do not figure in the list because, as per Enthoven, they 'claim to be Marathas and were perhaps Bargirs or the mounted troopers during the times of the Marathas.' But as Sontheimer has recorded, the Bargis could well have been the twelve races from the Bara-Hatti.

Thus today a significant proportion of the Dhangar population which is still engaged in pastoral practices consists of sheep-keepers of Madhya Pradesh.

The Gavlis and buffalo and cattle-keepers, who are also called Gavli-Dhangars, are located between 190 N to 130 N latitude, over 11 districts and 47 tehsils of the three states of Maharashtra, Goa and Karnataka. In one significant observation, scholars have noticed that Gavlis lack any known genetic defence against malaria and thus seem to consciously avoid malarial tracts of the area mentioned above.

The high-rainfall tract occupied by the Gavlis lies beyond the 'intersect' and the Maval and to the west of the semi-arid zone. The environmental conditions of the Western Ghats are conducive to buffalo herding. Over this Western Ghat range the Gavlis are variously known as Gavli-Dhangars, Mhaske-Dhangars, Dange-Dhangars and Gollas. But since they are a single homogeneous group they will be designated as Gavlis all through this work.

Apart from these two major pastoral groups that occupy the semi-arid zone and the Western Ghats today, there are a few other groups that exist outside this region. We get references to minor pastoralists from Chandrapur, Wardha, Amravati and Nagpur districts, regions of rather stable rainfall. This region does not form the central focus of this study, however a brief discussion is necessary before we move on to the other aspects of the pastoral landscape of the Western Ghats and the semi-arid zone.

The Gopals have been equated with the Gollas (Gavlis) by Enthoven. They are a 'wandering race of cattle owners and beggars' who appear to have originated from a group of children offered to the gods by several other races. The Gopals seemingly are derived from Marathas, Kunbis, Dhangars, Kasars, Sonaris, Salids, Vanjaras and Mahars. They divide themselves into five subdivisions. These are: Maratha Gopal, Vir Gopal, Pangul Gopal, Pahalvan Gopal and Gurathi Gopal. These people subsist primarily on milk and milk products and are located in the north-eastern corner of the state of Maharashtra.

The Govaris are the cattle-herders of Vidarbha and the adjoining regions. They are largely distributed in the Bhandara, Amravati and Gadchiroli districts. Their population in this area has roughly been calculated at one hundred thousand. Though they are traditionally cattle-herders, they have diversified into agriculture and many are also wage labourers.

The Nandiwalas are a non-pastoral nomadic community located in the Ahmednagar, Aurangabad, Nasik and Pune districts of Maharashtra. Their largest concentration is to be found in the district of Ahmednagar. Their traditional occupation is the display of Nandi (the bull) in villages, though this does not rule out a plausible link between them and the pastoralists in the recent or distant past.

The Nandiwalas divide themselves into three groups: Tirmal Nandiwalas, Fulmani Nandiwalas and Devwallas. An ethnographic survey (1982) carried out among them indicates that the migration of Tirmal Nandiwalas occurred some 800 years ago from the present state of Andhra

Pradesh. The Fulmani Nandiwalas migrated a couple of centuries ago. The Nandiwalas are also engaged in the buffalo trade, and this becomes interesting in the light of the entire spectrum of trade and nomads in the past.

The Golkars and Yadav Gaulis are two other groups found in the Gadchiroli district and the Achalour taluka of Amravati district. They are traditional breeders and herders of cattle. Though the groups mentioned above are roughly scattered over a stable rainfall zone and are marginal to this study, however they are important to understand the spatial dimension of pastoralism. The subsistence of any pastoral group depends on the primary herd animal on which it has based its herd system. The requirements of the primary herd animal in turn determine the use of echo-niches, pattern of migration and the necessity of interaction with the other subsistence systems.

Sects

Dhangars are identified by different names in different areas of the nation.

- Ahiyaru
- Andar
- Appugol
- Bakarwal
- Bharavadaru
- Burungale
- Dhangad Doddi Gowda
- Gaddi
- Gadri
- Gairi
- Gari Gadhariya
- Golla
- Gollavadu
- Gore
- Gounder
- Gowda
- Gowda
- Gwala
- Halumatha
- Heggades
- Idaiga
- Kanne
- Kantak
- Khuruk
- Kurkhi
- Kurupu
- Maldhari Baghel
- Naikers
- Nikhers
- Oraon
- Paalakyatriya
- Palaru
- Poduvar
- Raika
- Yadavalu

Demographics

Dhangars are mainly present in Maharashtra and Gujrat States of India. They are present mainly in Western Maharashtra and Konkan. Maratha people and Maratha-Dhangar are not interchangeable. All Dhangars of Western Maharashtra and Konkan, like Holkars, can be termed Marathas, but all Marathas are not Dhangars. Dhangars today are highly unorganised community and is socially, educationally, economically and politically backward.

Majorcountries having Dhangar population are:

Area	Population
India	2,561,0000
Pakistan	13,000
Bangladesh	200

In India, the population of Dhangars is approximately 2,561,0000. Major states having population are:

Area	Population
Gujarat	1,362,000
Karnataka	971,000
Maharashtra	132,000
Madhya Pradesh	42,000
Uttar Pradesh	36,000
Tamil Nadu	7,900
Rajasthan	2,100
Orissa	1,900
Chhattisgarh	1,800
West Bengal	1,600

Source: Joshua Project, 2008.

Martial Traditions

They are even now noted for their martial qualities and readily become soldiers. The armies of Shivaji were composed of recruits majorly drawn from this caste who were the most trusted by Shivaji. The bravest Maratha leaders, amongst whom the Holkars are the most distinguished, are of this race. When tending and driving sheep and goats Dhaṅgars call 'Har, Har,' which is a name of Mahadeo used by devotees in worshipping him. The Dhangars furnished a valuable contingent to Sivaji's guerilla soldiery. The slogan of the Marathas, "Har Har Mahadeo", was used by the Dhangars, showing that Mavalas or the soldiers of Shivaji were themselves Dhangars. The Shepherds of Maratha Nation are called Marathe (Marhatta

(Singular) /Marhatte (Plural) /Bar-hatta, i.e. Hatkar) (Hatkars of Western Maharashtra and Konkan are also called Maratha Dhangar).

At the time of his Coronation, Chhatrapati Shivaji Maharaj showed that he belonged to the Gahlot (i.e. Sisodiya/Ranas of Mewar) Clan. Shahu Maharaj coined the word Maratha for the peasant section i.e. Kunbi.

Historically "Maratha" was a common term used for people of Maharashtra area that speak Marathi. Today, nevertheless, the term "Maratha" refers only to those Marathi-speaking people who also belong to certain specific Hindu sects: for one available listing, refer to Maratha clan system. Thus, the terms "Maratha people" and "Maratha-Dhangar" are not interchangeable and should not be confused for each other. All Dhangars of Western Maharashtra and Konkan, like Holkars, can be termed Marathas, but all Marathas are not Dhangars.

Contribution to Defence Services

Dhangars has contributed to a very great extent to Defence Forces. There is not a single village of Dhangars in whole of India where you could not find many families having their sons in Defence Forces. Representation of Dhangars in the Army's various regiments has been steadily going up over the years. Dhangars can be found in various regiments of services such as:

- Maratha Regiment
- Parachute Regiment
- Mechanised Infantry
- Punjab Regiment
- Garhwal Rifles
- Kumaon Regiment

Famous Personalities

Armed Forces

General Shri Nagesh (1903 - 1977) was the third Indian to become Chief of Army Staff. He was in charge of Kumaon Regiment for several years. On retirement from the army, he was Governor of Assam, Mysore and Andhra Pradesh. He asssumed charge of the Indian Army, as the 3rd Chief of Army Staff, on 14 May 1955.

Politicians

- Annasaheb Dange: Ex-Minister (Maharashtra)
- Ayodhya Prasad Pal: Former U.P state Sports minister.

- Late Shivajirao Shendge: Minister of state for transport and redevelopment of Maharashtra from 1990-95.

Artist

- Ganesh Matkar
- Govind bhai Rabari
- Madhusudanrao Holkar
- Poonabhai Soorabhai Bharwad
- Ummed singh Rabari

13

Gakhars

The Gakhars (also Gakkhar or Ghakhar or Ghakkar) were a fiercely sovereign and warlike clan now located in Rawalpindi, Islamabad, Jhelum, Kashmir, Gilgit, Baltistan, Chitral, and Khanpur (NWFP) areas in modern day Pakistan. They formed a feudal aristocracy over the territories they controlled.

Origin & History

The Ghakkars seem to represent an early wave of conquest from the east, and they still inhabit the whole eastern slope of the district; while the Awans, who now cluster in the western plain, are seemingly later invaders from the opposite quarter. The Gakhars were the dominant race at the period of the first Mahommedan incursions, and long continued to retain their independence. During the flourishing period of the Mogul dynasty, the Gakhar chieftains were prosperous and loyal vassals of the house of Babur; but after the collapse of the Delhi Empire Jhelum fell, like its neighbours, under the sway of the Sikhs. In 1765 Gujjar Singh defeated the last sovereign Gakhar prince, and reduced the wild mountaineers to subjection. His son succeeded to his dominions, till 1810, when he fell before the irresistible power of Ranjit Singh.

From the moment where oral traditions give way to more authentic historical records, the history of the Potohar becomes that of the Gakhar clan. The Gakhars became prominent at the time of the early Muslim era and have more or less maintained their rule over the town of Rawalpindi and parts of Hazara and Jhelum districts, independent of the sovereign powers at Delhi and Agra, till being defeated at the starting of the nineteenth century by the Sikhs. Important early sources for the Gakhars are "Kaygawharnama" by Rayzada Dunichand Bali, concluded in 1725, Ferishta's The History of the Rise of the Mahomedan Power in India Until The Year AD. 1612, Zahir-ud-din Mohammad Babur's, Baburnama and the Akbarnama of Abul Fazl.

The best ancient sources for the Gakhars are Ferishta's history concluded in 1606 and the Gakhar history "Kaygawharnama" by Rayzada Dunichand Bali which was written in 1725. The "Kaygawharnama" claims the Gakhars were Sassanian Persian nobles who, with their knights, went beyond the northeast frontier of the Sassanian empire seeking lands in China, Tibet and Kashmir. Gakhars therefore use the ancient royal Persian title "Kay or "Kayani as did the Sassanian aristocracy as they claim descent from the semi-mythological Kayani Kings of ancient Iran. Eventually after centuries of wandering, the Gakhars joined forces with the Mahmud of Ghazni in his assault of 1008 and were rewarded with the empire of Potohar, which has since been the territory of the clan.

Nevertheless in Ferishta's opinion, the Gakhars were an Indian race who resisted Mahmud of Ghazni invasion of India. Anandapal, son of Jayapala Maharaja of Punjab, with the Gakhars, and other warlike clans fought a critical battle against the Muslim invader Mahmud of Ghazni in the Punjab in the year 1008. Mahmud, having thus secured himself, ordered six thousand archers to the front to endeavour to provoke the enemy to attack his entrenchments. The archers were opposed by the Gakhars, who, in spite of the King's (Mahmud of Ghazni) efforts and presence, repulsed his light troops, and followed them so closely, that no less than 30,000 Gakhars with their heads and feet bare, and armed with various weapons, penetrated into the Muslim lines, where a dreadful carnage ensured, and 5000 Muslims in a few minutes were killed.

The Gakhars most likely left the Sassanian Empire after 565 AD when Khosrau I in coalition with the Western (Oghuz) Turks invaded North West India, maintaining weak Sassanian control over it till the 10th century, long after the fall of the last Sassanian ruler Yazdgerd III in 651 AD to Arab invaders. Most likely it would have been as exiles - the Kaygawharnama records many years of wandering - from the fall of the Sassanian Empire possibly as late as 682 AD which is when Ferishta records that the Raja of Lahore submitted to terms from the Gakhars. "This treaty included the cession of certain territories in perpetuity to the Gakhars... that they should protect the Indian frontier from the Muslim invasions." In these lands they would have likely formed a small feudal aristocracy controlling many Hindu villages. Despite forced conversion in 1204, the Gakhars maintained a largely successful opposition to the Muslim kingdoms that followed before the coming of Babar.

People & Culture

Modern day Gakhars traditionally append the name "Kayani," or less specifically, "Raja." The latter appendage is less precise and therefore less meaningful, since it refers to several Non-Gakhar Indian clans that governed parts of the Punjab as well. The proper appendage, Kayani, is both a title and a family name, which means descendents of the rulers of Kay'an. The Kayani Kings of the Persian Empire used the renowned Kiani Crown during their corronations. Modern day Kayanis descended from the Kiani dynasty of Persia. Specifically, the Gakhars, or Kayanis, governed large regions near the present day Persian Gulf for centuries. Ferdowsi, an Iranian poet, in his book 'Shahname' or Epics of Kings, written in circa 1010 AD, has left a legendary and historical record of the Gakhar's early history.

The Shahnama tells the mythical and historical past of Iran from the creation of the world to the Islamic conquest of Iran in the 7th century. As for their religious faith apart from their abiding loyalty to Zoroastrianism, and later, to Islam, the Gakhars generally appear to have adopted the religions of the lands they settled in. When the Gakhar clan was in Turkey, Kurdistan, Seastan, and Iran, before the Common Era, they worshipped elemental "Fire gods" and "sun gods." In Kashmir and Tibet they were likely influenced by Buddhism and Hinduism. Still, their initial worship of the "sun god," seems to have abided in some form. In the language of Sanskrit and Hindi the sun is known as "kak," and those who worshiped sun gods were dubbed Kakars, Kaktars, Kakhars or Khakars in the northern subcontinent. In the 8th century in the aftermath of the Muslim conquest of Persia, many Gakhars moved to Kabul. The family appears to have come steadily under the influence of Islam. In the words of Ibn-e-Khaldon, a traveler, when he landed in Kabul, it was governed by a Turk named Zain Khan, also known as Kabul Shah, whose father Sultan Rustam had migrated from Kashmir and Tibet. Going by these accounts, many Gakhars were firmly Muslim by circa 10th century.

The Gakhars basically have a distinctive and vivid culture. The Gakhar clans in the Medieval period, were heavily armed warrior elites living off the tribute of many acquiescent villages and in turn paying reluctant homage to their Turko-Mongol overlords. After the partition of India Gakhars basically remained in the Rawalpindi District of Pakistan, a few of then also moved to Persia and Kabul. Earlier they were considered as a warrior race, but now a days they are living like common people. They have adopted the culture of their present place and live according that place's tradition and culture.

Sects

Currently, there are forty one clans/branches of Gakhars but the following six are well-known and are the most important ones:

1. Adamal (descended from Sultan Adam)
2. Sarangal (descended from Sultan Sarang)
3. Hathial (said to be descended from Sultan Hathi)
4. Bogial (said to be descended from Malik Boga)
5. Firozal (said to be descended from Malik Firoz)
6. Iskandrial (said to be descended from Malik Sikandar)

Demographics

The Gakhars are generally settled in Rawalpindi, Islamabad, Jhelum, Kashmir, Gilgit, Baltistan, Chitral, and Khanpur regions in modern day Pakistan.

In Pakistan, the population of Ghakars is approximately 48,000. Major states having Ghakar population are:

Area	Population
North-West Frontier	43,000
Punjab	2,900

Source: Joshua Project, 2008

Martial Traditions

As we know that Gakhars were a warrior race and have greatly contributed in historical wars of India in medieval times. They served under the Mughal Kings and fought for them. Humayun, Baburs son governed from 1530–1540. Humayun lost his Indian territories to the Afghan Sultan, Sher Shah Suri, and, with Persian aid, regained them fifteen years later. As per the Akbarnama, Sher Shah Suri started a genocidal war against Sultan Sarang Khan Gakhar who remained loyal to Humayun, building the massive Rohtas Fort in 1541-43 in an effort to crush the Gakhars, to whom the fort was finally surrendered ten years after Sher Suri's death. Sultan Sarang built Rawat Fort nearby and is buried there with many of his sons.

From therefrom he (Sher Shah Suri) advanced as far as Khushab and was for some days in Bhera. He sent a summons to Sultan Sarang Ghakkar and Sultan Adam who were the leading landholders in that neighbourhood, but as they had been clients of his Majesty Giti-sitani Firdusmakani, and had prospered by the favour of that exalted family they did not listen to his overtures. He advanced as far as Hathiapur in the Ghakkar territory and sent a large force against them. The Ghakhars fought bravely and defeated the Afghans so much that many of them were captured and sold. Sher Khan (Sher Shah Suri) wanted to march against them in person. He consulted his followers and they advised that as this race had strong mountains and remote heartlands they should be dealt with by degrees and by policy. The proper course was to leave a large army in that neighbourhood which could both watch the royal army and devastate the nation of the Ghakkars. It was also desirable that a strong fort should be built for the carring out of these two objectives. In consequence of this advice he laid the foundations of the Fort of Rohtas and having left a large force there he marched back and came to Agra.

Jalaludin Muhammad Akbar also known as Akbar the Great was the son of Humayun whom he succeeded as ruler of the Mughal Empire from 1556 to 1605. He was the grandson of Mughal conquerorZaheerudin Babur who established the Mughal dynasty, a contemporary of Elizabeth the 1st of England and widely considered the greatest of the Mughal emperors.

The first act of homage by the Gakhars to Akbar was the capture and surrendering of the traitor Mirza Kamran, brother of Humayun who had joined with the Afghans. In order to further cement his relations with the Gakhars and use them as an ally against the tubulent Afghans, Akbar in accordance with his well-known policy, contracted matrimonial alliances with them. Prince Salim was married to a daughter of Sayd Khan, a brother of Kamal Khan. Sayd Khan had fought under the Mughal General Zayn Khan against the Afghans in Swat and Bajaur. Later Aurangzeb also honoured the Gakhar chief Allah Kuli Khan (1681-1705) by marrying one of his daughters to his son prince Muhammad Akbar. Thus two Gakhar women found their way into the Imperial harem.

Akbar's policy of pacification and reconciliation had its desired effect and we find the Gakhars leading a peaceful and uneventful life during the major part of the Mughal rule. They seem to have have only reluctantly accepted Mughal rule nevertheless as a celebrated Gakhar warrior-chief, Mukarrab Khan, sided with Nadir Shah and took part in the Battle of Karnal (1739), which showed up the crumbling fabric of the Mughal empire. As a reward for his services, he was confirmed in his possession of the fort of Pharwala and on his return to Kabul, Nader Shah conferred upon him, as a mark of further favour, the title of Nawab (this seems to have been a personal title as no later Gakhar chief ever used it). In his days the Gakhar power was greater than it had perhaps ever been before. He defeated the Yusafzai Afghans and Jang Kuli Khan of Khattak, and captured Gujrat, overrunning the Chib nation as far north as Bhimber. He was finally beaten by the Sikhs at Gujrat in 1765 and had to surrender the whole of his possessions up to the Jehlum.

Contribution to Defence Services

Gakhars are considered martial race since the days of British colonial rule and form a major part of Pakistan Army. The Pakistani military has always heavily recruited Gakhars and as is consistent with the past, the race continues to produce a considerable number of recruits who occupy many of the senior ranks of the Pakistani Army.

Famous Personalities

Ghakars have contributed to all fields of life and have produced some famous personalities, a list of which is given below.

Armed Forces

Gallantary Award Recipients

Major Mohammed Nawaz Kayani was a Highly Decorated soldier of Burma War. Awared the British **Military Cross** for bravery on enemy lines in 1946.

Major Masud Akhtar Kiani was awarded **Sitara-e-Jurat** 19 Lancers: slained in action at Jasoran, Chawinda sector during the 1965 war.

Air Commodore Raees A. Rafi: Sitara-e-Jurat Recipient in 2008.

Col. Rasheed Kayani: **Sitara-e-Jurat** Recipient

Lt.Col Haq Nawaz Kayani Shaheed: Sitara-e-Jurat Recipient

Others

Admiral Tariq Kamal Khan (retired): Ex Chief of Naval Staff and Ambassador; son of Col. Sir. Sher Muhammad

Lt. General Jamshed Gulzar Kiani: Ex-corp commander and former chairman Federal Public Service Commission

General Ashfaq Parvez Kayani: Chief of Army Staff

Air Marshal Shahid Hamid: Chairman of the Alternative Energy Development Board

Brigadier Riaz UL Haq Kayani: Ex-Chairman CDA and Center Comdt Engrs Center, Son of Fazal Ellahi from Dadochha

Capt. Shahjehan Kayani: Indian Army from Dadochha. Decorated for bravery in WWI

Major General Zaheer Ahmad Khan: Director General Military Vehicles Research and Development

Politicians

- Raja Hassan Akhtar: Bureaucrat, Deputy Commissioner and later Member of the National Assembly; President of the West Pakistan Muslim League
- Raja Nargas Zaman Kiani: Ex Senator
- Afzal Khan Kayani: Ex-Lord Mayor of the City of Manchester, England

Artists

Hadiqa Kayani: Singer

14

Gujjars

The Gujjar or Gurjar are an ethnic group in India and Pakistan. Alternative spellings include Gurjara, Gujjar and Goojar. The Gujjars follow Hinduism, Sikhism and Islam. The Hindu Gujjars belong to the traditional Kshatriya Varna in Hinduism, while the Muslim Gujjars are considered to be a Potwari race in India and Pakistan.

Origin & History

The ancestry of the Gujjars are uncertain. The Gujjar clan appeared in northern India about the time of the Huna invasions of northern India. Some scholars believed that the Gujjars were foreign immigrants, possibly a branch of Hephthalites. D. B. Bhandarkar believed that Gujjars came into India with the Hunas, and the name of the race was sanskritized to Gujjar. He also believed that several places in Central Asia, such as "Gurjistan", are named after the Gujjars and that the reminiscences of Gujjar migration are preserved in these names. General Cunningham identified the Gujjars with Yuezhi or Tocharians.

In the past, Gujjars have also been hypothesized to be descended from the nomadic Khazar clans, although the history of Khazars shows an entirely different politico-cultural ethos In Gazetteer of Bombay Presidency, the British civil servant James M. Campbell identified Gujjars with Khazars.

Some Gujjars also claim that the Gujjar caste is related to the Chechens and the Georgians, and argue that Georgia was traditionally called "Gujaristan" (actually Gorjestan). The state of Gujarat in Western India, gets its name from the Gujjars or Gujjars who migrated and settled from Central Asia. Some of them also claim that Germans are Gujjars. Nevertheless, there is no evidence for such claims. The word "Georgia" derived from the Arabic and Persian word Gurj, and not Gujjar or Gurjar.

As said by many historinans (alomost all), It is claimed that Gujjars originated in Central Asia, came into India via Afghanistan and founded an empire in Rajasthan until beaten by the Muhammadans. They then settled in Gujarat, and this provides one explanation of the name, but this is contested. They are first referred to in the 7th century as warriors, who later migrated to the mountains for pasture for the animals. Their language is called Gujjari, close to Pahari and Urdu. The census of India 1941 sates: Historians seem to be satisfied that the communities called "Gujjars" were founded in the region near Mount Abu in Rajasthan, around 6th century AD. onwards. It is believed that these and other sections of the race were the ancestors of those now known as Gujjars in this state. The "Gujjars" were Hindus at the time they are first noticed in India. They had founded an empire of their own at the time of Harsha of Thaneswar (606-647) around 640 AD. It seems that the Gujjars successfully resisted the Arab invasion from the north early in the eighth century AD. It is alleged that around 750 AD. the Chapa dynasty of the Gujjars which had been in power for around 200 years, was displaced by the Pratiharas who seem to have carried on until around 1000 AD., when their power was broken by the coming of Mahmud of Ghazni.

Nothing much appears to be known of the Gujjars in the Punjab till 980 AD. When Raja Shankervarman of Kashmir is said to have invaded Gujarat, the Gujjar Empire was governed over by one Lakhandev. A area known as Takka, situated in the region now known as the Punjab was ceded by Shankervarman. It is reasonable to presume that Gujjar communities had extended to the Punjab and it is probable that such places as Gujarat, Gujrat, Gujranwala and Gujjar Khan and Gurdaspur, where Gujjar families are still found derived their names from this fact. The Gujjar Empire ceased to exist by the time of Akbar when their nation was annexed. By this time a number of Gujjars, had embraced Muhammadism and from now onwards the connection of the northern sections with their Hindu ancestors becomes less and less. The migration of a part of the race to the territories now known as Jammu and Kashmir is attributed to the outbreak of a serious famine in the area inhabited by the race, now known as Rajputana, Gujarat and Kathiawar. The exact period has not been fixed but it is known as the Satahsiya famine. It is stated that some part of the migrating races moved to the Punjab whilst others moved further north to the regions now known as Kaghan, Swat, Hazara, Kashmir and Gilgit.

In the vast nation of sub-continental dimension, which had been familiar as Aryavarat, regional provincial and religious fervour influence variously to shape customs, manners, behaviour and political ideologies. As per a saying a bride married to family living at distant places as far as 50 miles, while taking leave of her parents address plaintively with tears rolling down from their eyes to asks her father why she has been given in marriage to a family at a far off place, and how she could be able to maintain and uphold common traditions of the same ancestry, spread from Hindukush to Arakan. It is, nevertheless, remarkably striking to note that the Gujjars all over the sub-continent claim to be natives of the land since time immemorial. Learned amongst them also claim with confidence that they are Kshtriyas by ancestry, without having any traces of tradition of so called foreign ancestry.

The Jhalwan Gujjars speak both Balochi and Sindhi languages and claim to be natives of these regions without having ancestry of any foreign element in so far as their ethnic traditions are concerned. In the region the Zamindars (landlords) are called Baloch. The other Pakistani Blauch and adjoining Irani Bluches are of one ancestry but against this we hail from separate Gujjar community. As per one tradition they have come from Delhi to this area and speak Sindhi language. In Markan, near border of Iran, the Gujjars are Ziki by faith and claim to have come from Mewar during the time of Akbar, the elderly Gujjars added.

In the North-Western Frontier Province, the Gujjars are no less in number than the Pathans. Every Gujjar remembers his gotra (family name or sub-caste). Gujjars of almost all gotras are found here. Their pronunciation is quite the same as in other parts of the sub-Continent. The language, they speak amongst themselves, is Hindi. In Peshawar proper, this language is called Hindky. It is spoken side by side with Pashto. In Kashmir the Gujjars speak the same language. Here it is called Gujjari having the difference that Gojari in Hindi spoken in the tone of Mewari or Brij Bhasha in which oftenly "a" is changed into "o" and Hindky is Hindi inter-loaded with Punjabi words.

In Hazara district of the Frontier Province, it is noticeable that Jats and Ahirs are included amongst the Gujjars. They marry together, speak the same language and claim their ancestory from the common Indian ancestry, the Kashatriyas.

In district Gujrat (West Punjab), there are forty villages of Khatana Gujjars are heirs of Jaipal who fought against Mahmud of Ghazni, but the peathingy hypothesis could not be solved by them. Gujjars firmly claimed that they were descendents of Jaipal's family and revealed that (Peathingy) was their royal insignia. To the people of mountainous area from Kashmir to Afghanistan, peathingy was loveable bird. Shah Mir who claimed his descendancy from Pandu, in Mahabharat family, was the first local Muslim ruler. By and by, the Muslims from aboard poured in Kashmir and began hunt of the peathingys. Shah Zain-ul-Abdin, the grandson of Shah Mir put a ban on the killing of the peathingys. Severe punishment was imposed on the defaulters. Except at Zoo, the peathingy is now extinct in Pakistan but at Katas in district Jhelum, there is a Hindu temple around which there are peathingys since long. On request of the Hindu custodians of the temple, the Government of Pakistan has prohibited the killing of the bird in the region around the temple.

In Central Asia there are many communities such as Tajik, Uzbeck, Kirgis, Khazer etc etc, each having their sub-sects or races. Their racial names do not even resemble with any subcaste of the Gujjars, Pathans, Shina and Dard etc. the people on Southern side of the northen Mountains. It was surprising to note that Noor and Bostan Khan during talks called the whole population of Central Asia as Uzbeck implying thereby uncivilised people. The word Uzbeck is used in the same sense in large regions around Delhi.

The whole Western part of the Sub-Continent, Gorakhpur to Chitral and Banaras to Zehidan and found that the Gujjar have no tradition of their being originally foreigners. Morever, the Arabs and the Chinese travellers and their adversaries of the past and the Muslim historians in India during their centruries long rule had mentioned the Gujjars to be the Indian people by ancestry. Now, the question arises why and how the theory of foreign ancestry of the Gujjars was profounded during British rule in India.

In cities and towns the families of the foreigners settled holding all the lands around them. None of the natives had proprietory rights of land, they were only tenants, slave cultivators who were given a scanty quantity of grains of the lowest kind, such as millet, jawar and barley. Moreover, it also depended on the willingness of the masters to give or not to give at all. K.M. Munshi in his book Glory That Was Gujjar Desa has rightly stated that many local famillies of high rank became out-law in the forests. Conversion to Islam did not help the people, the Shudas remain shadras. Kashatriya people became graziers and shepherds, anyone can see even today the Muslim Gujjars with their buffalos, cows, sheep and goats wandering from Dehra Doon to Swat. A mosque may be built jointly by the habitants of the whole village but the local.

It is to be seen during to the period of foreing Muslim Rule. Direct control was difficult over Gujjar Desa being a vast desert. So to suppress Kshatriyas it was handed over (in the early years of the Fouteenth Century AD.) to those natives who cooperated with the foreigners. These native Jagiradars called Rajput found the new cities, Bikaner, Jaisalmer, Jaipur, Jodhpur, Kota, Bundi etc during Musilim Rule in India. The forign Muslims wrote histry books using the word Rajput for the ancient Rulers of India, surely to degrade the Kshatriyas, elevated to high position, during Mughal period in the Seventreenth and Enghteenth Century AD. the Rajputs got prepared their pedegree trees connecting them with ancient royal houses of Sialkot, Ajmer, Bhatinda, Delhi, Multan, Kannauj, Khera, Ujjain, Bhilmal, Baroach and Anahilwara.

Such was the state of affairs in the nation when the Britishers (East India Company) founded an empire by fighting, negotiations or conspiracies. They never declared holy war. Genghiz Khan can repent and can have pity on the defeated, but a holy warrior cannot do, because he is blessed more and more by God on his most brutal and heinous exploits, infllicted on the defeated.

As such the Britishers did not dismantle the worship places of any relilgion, men were not made slaves and the women were respected. The local old books were searched out and were translated into English. The Britishers were men of larning and loved the learned.

In 1805 AD. Colonel James Todd was appointed as Surveyor General in Gujjar Desa (present Rajasthan). There he took great interest in Archaeology. The Sanskrit inscriptions since sixth Century AD. on ancient palaces, forts. Temple and baolies revealed that those buildings had been built by the Gujjars and not by the Rajputs as had been propagated by the foreign Muslims in India and the Rajputs as well, to such an extent that every Indian Ruler of the past and the present was being called Rajput all over the Sub Continent, it puzzled Colonel Todd. As mentioned above, the poverty and illiteracy prevailed in the Indian Society so there was no local History book. Some famillies of the ancient past are common amongst the Gujjars, Jats, Ahirs and the Rajputs. How to adjust in history the Rajputs, who then held the highest position in political fields amongst the Hindus? Perchance he got a book Prithvi Raj Raso written by a Bard Chand Bardai in 15th or 16th Century AD having a story stating that the Parmar, Solanki, Pratihar and Chohan were born of a fire pit at Mount Abu. Haphazardly, it was supposed. There is no mention of Gujjars before sixth century in therefore, the Gujjars came with the Hunas, Scythians and Epithalites etc. Who in Sixth Century AD. invaded. They were converted to Hindusim at Mount Abu. The higher ones were made Rajput and rank and file remained Gujjar and Ahirs.

This supposition or thought of Colonel James Todd in the book Annals and Antiquities of Rajasthan was readily accepted by the historians Europeans and Indians with further remarks. Some said they came from Gurjistan and others took them to be Khazers of Central Asia. General Cunningham stopped further and said.

There is Kushan family amongst the Gujjars, so he fixed their arrival into India with Kushan, Yu-Chi and Tatars in the First Century AD. when the Kushans emerged into history.Mr. C.V. Vaidaya was the first scholar who challenged this so called theory.

Honourble K.M. Munshi in 1944, first of all, called all the rulers of Gujjar Desa from 6th Century AD. to 1300 AD., by the Gujjar name. But he put forward a new theory, Gujjar primarily was the namae of a territory whose habitants were divided into four sects, Gujjar Brahman, Gujjar Kshatriya, Gujjar Vaishya and Gujjar Sudras.

Sri Yatindra Kumar Verma challenged this theory in his Gujjar Itihas and proved that Gujjar was name of a Kshtriyan race. It has been said that Rajputs originated on Mount Abu in the begining of 6th Century AD. but from 500 AD. to 1300 AD. there was no community by the name of Rajputra or Rajput in India whereas Gujjar and Ahirs are mentioned even before Christ.

A Jat-Asur is mentioned in the book Mahabharat 3101 BC. If a Kshatriya becomes Jat (illiterate) or Asur (non-believer) or thief (as per Chachnama) his ancestry will remain the same. Nevertheless, we find a Jat king ruling at Takatpur in around 975 AD. in Northren Sind. Abhirs or Ahirs are well known to history. It is universally known that Sri Krishna was brought up by Baba Namd Ahir and his wife Yeshoda (3100 BC.). Nevertheless, we find Ahir kings ruiling in Saurashtra side by side with the Gujjars.

The Agni Kul (fire born) ruling families were Gujjars as per epigraphic and Antiquary records from 500 AD. to 1300 AD. During this whole period, they never called themselves fire-born. They always called themselves Brahm Kashtra. Raghava (Raghu) and Surya Vansh.

The groups of people are formed of old races with new names under different circumstances. Here it is meant that the groups of ancient Kshtriyas, the Gujjars and Ahirs are older than the present groups of the

Rajputs. Therefore, the Rajputs have no concern with Agni Kul legend. It is noteworthy that there is not at all the word Rajput found anywhere in the book Prithvi Raj Raso in which the legend is recorded.

Hun is no doubt as sub-caste of the Gujjar caste. The Gujjar caste consists of hundreds of gotras (sub-caste). Hun no doubt governed some small principalities whereas the Gujjars founded empires, of them four are famous to history and the Huns were their subordinate rulers, then how the Hun can be called the master of the Gujjars and Ahirs. Hun is a Sanskrit word denoting a person who does not listen to the opinion or advice of the others but acts upon his own wishes. Hun Mat a proverb is still in use implying thereby the wisdom of an unruly. Hun clan is mentioned in the Mahabharat, Puranas, in history of Guptas of Patna, and Palas of Bengal.

In the time of Gujjar Mihir Bhoj, Hun's principality was that now called Mianwall district on the eastern bank of River Indus. In the book Mahabharats approximately 200 Kshatriyan races are mentioned in the Sub-Continent, of whom Chib, Hun, Dard, Shina (China or Channa) Dakh, Pakhtu and Kombed are described in the regions, south of Palmir and Oxus River. Kombel were in the West near the border of Iran who migrated inside the nation in 10th century AD., but all the other clans under same name are living in those regions until today. The Huns in Hunza have lost their identity and are called Ismailies or Aghan Khani a sect of Shia Muslims. The Husns in other parts are a part and parcel of Indian society from ancient time to this day. Once one educated Nawarai Hun (in Gujrat Kathiawar) went to the house of Muslim saint namely Jahanyan Jahan

Georgia was called Gurjistan by the Persians. It is merely a coincidence with the word Gurjar so is Khazer with Gujjar. The words Gurjar and Gujjar are the same.

Gujjar is Prakrit form of the Sanskrit word Gurjar. Such as Brahman, Bahman, Krishan = Kishan, Rajputra = Rajput etc., but Gurjistan and Khazer are two separate words, it is merely a tampering to connect these words with Gurjar of Gujjar.

An Arab historian Ibn Khardadbah in his history book Al-Masalik-w-Al-Mamalik states: The tititle of the kings of Turkj, Tibet and Khazer is Khaqan. They are all the descendents of Faridum. He further states in Hind, Balhara is the greatest of all kings, there are also, other kings such as, Chap, Tank, Juzae, Jaba, Brahma, Kamrup. He again writes Draham (coin) of Malikul- Juzer is Tatri.

Balhabra is Valbhi Eai, Juzar is Gujjar (In Arabic there is no G and P) Jaba is Chap, Kamrup is modern Assam. If read thoroughly the above statement pertains to seventh Century AD. It is clear that Khazer and Gujjar were quite different races.

In Bible (Old Testament) the nation, adjacent to Iran in the east, is Kush. It shows that modern Afghanistan was called Kush in the time of Bible. Afterwords, the whole valley of Sindh was called Hind by Persians. Persian language is Prakrit or a branch of Sanskrit. Alphabet's is changed into in Persian such as Sapt = Haft (seven), Saptah = Hafth (week) Sahsar =Hazar (thousand), Sind = Hind, Dash =Dah Ten. Sam Karya =Hamkar (man of the same profession).

The name Hind was applied to the whole land to the east of Sind Valley. The Arabs called the people of Hind, Ahl-ul-Hindu but the Persians particularly Central Asians called its habitants Hindu. So they called Kush by the name of Hindu Kush. Hindu Kush is called by the same name until today. The Kushan were Hindu who reached Patliputra under their leader Kanishk. It is strange in history when a Hindu of Peshawar which is inside Aryavarta conquers Patna he is supposed to be foreigner but when Chandra Gupta a Hindu of Patna conquers Peshawar, he is not foreigner. It must take into view that Peshawar was as inside Aryavarta in the West as Patna was inside Aryavarta in the East. Kanishk is a Hindu name. His father was Vijhisk.

Their ancestor Kidphysis is a wrong imagination of the Europeans. It is also said that Kaniskh wore heavy cloth and boots. Yes, in snowy valleys of Kailash and Hindu Kush, a Patna Dhoti (loin) cannot be worn The Kushan, sub-caste of the Gujjars, was a native family at Peshawar, that is why Kanishk spared Subahu Nagar, the Ruler of Patna. The family was called Devaputra, the Aryan.

Gujranwala was a new settlement coming into existence in the 18th Century AD. but Gujrat Mardan and Gujrat Chenab are ancient names of the territory. The Gurjar (Gujjar) and Gurjjaratra (Gujrat) are pure Sanskrit names. If the Gujjars coming from the foreign lands established these cities with Sanskrit names, where had they been taught Sanskrit language.

In Urdu, Hindi and English the word Gurjar or Gujjar is in use but in all the ancient records upto 1300 AD. It is Gurjar, its Prakrit is Gujjar which is generally spoken by the people. A group of Kshatriyas in ancient times destroyed the enemies of the nation, the invaders on the western border, so the people entitled them as Gujjars. There are examples in history, when a Kshatriya of that Area rose to highest power and adopted the title Gujjar, Gujjarasver, Gujjar Nath, Gujjar Senani, Gujjarendra and Gujjar Path. The Gujjars were not only the conquerers, victorious and rulers but were the best administrators and lovers of sciences in the whole world at that time.

The Rashtra Kuts of Deccan were the adversaries of the Gujjars. In an inscription Govind III the Rashtra Kut states my grand father defeated the Gujjars who were the highest ranking amongst the Kshatriyas.

There is ample contemporary evidences to show that the people had the knowledge about the Gujjars being Kshatriyas of the ancient highly reputed families ie Yadu, Raghu, Iksvaku, Paru etc, Hieun Sang the Chinese traveller is considered an honest writer. He himself was a Buddhist and king of Sind at that time was a Buddhist but Hieun Tsang honestly wrote him a Sudra by ancestry. He states, the Gujjar rulers of Bhinmal, Valbhipur, Baroach, and Vatapi were Kshatriyas by ancestry.

It is also wrong to say that the Gujjars were against Buddhist History scholars. In 7th Century AD., the Gujjar empire of Bhinmal was the second biggest empire in the Sub-Continent. Its Ruler was Buddhist. The ruler of Valbhipur was also Buddhist as per statement of the Chinese traveller. Moreover, in the middle of 12th Century AD. the Chaun of Naddul had adopted Jainism.

In some Puranas a Kshatriya group has been described by the name of Gushavar (master of the enemy). Prakrit form of this word is Gurshar as Ishar = Isar, Sanskrit with Prakrit is a vast language, so the people change the sound of a pesonal name or caste name as per deeds or misdeeds of the person, when the Gurshar repulsed or defeated the invaders in most ancient times, the people changed the word Gurshar with a strong sense into Gujjar (destroyer of the enemy) oftenly S or Sh are changed into J. As far as the word Gujjar goes in its present form, it is found in Panch Tantra. It was translated into Pehalvi by Borozoya, the Minister of Khust I, in 4th century AD. An English author of the book stories told that world over described Panch Tantra was written in 200 BC. Almasoodi writes that the book was written in the time of first successor of Poras who fought against Alexander. Almasoodi takes the book upto 300 BC. In this old book, there is a mention of Gujjar Desa. Date of Gujjar Desa prior to Panch Tantra and date of Gujjars prior to Gujjar Desa lead us many centuries before Christ.

Gujjar Desa was a desert where camels were in abundance, so it consisted of west Punjab (now in Pakistan) and west Rajasthan. West Punjab was also a desert before the canal system was intoduced.

There is a stone inscription of 150 AD. of Rudra Dama on a rock in Girnar Hills in Sorashtra. It reads that Rudra Dama defeated Yaudheyas who has adopted the title of Vir amongst the Kshatriyas. In all the lists of 36 royal families Gujjar with Vir title is mentioned. Sau Vir. Thus it is evident that around this time i.e. 1st century AD. Vir title had been a custom amongst the rulers of Gujjar Desa.

In 3rd and 4th century AD. the Chap famiuly had begun to rule at Baroach. Their history has come to light in full in 6th century AD. Gujjar Empire with its capital Bhimal was the second biggest Empire in the sub-continent. The Kingdoms of Chalukya in Deccan, parmars of Ujjain and the other Kingdoms of the Gujjars upto 1300 AD. have come to light with full details. The Gujjar Desa later on expended upto Peshawar in the north, Baroach in the south and the Kanauj to the East. The details may be seen in history books.

There are many causes of down fall of the Gujjars. One of them is lack of national unity. The Gujjars and the whole Hindu society as well, were so jealous that they were happy to see the fall of each other, even at their own cost, at the hands of the foreigners, some examples are as follows:

It is an after thought story invented by foreign Muslim historioans that Jaipal was assisted by all Indian princes. As a matter of fact, neither a single prince understood the aspect of the postilence which befell on Jaipal and his son Anand Pal, no prince came forward for assistance of this Shahi dynasty.

Ghaznavite governed north of Sutlej from Lahore to Kabul for approximately 150 years, but the Gujjar rulers never thought of liberating that territory from the foreigners. The local people from the area were pouring in the adjoinig Hindu States but nobody paid any attention. The people of Ghor in Afghanistan threw the yoke of the Turks (Ghaznative) dug the graves of Subuktgin's descendents and by putting on a heap of woods burned to ashes the dead bodies and bones.

In 1178 AD. Mohammad Ghori by crossing the river Sutlej entered Chauhans Empire. The informers informed Ajmer that Ghoris were marching on Anahilwara, The Chauhans were happy to see their adversaries, the Solankis of Anahilwara, in trouble, so they did not check the advance of Ghoris. Ghoris were defeated and crossed again the Chauhans territory without any harm, in 1189 Bhillam Yadva of Devagari (Deccan) attacked Anahilwara which was narrowly saved, so Bhillam was boastifully called cloud to the Gujjar swans.

In 1192 AD. Prithvi Raj Chauhan was defeated and killed by Ghoris. When the news reched Kanauj its ruler jai Chand Gahdwa was pleased and ordered for celebrations in the capital (later he himself was killed by the national enemies).Ghoris further marched on Anahilwara and looted the whole nation. After their return, Singjian grandson of Bhillam Yadav, the ruler of Devagiri (Deccan) invaded Gujrat but was replused. After the death of Bhim Solank. Vaghelas, a branch of Solanki became the rulers of Gujrat (Kathiawar).

Maharana Karna Vaghela governed Gujrat 1296 to 1304 one of his Ministers was Madho Brahman. The Minister's brother died leaving a widow Deval Devi and a minor daughter. Karna enamoured by the beauty pf the widow fell in love with her and kept her in his palace. Madho was enraged and avowed. I will not drink water, nor will take food unless and till I take Turks to Gujrat. So he went to Delhi and Khilji forces invaded Gujrat. Karna faced the foreigners with huge army gallantly, but was defeated.

When the news reached Anahilwara the queens and all the ladies of the town sat on pyre but Karna fled with Deval Devi to Baklana. Sultan's army levelled Anahilwara to the ground forever, even its remains are not to be seen today. The whole nation was plundered. With a heavy loot the invading army returned to Delhi. Gujrat became a province of Delhi Sultanate.

The spies informed the whereabouts of Kanran to the Sultan who again despatched an army. The army stealthily surrounded Baklan. Deval Devi with her daughter was caught and taken to the Harem of the Sultan. What happended to Karna is not known. The tragedy did not end. Jag Mal joined Akber's army against his own brother Rana Partap. The Sikh rulers in the south of Upper Sutlej preferred subordination of the Britishers to the alliance of Sikh Maharaja Ranjit Singh.

As per some historical accounts, the empire with capital at Bhinmal (or Srimal) was founded by the Gujjars. A minor empire of Bharuch was the offshoot of this Empire. In 640-41 AD, the Chinese traveller Xuanzang (Hieun Tsang) described the kingdoms of Su-la-cha (identified with Saurashtra) and Kiu-che-lo (identified with Gujjar) in his writings. He stated that the Gujjars governed a rich and populous empire with capital at Bhinmal (Pilo-mo-lo). As per his expositor, M. Vivien de St. Martin, Su-la-cha represents the modern Gujarat, and Kiu-che-lo (Gurjjara), "the nation of the Gujjars", represents the area between between Anhilwara and the Indus River, i.e. Sindh area.

Vincent Smith believed that the Pratihara dynasty, which governed a large empire in northern India from the 6th to the 11th centuries, and has been mentioned as "Gujjar-Pratiharas" in an inscription, was certainly of Gujjar ancestry. Smith also stated that there is possibility of other Agnikula Rajput clans being of same ancestry. Dr. K. Jamanadas also states that the Pratihara clan of Rajputs descended from the Gujjars, and this "raises a strong presumption that the other Rajput clans also are the descendents from the Gujjars or the allied foreign immigrants". D. B. Bhandarkar also believed that Pratiharas were a clan of Gujjars. In his book The Glory that was Gujardesh (1943), Gurjar writer K. M. Munshi stated that the Pratiharas, the Paramaras and the Solankis were imperial Gujjars.

Nevertheless, some other historians believe that although some sections of the Pratiharas (e.g., the one to which Mathanadeva belonged) were Gujjars by caste, the imperial Pratiharas of Kannauj were not Gujjars and there was no Gujjar empire in Northern India. H. A. Rose and Denzil Ibbetson stated that there is no conclusive proof that the Agnikula Rajput clans are of Gujjar ancestry; they believed that there is possibility of the indigenous races adopting Gujjar names, when their founders were enfiefed by Gujjar rulers.

Over the years, the Gujjars were assimilated chiefly into the sects of Kshatriya varna, although some Gujjar groups (such as Gaur Gujjars of central India) are classified as Brahmins. During the Muslim conquest in the Indian subcontinent, many of the Gujjar Hindus converted to Islam.

British Rule: In the eighteenth century, several Gujjar chieftains and small kings were in power. During the reign of Rohilla Nawab Najib-ul-Daula, Dargahi Singh, the Gujjar chieftain of Dadri possessed 133 villages at a fixed revenue of Rs. 29,000. A fort at Parlchhatgarh in Meerut District, also known as Qila Parikishatgarh, is ascribed to a Gujjar Raja Nain Singh. As per a legend, the fort was built by Parikshita and restored by Nain Singh in the eighteenth century. The fort was dismantled in 1857, to be used as a police station.

The Imperial Gazetteer of India states that all through the Indian Rebellion of 1857, the Gujjars and Musalman (Muslim) Rajputs proved the "most irreconcilable enemies" of the British in the Bulandshahr region. A band of rebellious Gujjars ransacked Bulandshahr after a revolt by the 9th Native Infantry on May 21, 1857. The British officers initially left for Meerut but later sent a small force to retake the city. The British forces were able to retake the city with the help of Dehra Gorkhas, but the

Gujjars rose again after the Gorkhas marched off to assist General Wilson's column in another region. Under the leadership of Walidad Khan of Malagarh, the British garrison was driven out the district. Walidad Khan held Bulandshahr from July to September, till he was expelled after an engagement with Colonel Greathed's flying column. On October 4, the Bulandshahr District was regularly occupied by the British Colonel Farquhar and measures of repression were adopted against the armed Gujjars.

During the revolt of 1857, the Muslim Gujjars in the villages of the Ludhiana District showed dissent to the British authorities. The British interests in Gangoh town of Saharanpur District were threatened by the rebel Gujjars under the self-styled Raja Fathua. These Gujjars rebels were beaten by the British forces under H. D. Robertson and Lieutenant Boisragon, in June 1857. The Gujjars of Chundrowli rose against the British, under the leadership of Damar Ram. The Gujjars of Shunkuri village, numbering around three thousand, joined the rebel sepoys. As per British records, the Gujjars plundered gunpowder and ammunition from the British and their allies. In Delhi, the Metcalfe House was sacked by the Gujjar villagers from whom the land was taken to erect the building. The British records claim that the Gujjars carried out several robberies. Twenty Gujjars were reported to have been beheaded by Rao Tula Ram for committing dacoities in July 1857. In September 1857, the British were able to enliist the support of many Jats and Gujjars at Meerut.

The British classified the Gujjars (and around 150 other Indian communities) as "criminal race" through the Criminal Tribes Act, 1871 (later repealed by the Government of independent India.

People & Culture

Majority of Gujjars are at present spread over north-western parts of India, extending from Indus to Ganges and from the hills of Hazarah to Gujrat. Bengal too had once remained the centre of Gujjars but they are now converted into other sects. The regions on the banks of Ganges and Jamna rivers, and district of Sharanpur, which was at one time known as Gujrat, is dominant with Gujjars. On the east of Bundel Khand region in the mini State of Simther and the northern district of Gwallior, which is even now known as Gujjargadh, Gujjars are settle in large numbers. The State of Rampur in U.P and Bundel Khand too have abundance of Gujjars who belong to both the faiths the Hindus and the Muslims. In Rampur U.P a very big Mohalla, Gujjar Tola is domiciled by the Gujjars.

Small Groups of Gujjars are also sprinkled and spread out on a wide region of eastern Rajputana. The Gujjars, nevertheless, constitute a majority population in western States and Gujrat. On the south of Delhi the kings came from Rewadi Gujjars. In south of Punjab, Gujjar population is quite small. Nevertheless, on the northern side their number is large enough inasmuch as several districts are familiar with Gujjar names such as Gujaranwalla in Rachna Duab (tract of land between two rivers), Chahaj Duab in Gujrat, Gujjar Khan in Daab of Sindh Sagar. In the district of Jhelum, regions Hussan Ibdal and even Hazara they are dominantly inhabited by Gujjar.

From Peshawar to Swat Benaer, Gujjars are found coherently or incoherently settled. Hazara as per Aee-n-Akbari is known as Hazara Gujjar. Besides Gujjars are settled in mountain tracts of Hazara district Kashmir and thingych. They are also found in good numbers in Chitral valley, Sheshi Koh, and Pushgal. Gujrat and Kathiawar too have remained the centre of Gujjars from ancient times although they have now changed their sects.

Gujjars are settled far and wide alongwith the sea-shores somuchso the seashore from Beirut to Mahazi had been halting place of Chechi clan of Gujjars. This clan has now mingled with other clans. Many groups of Gujjars exist in the valley of Sheshi Koh and Shigal. In the State of Abna and Chitral too Gujjars are found. Kashmir and Gwallior is the abode of Gujjars. They are also found in the vicnity of Taxla near Tairi Shahan and around. Gujjar constitute a dominant race there.

Gujjars are conspicuous by their large number in the Sindh Parganas of Chilas and Pilas and on the western side of river. The southern part of Hindukush is known by the name of Kujal due to Gujjar settlements in large numbers in the region. A big segment of Gujjar migrants had gone and settled in Bengal too. Undoubtedly this fact with the name of Gorran refreshes the memory.

In the Central Asia, Khuwarzim, Azar Baijan are their native home. Gujjar Khasi is situated on the roadside of Sestaan, while as Gurjaristan is a place of historic significance dating back ten thousand years. In the bygone days they were settled in Kabul at a village known as Gurjani. In other countries where Gujjars are settled include Russia, China, Turkistan, Iran, Tibet, Egypt etc. Sea of Khazzar is still remembered with the Gujjar name Khazzar. From the census reports precise and elaborate details about their number etc of Gujjars could be ascertained.

Any race while migrating to other places for accomplishing certain objectives or invades some other nation, a chunk of its population continues to say away at their native land, is a fact that can not be denied. We have already stated that Gujjars have come from Central Asia and as such this race still continues to exist there. On the banks of river Halmand two settlements of the name of Gujarastan and Gujjar Khasi still stand. Traces of another locality of Gurjistan was found in the vicinity of Gazni. In the frontier regions a clan of Gujjar Khail also exit.

The earliest Gujjar settlement seems to have been in the Punjab and in the United Provinces from the Indus to Mathura, where they still differ greatly in dress and language from most of the other habitants. From Mathura, the Gujjars seem to have passed to east Rajputana, and from there, by way of Kota and Mandasor to Malwa, where though their original character is considerably altered, the Gujjars of Malwa still remember that their ancestors came from Doab between the Ganges and Jamna. In Malwa they spread out as far east as Bhilsa and Saharanpur, from Malwa they passed south to Khandesh and west, probably by the Ratlam-Dohad route to the province of Gujrat. In the other direction, the Gujjars extended north and are now found roaming over the Himalayas north of the Punjab and over the hills of Kashmir. It is an interesting fact that where they have not been absorbed into the rest of the population as in the plains of Punjab (where two districts, Gujrat and Gujaranwala are named after them), they are always found to speak some dialect of one and the same language, closely connected with eastern Rajasthani and with Gujarati. The grammar of the Gujjars of Swat is almost the same as that of Rajputs of Jaipur.

Gujjars traditionally belonged to the Kshatriya caste, and governed over the Gujjar-Pratihara Empire. Gujjars have a glorious past, a truth no doubt. Although fairly unpopular for their violent conduct, Gujjars have lived on their productive labour. In recorded history, Rajasthan's Gujjars are an integral part of the mainstream caste in the area's society.

The Van Gujjars, meaning forest Gujjars, actually live in forests as quasi-nomads. During the winter they come down to the plains along with their cattle, and return to the upper Shivalik hills during summer. To Van Gujjars, cattle rearing are an absolute necessity as that is the only source of sustenance they know. There is no way Van Gujjars could do farming in the Shivalik hills, neither have they thought of immigrating to the mainland. They have remained with their occupational culture for ages, and arguably, are quite content.

But, as part of mainstream society, to the Rajasthan Gujjars, cattle rearing is not a necessity as they have fairly good land holdings, and other opportunities of enterprise available around them. Rooted in their tradition, cattle rearing is a cult among Rajasthan Gujjars.

Even if a Gujjar family had for example, a hundred acres of land, and additional sources of income, by tradition, the family must have a couple of cows or buffaloes, even few goats. In the Gujjar world, home produced pure milk is as dire a necessity as oxygen to most of us. Cattle rearing thus become an absolute necessity to a Gujjar household.

Not much has been researched or written about the predicament of the cattle rearers. In India, cattle rearing is not recognised as an organised industry. By nature, even those with a single animal require the services of small hands, of children, at some stage or the other during the day. Understandably, there cannot be a cow or buffalo that will give milk round the year. So, if a family has one cow, the logic of the availability of pure-milk all through the year demands another cow. In the process, often, all the members including children are involved in taking care of the cows. Children are less likely to enroll in schools. Those who have enrolled are likely to drop out. The few, who still manage to get a degree, tend to under-perform and therefore are unfit in the job market.

Rajasthan Gujjars, or the Gujjar community as a whole with few exceptions though, is trapped in the tradition of cattle rearing. Since the mainland Gujjars live in mainstream society, they watch members of other communities getting into government jobs, which brings instant prestige and recognition in society. The Rajasthan Gujjars now aspire for government positions but without abandoning their tradition of cattle rearing.

Sects

The following is a list of better-known clans of the Gujjar community listed in alphabetical order:

- Adhana
- Aheer
- Ajar
- Ambwata
- Andarwar
- Antu
- Asaria
- Aswaal
- Dharawata
- Dhind
- Dhinda
- Dhonchak
- Diya
- Dogay
- Dorata
- Fagna
- Khaila
- Khari
- Kharol
- Kharra
- Khattana
- kheppar
- Khokhar
- Koli

- Awaar
- Awana
- Ayeri
- Baaru
- Baddi
- Baghela
- Bahrowal
- Bainsla
- Baisoya
- Banslay
- Baswaal
- Bathoya
- Bawaar
- Bawla
- Beeten
- Bensla
- Bhaati
- Bhadana
- Bhalot
- Bhanbar
- Bhati
- Bhatria
- Bhatti
- Bidhuri
- Butt
- Chalok
- Chandela
- Chandna
- Chaprana
- Charan
- Gaigi
- Gaj
- Gajgahi
- Galeria
- Gangoh
- Garahwaal
- Gararr
- Garasia
- Gehlot
- Ghaakla
- Ghabela
- Gharwaal
- Ghorey
- Ghorsi
- Gogi
- Gola
- Goop
- Goras
- Gori
- Gurs
- Gus
- Hakla
- Hakum
- Handu-Aane
- Harsana
- harthala
- hathwal
- Hun
- Jabarhera
- Jagal
- Kulyana
- Kundwana
- Laadhi
- Ligree
- Lohia
- Lohmod
- Lomwar
- Lumbar
- Maal
- Mahrane
- Maitrak
- Malik
- Mawai
- Meed
- Mehar
- Miyana
- Mothsar
- Nalia
- Nekadi
- Nitad
- Nooniara
- oheelu
- Padana
- Pamad
- Patel
- Rana
- Ratala
- Rawal
- Rawat
- Sahi

- Charr
- Chaudhary
- Chaudhri
- Chechi
- Chhawari
- Chhokar
- Chohan
- Chouhan
- Dahima
- Dargas
- Dedha
- Dedhar
- Dhaliya
- Dharandia
- Jangal
- Jangee
- Jat
- Jatu
- Jindar
- Kahrana
- Kalas
- Kangas
- Kanwar
- Kapasi
- Karahna
- Kasana
- Kasana
- Kataria
- Sangu
- Saradhana
- Shukkal
- Siroh
- Sisodia
- Solanki
- Tanvar
- Tanwar
- Tomar
- Vihun
- Virana
- Vokkan
- Warraich

Demographics

Gujjars are chiefly concentrated in the Indo-Gangetic plains, the Himalayan area, and eastern parts of Afghanistan, although the Gujjar diaspora is found in other places as well. A majority of Gujjars follow Hinduism and Islam, though small Gujjar communities following other religions exist.

In India, Gujjar populations are found chiefly in Delhi, Jammu and Kashmir, Himachal Pradesh, Punjab, western Uttar Pradesh, Haryana, northern Madhya Pradesh, Uttarakhand, Rajasthan, Gujarat and Maharashtra. The semi-nomadic Gujjar groups are found in the states of Jammu and Kashmir, Himachal Pradesh, and north-western Uttar Pradesh. The name for the state of Gujarat has derived from "Gurjar."

In Pakistan. Gujjars have given their names to several places in Pakistan, including Gujranwala, Gujjar Nallah, Gujjar Khan, Gojra and Gujrat. Stephen M. Lyon of University of Kent has written about what he calls "Gujarism", the act of Gujjars seeking out other Gujjars to form connections, and consolidate ties with them, based strictly on clan affiliation. The Gujjars have migrated and settled in many urban regions of Pakistan. Islamabad, Lahore and Karachi has now large Gujjar population.

Majorcountries having Gujjar populations are:

Area	Population
India	6,66,0000
Pakistan	2,299,000

Source: Joshua Projects, 2008

Martial Traditions

There is no denying the fact that this community has a history of a pastoral community and they have distinct culture and existence. On this ground they are treated by some scholars among the old communities of India.

This community is a brave community with an irresistible desire to excel in all fields. They are generally strong and larger in physique compared to others. They have a very good self esteem and are generally proud of their culture and community. This community has given India some of the grand leaders like King Mihir Bhoj, Sardar Vallabh Bhai Patel, Vijay Singh Pathik, and a recent Congress leader Rajesh Pilot (from Rajasthan).

If we think about this community as per the Varna System of the Hindus, one can classify them as Kshatriya or the Warrior class. All the three variations of Gujjars (Gujjar, Gurjar, and Gujar) traditionally fall in this category. They formerly governed Gujjar-Pratihara empire which included much of the Northern India during eighth and the ninth centuries.

Gujjars are not limited to India. They also live in other parts of the globe like Afghanistan, Iran, Ukraine and Pakistan. They are represented in the fields like agriculture, urban professions, civil services and officer classes. There is no supporting data as to whether they are well represented or lagging behind.

In India their population is approximately 3.3 crores. Uttar Pradesh, Rajasthan, Gujrat, Madhya Pradesh, Haryana, Karnataka, Jammu and Kashmir, Delhi, and Orissa have Gujjar population, nevertheless, majority of their population reside in UP, Rajasthan, and Gujrat. In India, only Gujjars of Jammu and Kashmir are Muslims. The rest of the community are (nearly all) Hindus. Some Gujjars are also Sikhs.

Despite this fact, all Gujjars speak their mother tongue "Gujjari, also spelled Gurjuri, Gojuri, and Gojiri" regardless of their religion and area. There are approximately 500 subcastes or gotras within the Gujjars,

Kasana, Bhati, Nagar, Chechi, Chauhan, Poswal to name a few. The cultural and phonetic evidences tells that the word Gujjar is a derivation of Gujjar and sounds like Georgia which indicates that the Gujjar community is of central Asian ancestry (Georgia,Chechnya,Ukraine etc).

This theory of ancestry of Gujjars is supported by among the known historian Dr Huthi of Georgia. He visited India and studied on the Gujjars living in Northern part of India. He found Indian Gujjars' langauge accent, their dress and their bullock carts resembling that of the Georgians. Dr. Huthi believes that the Gujjars came to India when "Timur" let loose a reign of terror over them. They were subsequently pushed to India he believes. They came to India to protect their lives and religion and called themselves "Georgian" which with the passage of time became Jorjars. Later this word was changed into "Gurjar" or "Gujjar".

Contribution to Defence Services

Gujjar community is known for its valour and has always remained patriotic towards the country. Gujjars join the Indian armed forces in large numbers. At present there are 30,000 of them in the Indian armed forces. Gujjars has contributed heavely to defence forces. There is not a single village of Gujjars in whole of India where you could not find many families having their sons in defence forces. Representation of Gujjas in the Army's various regiments has been steadily going up over the years. Gujjarss can be found in various regiments of services such as:

- Brigade of the Guards
- Parachute Regiment
- Mechanised Infantry
- Punjab Regiment
- Garhwal Rifles
- Kumaon Regiment
- Sikh Regiment

Famous Personalities

Gujjars have contributed to all fields of life and have produced some famous personalities, a list of which is given below.

Armed Forces

Gallantary Award Recipients

Kamal Ram Gurjar was recipient of Victoria Cross in II WW on 12 May 1944 at the River Gary, Italy.

Brig. Kuldeep Singh Chandpuri was **Maha Vir Chakra Recipient** in the Battle of Longewalla in 1971.

Politicians

- Ch. Fazal Elahi Gurjar: Ex President of Pakistan
- Chaudhry Amir Hussain: Speaker of National Assembly of Pakistan since 2007.
- Choudhary Rahmat Ali: a Gujjar of Gorsi goth who coined the name of Pakistan.

Artists

- Ranjeet: Popular Villain in Hindi Film Industry.
- Arjun Rampal: Super Model Turned Actor.
- Saher Ludhyanvi: Legendary Revolutionist Urdu Poet, Many Songs Have Filmed in Hindi Film Industry.
- Hazrat Mian Muhammad Buksh Poswal: Famous Punjabi poet (Author of "Saif - ul - Malook").

15

Kambojs

The Kambojs are an ethnic community of the Punjab area. They are the modern representatives of ancient Kambojs, a well known Kshatriya race of Iron Age India, said to have Indian as well as Iranian affinities. Kamboj is frequently used as surname in lieu of the sub-caste or the gotra name by many Kambojs of Punjab, India. Their Muslim counterparts living in Pakistan mostly use last name Kamboh instead of the gotra name.

Origin & History

Analysis of ancient Sanskrit texts and inscriptions place the Kambojs, Gandharas, Yavanas (Greeks), Madras, and the Sakas in the Uttarapatha - the northern division of Jambudvipa (the innermost concentric island continent in Hindu scripture). Geographically, this region sat along, and was named for, the major trade route from the mouth the Ganges to Balkh, now a small city in Northern Afghanistan. Some writers hold that Uttarapatha included the whole of Northern India and comprised very region of Central Asia, as far as the Urals and the Caspian Sea to the Yenisei and from Turkistan and Tien Shan ranges to as far as the Arctic.

Linguistic evidence, combined with this literary and inscriptional evidence, has led many scholars of note to conclude that ancient Kambojs originally belonged to the Ghalcha-speaking region of Central Asia. For instance, Yasaka's Nirukata attests that verb Savati in the sense "to go" was used by only the Kambojs. It has been proven that the modern Ghalcha dialects, Valkhi, Shigali, Sriqoli, Jebaka (also called Sanglichi or Ishkashim), Munjani, Yidga and Yagnobi, chiefly spoken in Pamirs and countries on the headwaters of Oxus, still use terms derived from ancient Kamboj Savati in the sense "to go". The Yagnobi dialect spoken in Yagnobi around the headwaters of Zeravshan in Sogdiana, also still contains a relic "Su" from ancient Kamboj Savati in the sense "to go." Further, as per Sir G Grierson, the speech of Badakshan was a Ghalcha until around three centuries ago when it was supplanted by a form of Persian.

Thus, the ancient Kamboj probably included the Pamirs, Badakshan, and possibly parts of Tajikstan, including Yagnobi area in the doab of the Oxus. On the east it was bounded roughly by Yarkand and/or Kashgar, on the west by Bahlika (Uttaramadra), on the northwest by Sogdiana, on the north by Uttarakuru, on the southeast by Darada, and on the south by Gandhara.

Later, some sections of the Kambojs crossed the Hindukush and planted Kamboj colonies in Paropamisadae and as far as Rajauri. This opinion is fully supported by the Mahabharata, which specifically draws attention to the Kambojs located in the cis-Hindukush area as neighbors to the Daradas, and the Parama-Kambojs located across the Hindukush as neighbors to the Rishikas (or Tukharas) of Ferghana/Sogdiana.

Dr J. C. Vidyalanakara, Dr V. S. Aggarwala, Dr K. C. Mishra, Dr J. L. Kamboj and many other scholars locate Kamboj in Pamirs and Badakshan and the Parama Kamboj further north, in the Trans-Pamirian territories comprising Zeravshan valley, towards Sogdhiana/Fargana,in the Sakadvipa or Scythia of the classical writers. Dr H. C. Seth identifies the mountainous area between the Oxus and Jaxartes (old Sogdiana) as the locale of the ancient Kambojs. This may primarily equate to the Parama Kambojs of the Mahabharata.

Scholars like Dr Buddha Parkash, H. C. Seth, Kirpal Singh etc identify the Ptolemian Komedei with the Komudha-dvipa of the Puranic literature and also connect it with the Iranian Kambojs. The two separate Kamboj settlements (one on either side of the Hindukush), are also substantiated from Ptolemy's Geography itself, which also references geographical term Tambyzoi located north of Hindukush on the river Oxus in Bactria, and Ambautai people living on the southern side of Hindukush in the Paropamisadae. Scholars have identified both the Ptolemian Tambyzoi and Ambautai with Sanskrit Kamboj.

The Yidga sub-dialect of Galcha Munjani is still spoken on the southern sides of Hindukush in Paropamisadae, further strengthening the opinion that some Kambojs crossed south of the Hindukush. Still further, Ptolemy attests people called Khomaroi and Komoi located north of Bactria in Sogdiana. It has also been pointed out that the Ptolemian Komoi is classical form of Kamboi (or Kamboika: from Pali Kambojika, Sanskrit Kamboj). This settlement of the Kamboj may have resulted in the wake of movement of the Scythian Komedes (which included Parama Kambojs) from the Alai Valley/Alai Mountains into the west around second century BC.

With time, the trans-Hindukush Kambojs remained essentially Iranian in culture and religion, while those in the cis-Hindukush area came partially (or partly) under Indian cultural influence. Numerous scholars have remarked that the ancient Kambojs had both Indian as well as Iranian affinities.

Still later, some sections of the Kambojs seemingly moved even farther, to Arachosia, as attested by the Aramaic version of Greco-Aramaic inscription of king Ashoka found in Kandahar. Some scholars have identified the original Kamboj with Arachosia (Kandahar), but this opinion does not seem to be correct.

A branch of Central Asian Kambojs seems also to have migrated eastwards towards Tibet in the wake of Kushana (1st century) or else Huna (5th century) pressure and therefore their notice in the records of Tibet (Kam-po-tsa, Kam-po-ce, Kam-po-ji) and Nepal (Kambojdesa). Burmese records refer to them as Kampuchih. Later, these Kambojs appear to have moved towards Assam from where they may have invaded Bengal during the bad days of the Palas and wrested north-west Bengal from them. Brahma Purana of 5th c AD mentions the Kambojs around Pragjyotisha and Tamraliptika. Buddhist text Sasanavamsa also attests the Kambojs in/around Assam. These Kambojs had made first bid to conquer Bengal during the reign of king Devapala (810 AD-850 AD) but were repulsed. A latter attempt was crowned with success when they were able to deprive the Palas of the suzerainty over North and West Bengal and set up a Kamboj dynasty in Bengal towards the middle of 10th century AD.

Historians believe that, there was a movement of the Eurasian nomads in Iran in the early centuries of first millennium BC, in which the Cimmerians and Yautiya figured prominently. Driven by Medes, these Eurasian nomads bifurcated into two wings, the right one pushing north-westwards up to Transcaspiana and the left one wheeling towards the south-east and penertrating into Afghanistan and Punjab.

Closely allied to the Iranian Yautiya were the Kurus, Kambojs and some other clans of the Scythians, which in later centuries, had sided with Achaemenid Teispes (Cispi), and contributed to the formation of Achaemenian empire in Iran. Soon these early Scythians merged with sedentary population of Iranians and became an integral part of them thus losing all traces of this ancient incursion except for some place-names, noted by a grammarian, interested in linguistics or some faint traditions lost in the multitudinous amalgam of legendary lore. As per Dr

Buddha Prakash, the Indian epic Mahabharata, in reality, is a record of Scytho-Iranian invasion of Vedic India of the 9th BC. Mahabharata abundantly attests that the Kambojs and their kindered Scythian communities like the Sakas, Tusharas, Khasas etc had played a very prominent role in the Kurukshetra war where they had all fought under the supreme command of Sudakshina Kamboj.

Scholars believe that the nomadic invaders who had invaded Iran several centuries prior to Christian era were Scythian people of the "Kambysene" territory from west of Caspian area i.e. ancient Armenia. Name Kambysene has been attested anciently by Strabo which he specifies as a area bordering on Caucasus mountains. It comprised a rugged area through which a road connecting Albania and Iberia passed. The Greek form of the name is believed to have been derived in the Hellenistic period from an indigenous name, corresponding to Armenian Kamboean. In Georgian, it is written Kambeovani, in Arabic, Qambzan. In Sanskrit, it was transliterated as Kamboj. Though not attested prior to Strabo, the area Kambysene is believed to have born this name since remote antiquity. The people living around this area were also called by the same name. Strabo also attests two rivers viz: Cyrus (modern Kura) and Cambyses (modern Jori or Jora), the latter being a tributary of the former.

The territorial name Cambysene or Kambysene as well as the river names Cyrus and Kambyses of Strabo's Geography occurring north of Iran, and the ethnics inhabiting therein have been connected to the ethno-geographical name Kambuja/Kamboj and Kuru of the Sanskrit texts. As per Ernst Herzfeld also, Cyrus and Cambyses, the names of two rivers, as well as the Achaemenid names Kurush and Kambujiya, were derived from two ethnics i.e Kurus and Kambojs of ancient Sanskrit texts. The name Cambyses occurs in Old Persian as Kambujiya or perhaps Kambaujiya, in Egypt as Kambuza, Kembatet (or rather Kambuzia) and Kambunza, in Elemite Kanbuziya, in Akkadian Kambuziya and Aram. Knbwzy etc. In Zend Avestan, the name takes the form of Kavaus and in modern Persian as Kavus and Kaus. Kabus, which was born by the Dilemite sovereigns is the same with the Kaus of Romance; yet the more ancient form is Kaubus or "Kabuj" which latter name renders the identification with Sanskrit Kamboj also most certain. The Georgians, even to the present day, name the hero of romance Kapus, still retaining the labial which has merged in the Persian. In modern times, the name appears as Kamoj in Kafiristan and Kamboj/Kamboh in Punjab.

Scholars also say that Kambysene of the Greeks transliterates into Kamboj and the Cyrus into Kuru of the Sanskrit texts. They further note that the hordes, who had participated in the earlier invasion of Iran along with Yauteyas were the Nordic Scythians, living around the Kambysene area, near Mt Caucasus in ancient Armenia. They were the Kuru-Kambojs of the Sanskrit texts. These Nordic Kuru-Kamboj hordes later got mixed with the Alpine base "Parsa-Xsayatia" (Purush-Khattis) Iranians and gave birth to the renowned Achaemenian dynastic line of Persia. This might explain as to why the Achemenians chose to name their renowned kings as Kambujiya (Cambyses) and Kurush (Cyrus).

Kambohs of Punjab are the modern representatives of these Scythian Kambysene, whom he calls Scythian Kambojs. Chandra Chakravarty further asserts that a branch of these Scythian Kambysenes which had settled in the north-west India (in northern Afghanistan) became known in ancient Sanskrit/Pali texts as Kamboj; and yet another branch of them reached Tibetan plateau where they mixed with the locals; and some Tibetans are still called Kambojs. And through Tibet, they went further to Mekong valley where they were called Kambujas (Cambodians), now represented by the Chams, still a tall, fair, dolichocephelic people with non-mongoloid eyes of the Mon-Khmers. In ancient Indian traditions, the Kambojs are portrayed as belonging to the Kshatriya caste of Indo-Aryan society.

People & Culture

The modern representatives of Ancient Kamboj who still call themselves Kamboj (or prikritic Kamboh, or Kamoz) or Kambhoj are estimated to be around 1.5 million and the rest of the Kamboj population, over the time, has submerged with other occupationalized sects/groups of the Indian sub-continent. Consequently, one can notice numerous of their sub-caste names over-lap with those of other communities of northern India like the Khatris, Rajputs, Jats, Brahmins, Arains etc.

The Kambojs, by tradition, are divided into fifty-two and eighty-four clans. fifty-two line is stated to be descendents of Cadet branch and eighty-four from the elder Branch. This is claimed as referring to the young and elder military divisions under which they had fought the Bharata War. Numerous of their clan names overlap with other Kshatriyas and the Rajput sects of the north-west India, thereby suggesting that some of the Kshatriya/Rajput clans of north-west must have descended from the Ancient Kambojs. The Kambojs/Kambohs practiced weapon-worship in the past but the practice is now going out of vogue.

The Kamboj or Kamboh living in upper India (Greater Punjab) are identified as the modern representatives of the ancient Kambojs. They are found as Hindus, Sikhs, Muslims, Buddhists and the Jains. Kambojs are known as adventurous and enterprising people. Therefore, as a colonists, servicemen, politicians and businessmen, they have also spread out, after the partition, into various parts of India, including a belt of Haryana from Sirsa to Hisar and Karnal to Yamunanagar, Delhi, Uttar Pradesh, Ganganagar in Rajasthan, Nainital, Dehradoon and Shaheed Udham Singh Nagar in Uttarakhand and Madhya Pradesh.

There is also minuscule Kambhoj (jaina) community living since olden times near Nanded in Maharashtra, possibly the dwindling remnant of ancient Kambojs who had settled southwest India around the Christian era. The community obviously seems to have mixed with the local communities over time and imbibed local cultures and languages. The Tajiks, Siyahposh clan (Kam/Kamoz, Katir/Kamtoz) of Nuristan, Yashkuns, Swatis, and the Yusufzais of Eastern Afghanistan and NWFP of Pakistan are said by various scholars to have descended from the ancient Kambojs.

The Kambohs are stated to be the ancient habitants of Persia. The Sikh Kamboj of Kapurthala & Jullundur (Punjab) claim descent from Raja Karan. They also have a tradition that their ancestors came from Kashmir.

Hindu Kambohs claim to be related to the Rajputs and to have come from Persia through southern Afghanistan. The Chapter III of Gazetteer of Muzaffarnagar (UP) based on British India census reports of 1881 1891 etc note that approximately 1200 Muslim and Hindu Kamboj were living in Saharanpur who also claimed to be Rajputs. The Kamboj in Phillaur, District Jullundur, too claimed to be Suryavanshi Rajputs. The Kambohs of Bijnor claim that they came from Trans-Indus nation and Mr Purser accepts this as evidently true. Many of the Bijnor Kambohs also have a tradition that they are of the same ethnic ancestry as the Chattris or Khatris. "In the Census of 1891, it is reported that the Kamboh who lived around Mathura in the United Province (Uttar Pradesh), were originally Kshatriyas." The Rajasthan district Gazetteers asserts that the Kambohs are probably related to the Khatris. The Hindu Kambohs from Karnal claim their ancestry from Garh-Gajni. Their Pandits still pronounce the following couplet at the phera during their marriage ceremony to give information about their original home: Garh Gajni nikaas, Lachhoti Ghaggar vaas (Trans: Originated from the fort of Gajni, and settled down in Ghaggar area (in Haryana or Punjab). One Gajni or Ghazni is located in Afghanistan, but based on another tradition of the Karnal Kamboj, th eminent ethnographers like H. A. Rose and several other scholars have identified this Gajni in Kambay in Saurashtra (port of Vallabhi)

Muslim Kambohs have a tradition that they descended from ancient Kai dynasty of Persia, to which the emperors Kaikaus, Kaikhusro, Kaikubad, Kai-lehrashab and Darius all belonged. On the last king of the dynasty having been dethroned, and expelled from the nation, he wandered about some time with his family and dependents in the neighboring countries and finally settled in Punjab.

The modern Kamboj are still found living mainly by agriculture, business and military service which were the chief professions followed by their Kamboj ancestors some 2500 years ago as powerfully attested by Arthashastra and Brihat Samhita. Numerous foreign and Indian writers have described the modern Kambojs/Kambohs as one of the finest class of agriculturists of India. British colonial writers such as H. A. Rose and Denzil Charles J. Ibbetson note the Kamboj and Ahir agriculturists as the first rank husbandmen. They occupy exactly the same position in general farming as the Ramgarhias occupy in general industry. The Kambojs have made grand contributions in agriculture and military fields. The majority of Krishi Pandit awards in Rajasthan/India have been won by the Kamboj agriculturists. Several foreign and indigenous observers have described the modern Kambojs as very industrious, stiff-necked, hardy, turbulent, skillful, provident and an enterprising race.

There is a medieval era Persian proverb (verse) current in the north-west to the effect that of the Afghans, the Kambohs (Kamboj) and the Kashmiris... all three are rogues. This old proverb seems to convey the historical fact that in the distant past, the Persians, the Afghans, the Kambojs/Kambohs and the Kasmiris lived more or less as neighbors and belonged to one inter-related racial group. The honesty and integrity of the Kamboj/Kamboh community of Punjab is proverbial.

The Kambojs have also been noted for their courage, tenacity and stamina for fighting. They (Kamboj) make excellent soldiers, being of very fine physique and possessing grand courage.....They have always been noted for their cunning strategy, which now, being far less 'slim' than in former times, has developed into the permissible strategy of war.

Modern Kamboj are a generally tall, well-built, sharp featured, and generally very yellow (gaura varna) race. "Pure blood Kamboj ladies are very beautiful and attractive". Kamboj women have especially been noted for their beauty in ancient times too. In ancient references, the Kambojs have been described as a very handsome race. Ancient Kamboj princes have also been noted as tall like towers, exceedingly handsome and of gaura varna, having faces illustrious like the full moon, lotus eyed, handsome like the lord-moon amongst the stars. Even Ramayana calls the Kambojs ravisanibha i.e. with faces illustrious like the Sun.

Sects

Traditionally, Kambojs are divided into fifty-two and eighty-four clans. Line of Fifty-two clan is stated to be descendents of Cadet branch and that of eighty-four from the elder Branch.

Fifty-two Gotras:

1. Azad
2. Abdal
3. Ajpal
4. Angiarey
5. Asoi
6. Bahujad
7. Bage
8. Ban
9. Barar
10. Batti
11. Basra
12. Chandi
13. Chandna
14. Chatrath
15. Daberah
16. Dhanju
17. Dhot
18. Dulai
19. Handa
20. Jaspal
21. Jatmal
22. Josan
23. Kadi
24. Karanpal
25. Kaura
26. Khinda
27. Kirgil
28. Mardak
29. Mehrok
30. Momi
31. Mutti
32. Nadha
33. Nagpal
34. Nagri
35. Nandan
36. Nibber
37. Padhu
38. Patanroy
39. Ratanpal
40. Sandha
41. Sandher
42. Sandheyer
43. Sawan
44. Sohi
45. Shahi
46. Tarikha
47. Thind
48. Tume
49. Turne
50. Vinayak
51. Pathan
52. Unmal

Eighty-four Gotras:

1. Aglawe
2. Ambri
3. Angotre
4. Bahia
29. Gandheyor
30. Gaure
31. Gayile
32. Ghangra
57. Momsarang
58. Multani
59. Naipal
60. Nauhriye

5. Bala
6. Bangar
7. Bangwaye
8. Banjahal
9. Barham
10. Bassi
11. Bastorh
12. Beeharh
13. Bhujang
14. Brahman
15. Chaupal
16. Chhanan
17. Chhichhoti
18. Chichare
19. Chimne
20. Churawat
21. Churiye
22. Dange
23. Dehgal
24. Dhare
25. Dhehte
26. Doliyan
27. Fokni
28. Gadre

33. Ghasitey
34. Gogan
35. Gosiley
36. Harse
37. Jade
38. Jagman
39. Jande
40. Jhand
41. Kakra
42. Kalra
43. Kalsia
44. Khokhar
45. Kukar
46. Lahinde
47. Lakhi
48. Lata
49. Lehri
50. Machhle
51. Mage
52. Mahes
53. Makkar
54. Mall
55. Malle
56. Mandey

61. Nigambar
62. Nuri
63. Padhasi
64. Pandey
65. Rindi
66. Sainik
67. Sandle
68. Sarang
69. Sarkude
70. Sathand
71. Satte
72. Senapati
73. Soki
74. Soni
75. Suage
76. Sulehre
77. Sulhiro
78. Sunehre
79. Tande
80. Taparhiye
81. Thathai
82. Thingrey
83. Topchi
84. Tugal

Demographics

Kambojs are mostly found in North West, Upper India and governed India comprising of North of Kashmir, Hindukush mountains and its adjoining geographical regions comprising Afganistan, Parts of Tajikstan, Ujbekstan, Kafirstan & Pamir Badakstan States, Iran and Cambodia/ Campuchia. Kambojs have also found in Gujarat, Sindh, Rajasthan, Kashmir, Punjab, Haryana, Himachal Pradesh, Delhi, Western Uttar Pradesh, Bengal, Bihar, Orissa, Madya Pradesh, Dinajpur in Bangladesh and regions between Bengal & Myanmar.

Majorcountries having Kamboj population are:

Area	Population
Pakistan	7,79,600
India	4,87,000

Source: Joshua Project, 2008

In India, major states having Kamboj population are:

Area	Population
Rajasthan	1,15,000
Punjab	88,000
Haryana	81,000
Delhi	79,000
Gujarat	7,300

In Pakistan, major states having Kamboj population are:

Area	Population
Punjab	682,000
Sindh	69,000

Source: Joshua Project, 2008

Martial Traditions

The earliest and most powerful reference endorsing the Kshatriyahood of the Kambojs is Panini's fifth century BC Ashtadhyayi. Panini refers to the Kamboj Janapada, and mentions it as "one of the fifteen powerful Kshatriya Janapadas" of his times, inhabited and governed by Kamboj Kshatriyas.

The Harivamsa attests that the clans of Kambojs, Sakas, Yavanas, Pahlavas, Paradas were "formerly noble Kshatriyas". It was king Sagara who had deprived the Kambojs, and other allied races, of their Kshatiyahood (sarve te Kshatriya tata dharma tesham nirakrta) and forbade them from performing Svadhyayas and Vasatkaras.

The Harivamsa calls this group of Sakas, Kambojs, Yavanas, Pahlavas and Paradas as "Ksatriya-pungavah", i.e., foremost amongst the Ksatriyas. Vayu Purana calls them as "Ksatriya ganah" (Kshatriya hordes).

The Manusmriti attests that the Kambojs, Sakas, Yavanas etc were originally "noble Ksatriyas", but were steadily degraded to the status of

"Vrisalah" (degraded Ksatriyas), on account of their neglect of revered rites and non-entertainment of the Brahminas in their countries.

The Mahabharata likewise, also notes that the Kambojs, Sakas, Yavanas, Pahlavas, et al. were originally "noble Kshatriyas", who later got degraded to barbaric status because of the wrath of the Brahmanas (Saka Yavana Kambojs tastah Kshatriya-jatayah, vrishalatvam parigata Brahmananamadarshana).

Furthermore, while making a reference to a Kamboj king called Kamatha, the Sabha Parva of Mahabharata also styles the Kamboj prince as one of the foremost Kshatriya princes (tatha.eva.ksatriya ShresthADharma.rajam.upasate) present amongst the princely invitees of the Pandava king Yudhisthira on the inauguration ceremony of the royal palace.

The legend of Daivi Khadga or Divine Sword detailed in Shantiparva of Mahabharata again powerfully endorses the Kshatriya-hood of the Kambojs. The sword as the "symbol of Kshatriya-hood" was wrested by the warrior king Kamboj from the Kosala king Kuvalashava alias Dhundhumara, from whom it went to another warrior king called Muchukunda.

The Arthashastra of Kautiliya attests the Kshatriya Shrenis (Corporations of Kshatriyas or Warriors) of the Kambojs, Surashtras, and some other nations, and mentions them as living by agriculture, trade and warfare.

Also, as per numerous Puranas, the military Corporations of the Shakas, Yavanas, Kambojs, Pahlavas and Paradas, known as five hordes (panca-ganah), had militarily supported the Haihaya and Talajunga Kshatriyas in depriving Ikshvaku king Bahu (the 7th king in descent from Harishchandra), of his Ayodhya empire. A generation later, Bahu's son, Sagara recaptured Ayodhya after totally destroying the Haihaya and Talajangha Kshatriyas in the battle. Story goes that king Sagara had punished these foreign hordes by changing their hair-styles and turning them into degraded Kshatriyas.

Bhagavata Purana makes reference to a Kamboj king, and calls him a "powerfully armed mighty warrior" (samiti-salina atta-capah Kamboj).

Kalika Purana refers to a war between the Buddhist king Kali (Maurya Brihadratha) and the Brahmanical king Kalika (Pusyamitra Sunga), where the Kambojs came as military supporters to Brihadratha, (187-180) BC. The Purana notes the Kamboj warriors as Kamboji...bhimavikramaih, i.e.

the Kambojs of terrific military prowess", again confirming the Kshatriya-hood of the Kambojs.

Brahmanda Purana talks of twenty-one battles waged by Brahma-Kshatriya sage Parsurama against the ancient Haihaya dynasty clans of the Indian subcontinent. The list of Haihaya dynasty clans whom sage Parsurama fought with includes the Kambojs as well. This ancient evidence again verifies that Kambojs were a Kshatriya clan.

There are numerous similar references in the Puranas, Mahabharata, Ramayana and other ancient Sanskrit and Pali literature, that further document the Kshatriya-hood of the Kambojs.

Chudakarma Samskaara of Paraskara Grhya-Sutram, Vamsa Brahmana of the Sama Veda, the Epic Ramayana as well as Mahabharata and some other ancient references profusely attest that a section of the ancient Kambojs also had adopted the profession of learning and teaching. Thus we see that the ancient Kambojs are known to have been grand scholars and teachers. Undoubtedly, they were intimately connected with ancient renowned University of Taxila in Gandhara.

In Paraskara Grhya-sutram, the Kambojs have been listed at par with the Vasishthas,the cultural heroes of ancient India. Their social customs are stated to be identical. Rsi Upamanyu, the composer of Rigvedic Hymn; and his son/descendent Kamboj Aupamanyava a hallowed sage and teacher mentioned in Vamsa Brahmana of the Sama Veda are some of the very distinguished ancient philosophers/scholars and teachers born of the Kamboj lineage.

The Kambojs have been renowned in ancient time for their excellent breed of horses as well as as a remarkable horsemen or cavalry troopers. They have been portrayed as renowned Central Asian horsemen located in the Uttarapatha or North-west. In the Epic and Pali literature, they repeatedly appear in the characteristic Iranian roles of splendid horsemen and breeders of notable horses. The Mahabharata, the Puranic texts and numerous other ancient literature profusely attest the Kambojs amongst the finest horsemen. They are known to have been constituted into Military Sanghas and Corporations to manage their political and military affairs as Kautiliya and Mahabharata amply attest for us. They are also attested to have been living as Ayuddha-jivi or Shastr-opajivis, which means that the Kamboj cavalry offered their military services to other nations as well. There are numerous references to Kamboj having been requisitioned as cavalry troopers in ancient wars by outside nations.

The horses of the Kambojs were renowned throughout all periods of ancient history. Ancient literature is overflowing with excellent references to the famed Kamboj horses. The Puranas, the Epics, ancient Sanskrit plays, the Buddhist Jatakas, the Jaina Canon, and numerous other ancient sources, all agree that the horses of the Kambojs were a foremost breed.

In Buddhist texts like Manorathpurani, Kunala Jataka and Samangavilasini, the Kamboj land is spoken of as the "birth place of horses." The Aruppa-Niddesa of Visuddhimagga of Buddhaghosa mentions Kamboj as the "base of horses". In the Mahavastu, the superb horses of Kambojs (Kambojka Asvanara) are also referred to and glorified. The Jaina Canon Uttaradhyana-Sutra tells us that a trained Kamboj horse exceeded all other horses in speed and no noise could ever frighten it. The Bhishamaparva of Mahabharata lists the best horses from various lands, but places the steeds from Kamboj at the head of the list, and specifically designates them as the leaders amongst the best horses. In the grand battle fought on the field of Kurukshetra, the fast and mighty steeds of Kamboj were of greatest service.

Besides, the Ramayana, Kautiliya's Arthashastra, the Brahmanda Purana, Somes'ara's Manasollasa, Ashva. Chakitsata by Nakula, Raghuvamsha and Mandakraanta of Kalidasa, Karanabhaar of Bhaasa, Vamsa-Bhaskara, Madhypithika, Karnatakadambari of Nagavarman and numerous other ancient texts and inscriptions also make highly laudatory references to Kamboj horses, and state them the finest breed.

Vishnu Vardhana (twelfth century), the real founding father of Hoysala greatness, who later on became ruler of Mysore, made the earth tremble under the tramp of his mighty Kamboj horses. There were Kamboj steeds in the cavalry of Pandya king Vallabhadeva who is referred to as the proud possessor/rider of the Kamboj horses and elephants. These references amply demonstrate that Kamboj horses were sleek, very mighty and a foremost breed. They have been especially noted for their grand fleetness and remarkable behavior on the battle field. No doubt, Kamboj steeds were the prized possession of kings and warriors in ancient times. It was on account of their supreme position in horse (Ashva) culture that the ancient Kambojs were also popularly known as Ashvakas, i.e. horsemen. Their clans in the Kunar and Swat valleys have been referred to as Assakenoi and Aspasioi in classical writings, and Ashvakayanas and Ashvayanas in Panini's Ashtadhyayi.

The Mahabharata specifically refers to the Kambojs as Ashva-Yuddha-Kushalah, i.e., expert horsemen or cavalrymen. Similarly, Vishnudharmotra Purana also attests that the Kambojns and Gandharans were expert horsemen i.e. proficient in cavalry warfare (Ashva-Yuddha). The Mahabharata, Ramayana, numerous Puranas and some foreign sources amply attest that "Kamboj cavalry-troopers were frequently requisitioned in ancient wars". Therefore, there is no exaggeration in the Mahabharata and Vishnudharmotra Purana statements portraying the ancient Kambojs as horse-lords and masters of horsemanship.

Because the Kambojs were renowned for their horses (ashva) and as cavalry-men (ashvaka) they were also popularly called "Ashvakas". The Ashvakas inhabited Eastern Afghanistan, and were included within the more general term Kambojs. French scholars like Dr. E. Lamotte also identify the Ashvakas with the Kambojs.

The Kambojs entered into conflict with Alexander the Great as he invaded Central Asia: "The Macedonian conqueror made short shrifts of the arrangements of Darius and over-running Achaemenid Empire, dashed into Afghanistan and encountered stiff opposition of the Kamboj races called Aspasios and Assakenois known in the Indian texts as Ashvayanas and Ashvakayanas". These Ashvayana and Ashvakayana Kamboj clans fought the invader to a man. When worse came to worst, even the Ashvakayana Kamboj women took up arms and joined their fighting husbands, thus preferring "a glorious death to a life of dishonour". Diodorus gives a detailed graphic accounts as to how the Ashvakayanas had conducted themselves when faced with the sudden treacherous onslaught from Alexander.

Commenting on the heroic opposition and courage displayed by the Ashvakayanas (Kambojs) in the face of treacerous onslaught of Alexander, Dr Buddha Prakash remarks: "Hardly could any Thermopylae be more glorious!" The Ashvakas had fielded 30,000 strong cavalry, 30 elephants and 20,000 infantry against Alexander. The Ashvayans (Aspasios) were also good cattle breeders and agriculturists. This is clear from large number of bullocks, 230,000 as per Arrian, of a size and shape superior to what the Macedonians had known, that Alexander captured from them and decided to send to Macedonia for agriculture.

King Ashoka sent missionaries to the Kambojs to convert them to Buddhism, and recorded this fact in his Rock Edict V. Dipavamsa and Mahavamsa attest that Ashoka sent thera Maharakkhita to Yona, and Majjhantika to Kashmra and Gandhara, to preach Dharma amongst the Yonas, Gandharas and Kambojs. Sasanavamsa specifically attests that Maharakkhita thera went to Yonaka nation and established Buddha's Sasana "in the lands of the Kambojs and other countries." Thus, the Zoroastrian as well as Hindu Kambojs appear to have embraced Buddhism in large numbers, because of the efforts of king Ashoka and his envoys.

Particularly during the second/first centuries BC, in their advance from their original home, one stream of the Kambojs, allied with the Sakas and Pahlavas, had proceeded to Sindhu, Sauvira and Surastra; while the other stream allied with the Yavanas appears to have moved to Punjab and Uttar Pradesh. There are important references to the warring Mleccha hordes of the Sakas, Yavanas, Kambojs, Pahlavas etc in the Bala Kanda of the Valmiki Ramayana. Indologists like Dr H. C. Raychadhury, Dr B. C. Law, Dr Satya Shrava and others see in these verses the clear glimpses of the struggles of the Hindus with the mixed invading hordes of the barbaric Sakas, Yavanas, Kambojs, Pahlavas etc from north-west. The time frame for these struggles is second century BC downwards. Dr Raychadhury fixes the date of the present version of the Valmiki Ramayana around/after second century AD.

The invading hordes of the Sakas, Yavanas, Kambojs, Pahlavas, Abhiras etc from the north-west had came to Punjab, United Province, Sindhu, Rajasthan and Gujarat in large numbers, wrested political control of northern India from the Indo-Aryans and had founded their respective kingdoms/principalities as sovereign rulers in the land of the Indo-Aryans,a fact also sufficiently attested by other Hindu texts like the epic Mahabharata as well as Kalki Purana. There is also a literary as well as inscriptional evidence supporting the Yavana and Kamboj overlordship in Mathura in Uttar Pradesh. The royal family of the Kamuias (Pali: Kambojikas or Sanskrit: Kambojs) referenced in the Mathura Lion Capital inscriptions of the Saka Mahakshatrapa Rajuvula, are believed to be linked to the royal house of Taxila/Swat in Gandhara/Kamboj. The Maitraka Dynasty of Saurashtra/Gujarat, in all probability, belonged the Kambojs, who had settled down in south-western India around Christian era. In Mediaval era, the Kambojs are known to have seized north-west Bengal (Gauda and Radha) from the Palas of Bengal and founded their own Kamboj-Pala Dynasty. Indian texts like Markandeya Purana, Vishnu Dharmottari Agni Purana, Garuda Purana, Arthashastra of Barhaspatya and Brhatsamhita of Vrahamihira etc etc profusely attest Kamboj references in the south-western and southern India. The inscriptional references of the medieval era rulers of Vijayanagara of southern India also attest a Kamboj empire abutting on the borders of the Vijayanagara Empire which possibly alludes to a Kamboj empire near/around Gujarat/Saurashtra. These facts sufficiently prove that the Kambojs from Central Asia had migrated into western and interior India around Christian times and had permanently made India their home.

There are also several ancient inscriptional references found in Rohana province (in Ceylon), belonging to second BC, which illustrate pre-Christian Kamboj presence in various parts in Sri Lanka and also powerfully attest one Kamboj Sangha as well as grand Kamboj guilds located in the island, thus indisputably proving that the Kambojs had also migrated to Ceylon during pre-Christian times and must have played active role in the social, economical and political arena of the island. The Sihalavatthu, a Pali text of around the fourth century AD, also attests a group of people called Kambojs living in Rohana province in Sri Lanka. This above pieces of evidence give mighty support to Kamboj dominance of Sri Lanka and also to the view that the Kambujas who had established the ancient Kambuja empire, in Indochinese peninsula, were none-else than the north-western Kambojs, who had probably migrated to Indochina via Sri Lanka or Ceylon.

The Kambojs were a people of Iron Age India, frequently mentioned in (post-Vedic) Sanskrit literature, making their first appearance in the Mahabharata and contemporary Vedanga literature (roughly from the 5th century AD). Their Kamboj Kingdoms were likely located in areas on both sides of the Hindukush. They seemingly qualify as an Indo-Iranian people, better as Iranians, cognate to the Indo-Scythians.

Together with the Indo-Scythian invasion of India during the pre-Kushana period, Kambojs appear to have migrated to Bengal, Sri Lanka and Cambodia in the period spanning the 2nd century AD and the 5th century AD. Their descendents held various principalities in Medieval India, the one in north-west Bengal being seized, around middle of tenth century AD, from the Palas in Bengal.

Several foreign and indigenous observers have described the modern Kambojs as very industrious, stiff-necked, hardy, turbulent, skillful, provident and an enterprising race. There is a medieval era Persian proverb (verse) current in the north-west to the effect that of the Afghans, the Kambohs (Kamboj) and the Kashmiris... all three are rogues. It seems that in the distant past, the Persians, the Afghans, the Kambojs/Kambohs and the Kasmiris lived more or less as neighbors and belonged to one inter-related racial group.

The Kambojs have also been noted for their courage, tenacity and stamina for fighting. They (Kamboj) make excellent soldiers, being of very fine physique and possessing grand courage.....They have always been noted for their cunning strategy, which now, being far less 'slim' than in former times, has developed into the permissible strategy of war..

Modern Kamboj are a generally tall, well-built, sharp featured, and generally very yellow (gaura varna) race. "Pure blood Kamboj ladies are very beautiful and attractive". Kamboj women have especially been noted for their beauty in ancient times too. In ancient references, the Kambojs have been described as a very handsome race. Ancient Kamboj princes have also been noted as tall like towers, exceedingly handsome and of gaura varna, having faces illustrious like the full moon, lotus eyed, handsome like the lord-moon amongst the stars. Even Ramayana calls the Kambojs ravisanibha i.e. with faces illustrious like the Sun.

Very curiously, besides the Kamboj/Kamboh people, many clans of the Jatts, Rajputs, Arains and other peoples of Punjab also boast of their descent from the same Raja Karan. If this Raja Karan was indeed the ancestor of the Kamboj people as is thoughtlessly asserted and propagated in the writings of these British colonial writers or their lieutenants like Ahmed Abdulla, Syed Abdul Quddus etc in order to establish a hypothetical connection between the Kamboj and the Arains, then, an inevitable consquence of this misdemeanor must also be faced, that is, besides the Arains of Pakistan, many clans of the Jatts and Rajputs like the Dhillons, Gorayas, Sandas, Thathus/Thathas/Thathials, Naru/Narma/Narwa, Babbar, Khakh, Janjuhan (Janjua?), Kharrals, Harrals, Lakas, Langhas/Lahnghas, Bhuttas, Varyas/Barias, Barah/Warah, the Kathias of Ravi/Jhang, the Punwars, the Baghelas, the Balwanas, Pawars, many sections of the Rajputs from Kathiawar and the Kakezais of the Afghans etc,- all these must also be treated as a Kamboj breed. This may also make a sense since the people like Kambojs (and the Kathis and the Gujjars etc) are the oldest surviving identities and rest of the people are simply the (later-time) derived sects/units from the ancient classical races like the Kambojs, Sakas, Yavanas, Pahlavas, Paradas, Rishikas, Hunas, Gujjars etc etc. The process of "occupationalization" (caste-formation) surely and slowly went on as the centuries rolled by, thus, finally emerging into a picture as we see it today.

There is no connection between the Arains and the Kamboj. The Kamboj have persistently denied any relation as Mr William Crook has commented. Whereas the term "Arain" is an occupational caste and is a mixture of diverse ethnic elements which took place over the time, the term "Kamboj" represents purely a sect name. Of the numerous sects of the Kamboj, only approximately twenty unimportant clan names overlap with the Arains.

Thus, Gaure, Momi, Handa are the only important clans of the Kamboj shared with the Arains. On the other hand, over sixty of Arain clans overlap with those of the Punjab Jatts, and approximately twenty with those of the Rajputs. Some important Arain clans overlapping with the Rajputs are Siroha, Janjua, Chauhan, Bhatti, Bhutta (or Bhutto), Chachar, Indrai/Indhar, Joiya, Khokhar etc. Therefore, like the Rajputs and the Jatts, the Arains also represent an occupational caste, rather than a single ethnic group which the Kamboj undoubtedly are, and therefore, the Arains, in all probability, are a mixture of numerous diverse ethnic elements from the ancient Sakas, Kambojs, Yavanas, Pahlavas, Hunas, Gujjars etc. It is notable that the title of Mahar is prevalent both amongst the Arains as well as the Gujjars.

Contribution to Defence Services

Chandragupta Maurya constituted his army based on the principles and recommendations of Arthashastra. This is evident from the fact that the martial clans of Kambojs find prominent mention in Maurya army as is attested by Mudrarakshasa play of Visakhadutta. Both Mudrarakshasa as well as Jaina work Parisishtaparvan refer to Chandragupta Maurya's alliance with the Himalayan king Parvatka. This alliance gave Chandragupta a composite army made up of the Republican Kambojs besides also of other warrior clans such as Yavanas, Sakas, Kiratas, Parasikas and Bahlikas.

With the help of these frontier warlike republican clans from the northwest, whom Justin (Marcus Junianus Justinus) brands as "a band of robbers", Chandragupta Maurya was able to defeat the Macedonian straps of Punjab and Afghanistan and later following this, the corrupt Nanda ruler of Magadha, thus laying the foundations of a great Maurya Empire in northern and north-western India.

Kambojs has contributed heavely to defence forces. There is not a single village of Kambojs in whole of India where you could not find many families having their sons in defence forces. Representation of Kambojs in the Army's various regiments has been steadily going up over the years. Kambojs can be found in various regiments of services such as:

- Parachute Regiment
- Mechanised Infantry
- Punjab Regiment
- Sikh Regiment

Famous Personalities

Armed Forces

- **Capt Rajdeep Singh Kamboj:** Deputy Director, Sainik Welfare
- **Lt Col Shrish Kamboj:** A highly recognized Officer

Politicians

- Dr. Kamla Verma: Leader
- Hansraj Jossan: MLA
- Lal Singh: Popular Leader
- Subhash Kamboj: Leader

Artists

- Dr. Jiya Lal Kamboj
- Kirpal Singh Dardi
- Lajwant Singh Thind
- Kaleem Ahmad Kamboj

16

Kurmis

Kurmi, which is the name of one of the sects of the Hindus. Basically, In hindu society structure, there are four varna named as: Bharmanya, Kshatriya, Vaisya and Kshdrya, which was decided on the basis on thier work. People from Kurmi community belong to Kshatriya varna. They were suppose to do administration related works, but with the due course of time, they got engaged with agriculture related works. The "Kurmi" is known as the chief ancient agricultural caste of India. Colonel Dalton regards them as the descendents of some of the earliest Aryan Colonists - a brown tawny coloured people, of an average height, well proportioned and with fair amount of good looks. They show well-shaped heads and high features and except when they have obviously intermixed with aborigins, they are unquestionable Aryans in looks. Grey eyes and brownish hair are sometimes met with among them. The women usually have small and well formed hands and feet

The link between Kshtriyas and agriculture has been justified on the grounds of linguistic affinities between the root "ar" (bravery, heroism, found in English and Greek hero, Russian geroj and Sanskrit arya) and other words for cultivators i.e. those who labour nobly (Russian oratel or ploughman, Airga in the Zend-Avesta), as well as in the legend of King "Prithu", who tamed the earth to make fertile again. It is for this reason that the Sanskrit word for "earth" is "Prithvi", in honour of the Aryan king "Prithu" who first cultivated the earth. And, in the words of Thomas Jefferson, "cultivators of the earth are the most virtuous and independent citizens".

Origin & History

Kurmis are the direct descedants of the wellknown Kshatriya dynasties of Lord Rama. The physical appearance of the kurmis tends to support the opinion of their Kshatriya Ancestry. Another ancestry of

Kammas is speculated as: Buddhist Kurmis from the Gangetic plains migrated to the Krishna river delta in large numbers to escape the persecution of Pushyamitra Sunga (184 AD). Buddhism was already flourishing in Dharanikota, Bhattiprolu, Chandavolu etc in this fertile region. Historians surmised that the Sanskrit word Kurmi/Kurma became Kamma in later years. The first records of the word Kammarashtram appeared in the Jaggayyapeta inscription of the Ikshvaku King Madhariputra Purushadatta (3rd century AD). Kammarashtram extended from the Krishna River to Kandukur (Prakasam Dt.). The next record was that of Pallava King Kumara Vishnu II followed by that of Eastern Chalukya king Mangi Yuvaraja (627-696 AD). The subsequent inscriptions of Telugu Cholas/Chodas and Kakatiya dynasty mentioned 'Kammanadu'. This area is also known as Pallavanadu/Palanadu/Palnadu because of Pallava rule.

The industrious Kurmis developed the land quickly. To maintain a record of the annual crops on each Pat (a parcel of land) the ruler appointed a record keeper known as the Patlik. This name was later shortened to patel.

There are several sub-sects within the Kurmi communities. Bhumihar Brahmins are land-owning Brahmins and they are different from brahmin that live from donations. Due to vast regions of land belong to bhumihar the kurmi work on some or part of the bhumihar land for a wage. The Kurmi, Kanbi, Patel, Matya etc of Gujarat probably followed the various land-owning Brahmin sects that went to Gujarat and other places to the south of the Vindya mountains a long time in the past.

The Kurmi's of Bihar are the same genetic ancestry as the various Kanbi Patel sects in Gujarat excluding the Koli Patels. Kurmi's constitute around 1.4% of the Indian population. Kurmi word has been derived from "Krish Dhatu" of Sanskrit.From history Kurmi are agrarian, thats is the meaning of word Kurmi.

People & Culture

Kurmi and their descendents residing all over the world and especially in India are compassionate, industrious and very resourceful people. Kurmi are involved in various Agricultural and Business. Kurmi didn't forgotten their culture and rich heritage, therefore other Samaj are changing with the time and left there culture.

The surname Patel is the most widely used name today. Originally the Kurmis of Punjab, after having settled in Gujarat around 1400 AD. were allocated the uncultivated land in Petlad Taluka by the Solankis, the rulers of Gujarat at the time. The Solanki ruler allocated land equivalent to one village to each family for cultivation. The Kanbi family being highly motivated and industrious to succeed cultivated the land and prospered. The King has an agreement with Kanbis and had appointed a headman, whose responsibility was to keep the records of the crops on a Pat. The person keeping the record was known as Patlik, and was shortened to Patal, and eventually to Patel. Prior to the introduction of the name Patel in Gujarat, they were known as Kanbis. Paste is not a cast, but a surname adopted by the most of original Kanbis.

Kurmi means "owner of land". 'Pati' means land and 'Dar' means the person who owns it. In Mehamdavad, Kheda district, around 1700 AD., the ruler of Gujarat, Mohammed Begdo, selected the best farmer from each village and gave them land for cultivation. In return, the Kurmi would pay the ruler a fixed income for a certain period of time, after which, the Kurmi would acquire the ownership of the land. The Kurmis would hire a industrious and knowledgeable work force to cultivate the land and in due course of time, they would become the owners of the land. These Kurmis were from then onwards identified as Patel Kurmis.

The History proves that the Kurmis are very industrious, enterprising, and very resourceful people who do not wait for an opportunity, rather creates one and makes success for it. Kurmi have come from state of Gujarat to various areas of in India. Kurmi chiefly live in the state of Madhaya Pradesh, Gujarat, Rajasthan and Maharashtra of India. Kurmis are also found in the rest of the world including America.

Sects

- Chandrakar
- Gangwar
- Jaiswar
- Kamma
- Kanbi
- Katiyar
- Kulambi
- Kulwadi
- Kunbi
- Kutumbi
- Mahanta
- Mahato
- Mohanta
- Naidu
- Niranjan
- Patel
- Reddy
- Sachan
- Singraur
- Umrao
- Verma
- Vokkaliga

Demographics

In India, their population is approximately 16,500,000 major states having Kurmi population are:

Area	Population
Uttar Pradesh	5,852,000
Bihar	3,122,000
Jharkhand	2,006,000
Madhya Pradesh	1,714,000
West Bengal	1,216,000
Chhattisgarh	770,000
Andhra Pradesh	698,000
Assam	221,000
Orissa	50,000
Karnataka	48,000

Source: Joshua Project, 2008

Martial Traditions

The kings and military persona of Kammanadu started using the title Nayaka/Nayakudu from 10th century onwards as observed in many inscriptions. There are approximately 1200 Kamma surnames (Intiperu) which are discernible from this time. The surnames and Gothras of Kammas and Velamas were catalogued by Badabanala Bhatta in 1068 AD. The names of the ancestral villages were adopted as Gothras. This shows that the ancestors of Kammas and Velamas were either Buddhists or Jains who did not follow Gothra system and that both the social groups had a common history. The historical reasons for the dichotomy of the two groups are not known, although many stories abound.

The inscriptions of many Kamma Nayaks mentioned that they belong to Durjaya clan (Vamsa). For example, the inscription (1125 AD) of Pinnama Nayudu in the temple of Sagareswara in Madala village mentioned that he belonged to Durjaya clan and Vallutla Gothra. Another inscription (1282 AD) in the same temple mentioned that Devineni Erra Nayudu, Kommi Nayudu, Surappa Nayudu and Pothi Nayudu belonged to the lineage of Buddhavarma, Durjaya clan and Vallutla Gothra. The inscription at Ravuru mentioned that the bodyguards of Queen Rudrama Devi, Ekki Nayudu, Rudra Nayudu, Pinarudra Nayudu and Pothi Nayudu belong to Durjaya vamsa and Vallutla Gothra. It is worth mentioning here that many of the martial clans of Kammas belong to Vallutla Gothra. Many of the Telugu Chodas of Kammanadu had relations with Eastern Chalukyas and later with Kakatiyas.

As per many inscriptions and "Velugotivari Vamsavali" Kammas with surnames such as Yalamanchi, Gollapudi, Yalampati, Sammeta, Maccha, Konda, Choda, Vasireddy, Katta, Adapa etc., belong to Choda-Chalukya ancestry. The Vasireddy Clan had a title "Chalukya Narayana". Historians surmised that by the end of 10th century Durjayas, Chodas, Chalukyas and Haihayas of Kammanadu merged into Kammas. Kammanadu is an ancient geographical area in the present day South Indian state of Andhra Pradesh. A Gotra indicates lineage in the Hindu community. A replica of an ancient statue found amongst the ruins of a temple at Sarnath Buddhism is a philosophy based on the teachings of the Buddha, Siddhartha Gautama, a prince of the Shakyas, whose lifetime is traditionally given as 566 to 486 AD.

The Rig Veda, refered to an Aryan people living in the highlands of Pamir in Central Asia. Almost 1000 years later, the Aryans migrated in three different directions. One journeyed towards present-day Iran, another towards Europe, and through Afghanistan. Those Aryans who settled in Punjab became a very happy and prosperous people. They organized themselves around a caste syatem that described four specific functions of the community. The Kshatriyas of that system were the protectors of the land. Nevertheless, in peace time many of their members framed the land and raised cattle.

These people, named Kurmi Kshatriyas, eventually migrated to the fertile land of Ganga and Jamuna, eventually reaching Bihar and Bengal. From 600 BC to 200 BC, the kings of Iran and Greece repeatedly attacked Punjab, forcing most of the Kurmi Kshatriyas (also known as the Kurmis) to flee even further south to Gujarat in Vadnagar and Charator in the Kheda district. Around 1400 AD, the ruler of Gujarat granted the uncultivated land of petland Talukas to the Kurmis as their new home.

Kurmis helped various kings during the wars and engaged in farming during peacetime. After the decline of major kingdoms, Kammas controlled large fertile areas, as a legacy of their martial past. The British recognized their prominence and made them village heads also known as Chowdary to collect taxes. The association of Kurmis with the land and agriculture is legendary. The martial prowess of Kurmis was put to good use to tame the lands in modern times. There are many proverbs which speak of the Kurmis' adeptness in agriculture and their emotional attachment to the soil.

Contribution to Defence Services

Kurmis are among the bravest of the Indian army's recruited communities. They have always been represented in the armed forces.

They can be found in various regiments of Indian Army such as:

- Parachute Regiment
- Punjab Regiment
- Maratha Light Infantry
- Bihar Regiment

Famous Personalities

Kurmis have contributed to all fields of life and have produced some famous personalities, a list of which is given below.

Armed Forces

Gallantary Award Recipients

- Rifle man Rishi Patel: Maha Vir Chakra Recipient

Others

- Lt. General Markande Katiyar
- Lt. General Shoarya Patel
- Brig. Jaipal Kurmi
- Brig. V.S Sinha
- Mahamritunjaya Engineer

Politicians

- Beni Prasad Verma: Famous Leader and Founder of Samajwadi Kranti Dal
- Keshu Bhai Patel: Famous BJP Leader and Former Chief Minister of Gujrat
- Lalji Verma: Famous BSP Leader and Cabinet Minister in Mayawati Government in UP
- Sone Lal Patel: Famous Leader and Founder of Apna Dal
- Vinay Katiyar: Famous BJPleader and founder of Bajranj Dal
- Yashaskara

Artists

- Lalita Pawar: Former Bollywood Actress
- Sayali Bhagat: Miss India
- Smita Patil: Former Bollywood Actress
- Smt Kumud Pawade: Renowned Sanskrit scholar
- Smt Prabha Rau: Musician
- Ujjwala Raut: Supermodel

17

Mukkulathors

Origin & History

There are diverse theories with regard to the ancestry of Mukkulathors. Dr Spencer Wells and Dr. Pitchappan have found an ancient DNA marker in the blood of Kallar that links them to the very first modern humans who migrated out of Africa about 60,000 years ago and travelling through the southern coastline of Asia had eventually reached Australia. Based on this theory, it is assumed that the Piramala Kallars are the oldest human habitants of the subcontinent. Yet, this is an isolated case found only amongst the individuals of the Kallar caste.

The downfall of the Mukkulathors took place in 1345 with the fall of Vira Pandyan IV and the subsequent conquest of Madurai by the Delhi Sultanate. Nevertheless, the southern territories of the Sultanate soon asserted their independence and the Mukkulathors recovered under the Vijayanagar Empire and later under the Nayak dynasty during whose period they served as Polygars or chieftains.

The Nayaks were actually governors appointed by Vijayanagar kings and were Naidus of Telugu ancestry. Later, after the fall of Vijayanagar, they established some measure of independence in the provinces which they governed and appointed individuals from the warrior Mukkulathor clans as their military chieftains and governors. After a century of peace and prosperity, the Nayak empire disintegrated and regional Polygar chieftains most of whom were from the Mukkulathor communities, making use of this opportunity, established their dominance and rule in the regions which they governed. Nevertheless, just as their sun was in its ascendancy there arose a serious obstacle in the form of the British East India Company who desired to force the Polygars into submission and annex their territories to the Madras Presidency.

There was a clash of interests between Mukkulathor Polygar chieftains seeking to recover their lands after 400 years of foreign rule and the British East India Company, an emerging power seeking to expand its influence and power into new territories and to arrest the growth of French influence in India ahead of the Seven Years War.

The first direct challenge was thrown by Puli Thevan in 1755. This was precipitated by the support the British East India Company lent to Puli Thevar's enemy, the Nawab of Arcot. Puli Thevar is remembered as the first king to have fought and defeated the British in India. His exploits have since become legendary.

Opposition to British rule was also offered by Padal Vellaiya Devan who fought the British along with Kattabomman. His son Desakaval Senbaga Devar is also remembered for his exploits.

Queen Velu Nachiyar, Queen of Sivaganga, is another noted personality who fought with the British during early British Era. The Maruthu Pandiyar brothers are notable for their role in the Polygar Wars. They were eventually captured by the British and hanged in 1801. In 18th century Vallambars (Nattars) helped the Maruthu brothers in War against Britishers. So they presents some regions to them, to manage the administration of places near to Karaikkudi. Then Vallambars are also called as Palaya Nattars.

Marriages happen between people with the same surname. The Kallar with surname of "Vanniar" or "Vanniyar" still follow the traditional ways. In Thanjavur district the oldest person in the village is treated as "Arasukarar" (king), and they have been given the first respect during the "Pongal" festival.This has been followed all the way from chola empire as heared. Every surname has it's own description, for instance The people who hold sword (vaal) and patrol the city during the Chola period are called "Valludayar" later it becomes "Vandayar".

People & Culture

These are believed to be the ancient habitants of the plains, who became subject to Hinduism by the influx of Brahmins amongst them from the north; who, having emigrated from their native place, settled down on the banks of the fertile rivers, carrying with them a knowledge of civilisation, and instructing the people in the knowledge of letters and divisions and subdivisions of sects, probably some six or seven centuries prior to the Christian Era. The Maravers are believed to constitute the greatest bulk of the population of the Tinnevelly district, numbering over one hundred thousand, and to be descendents of lineal representatives of the Pandean dynasty, which flourished from BC. 500 to the fifteenth century. Subsequently the capital of the Pandean empire was founded at Madura, embracing the Madura and Tinnevelly districts. The Maravers are a robust hardy race, dark skinned (almost black), athletic, active, of medium height; muscular system fully developed; forehead rather low; cranium rounded, narrow in front; eyes large and full. They are believed to be by birth and profession thieves and robbers; and have been from time immemorial employed as village watchmen, for which service they are paid in kind by the villagers for the protection of their property.

They are honest and honourable to their trust in their own village; but at night form large gangs, of from fifty to one hundred, at remote places, with a view of pillaging villages. If thwarted in their designs on these occasions, they become reckless, and frequently commit murder. To avoid being taken, they divest themselves of clothing and oil their skins freely. Some notorious character having been selected for a leader, their meet takes place at some distance, and quite in a different direction, from the village intended to be plundered, so as to throw off suspicion. They carry short stout sticks, having one end loaded with two, three or more iron ferrules, in the use of which they are great experts, more especially in the manner of throwing their sticks; they often kill game at full speed in this way. They make use of all flesh meats, except beef.

Although a great many of the members are still agriculturalists, many have also progressed up the social ladder as doctors, engineers, entrepreneurs, politicians and civil servants. Large number of people from the community are serving the nation as military men. Large number of people serving the tamilnadu police department. They are traditionally Hindus. Today they constitute a significant part of the Tamil community in India, Sri Lanka, and in other parts of the world.

Sects

The Kallar, Maravar and Agamudaiyar communities constitute the Kshatriya or warrior class of Tamil Nadu, South India. They are a prominent social group of India. They descent from the ancient royal dynasties of the southern area. They have proven Indian histories of more than 3000 years

Kallar: Kallar is one of the three communities which constitute the Mukkalathor confederacy. European eyewitnesses of the 18th century have made mention of Kallars as "a fearless race show many signs of independence and non-submission to any form of subjugation". They were expert soldiers and constituted the bulk of Chola and Pandya armies.

One of the principa! weapons of the Kallars is the boomerang. This has evoked comparisons with the Australian aborigines and vouch for the theory that Kallars were one of the earliest people to inhabit the Indian subcontinent. The principal occupation of Kallars is farming.

Kallars are found largely in Madurai, Sivagangai, Pudukkottai, Thanjavur, Trichy, Theni and Ramanathapuram districts of Tamil Nadu. One of their popular deities is Kallazhagar who is a warrior form of Lord Thirumala or Venkadavan.

There are various sub-sects of Kallars, among whom the Ambalakarar is the most important. They were a warlike people who strongly resisted every British attempt to subjugate them. They are found in Madurai and Sivaganga districts. In these districts, each village is headed by an Ambalakarar (president of an assembly) and the Ambalakarars took upon themselves the power to adjudicate disputes that arose amongst the habitants in the "nadu", belonging to different sects. They used to hear complaints, hold inquiries and punish the offenders. They wielded considerable powers to intervene in any kind of transaction or transfer of property amongst the people. No land could be alienated from one man to another without the permission of the Ambalakarars. Another important Kallar subcaste is the Piramalai Kallar. They are highly conservative and have preserved their customs and traditions to the present day. They are also believed to be the oldest habitants of the Tamil nation with reports of their presence going back to Tamil literary works of the 4th century BC. They are found chiefly in the districts of Madurai and Theni. Their popular deity is Amman, the Mother Goddess.

There are kallar settlements in Aziz Nagar (near Ulundurpettai), Pammal (near Tambaram) and Prisly Nagar (Otteri,Chennai). Kallars (Thevar pattam) in these settlements are belived to be migrated from southern parts of Tamil Nadu to a place called Veppur (Cuddalore district). A temple ("Nallathangal kovil") laid down by them at Veppur on their migration and a Nallathangal temple found in a southern district is the only link to establish their migration.

Maravar: Maravar (meaning "veerar",upper caste), are one of the oldest social groups to be mentioned by the Sangam Tamil literature. This indicates a connection with the Tamil land which is at least 2,000 years old. The writers of the Sangam Age place them in rural settlements withdrawn from cities. Maravar, in Tamil, means a warrior. Maravars are the courageous breed and were involved in the major wars that Tamilnadu witnessed.The maravar are popularly given the title 'Thevar.Other historians postulate that Maravar is derived from Tamil language term Marutham (called as Thinnai). They originally lived in.

The name of the city Madurai is also postulated to be derived from Maruthai and honourific title of local Pandya kings..They were the rulers of ancient tamilnadu.They governed the vast land mass of tamilnadu along with Paravar,the coastal rulers.Both these races have same ancestry and they are renowned all over south India for their valour.They were bloodly related akins.The Maravar and Paravar constitute the Kshatriya varna of Tamil caste system.The southern styles of Kalarippayattu,silambam,varma kalai have been practiced primarily by nairs ezhavas,Kallars and Thevars of erstwhile Travancore regions.The Maravar have close relation with kalabhras but they were non-aryan,non-kalabhar group.They were ancint rulers of Pandya empire from the first sangam age.Another predominant caste called the Paravars and Maravars were collectively called as Meenavar and Villavar of the past.

They both have same ancestry and they had control over pandya empire.Their leaders were given the title"Meenavan" or "Pandyan".Later years the paravas diversified to various fields like pearl fishing,sea trading,also renowned sailors came from that caste.But the maravas of meenavar still remained in their tradition.Veera Maravar are the fore fathers of varma kalai.

The Maravas were unbeaten in the History of tamilnadu.They governed Chera,Chola and Pandya kingdoms in later years and they were the Muvendar.Later Naga invasion,Nairis (the present day Nair caste) came to south India as allies to Maravar. But Later they changed their diplomatic stance to enemy and the cowardice attack of Nairs made Maravar lose Chera empire.Edgar Thurston (1855-1935) a British museologist and ethnographer identified the use of the boomerang by Kallar and Marawar.

Agamudayar: Agamudayar also known as Agam Padaiyar is one of the three Mukkulathor communities. W. Francis writes about Agamudaiyans that they are "a cultivating caste found in all the tamil districts'. nevertheless, most agamudaiyars are found in Thanjavur, Madurai and Tirunelveli districts."

There are various derivations of the word "Agamudaiyan" or "Ahamudaiyan". " derived from the root aham, which, in Tamil, has many significations.In one of these, it means a house, in another earth, and therefore it has two meanings, householder and landholder; the suffix Udeiyar indicating ownership. The word is also used in another form, ahambadiyan, derived from another meaning of the same root, i.e., inside. And, in this derivation, it signifies a particular caste, whose office it was to attend to the business in the interior of the king's palace, or in the pagoda".

Of the Mukkulathor, the Agamudaiyans are the community most influenced by Brahminism. The ordinary title of the Agamudaiyans is Servaikkaran, but many of them call themselves Pillai. In Thanjavur district, agamudaiyans are also called "Terkittiyar" or "southerners". The Agamudaiyans are divided into the following sub-sects: Aivali Nattan, Kottaipattu, Malainadu, Nattumangalam, Rajaboja, Rajakulam, Rajavasal, Kalian, Sani, Maravan, Tuluvan (cf. Tuluva Vellala) and Servaikkaran.

Surnames: The surnames used by the Thevar people are Ambalakarar, Servai, Vandaiyar, Mannaiyar, Nattar (not Nadar), etc. It is a general practice in Tamil Nadu to address a Thevar woman as "Nachchiyaar". The Kallars of Dindigul, Trichy, Thanjavur, Theni, Madurai, Sivaganga, Pudukottai and Ramnad Districts have very distinct surnames. Some of the most common names are Anjathevar,Olivarayar, Vanathirayar, Sendapiriyar, OOnayaar, Alathondamar, Ambalam, Aarsuthiyar,Kaadavaraayar, Kalingarayar, Vandaiyaar, Vallundar, Thanjaraayar, Chozhangaraayar, Kandiyar, Pursaar, Vaanavaraayar, Mazhavaraayar, Payer, Kommatti, Mootar, Patti, Kannakkarar, Irungular, Singilaar, Pallavaraayar, Ponnapoondar, Pullavaraayar, Servai, Karaimeendar, Vanavarayar,Vairayar, Ponpethiar, Gopalar, Thondaimaan, Thevar, Kandapillai, Vayaadiyar, Vanniar, Nattaar, Alankara Priyar, mavaliyar, Munaiyatriyar, Keerudayar, Saaluvar, Manraayar, Kaadavaraayar, Madhavarayar, Onthiriyar, Servai, Serumadar, Sethurayar,Vambaliar, Thenkondaar, Mankondaar, Kaaduvetiyaar, Sozhagar, Chozanga Nattar, etc. There are over 700 surnames in use.

Demographics

Kallar, Maravar, Agamudaiyar basically are the Pandiya and chola caste who governed the pandiya nadu and chola nadu. Kallar chiefly lived and are still populas on the northern pandian territory or Thanjavur, Thiruchirappalli, Dindugal, Madurai districts.

Agamudaiyar formed the police force and did security jobs. They bascially stood guard for Temple, Farm lands, Nadan hamlets. They are called servai in Thirunalveli, Thoothukudi districts. Maruthu Sagothararkal are marked for their guard of Kalayar koil against the war with British. They are scaterd all thro Pandiyan Territory chiefly to all temple cities.

Maravar are brave warriors who met head-on. They lived and are still populas on the northern Pandian Territory next to Kallar belt in the districts of Ramnad, Madurai, Raja Palayam, Thirunelveli. They shared the ruling titles of Pandiyans for their bravery.

When the Pandian suffered defeat at the hands of Nayaks and Muslims of Vijayanagar Empire, These 3 castes stood guard and gave their life in protecting the assets of Madurai Meenakshi temple and its chain of temples down south. They retained the pandian control and still are dominant in the southern pandiyan districts of Tamilnadu.

Martial Traditions

Avippali, Thannai, Verttal, Vallan pakkam, Pun Kilithu Mudiyum Maram and Marakkanchi: the forms of martial suicide and suicidal battle of the warrior as the ultimate expression of his loyalty to his commander. These six forms of martial suicide are defined as described by the works referred to above.

Pulla Vazhkai Vallan Pakkam – the martial attitude of the warrior who goes forth into suicidal battle is mentioned by Tholkappiyam. The other works refer to it as Thannai Verttal. Duarte Barbosa describes the practice amongst the Nayar (of the Chera empire). It was later noticed by British officials as well. It was also prevalent amongst the Maravar (of the Pandya empire) from whom the suicidal Aapathhuthavi bodyguard was selected. Thannai Verttal also refers to the suicide of a warrior on hearing that his king or commander has died (Purapporul Venpa Malai). Punkilithu Mudiyum Maram is the martial act of a warrior who commits suicide by tearing apart his battle wound.

Another form of martial suicide mentioned by all the works except Veera soliyam, is Avippali. Tamil inscriptions speak of it as Navakandam. Inscriptions found in many parts of Tamilnadu provide greater information on the practice. Navakandam is the act of a warrior who slices his own neck to fulfil the vow made to korravai – the Tamil goddess of war – for his commanders' victory in battle. The Kalingathu Parani – a work which celebrates the victory of the Chola king Kulotunga and his general Thondaman in the battle for Kalinga, describes the practice in detail. "The temple of korravai is adorned with lotus flowers which bloomed when the warriors sliced their own necks"; "they slice the base of their necks; the severed heads are given to the goddess"; "when the neck is sliced and the head is severed, the headless body jumps with joy for having fulfilled the vow".

The epics of Chilapadikaram and Manimekalai mention the practice. To ensure the complete severing of the head, the warrior tied his hair to a bamboo bent taut before he cut his neck. Hero stones depicting this practice are found all over Tamil Nadu, and are called Saavan Kallu by locals. The warriors who thus committed suicide were not only deified in hero stones (saavan kallu) and worshipped but their relations were given lands which were exempted from tax.

An region handbook (Tharamangalam) of the Tamilnadu archeology department notes that "the Nava Kandam sculpture which is found widely all over Kongu Nadu (Coimbatore, Salem) is to be seen at the Tharamangalam Kailasanathar kovil also. The people call it Saavan Kallu. "The practice of Nava Kandam existed in Kongu Nadu until the early part of this i.e., 20th century."

A Saavan Kallu at Thenkarai Moolanatha sami Kovil in Madurai, depicting the act of a warrior holding his hair with his left hand and slicing his neck with his right – 14th century – is said to be annually worshipped by the Conjeevaram Mudaliyars. The Conjeevaram Mudaliyars are Kaikolar, a presentday weaving caste which was militarized under the Chola empire and was made into a special military body; there are indications that Kaikolar warriors practiced Nava Kandam.

Apart from these codified forms of martial suicide, a method called Vadakkiruththal is mentioned in Tamil heroic poetry. It is the act of a warrior king fasting to death, if some dire dishonour were to come upon him. The Tamil teacher, and the Dravidian propagandist, turned the song of the legendary Chera king Irumborai who committed suicide when he was taken captive by his enemies into a compelling theme in Tamil renaissance.

The Avippali form of martial suicide as the ultimate expression of loyalty to one's commander, is deeply embedded in the Tamil psyche. Senchorru-kadan (the debt of red rice) is a phrase that is widely used today by Tamils as an expression of loyalty. One frequently hears of it in a popular Tamil song. The phrase sands for the ritual of partaking of rice by which Maravar and other Tamil military caste warriors bound themselves to their king or commander to die in suicidal battle for him, or to commit suicide on the day he was killed.

The ritual of red or blood rice was described by two Muslim travellers who had visited the Tamil nation in the 9th century. "A quantity of cooked rice was spread before the king, and some three or four hundred persons came of their own accord and received each a small quantity of rice from the king's own hands, after he himself had eaten some. By eating of this rice, they all engage themselves to burn themselves on the day the king dies or is killed; and they punctually fulfill their promise." In modern times it has been observed that "when a Maravar takes food in the house of a stranger, he will take a pinch of earth and put it on the food before he commences his meal." This act freed him from the debt of blood rice. Some also committed suicide by eating bricks.

Contribution to Defence Services

The achievements of the Mukkulathors are considerable. Awards and decorations are not always an accurate gauge of their supreme sacrifices. Almost every regiment of army have Mukkulathors. They have their presence in various regiments such as Infantry Regiments, Armoured Regiments, and Engineering Regiments

Famous Personalities

Armed Forces

Gallantry Award Recepients

Naik Radhakrishan C. from the Madras Regiment was the commander of a search team in Kupwara district (J&K) on 18 October, 2006. In a close fire fight he killed three terrorists unmindful of the injury he sustained in the operation.He was awarded **Maha Vir Chakra** for this deed.

Subedar Manohar P. was awarded **Shaurya Chakra** forhis actions in counterinsurgency operations in 2007.

Politicians

- Azhagu Thirunavukkarasu: Ex-Minister
- C. Mahendran: Communist Party of India
- Nallakannu: Communist leader
- Natarajan: Editor Pudiya Paarvai
- S. S. Palanimanickam: Minister for finance, India
- Sridhar Vandaiyar: Mooventhar Munnettra Kazhagam
- T.R.Baalu: Honourable Minister for Shipping and Road transport of India
- Thamizhachi thangapandian: Poet and a budding politician

Artists

- Sivaji Ganesan: Actor

- Chinnappa Thevar: Producer, Founder of Thevar films
- R. Muthuraman: Late actor
- S.S.Rajendran: Actor
- O.A.K. Thevar: Late actor
- Chandrabose: Music director
- Karthik Muthuraman: Actor
- Prabhu Ganesan: Actor

18

Nairs

Nayar (most commonly spelt Nair) is the name of a Hindu upper caste from the southern Indian state of Kerala. The Nairs were a martial nobility and figured prominently in the history of Kerala. Before the British conquest in 1792, the Kerala area contained small, feudal kingdoms, in each of which the royal and noble lineages, the militia, and most land managers were drawn from the Nairs and related sects. Nairs were prominent in politics, government service, medicine, education, and law.

Nairs were traditionally matrilineal. Their family unit, the members of which owned property jointly, included brothers and sisters, the latter's children, and their daughters' children. The oldest man was legal head of the group. Rules of marriage and residence varied somewhat between kingdoms.

The Nairs were renowned for their martial history, including their involvement in Kalaripayattu and the role of Nair warlords in the Mamankam ritual. The Nairs were classed as a martial race by the British, but were de-listed after rebelling against them under Velu Thampi Dalawa, and thereafter were recruited in low numbers into the British Indian Army. Only Nairs were recruited into the Thiruvithamkoor Nayar Pattalam (Travancore State Army), till 1935 when non-Nairs started to get admitted. This State Force (known also as the Nair Brigade) was merged into the Indian Army after independence and became the 9th Battalion Madras Regiment, the oldest Battalion in the Indian Army.

It is believed that the Kshatriya Kolathiri and Travancore kingdoms had Nair ancestry. The Zamorin Raja was a Samanthan Nair and the Arakkal empire of Kannur, which was the only Muslim empire in the Kerala area, also had Nair ancestry. Nair feudal families such as the Ettuveetil Pillamar were extremely influential in the past and often had greater influence than the Raja.

Origin & History

A number of sociologists are of the opinion that the Nairs are not indigenous to Kerala, as many customs and traditions distinguish them from other Keralites. As per one theory, Nairs are descendents of the Newars of Nepal, who joined the Munda exodus and later migrated to Kerala. The most prominent arguments given in support of this theory are the presence of distinct pagoda-like architectural style of Nair Tharavaadus and Temples and the practice of Marumakkathaayam (matrilinial) system of inheritance similar to both Nairs and Newars.

There is also a hypothesis on the basis of mythology that the Nairs are Nagas and were Kshatriyas belonging to the Serpent dynasty (Nagavansham) who removed their revered thread and migrated south to escape the wrath of a vengeful Parashurama. A Naga ancestry from Rohilkhand has been suggested. The affinity of the Nair community towards serpent worship, their martial past, and the absence of the revered thread lends support to this theory. In addition, the Travancore State Manual states that there were indeed serpent-worshiping Nagas in Kerala who fought with the Namboothiris until they reached a consensus. The Nairs have also been classified as of Indo-Scythian (Saka) ancestry as well as being linked to the Nagas.

As per Chattampi Swamikal, who interpreted old Tamil texts, the Nairs were Naka (Naga or Snake) Lords who governed as feudal lords in the Chera empire. Therefore this theory proposes Nairs to be descendents of the rulers and martial nobility of pre-Brahmin Kerala who, after the arrival of the Namboothiris (and establishment of the Varnas/Caste System), got categorized as sat Sudras. Nevertheless, Nairs have also been classed as Kshatriyas by some sources. One finds mention of the Nairs during the reign of the King Rama Varma Kulashekhara (1020-1102) of the second Chera dynasty, when the Chera Empire was attacked by the Cholas. The Nairs fought by forming suicide squads (Chavers) against the invading force. It is not clear whether the Cheras themselves were Nairs, or if the Cheras employed the Nairs as a warrior class.

The Sanskrit Kerala Mahatmayam, an upa purana of the Bhoogola Purana, calls them the progeny of Namboodiri men with Deva, Rakshasa and Gandharva women.

It may not be easy to trace out the exact date of the ancestry of Nairs. It is certain that they belonged to the Dravidian group, not the Aryan. It is believed that in the Aryan society the rulers were Kshatriyas. Chera rulers who governed over Kerala from AD 130 to AD 1100 were not Kshatriyas. But they belonged this place. So it can reasonably be presumed that they were Nairs. Greek ambassador in the court of Chandra Gupta, Megasthenes refers in around 300 BC about the Nairs and the empire of Cheras, where there were female sovereigns, in his account of ancient India. There is no ample evidence to prove the advent of Aryans to Kerala or their establishment of kingdoms here. But there are clear evidences for the involvement of Nairs in the rule of the country.

It can be assumed that as a result of the Aryan insurgency to the south the Non-Kshatriyas of Kerala were converted as Kshatriyas. Though the rulers of Venad, Onat (Kayamkulam), Deshinganad, Ilayidathu Swaroopam, Thekkumkur, Vadakkumkur, Kochi, Kozhikode and Kolathumadu were known as Kshatriyas, they were actually Nairs. The profession of the Ksyathriyas was warfare. As per this interpretation, Nairs would seem to be more like Kshatriyas since they were a martial class as well. The rulers of Thekkumkur and Vadakkumkur were saluted as "Naeri".

The word 'Nair' was authoritatively recorded in the 9th century Thirukodithana (Trikodisthanam) command of Vijayaragadeven. Mention to Nair was also seen in the Thirunelli Pattayam of Bhaskararavi Varma. There are inferences about to 'Padanairs' (warriors) in two stone carvings of Nedumpuram Thali. In the stonewall of Suchindram Dwaraka Temple which belongs to AD 400, it was recorded that 'Pallikkkan Nair' was the temple uralan. During the starting of the 19th century Nair became a caste name in Venad. Before that, the word was used to mean "warrior".

One finds mention of the Nairs during the reign of the King Rama Varma Kulashekhara (1020-1102) of second Chera dynasty, when the Cholas attacked the Chera Empire. The Nairs fought by forming suicide squads (Chavers) against the invading force.

Whatever may be arguments on the ancestry of Nair community, it is an undisputable fact that Nairs were strong group of people having deep-rooted influence over Kerala. No other society had possessed their status or standard. They were deeply immersed with the history and culture of Kerala. Truly speaking, the history of Nairs is indeed the history of Kerala. The 17th century the Brahmin-inspired Keralolpathi and Grama Padhati describes the Nairs of Kerala and the similarly matrilineal Bunts of southern Tulu Nadu as descendents of the Sudras who accompanied the Brahmins to Kerala and Tulu Nadu respectively from Ahichatra/ Ahikshetra in southern Panchala.

The Manual of Madras Administration Vol II (printed in 1885) notes that the Nadavas are the same people as the Nairs of Malabar and the Bunts of southern Tulu Nadu:

They appear to have came to Malabar from the North rather than the South and to have peopled first the Tulu, and then the Malayalam nation. They were probably the off-shoot of some colony in the Konkan or the Deccan. In Malabar and south of Kanara as far as Kasargod, they are called Nayars and their language is Malayalam. From Kasargod to Brahmavar, they are termed as Bunts and speak Tulu. To the north of Brahmavar, they are called Nadavars, and they speak Kanarese.

The Nairs have disappeared as an entity from Tulu Nadu but the inscriptions found in Barkur from the medieval period as well as the Grama Padathi, which gives the history of Brahmin families in Tulu Nadu, have made several references to the Nairs. They seemed to have intimate connections with the Brahmins and acted as their protectors, perhaps brought to Tulu Nadu by the Kadamba kings in the 8th century. Kadamba king Mayuravarma, who is credited with bringing Brahmins from Ahichatra (from the north), also settled Nairs in Tulu Nadu. Yet, there is no written proof for this occurrence and the only mention of the Nairs in the inscriptions comes after the Alupa period (early part of 14th century). It is postulated that the Nairs were later absorbed into the social stratum of the Nadava community.

Historians, and foreign travellers referred to the Nairs as dignified martial nobility. The earliest reference to Nairs comes from the Greek ambassador Megasthenes. In his accounts of ancient India, he refers to the "Nayars of Malabar" and the "Kingdom of Chera".

Irrespective of the different theories that seek to explain the ancestry of Nairs, it is clear that until the early 20th century, Nairs exerted their influence in medieval Kerala society as feudal lords and owned large estates. The position in society of the Nairs as that of a martial nobility in medieval Kerala has been likened to the position in society of the Samurai in medieval Japan. Nairs dominated the civil, administrative and military elite of the pre-British era in Kerala.

The decline of Nair dominance came about in multiple stages. During colonial times, the British perceived that Nairs were an inherent threat to their hegemony in the area and therefore outlawed their right to bear weapons and by banning the Nair martial art of Kalaripayattu. Weapons were integral to the Nair psyche and power, and combined with repressive legislation led to a loss of social standing for Nairs, though some of the social legislation was in part inspired by the Nairs themselves, such as changes in inheritance law permitting the Karanavan to pass on some (and later all) of the fruits of his stewardship of the taravad to his own children. During post-colonial years, the Land reforms of 1950's led to massive loss of land-ownership by Nair feudal lords and some Nair gentry were relegated to poverty overnight. The decline of Nair dominance was nevertheless tempered by their conversion through the 20th century to the academic and professional classes and their high profile in Kerala politics.

Early in the British period, Nair armies were disbanded. Perhaps partly as a result, plural marital unions steadily died out in the 19th century. Children began to be maintained by their father, to support him in his old age, and to perform the ceremonies at his death. Laws passed in the 1930s enforced monogamy, permitted division of the matrilineal estate amongst male and female members, and gave children full rights of maintenance and inheritance from the father. By the mid-20th century it was increasingly common, especially in cities, for nuclear families to form separate residential and economic units.

Additional factors such as the impact of the market economy, the disappearance of traditional military training, the absorption of new values through the new system of education, the self-consciousness being generated amongst the lower sects and their cry for equality and privileges also contributed to the decline of Nair dominance.

People & Culture

There was a common belief that Nairs were a semi urban group having peculiar customs like wearing single dhothi, holding umbrellas made of palm leaves, with swords in their hands, females having four or five husbands, having alliance (sambandhams) with Brahmins, following matriarchal hereditary system, with belief in oracles and having fond of pulluvan pattu and maintaining kavus (snake parks) and ponds in their residential place.

But all these were about years ago. The Nairs who were proud of their ancestry and wealth and nursed their lords and Brahmins, who followed special practices of marriage are now living in an advanced and modern society, says Sri.Pattom G.Ramachandran Nair. This is in fact a realistic assessment. An in-depth journey through history will reveal the fact on the transition of Nair community to the present social situations.

A number of studies were made on the social set up of the races, the predecessors of Nairs. Blood relation determined the rights and privileges in such races. They maintained their heredity through father or mother. The system of marrying the uncle's daughter was common in some of the clans. The system of worshipping the dead souls was there. When person is dead, they used to put rice (in some places betel wine also) on his mouth. This practice might have from their strong belief that the soul of the dead person will live even after their death. They worshipped Deities (Devis and Devans). The advent of Dravidians to South India was between 1750 and 1400 BC. Before their advent, Nagas were the only people of the region. Historians say that radical changes took place in socio-cultural fields with the advent of Dravidians. The most important of them is the language. The South Indian languages including Malayalam originated from the early Dravidian language. During this period matriarchal and patriarchal systems were prevailing. The group who followed matriarchal system might have become Nairs.

During Sangha era (AD 1st to 6th Century), the social divisions like haves and have-nots, the superiors and subordinates came into existence. There are two opinions that during Sangha period the system of inheritance was matriarchal or patriarchal. The system of burning dead bodies was in practice during this period. The chastity of ladies was highly recognized during the period. Polygamy was in practice. There was independent style of life between men and women. Love marriages were not rare. The marriage function was grand like that of today. Females wore clothes made of cotton or silks. They wore ornaments too.

Both men and women tied their hair on top of the head. Men applied sandal paste on their chest. They were careful in wearing new dresses.

There was no major difference between Nairs and other sects in their social structure, belief, customs and practices. But still Nairs were considered as upper classes since they were soldiers and landlords.

By about 7th and 8th Century AD, a number of temples were founded in Kerala and they became the nerve centre of social life. Namboodiris Brahmins) were the priests and owners of temples. Untouchability was originated from the temples. It was during this period that caste system was also formed. Brahmins become more influential and mighty in the society. Kerala society divided into two. Those who recognized Brahmin supremacy stood on the one side and others who opposed them. The first was within the fold of Hinduism and latter was out of it. Those who embraced Hinduism were grouped into several races. Rulers or Kings became Kshathriyas. The trader group known Vaisyas was not there. All others who followed Brahmnical faith later came to be known as Sudras. They were Nairs. Nairs became prominent during the feudal period (17th to 19th century). A number of Naduvazhis (local rulers) emerged from Nair society. They became the leasers of Dewaswom land (land owned by temples) and soon became highly influential in socio-economic fields. During this period 'Thara' (village) was the lowest strata of society.

The activities of a Thara were managed by Tharakootom, a general body of the village headed by the distinguished family manager or managers of the village. The matters pertaining to a Thara was discussed and finalized here. The practice was to nominate the prominent elder of the Thara as 'Deshavazhi' and he was the decision-implementing officer of the Thara. A number of Thara constituted a Nadu, a certain region to an extent of a district or so. Naduvazhi is the ruler of the Nadu. Nattukoottangal assisted him. The chief amongst the Tharas were the members of Nattukoottangal. Various Nadus constituted a nation and Rajah was there above Naduvazhis. It was the Nairs or Kshathriyas who held the supremacy in all the stage from Thara to Rajah.

In the cultural field also, Nairs exhibited their talents during the feudal era. Festivals like Onam, Vishu, Thiruvathira were popularized during this period. Thiruvathira festival was confined only to the Nair society.

The changes that took place in the caste system of Kerala during the last decades of 19th century resulted in the revision of social system. There are several reasons for this change. Important amongst them was the progress in the field of education. Democratization and organized religions set up changed the caste-based society. The establishment of the Nair Service Society paved the way for bridging the disparity amongst the sub sections of Nairs. They overcame the existing Brahmin-Kshathriya supremacy and came in the forefront of the society as an influential group. The superiority in caste, high educational status, bureaucratic positions etc. paved the way for the rapid growth of nair community. They surpassed the other communities and emerged as a strong community.

The Nairs were the swordsmen, the military caste of the west coast of India. They constitute the majority of the Kerala Population. The ever so many rituals performed by this community reveal their matrilineality and their unique social setup. A Nair woman has to observe certain ceremonies during pregnancy. Puli-Kuti, literally meaning drinking tamarind juice, is one amongst them. It is performed on a particular day in the ninth month. Not only the day, even the hour is fixed by the local astrologer. The pregnant woman, after having bathed and properly attired, is seated facing eastwards in the principal courtyard (natu-muttam) of the Tharavaad (ancestral family house).

The Ammayi or maternal uncle's wife and the brother of the pregnant woman officiate this function. As soon as a child is born, the mother and the baby have to undergo some rite of purification. The baby is placed on the naked floor, and its father or uncle sprinkles a few drops of cold water on it. Pollution is observed for fifteen days after delivery, by all the members of the Taravad, during which period they are prohibited from entering temples and holy places or perfoming any ceremonies. The Naamakarnam is performed on the twenty-seventh day after the child's birth, when the Kaaranavan (senior most elder) of the Family gives to the child a spoonful or two of milk mixed with sugar and then names the child by calling it in the ear by the name three times.

The Annaprasaanam is choroonu takes place on an auspicious day in the sixth month, when the uncle or the father of the child first feeds it with rice. It is only after this ceremony that the child can be fed with rice. The ear boring takes place at the end of the first year after the child's birth,and the vidyaarambham in the third on fifth year.

Marriage amongst the Nairs used to mean either the formal ceremony of tying a Thaali round the neck of a girl, accompanied by festive celebrations, known as the Thaalikettu or Kettukalyaanam, or the ceremony of actual alliance as husband and wife known as the Sambandham or Pudavakoda. Now marriage is only the ceremony of alliance as husband and wife.

Kettukalyaanam is an indispensable rite in the case of every Nair girl before she attained puberty. This ceremony was performed within the age of eleven. The bridegroom who ties the Thaali can only be selected from certain well recognised families in the village called Machchampikkars. Those were the members of the earliest Nair families appointed for this purpose by Royal writs. This ritual has not been found in these days. A day was fixed for arranging the preliminaries of the wedding. When all the relations and men of the village were invited as also the astrologer (Kaniyaan), who forthwith fixed the most auspicious day for the celebration of the ceremony and noting it down in what was called a chaarthu or cadjan-writ, handed it over to the uncle or Kaaranavar of the family who then dismissed him with presents. The chaarthu stated that a boy should be selected as bridegroom whose natal star agreed with the girl's and also decided what star would be agreeable and fixes a muhurtham for the ceremony as well as for fixing the major pillar of the marriage pandal. A few days before the commencement of the building of the pandal, invitations were sent round to all the relations, friends and villagers. The major pillar of the pandal is generally made out of the jack or Mukampala tree which is cut for the purpose that same day and raised at the south west corner of the pandal,which itself has to be built on the eastern side of the house. A Kathir Mandapam, a raised floor with a grounded roof beautifully adorned with pictures, mirrors and glass globes,was erected inside the pandal, and it was here that the actual wedding occurred.

The first item in the celebration was what is called the Ayani oonu, a sumptous banquet given by the bride's people to the selected bridegroom or manavaalan as he was called. On the morning of the first day of the marriage the girl wa s taken to the bathing tank in regular procession headed by one of the machampi women (sisters-in-law) well dressed and decked with costly ornaments and holding a plate containing the girl's wearing apparel to be used after bath, a mirror and other toilet articles in her left hand and a metal hand-lamp called Changalavatta in her right. After bath the girl was taken back to the house and seated in a separate room, and then the assembled guests were served with a rich feast. Then came the rite called kaappukettu or tying prathisarabandham (a piece of string) round the wrist of the girl. This is done by Maaran, the Brahmani or sometimes the brother of the girl, accompanied by a song called Subhadra Veli (the account of the renowned marriage of subhadra by Arjuna) by the Brahmanis, a class of Ambalavaasis, who were accomodated inside the house and placing a garland around his neck formally invited him to start for the marriage pandal. A procession was then formed at an auspicious hour from the bridegroom's house, the bridegroom mounted on an elephant or walking on foot and holding in his hand a sword covered with a palmyra leaf or sword case.

Sects

Caste system was not prevalent in Kerala during initial history. In olden times when people resided in the Western Ghats, categorization on the basis of work done by them was in practice. There were seven such categories. Thudiyan (one who beats "thudi", a musical instrument), Parayan (one who beats "para", a kind of drum), Panar (singer), Kadambar (agriculturist), Valayar (fishermen), Vanikar (traders) and Uzhavar (workers) are these seven categories.

Though Brahmin migration to Kerala occurred during three or four centuries BC., they became mighty only during eighth century. Caste system began in Kerala only after this period. Sabdatharavali (1923) names the caste as Brahmins eight, Newna Vargam (minorities) two, Antharala Jathi (temple dwellers) twelve, Sudras eighteen, Shilpi six, Pathithar (untouchables) ten, Thana Jathi (lower caste) eight and 64 numbers of sub-sects.

Dr.P.K.Gopalakrishnan says that there was no caste system in Kerala until the end of Buddhist renaissance period. People were known by their profession like Panan, Parayan, Villavan, Ushavan, Paravathan, Ayar etc. Brahmins also migrated to this region and there was no caste amongst them. By about the second half of the 8th century, Brahmins become more influential and mighty in the society. This marked the starting of the caste system. Kerala society divided into two. Those who recognized Brahmin supremacy stood on the one side and others who opposed them. The first was within the fold of Hinduism and latter was out of it. Those who embraced Hinduism were grouped into several races. Rulers or Kings became Kshathriyas. The trader group known Vaisyas was not there. All others who followed Brahmnical faith later came to be known as Sudras. They were Nairs.

There is considerable controversy regarding the actual place of Nairs in the caste system. It is understandably, a very touchy subject. One of the major reasons is that the caste system in Kerala is very different from the caste system elsewhere in India. As per the caste system followed in the rest of India, only the lowest class, the sudras, were considered to be "untouchables".

Nevertheless, in the case of Kerala, anyone who was not a Namboothiri, was treated by the Namboothiris as an untouchable. The Namboothiris had different rules regarding the degrees of pollution for the different classes. A Namboothiri could only be "polluted" by the touch of a Nair, whereas the other classes had different distances after which they could be considered polluting. For instance, if an Ezhava got within 24 feet of a Namboothiri, the Namboothiri was considered to be polluted. In this regard, it would seem that the Nairs were like the sudras in the rest of India.

Nevertheless, the sudras in the rest of India were never a martial class, since warfare was the profession of the Ksyathriyas. As per this interpretation, Nairs would seem to be more like Kshatriyas since they were a martial class as well. Similar to Kshatriyas, they were second to the Brahmins (Namboothiris). Furthermore, many Nair families were aristocratic. They owned large feudal estates and in some cases, even took part in the ruling of Kerala. An example is the Paliam family of Kochi. The oldest male of the family, the Paliath Achan, served as the Prime Minister to the Raja of Kochi.

Classification based on Social Status

- Kiriyath Nair: Lords and warriors of the King
- Pannikodan Nair: Below Kiriyathu Nair
- Sudran: One who serves Brahmins
- Charna Nair: One who serves Kings
- Urali Nair: One who came from Tulunadu
- Muthaan: People of Palakkad who took trading as profession
- Tharavar: Merchents
- Mannadi: Mannadiyar
- Akathethara Nair: Ullakathu Nair
- Kaduppattan: Ezhuthachan
- Chaliyan: One who makes chela (cloth)

Classification based on Awards, Positions & Titles

Pillai is the award or title given by the Maharajah to the Nairs who hold Thirumukom.

Chembakaraman award was first introduced by His Highness Anizham Thirunal Marthandavarma.

Thampi is the title given to the children born to Travancore Maharajahs in Nair wives. The Thampis had the right to stand erect before the kings and to travel in Pallakks (carrying carts).

Kartha is one of the positions given to the Nairs of Travancore. It is also believed that Thekkumkur-Vadukkumkur rajahs gave the title to some landlords.

Kurup is one who gave Kalari training to the members of royal family.

Panicker is also one those who gave training in weapons to the royal family members. Panickers were also known as Asans. They enriched history as saviors of the land.

Kaimals were experts in warfare and financial management.

Unnithan, Valyathan, Menon, Menokki were also titles conferred on those who performed remarkable deeds.

Moopil Nair, Nayanar, Adiyodi, Kurup of Malabar, Menon, Marar of Cochin were also honours conferred by the rulers. Those who were in high positions in Nair community in Cochin won the titles of Karthavu, Kaimal, Thamban etc. because of their intimacy to the royal family and appeasement to Brahmins. Amongst the various groups like Akath Charnnavar, Purathu Charnnavar, Nambiar, Kurup etc. of the Nairs of Malabar, Nairs and Kurups were soldiers. Purathu Charnnavar and Akathu Charnnavar were servants of the royal family. Out of this, supremacy is for Purathu Charnnavar. Nair priests who performed rituals in Kalaries were known as Kuruppans, Unnikal, Kurukkal, Adikal etc.

Demographics

Nairs are chiefly found in South Indian States of Tamil Nadu, Kerala, and Orrisa. In India, the population of Nairs is approximately 6,895,000. Major states having Nair population are:

Area	Population
Kerala	5,559,000
Tamil Nadu	1,113,000
Karnataka	150,000
Maharashtra	52,000
Pondicherry	27,000
Goa	20,000
Delhi	14,000
Andhra Pradesh	10,000
Gujarat	7,100
Madhya Pradesh	1,500

Source: Joshua Project, 2008

Martial Traditions

There are differences of opinion about the ancestry of Nair community. One argument is that Nairs are descendents of Nagas, once a mighty group of India. Nagas were the oldest and strongest group resided in India before the Aryan insurgency. They were in India even before the era of Ramayana. They were warriors in the Mahabharatha battle and mention to this effect was seen in Harivamsa and Vishnu Markandeya epics. The Surya and Soma dynasties were related to the Nagas. There is mention in Ramayana that Nagas witnessed the sea crossing of Hanuman. The Nagas ladies were far famed for their beauty. There is a story in Mahabharatha that Arjuna during his journey met with Uloopy, a beautiful Naga girl and at once fell in love with her and later married her.

After the Mahabharatha battle the Nagas became more mighty. It was Nagas who slained the King Parikshit. There is historical evidence to believe that Nagas inhabited in all suitable places even from time immemorial. Their capital was Thakshasila. Their rule extended from Thakshasila to Assam on one side and from South India to Ceylone (Sri Lanka) on the other. The Nagas who came to Kerala became Nairs.

Snake worship is a special feature of Nairs. There were Sarpakavus (snake parks) attached to almost all the Nair Tharavads. The Nair ladies and men had a habit of combing and tying their hair just like a serpent's head. Nairs followed matrilineal (marumakkathayam) system.

Before the advent of Namboodiris, an organized war-like group of people exercised supremacy over Kerala. Their ancestry was unknown. Owing to the worship of Naga (snake), this set of people came to be known as Nagas. They exercised control over Adivasis, put them to hard fieldwork and made them slaves, says K.M.Panicker (Keralathile Swathanthrasamaram). William Logon has recorded in the Malabar Manual that Nairs were the Dravidian settlers who conquered Malabar and became landlords.

Kodungallur Kunhikuttan Thampuran in his book 'Keralathil' firmly ascertains that Nairs are same as Nagas. Sri Vidyadhiraja Chattambi Swamikal has reproduced some old ballards calling Nairs and Nagas in his book 'Pracheena Keralam'. He in his work 'Pracheena Malayalam', has reproduced the following details about Nagas found in the old vattezhuthu records.

Contribution to Defence Services

The Nairs are famous for their martial history, including their involvement in Kalaripayattu and the role of Nair warlords in the Mamankam ritual. The Nairs were classed as a martial race by the British, but were de-listed after rebelling against them under Velu Thampi Dalawa, and thereafter were recruited in low numbers into the British Indian Army. Only Nairs were recruited into the Thiruvithamkoor Nayar Pattalam (Travancore State Army), until 1935 when non-Nairs started to get admitted. This State Force (known also as the Nair Brigade) was merged into the Indian Army after independence and became the 9th Battalion Madras Regiment, the oldest Battalion in the Indian Army. The word "nair" was said to be derived from the word "nayakar" (troop leader) as the community was mainly serving as army peronnel of the then kings and local chieftains. The army of nairs was known as "nair pada" (pada means army). Even after India getting independence nairs have not fully left the tradition. They contribute a good percentage of the Indian army.

Famous Personalities

Armed Forces

Gallantry Award Recepients

Major K. N. Nair was awarded **Shaurya Chakra** for his bravery against terrorist in 1999.

Commandant Paikal Narayanan Nair was awarded **Shaurya Chakra** for his bravery against terrorist in 2002.

Major Krishnan Nair: Sena Medal

Lt. Jagadish G Nair: Sena Medal

Politicians

- Devan Nair: Former Head of the state of Singapore.
- P.K. Vasudevan Nair: Former Chief Minister of Kerala. Noted CPI leader.
- Sir C. Madhavan Nair: Administrator during British Rule.
- Sir Chettur Sankaran Nair: President of the Indian National Congress (1897-1898)

Artists

- Anita Nair: Writer.
- Balan Nair: Painter
- C. Gauridasan Nair: Noted political analyst, media critic
- M. Krishnan Nair: Literary critic
- Thikkurussi Sukumaran Nair: Actor

Bibliography

Anderson B.: *Imagined Communities: reflections on the origin and spread of nationalism*. London: Verso, 1983.

Anderson J. W.: "Military heroism: an occupational definition", *Armed forces and Society,* 1986.

Anon.: *Military Sketches of the Gorkha War, in India, in the years 1814, 1815, 1816*. London: R. Hunter, 1822.

Anon.: *On the deficiency of European officers in the Army of India. By one of themselves*. London: James Madden, 1849.

Appadurai A.: "Theory in anthropology: center and periphery", *Comparative Studies in Society and History,* 1986.

Asad T. and J. Dixon: *Translating Europe's Others. In Europe and its Others* (Vol. 1) (eds) F. Barker et al. Colchester: Univ. of Essex, 1985.

Badenach W.: *Inquiry into the state of the Indian army, with suggestions for its improvement, and the establishment of a military police for India*. London: J. Murray.

Baxter P. and R. Fardon (eds) 1991. *Voice, Genre, Text—anthropological essays in Africa and beyond*, Special issue, *Bulletin of the John Ryland's University Library of Manchester*, 1826.

Baynes J.: *Morale: a study of men and courage*. London: Cassell, 1967.

Ben-Ari E.: "On acknowledgements in ethnographies", *Journal of Anthropological Research*, 1987.

Bennett L.: *Dangerous Wives and Sacred Sisters*, New York: Columbia Univ. Press, 1983.

Bennett S.: "Shikar and the Raj", *South Asia*, 1984.

Biardeau M.: *Hinduism: the anthropology of a civilization* (trans. by R. Nice), Delhi: UP, 1989.

Bingley A. H. and A. Nicholls: *Caste Hand books for the Indian Army: Brahmans*, Calcutta: Supt. Govt. Printing, 1918.

Bishop E.: *Better to Die: the story of the Gurkhas*, London: New English Library, 1976.

Blake J. A.: "Military heroism: an occupational definition", *Armed Forces and Society*, 1987.

Bredin A. E.C.: *The Happy Warriors: the Gurkha soldier in the British army*, Gillingham, Dorset: Blackmore, 1961.

Bristow R. C. B.: *Memories of the British Raj: a soldier in India*. London: Johnson, 1974.

Bruce C. G.: *Foreword to Northey*, W. B. and C. J. Morris *The Gurkhas: their manners, customs and country*. London: John Lane, The Bodley Head, 1928.

Bryant G.: "Officers of the East India Company's Army in the days of Clive and Hastings", *Journal of Imperial and Commonwealth History*, 1978.

Burke K.: *A Rhetoric of Motives*, Berkeley: Univ. of Calif. Press, 1969.

Burroughs P.: "Imperial Defence and the Victorian Army: review article", *Journal of Imperial and Commonwealth History*, 1986.

Candler E.: *The Sepoy*. London: John Murray, 1919.

Caplan A. P.: *Priests and Cobblers: a study of social change in a Hindu village in western Nepal*, London: Intertext, 1972.

Cardew F. G.: "Our recruiting grounds of the future for the Indian army", *The Journal of the United Service Institution of India*, 1891.

Carnaticus (pseud): "General view of our Indian army", *The Asiatic Journal and Monthly Register*, 1821.

Chakravarti P. C.: *The Art of War in Ancient India*, Dacca: Univ. Press, 1941.

Chandos J.: *Boys together. the English public schools*, London: Hutchinson, 1984.

Chaudhuri K. C.: *Anglo-Nepalese Relations: from the earliest times of the British rule in India till the Gurkha war*, Calcutta: Modern Book Agency, 1960.

Clifford J.: *Review of E. Said's Orientalism, History and Theory,* 1980.

Collier P. and H. Geyer-Ryan (eds): *Literary Theory Today*, Cambridge: Polity, 1990.

Colson E.: *Heroism, martyrdom, and courage: an essay on Tonga ethics. In The Translation of Culture* (ed.) T. O. Beidelman. London: Tavistock, 1971.

Dabaral S. P.: "Gorkhali rule in Garhwal", *Regmi Research*, 1987.

Dahal D. R.: *An Ethnographic Study of Social Change among the Athpahariya Rais of Dhankuta*, Kathmandu: Centre for Nepal and Asian Studies, 1985.

Dandekar C.: *Military Related Social Research: an international review. Papers presented at the 1988 Munich Interim Conference of the Research Committee of the 01/ISA Armed Forces and Conflict Resolution* (ed.) Jurgen Munchen Kuhlmann, 1989.

Daniell D.: *Buchan and the popular literature of imperialism. In Literature and Imperialism* (ed.) B. Moore-Gilbert. Roehampton: English Department of the Roehampton Institute of Higher Education, 1983.

Das C. N.: *Traditions and Customs of the Indian Armed Forces*, Delhi: Vision Books, 1984.

Date G. T.: *The Art of War in Ancient India*, London: Humphrey Milford, 1929.

Davis P.: *A Child at Arms*, London: Hutchinson, 1970.

Dawson G.: *The Blond Bedouin: Lawrence of Arabia, imperial adventure and the imagining of English-British masculinity. In Manful Assertions: masculinities in Britain since 1800* (eds) M. Roper and J. Tosh. London: Routledge, 1991.

Dawson H. D.: "Who are the Gurkhas?", *Empire Annual for Boys*, 1917.

Des M. Chene: "In service to colonialism: the emergence of national identity among the Gurkhas". *Paper delivered at American Anthropological Association Conference*, 1988.

Donaldson E.: *Lepchaland*, London: Sampson Low, Marston, 1900.

Ellis J.: *The Social History of the Machine Gun*, New York: Arno, 1981.

Empson W.: *Some Versions of Pastoral*, London: Chatto and Windus, 1935.

Enloe C. H.: *Ethnic Soldiers: state security in divided societies*, Harmondsworth: Penguin, 1980.

Evans-Pritchard E. E.: *The Nuer*, Oxford: Clarendon, 1940.

Fabian J.: "Presence and Representation: the other and anthropological writing", *Critical Inquiry*, 1990.

Fardon R.: *Localizing Strategies: the regionalization of ethnographic accounts. General Introduction. In Localizing Strategies: regional traditions of ethnographic writing* (ed.) R. Fardon. Edinburgh: Scottish Academic Press, 1990.

Farwell B.: *The Gurkhas*, London: Allen Lane, 1984.

Forbes D.: *Johnny Gurkha*, London: Robert Hale, 1964.

Foucault M.: "What is an author?" *In Textual Strategies* (ed.) J. Harari. London: Methuen, 1979.

Fox R. G.: *Lions of the Punjab: culture in the making*, Berkeley: Univ. of Calif. Press, 1985.

Fraser J. B.: *Journal of a Tour through part of the Snowy Range of the Himala Mountains and to the sources of the Rivers Jumna and Ganges*, London: Rodwell and Martin, 1820.

Gaborieau M.: *Le Népal et ses populations, Bruxelles: Editions Complexe,* 1978.

Gaige F. H.: *Regionalism and National Unity in Nepal*, Berkeley: Univ. of Calif. Press, 1975.

Geertz C.: *Works and Lives: the anthropologist as author*, Cambridge: Polity, 1989.

Gilmore D. D.: *Manhood in the Making: cultural concepts of masculinity*, New Haven: Yale Univ. Press, 1990.

Girouard M.: *The Return to Camelot: chivalry and the English gentleman*, New Haven: Yale Univ. Press, 1981.

Goddard E.: "The Indian Army—Company and Raj", *Asian Affairs*, 1976.

Green M.: *Dreams of Adventure, Deeds of Empire*, London: Routledge, 1980.

Greenhut J.: "Sahib and sepoy: an inquiry into the relationship between the British officers and native soldiers of the British Indian army", *Military Affairs*, 1984.

Gregory C. A.: *Gifts and Commodities*, London: Academic Press, 1982.

Hamilton F.: *An Account of the Kingdom of Nepal and of the Territories Annexed to this Dominion by the House of Gorkha*, Edinburgh: Constable, 1819.

Hart K.: *On commoditization. In From Craft to Industry* (ed.) E. Goody. Cambridge: Univ. Press, 1982.

Hasrat B. J.: *History of Nepal: as told by its own and contemporary chroniclers*. Hoshiarpur, Punjab: the Editor, 1970.

Haycock R.: *British arms in India. In British Military History: a supplement to Robin Higham's Guide to the Sources* (ed.) G. Jordan. New York: Garland, 1988.

Heathcote T. A.: *The Indian Army: the garrison of British Imperial India, 1822-1922*, Vancouver: David and Charles, 1974.

Hickey M.: *The Unforgettable Army: Slim's XIVth Army in Burma*, Tunbridge Wells: Spellmount, 1992.

Hitchcock J. T.: *The idea of the martial Rajput. In Traditional India: structure and change* (ed.) M. Singer. Philadelphia: The American Folklore Society, 1959.

Höfer A.: *A new rural elite in Central Nepal. In Himalayan Anthropology: the Indo-Tibetan interface* (ed.) J. F. Fisher. The Hague: Mouton, 1978.

Holy L. and M. Stuchlik: *Actions, norms and representations: foundations of anthropological inquiry*, Cambridge: Univ. Press, 1983.

Hunter W. W.: *Life of Brian Houghton Hodgson: British Resident at the Court of Nepal*, London: John Murray, 1896.

Husain A.: *British India's Relations with the Kingdom of Nepal 1857-1947*, London: George Allen and Unwin, 1970.

Inden R.: "Orientalist constructions of India", *Modern Asian Studies,* 1986.

Jenkins L. H.: *General Frederick Young*, London: George Routledge and Sons,. 1923.

Jones R. L. and S. K. Jones: *The Himalayan Woman: a study of Limbu women in marriage and divorce*, Palo Alto: Mayfield, 1976.

Kabbani R.: *Europe's Myths of Orient*, Bloomington: Indiana Univ. Press, 1986.

Keegan J.: *The Face of Battle*, Harmondsworth, Penguin, 1976.

Keesing R. M.: "Exotic readings of cultural texts", *Current Anthropology,* 1989.

Kellett A.: *Combat Motivation; the behavior of soldiers in battle*, Boston: Kluwer Nijhoff Publishing, 1982.

Kirkpatrick W.: *An Account of the Kingdom of Nepaul*, London: William Miller, 1811.

Kolff D. H.A.: *Naukar, Rajput and Sepoy: the ethnohistory of the military labour market in Hindustan, 1450-1850*, Cambridge: Univ. Press, 1990.

Laver J.: *The Book of Public School Old Boys, University, Navy, Army, Air Force and Club Ties*, London: Seeley Service & Co., 1968.

Leach E. R.: Aspects of bridewealth and marriage stability among the Kachin and Lakher. In *Rethinking Anthropology*, London: Athlone, 1961.

Lindisfarne N.: Variant masculinities, variant virginities: rethinking "honour and shame". In *Dislocating Masculinity: comparative ethnographies* (eds) A. Cornwall and N. Lindisfarne. London: Routledge, 1993.

Macdonald A. W.: "Language, literature and cultural identity of the Tamang". Unpublished, 1991.

Macfarlane A.: *Resources and Population: a study of the Gurungs of Nepal*, Cambridge: Univ. Press, 1976.

Macmillan M.: Camp followers: a note on wives of the armed forces. *In The Incorporated Wife* (eds) H. Callan and S. Ardener. London: Croom Helm, 1984.

MacMunn G.: *The Martial Races of India*, London: Sampson Low, Marston, 1932.

Mangan J. A.: "The grit of our forefathers": invented traditions, propaganda and imperialism. In *Imperialism and Popular Culture* (ed.) J. M. Mackenzie. Manchester: Univ. Press, 1986.

Mannsaker F.: Early attitudes to empire. *In Literature and Imperialism* (ed.) B. Moore-Gilbert. Roehampton: English Department of the Roehampton Institute of Higher Education, 1983.

Mason P.: *A Matter of Honour: an account of the Indian army, its officers and men*, London: Jonathan Cape, 1974.

McDougal C.: *Village and Household Economy in Far Western Nepal*, Kirtipur, Nepal: Tribhuvan University, 1968.

McKeag H. T.A.: *Letters from the East, being records of journeyings and sojourns in India, Mesopotamia and Persia*. Belfast: Printed & published by the author, 1921.

Messerschmidt D. A.: *The Gurungs of Nepal: conflict and change in a village society*, Warminster: Aris and Phillips, 1976.

Moore-Gilbert B. (ed.): *Literature and Imperialism*, Roehampton: English Department of the Roehampton Institute of Higher Education, 1983.

Moran Lord: *The Anatomy of Courage*, London: Constable, 1945.

Morris C. J. (compiler): *Gurkhas: Handbooks for the Indian Army*, Delhi: Manager of Publications, Govt. of India, 1933.

Mrozek D. J.: The habit of victory: the American military and the cult of manliness. In *Manliness and Morality: middle-class masculinity in Britain and America, 1800-1940* (eds) J. A. Mangan and J. Walvin. Manchester: Univ. Press, 1987.

Nakane C.: A plural society in Sikkim. In *Caste and Kin in Nepal, India and Ceylon* (ed.) C. von Fürer-Haimendorf. Bombay: Asia, 1966.

Nandy. A.: *The Intimate Enemy: loss and recovery of self under colonialism*, Delhi: UP, 1983.

Nicholson J. B.R.: *The Gurkha Rifles*, London: Osprey, 1974.

Niven B. M.: *The Mountain Kingdom: portraits of Nepal and the Gurkhas*, Singapore: Imago Productions, 1987.

Northey W. B.: *The Land of the Gurkhas or the Himalayan Kingdom of Nepal*, London: Hefer and Sons, 1937.

Okely J. and H. Callaway (eds): *Anthropology and Autobiography*, London: Routledge, 1992.

O'Malley L. S.S.: *Bengal District Gazetteers*, Darjeeling: The Bengal Secretariat Book Depot., 1907.

Oppert G.: *Of the Weapons, Army Organisation, and Political Maxims of the Ancient Hindus: with special reference to gunpowder and firearms*, Madras: Higginbotham, 1880.

Ortner S. B.: *High Religion: a cultural and political history of Sherpa Buddhism*, Princeton: Univ. Press, 1989.

Padel F.: "Anthropologists of tribal India: merchants of knowledge". Unpublished, 1988.

Parkin D. J.: Toward an apprehension of fear. In *Sociophobics. the anthropology of fear* (ed.) R. Scruton. London: Westview, 1986.

Parry B.: *Delusions and Discoveries: studies on India in the British imagination 1880-1930*, London: Allen Lane, Penguin, 1972.

Pelly L. (ed.): *The Views and Opinions of Brig.-Gen. John Jacob*, London: Smith Elder, 1858.

Perkins R.: *Regiments of the Empire: a bibliography of their puhlished histories*, Newton Abbot (Devon): Privately Published, 1989.

Petre F, L.: *The 1st King George's Own Gurkha Rifles: the Malaun Regiment (1815-1921)*, London: Royal United Service Institution, 1925.

Pickford S. C.: *Destination Rangoon*, Denbigh: Gee and Son, 1989.

Pocock T.: *Fighting General: the public and private campaigns of General Sir Walter Walker*, London: Collins, 1973.

Poynder F. S.: *The Ninth Gurkha Rifles, 1817-1936*, London: Royal United Services Institution, 1937.

Praval K. C.: *Indian Army after Independence*, New Delhi: Lancer International, 1987.

Prinsep H. T.: *History of the Political and Military Transactions in India during the Administration of the Marquess of Hastings, 1813-1823*, London: Kingsbury, Porbury and Allen, 1825.

Proudfoot C. L.: *Flash of the Khukri: history of the 3rd Gorkha Rifles (1947 to 1980)*. New Delhi: Vision Books, 1984.

Rabinow P.: Representations are social facts: modernity and post-modernity in anthropology. In *Writing Culture: the poetics and politics of ethnography* (eds) J. Clifford and G. Marcus. Berkeley: Univ. of Calif. Press, 1986.

Rachman S. J.: *Fear and Courage*, San Francisco: Freeman, 1978.

Rana N. R.L.: *The Anglo-Gorkha War (1814-1816)*, Kathmandu: the Author, 1970.

Rathaur K. R.S.: *The British and the Brave: a history of the Gurkha recruitment in the British Indian army*, Jaipur: Nirola, 1987.

Richards J.: Films and the empire: Britain in the 1930s. In *Literature and Imperialism* (ed.) B. Moore-Gilbert. Roehampton: English Department of the Roehampton Institute of Higher Education, 1983.

Ridley H.: *Images of Imperial Rule*, London: Croom Helm, 1983.

Roberts Lord: *Forty-one Years in India: from Subaltern to Commander-inChief* (2 vols), London: Richard Bentley & Son, 1897.

Roland A.: *In Search of Self in India and Japan: toward a cross-cultural psychology*, Princeton: Univ. Press, 1988.

Rorty R.: Philosophy as a kind of writing: an essay on Derrida. *In Consequences of Pragmatism (essays: 1972-1980)*, Brighton: Harvester, 1982.

Rosaldo R.: From the door of his tent: the fieldworker and the inquisitor. *In Writing Culture: the poetics and politics of ethnography* (eds) J. Clifford and G. Marcus . Berkeley: Univ. of Calif. Press, 1986.

Rose L. E.: China and the Anglo-Nepal war: 1814- 1816. *Proceedings of the 24th Indian History Conference*, 1961.

Russell A.: *'The Yakha: Culture, Environment and Development in East Nepal'*, unpublished D. Phil thesis, Oxford University, 1992.

Said E.: *Orientalism*, London: Routledge, 1978.

Sangren P. S.: "Rhetoric and the authority of ethnography", *Current Anthropology,* 1988.

Saxena K. M.L.: *The Military System of India (1850-1900)*, New Delhi: Sterling, 1974.

Seidler V. J.: *Rediscovering Masculinity: reason, language and sexuality*, London: Routledge, 1989.

Singh K.: *Ranjit Singh: Maharajah of the Punjab*, London: George Allen and Unwin., 1962.

Singh T. N.: "The Gorkhas: an introduction by Lt.-Gen. Thakur Nathu Singh", *The Gorkha*, 1952.

Sinha N. K.: *Ranjit Singh*, Calcutta: Univ. of Calcutta, 1933.

Slim W.: *Courage and other Broadcasts*, London: Cassell, 1957.

Smith E. D.: *Britain's Brigade of Gurkhas*, London: Leo Cooper, 1973.

Smith T.: *Narrative of a Five Years' Residence at Nepaul* (2 vols), London: Colburn, 1852.

Stiller L. F.: *The Rise of the House of Gorkha: a study in the unification of Nepal 1768-1816*, Kathmandu: Ratna Pustak Bhandar, 1973.

Street B.: *The Savage in Literature: representations of 'primitive' society in English fiction 1858-1920*, London: Routledge, 1975.

Temple R.: *Journals Kept in Hyderabad, Kashmir, Sikkim, and Nepal* (2 vols.), London: WH Allen, 1887.

Tuan Y.: *Dominance and Affection: the making of pets*, New Haven: Yale Univ. Press. 1984.

Tuker F.: *While Memory Serves*, London: Cassell, 1950.

Turner E. S.: *Gallant Gentlemen: a portrait of the British officer, 1600-1956*, London: Michael Joseph, 1956.

Twiss L. O.: *Some of my Memories*, Privately published, 1961.

Vagts A.: *A History of Militarism: civilian and military*, London: Hollis and Carter, 1959.

Vance N.: The ideal of manliness. In *The Victorian Public School: studies in the development of an educational institution* (eds) B. Simon and I. Bradley. Dublin: Gill and Macmillan, 1975.

Wakeham E.: *The Bravest Soldier. Sir Rollo Gillespie, 1766-1814*, Edinburgh: William Blackwood, 1937.

Walton D. N.: *Courage. a philosophical investigation*, Berkeley: Univ. of Calif. Press, 1986.

Whelpton J.: *Jang Bahadur in Europe: the first Nepalese mission to the West*, Kathmandu: Sahayogi, 1983.

Wilkinson T.: *Two Monsoons*, London: Duckworth, 1976.

Index

C

D

E

F

G

R

S

T

U

V

W

Y

Z